TRANSPORTATION-LOGISTICS DICTIONARY

Joseph L. Cavinato, Editor

Associate Professor of
Business Logistics
The Pennsylvania State University

Published by
THE TRAFFIC SERVICE CORPORATION
1435 G Street, N.W., Suite 815
Washington, D.C. 20005
(202) 626-4500

Published by The Traffic Service Corporation
1435 G Street, N.W., Suite 815, Washington, D.C. 20005
(202) 626-4500

ISBN 0-87408-022-3
Library of Congress Catalogue Card Number 81-86142

Printed in the United States of America

THE TRAFFIC SERVICE CORPORATION, WASHINGTON, D.C.

New York   Chicago   Atlanta   Philadelphia
Boston   Westport   Palo Alto
Produced by Stephen R. Hunter

Contents

Preface

Only five years has passed since the first edition of this dictionary was published. In that short time span five major pieces of regulatory legislation were enacted that greatly affect transportation. Similarly, industry distribution personnel have adapted to these changes as well as continued to alter their organizations to adapt to the cost impacts of the 1970's and productivity push of the 1980's.

This second edition has two objectives: (1) reflect the changes in transportation and logistics during the last five years; and (2) present a stage for the fields in the future. There are 517 new entries added, 58 major alterations made and five deletions to the first edition material. Most of the new terms evolved in the transportation, hazardous materials and antitrust areas. More firms are entering into international procurement and distribution; and costs and productivity are now shop floor items of concern. In more firms traditional outbound distribution managers are now more closely linked with inbound purchasing and materials manager counterparts. And, the metric system is becoming more of the standard in the U.S. as each day passes. These major trends are captured in this edition. The nearly 600 changes and additions increase by almost 14% the body of transportation-logistics terminology used in the fields.

This edition is built upon the work of Wallace I. Little (1921-1977) who prepared the first edition and was known by many in the Pacific Northwest. He stated that there are no clear parameters to the scope of logistics and transportation. Even transportation terms share their origin and use with other operational areas of our economy. This dictionary is a needed facility that will grow. Its terminology should include all words or terms related to operations, institutions, equipment, modal systems, personnel, professional associations, functional responsibilities, academic terminology, applicable sciences, governmental institutions, historical terms, and on and on. Sometimes the terms may be succinctly stated in a few chosen words. Other times, an explanation of systems is mandatory. No apologies are made for the fact that some terms may have interpretations in addition to those presented. Some may even prefer another meaning.

This edition and new ones will meet the suggestions for improvement, correction, or addition; they are certainly invited. Refinement and expansion will be continuous and will appear in future editions.

Joseph L. Cavinato
State College, Penna. 1982

To Mary, Janet and Josh—

TRANSPORTATION-LOGISTICS DICTIONARY

—A—

A1 In transportation, a first-class vessel. The letter "A" specifies the class in which the hull is scheduled, and the numeral "1" refers to the stores and equipment. In Lloyd's Register, vessels are rated A1, A2, and so on down. In the American system, the registry descends from A by fractions—A1, A1¼, A1½, and so forth.

A.A.R. In insurance, against all risks.

ABAFT Refers to a location near the stern of the vessel.

ABANDONMENT This term has different meanings for different carrier modes. In most domestic transportation it specifies the abandonment of service underway in some designated form. In water transportation, it refers to constructive total loss. The insurer may treat such a loss as a partial loss, or abandon the vessel to the insurer and treat it as a total loss.

ABATEMENT A discount allowed for damage or overcharge in the payment of a bill is termed abatement. The extent of the abatement is usually designated before the bill is due. The amount of the abatement is deducted from the bill. The term abatement also refers to a suspension of proceedings.

AB INITIO From the beginning.

ABOARD A nautical word on or in a ship; also applied to railroad cars and other vehicles.

A-BURTON A stowage term used in designating cargo stowed athwartship instead of fore and aft.

ABC MANAGEMENT Application of Pareto's Law or the 80/20 rule; the ABC classifications are determined by descending rank order of all products according to each as a percentage of the total. "A" products are the most important or the highest in volume, "C" are the least. Ranking can be performed in terms of volume, dollars, pounds, tons, etc.

ABSOLUTE LIABILITY A condition in which the carrier is responsible for all liability and is not exempted from the normal exemptions found in bill of lading or common law liability.

ABSORPTION When the carrier absorbs the cost of special service or privileges and does not include the freight charge, it is called absorption. The special services which may be deducted may include bridge and ferry arbitraries, switching, lighterage, and wharfage.

ABSTRACT An abridgement of evidence omitting unessentials.

ACCEPTABLE QUALITY LEVEL A quality control and inspection term for the limit of item characteristics that can be accepted (includes tolerances, ranges).

ACCEPTANCE A time draft (bill of exchange) payable at a fixed or determinable future date. The acceptance of a draft is accomplished by stamping or writing the word "accepted" on the face of the draft, followed by the date and signature of the acceptor who must be the drawee. All acceptances carry an unconditional obligation of the drawee to pay the face amount at maturity.

ACCEPTANCE, BANKER'S A time or date draft drawn on and accepted by a banking institution. This signifies that bank's commitment to pay the face amount at maturity to a bona-fide holder.

ACCEPTANCE CHARGES A charge generally made by a Foreign Bank for presenting drafts for acceptance if the drafts are not left with them for collection.

ACCEPTANCE, DOCUMENTS AGAINST (D/A) An indication on a draft that the documents attached are to be released to the drawee only upon acceptance of the draft.

ACCEPTANCE NUMBER A quality control and inspection term for a number of faulty items in a lot that can be accepted while not rejecting the entire lot.

ACCEPTANCE OF HONORS A term expressing a third party's acceptance of a bill of exchange to save the honor of the drawee when the drawee fails to carry out his obligation to accept it.

ACCEPTANCE SUPRA PROTEST An agreement to pay a bill of exchange after it has been protested, to save the credit and honor of the drawer or endorser.

ACCEPTANCE, TRADE A time or a date draft which has been accepted by the buyer (the drawee) for payment at maturity. Trade acceptances, unlike bankers' acceptances, are drawn on the buyer, carry only the buyer's obligation to pay, and cannot become bankers' acceptances or be guaranteed by a bank.

ACCEPTOR One who, by his signature, makes acceptance of an order draft or bill of exchange.

ACCESS AISLE Passageway which allows access to storage areas.

ACCESS TIME This term is used in data processing. It is the time required in milliseconds to position read-write heads on a cylinder position.

ACCESSORIAL CHARGES A wide variety of services and privileges that are made available in connection with the transportation of goods are assessed accessorial charges. Examples would be charges for switching, loading, unloading, weighing, pickup, delivery, transit stop-off, storage, inspection, grading, repackaging, billing and fabrication. A demurrage charge is likewise thought of as an accessorial charge.

ACCESSORIAL SERVICE A service rendered by a carrier in addition to a transportation service, such as assorting, packing, precooling, heating, storage, substitution of tonnage, etc.

ACCIDENT REPORT ACT (MAY 6, 1910) Amended on August 26, 1937, this act requires monthly reports of railway accidents. The Department of Transportation is authorized to conduct the investigation of the accidents.

ACCOMMODATION BILL (OR PAPER) Sometimes known as a *wind mill* or kite, is a bill of exchange drawn, endorsed, or accepted without value being given for it, and for which no party is liable until value or consideration is given. The parties involved are known as *accommodation parties.*

ACCOUNT The general category of customer service as listed on the company books.

ACCOUNTING, CONNECTING-LINE Accounting for the movement of traffic on a through rate from point of origin to destination when two or more carriers participate in the haul. Each carrier receives a predetermined percentage of the revenue.

ACCOUNTING COST Any cost that is captured and reported in the accounting system.

ACCOUNT PARTY The purchasing party, the importer, the buyer in any transaction. Also "accountee."

ACCOUNTS AUDITED To check the procedures and inventory of a customer account for accuracy.

ACCOUNT STATED An agreed balance of account.

ACCREDITED CUSTOMER LIST A list of accounts authorized to draw directly upon the stock in the warehouse. Generally furnished by the owner of the goods or his designated agent.

ACCRUALS The accounts maintained for services rendered. The sum of the amount due.

ACID TANKER This specially constructed tanker is acid-resistant. When applied to motor transportation, it usually involves a considerably smaller trailer.

ACID TEST Measured by the ratio of liquid assets to current liabilities. The liquid assets include all accounts receivable, cash, securities, etc.

ACKNOWLEDGEMENT A voluntary declaration of the execution of an instrument before a proper officer.

ACOUSTIC CLOUDS The levels of the atmosphere which impede sound. It is said that this is responsible for the erratic pattern of fog signals and other sounds.

ACQUIESCENCE When a bill of lading is accepted or signed by a shipper or his agent without protest as to the conditions which appear thereon, he is said to acquiesce in the terms, giving a silent appearance of consent.

ACQUISITION The transfer of title of one company to another through a purchase.

ACQUITTANCE A written receipt in full, in discharge from all claims.

ACRONYM Term signifying that a name for something consists of the first letter or letters of a series of names applying to the item; example is COLA for cost of living adjustments.

ACROSS THE BOARD INCREASE An upward adjustment of all rates charged by a carrier on all commodities handled by it, with the exception of some that are subject to "hold down."

ACT Something done or established, as a statute passed by legislature. In traffic work: (1) a law, such as the Act to regulate Commerce, Ash Pan Act, Elkins Act, Shipping Act, Merchant Marine Act, Transportation Act, Accident Report Act, etc.; (2) the effect of the exertion of power, such as the *Act of God.*

ACTIVE INVENTORY The inventory from which goods are being picked as distinct from reserve inventory.

ACTIVE TIME This term applies to water transportation and involves the time a vessel spends loading and unloading at the dock.

ACT OF GOD Accidents of nature beyond man's control, such as flood, lightning, hurricane, snowslide, etc., are usually referred to as *acts of God.* The carrier is not legally responsible under most circumstances for damage incurred from acts of God.

ACT OF HONOR A term denoting the acceptance for honor of a bill of exchange.

ACT OF MAN This term used in water transportation refers to the deliberate action of the master of the vessel in sacrificing cargo or otherwise for the purpose of making safe the vessel for the remaining cargo. Those sharing in the spared cargo proportionately cover the loss.

ACT OF PUBLIC AUTHORITY One of the exemptions from carrier liability under bill of lading liability; covers delays from quarantines, court orders, etc.

ACT OF SHIPPER NEGLIGENCE One of the exemptions from bill of lading liability; it includes improper packaging, loading and misdescription of the goods.

ACT TO REGULATE COMMERCE An act, now known as the Interstate Commerce Act, passed by Congress on February 4, 1887, regulating carriers engaged in interstate traffic.

ACTION In law, a lawsuit.

ACTIVE COMPETITION Rivalry between two or more carriers, communities or commodities.

ACTIVE CORPORATION An actively operating business with the facilities and organization required for administering and operating the business.

ACTUAL DISPLACEMENT When a car is placed for loading or unloading at an available point other than on an industry track, due to inability of consignor or consignee to receive it, the carrier may, by giving customary notice, consider it as being placed at the point usually employed or designated.

ACTUAL LOSS The value of product loss and damage incurred by the shipper/consignee as distinct from the amount recovered or recoverable from the carrier.

ACTUAL PLACEMENT The placing of a car on a designated site for loading or unloading.

ACTUAL VALUE RATE A rate that carries with it the obligation for up to the full value of the goods in the event of loss and damage.

ADDED VALUE A term implying that at each production and distribution function, products are having value added to them in the form of time, place and form utilities from the various activities.

ADDITIONS AND BETTERMENTS A term which means that additions would include all raw equipment, tracks, etc., while betterments refers to their improvement.

ADDRESS In data processing, this refers to a label name or number to designate a location in a computer.

ADHESIVE FACTOR Also termed adhesion of drivers. A measurement of the extent force may be applied to rail wheels without slippage on the tracks. It is usually expressed as a percent of force to the weight on the drivers. This term was most commonly used for steam locomotives.

ADJACENT (Next to or bordering on.) Mexico and Canada are known as adjacent foreign countries for they border on the United States.

ADJUSTMENT Determining the amount of loss and liability; the settlement of claims.

ADJUSTMENT (OF RATES) The authorized basis, either percentage or arbitrary, on which rates are considered.

ADMINISTRATIVE FUNCTION The act of administering a court or a regulative body. Providing for the actual work or carrying on of the court or the regulative body.

ADMINISTRATIVE LAW JUDGE The official before whom cases are heard, or handled in many non-oral situations, at a regulatory agency.

ADMINISTRATIVE PROCEDURE ACT An act passed by Congress on June 11, 1946, setting forth the manner of procedures before federal agencies.

ADMIRALTY Jurisdiction over causes of action occuring in connection with contracts to transport by water, also other marine matters.

ADMIRALTY COURT A court that has jurisdiction over legal disputes arising out of navigation on public waters, is called an admiralty court. The United States District Court is referred to as the court of original admiralty.

ADOPTION When one carrier assumes the obligations and operations of another carrier it is called adoption. When this is undertaken, a legal document called an adoption notice must be filed with the Interstate Commerce Commission or the regulatory body in charge.

AD REFERENDUM A form of contract in which some points are left open for settlement at a future time.

ADVALOREM (ACCORDING TO VALUE) Customs duty that is based exclusively on the value of the goods that are subject to duty, irrespective of the quality, weight, or other considerations. Commonly, advalorem rates of duty are presented in percentages of the value of the goods. This is normally ascertained from the specified amount of the invoice.

ADVANCE When a partial payment is made by a merchant, broker, agent, etc., at the time of receiving the invoice and bill of lading it represents an advance. It is a process of paying part of the amount due on goods sent for sale.

ADVANCED ARRANGEMENT The mandatory advanced arrangement for the movement of some commodities by air carrier. Gold and other precious metals, live animals, and any other classes of shipment require such arrangements.

ADVANCE NOTICE Notifies warehouse of railcar or truck enroute, and the merchandise on the vehicles.

ADVANCED CHARGE The amount of freight or other charge on a shipment advanced by one transportation line to another, or to the shipper, to be collected from the consignee.

ADVANCED RATE A rate that has been increased since a specified time.

ADVANTAGE In traffic work a factor often considered in determining the reasonableness or unreasonableness of rates.

ADVANTAGE OF LOCATION An advantage which one city or shipper has over another because of situation with respect to nearness to markets of consumption, sources of supply, or agencies of transportation.

ADVENTURE Shipment of goods on shipper's own account. It is customary for exporters and merchants to keep a debit and credit account with each enterprise as *Adventure to Buenos Aires*. A *Bill of Adventure* is a document signed by the master of the ship which carries goods at the owner's risk.

ADVENTURE IN CO. Adventure in Co. is a shipment of goods at the joint risk of consignor and consignee, to be sold on their joint account.

ADVISE NOTE A letter telling the recipient that a particular business transaction has been completed, or is being undertaken on his behalf.

ADVISE ON SHIPMENT A notice sent to a local or foreign buyer advising that shipment has gone forward and containing details of packing, routing, etc. A copy of the invoice is usually enclosed and sometimes, if desired, a copy of the bill of lading.

ADVISING BANK The bank which advises the beneficiary that another bank has opened a letter of credit in his favor.

"A" END OF THE CAR The end of the car opposite the hand brake.

AERONAUTICAL RADIO, INC. A non-profit radio communications facility owned by the certified route air carriers.

AFFIANT One who makes the affidavit.

AFFIDAVIT A written statement sworn before a Notary Public.

AFFREIGHT To hire, as a ship, for the purpose of transporting freight.

AFFREIGHTMENT A vessel chartering contract that provides for the movement of the merchandise.

A-FRAME A metal hoist or support which is used to handle heavy objects from a rail car.

AFT Direction toward the stern of the vessel.

AGENCY The term *agency* signifies relations existing between two parties by which one is authorized to perform or transact certain business for the others; also applies to the office of the agent.

AGENCY STATION A railroad depot or station having a railroad agent would be termed an agency station. The term also applies to a motor-truck point where carriers share a dock or warehouse facility.

AGENCY TARIFF A tariff issued by a publishing agent for one or more transportation lines.

AGENT A person authorized to transact business for and in the name of another.

AGENT MIDDLEMEN The agent middleman negotiates purchases and/or sales but does not take title. They receive revenue from commissions or fees, which are paid by the buyer, or seller of the merchandise, but seldom both. The agent does not represent both the buyer and the seller in the same transaction. He may represent the seller and buyer in different transactions, however. The classes of agent middlemen are: (1) broker; (2) commission merchant; (3) resident buyers; (4) manufacturer's agents; and (5) sales agents.

AGGLOMERATION A term in location theory indicating that an area or locale contains certain economies of labor, skill or other cost factors because of the existence of a large firm or function there; this phenomenon serves to attract industries requiring the same inputs having the economies.

AGGREGATED SHIPMENT When a shipment is made from different shippers to one consignee in a consolidated action, and treated as a single shipment, it is called an aggregated shipment.

AGGREGATE OF THE INTERMEDIATE RATES Section 10726 states that a common carrier subject to Part I and III of the Act may not charge more for a through rate than the aggregate of the intermediate rates. Part II of the Act does not contain a provision relative to the aggregate of the intermediate rates, but the Commission has held a joint rate which exceeds the aggregate of the intermediate rates is unjust and unreasonable. This rule permits a traffic manager to find combinations of commodity rates that may be cheaper than a class rate, or even cheaper than a through commodity rate.

AGGREGATE OF THE INTERMEDIATE RULE Under the aggregate of the intermediate rule, which was an amendment to the Act in 1910, one cannot charge more for a through rate than the aggregate of the intermediate rates. This rule is applicable to regulated rail and domestic water moves. Rule 56(c) of Tariff Circular 20 states the aggregate-of-intermediate rule to prevent unattended violations of the principle. Traffic managers may use this rule to achieve reductions in rates. They do so by seeking a very low commodity rate on intermediate points which may, when combined with connecting class rates, or other commodity rates, give a lower combination rate.

AGGREGATE PLANNING A production scheduling term for the practice of intermediate term planning of work activity.

AGGREGATE SHIPMENTS Those under which aggregate tender rates apply.

AGGREGATE TENDER RATE A reduced rate on separate shipments that are included within a single motor carrier pick up move; the economies of the single consolidated pick up, and often part of the line haul, are passed on to the shipper in this lower rate.

AGREED CHARGES A form of rail contract rate in which a reduced rate is applied in exchange for the shipper routing a certain percent of total movements over a certain carrier.'

AGREED VALUATION The value of a shipment agreed upon in order to secure a specific rating and/or liability.

AGREED WEIGHT The weight which is prescribed for acceptance of a commodity shipped in specific containers or in a specific manner is the agreed weight. The agreement is between the shipper and the carrier.

AGRICULTURAL EXEMPTION An exemption from route and rate regulation in motor carriage (and with some products on railroads) when the carrier is hauling such goods; the motor carrier exemptions are found in part 1047 and the rail commodities are in part 1039 of Title 49 of the Code of Federal Regulations.

AIR BILL OF LADING Domestic and international shipments by air move under a standardized air waybill. It is the basic airline document covering the movements of shipments on international and domestic air freight. The contents of the document provide information needed for dispatch and the proper handling at points of origin, enroute and at destinations. It accompanies every shipment. Usually the air bill is prepared in sets of seven. They are respectively as follows: carrier's accounting copy, invoice, consignee's memo, delivery receipt, original station copy, and destination station copy. The airline normally provides the shipper with individual forms in blank, and the shipper makes out the air bill before the shipment is turned over to the air carrier. The air carrier receives the second copy when a uniform domestic bill of lading is applied, but when an air bill of lading is used, the airline retains six copies, with the shipper receiving the original.

AIRBORNE SPEED The method employed to measure the speed of aircraft. Computed by dividing the sum of the airport-to-airport distances by the flight hours. It is expressed in terms of great circle airport-to-airport distance.

AIR CARGO An all-inclusive term used in referring to mail and property carried in air service. The various services provided by AA in transporting Air Cargo include: Airmail, International Airmail and First Class Mail; Air Parcel Post and International Air Parcel Post; Air Express; Airfreight and International Air Cargo; and Company Material.

AIR CARGO, INC. This corporation was founded and is jointly owned by the scheduled air carriers of the United States. Its principal function is to execute contracts with the trucking companies that provide a connecting service.

AIR CARGO GUIDE The official listing of all carriers serving cities in the United States and Canada. Provides information relative to schedules, equipment, customs, maximum acceptable weight, etc.

AIR CARRIER A transportation carrier of cargo or personnel by air. The timer means airline.

AIR COMMUTER A class of airline that generally serves smaller market cities with airplanes ranging from four to about 30 seats, often same as air taxi.

AIR CONTAINER The container used to facilitate air transportation of cargo.

AIRCRAFT MILES The airport-to-airport distance for a flight.

AIRCRAFT PIRACY This term refers to aircraft hijacking, or the taking over of an aircraft while it is in flight or awaiting flight. It involves the use of the threat of violence.

AIRFRAME An aircraft, excluding its engine and accessories.

AIR FREIGHT Regular scheduled air cargo movements on a volume basis are referred to as Airfreight and International Cargo. The term *Airfreight* refers to freight shipments over certified airlines of the United States and Canada. The term *International Air Cargo* involves air cargo transport movements across the United States' border into Mexico over the route of A.A. de Mexico. Airfreight was pioneered by A.A. Most airlines now operate similar types of services and are involved in the interchange of traffic of air cargo movements. A.A. performs all functions of Airfreight service except the pickup and delivery functions. These services are handled by local cartage companies under contract with A.A.

AIR FREIGHT FORWARDER Classified as a transportation carrier, the freight forwarder assembles and consolidates small shipments into larger shipments. Its rates approximate those of the small shipment, but it receives service from the carrier on the basis of the consolidated larger shipment. It operates pickup and delivery services, as well as line haul operations.

AIR FREIGHT RATES These rates are simpler than those for other forms of transportation. The tariffs are put out by the Airline Tariff Publishers, Inc. as agents for the carriers. About six different tariffs are published. For example, SC 3 is a commodity rate tariff in charges per hundred pounds for minimum weights 100, 1000, 2000, 3000, 5000 and 10,000 pounds. Another example is CT 4 which is a container tariff. It applies on general and specific commodities, and presents rates about one-third off of existing rates for all weights in a container that exceed a specified amount. Other tariffs cover service transportation to the airport, local and joint airport to airport movements, and a rules tariff.

AIRLINE A commercial air transportation carrier, involving its equipment, personnel, and array of facilities.

AIRLINE EXCHANGE RAIL ORDER An order drawn on the agents of rail carriers by airline companies to provide for passenger services as a result of grounded airline service. Sometimes it authorized cash for the grounded service.

AIRLINE TARIFF PUBLISHERS, INC. This organization publishes airline tariffs, which present the station to station rates charged for the movement of cargo or personnel. Likewise published are the rules relative to air movement.

AIRLINE TERMINAL The airport building, runways, aprons, and all facilities, including parking, for passenger services.

AIR MAIL Airmail, Air Parcel Post and First Class Mail are carried in air service under contract to and through the agencies of the U.S. Post Office Department. International Airmail and International Air Parcel Post are carried beyond the boundaries of the U.S. under contract to and through the agencies of the U.S. Post Office Department.

AIR PARCEL POST The transportation by air of packages as air mail. Usually involves packages of five pounds or less. Packages cannot exceed seventy pounds in weight and 100 inches in combined length and girth.

AIRPORT The complete land facilities required to service the landing and take-off of aircraft. Includes runways, aprons, hangars, terminal buildings, and all accommodations for passengers—including parking.

AIRPORT NOTICE The statement of intent to serve a named point or points, authorized in the certificate. Filed with the Civil Aeronautics Board by the air carrier.

AIRSCAPE Pictures taken from an aeroplane.

AIR SLIDE Type of covered hopper car that uses forced air to loosen the bulk lading along the slanted floor so as to facilitate unloading through bottom hatches.

AIR TAXI OPERATOR An air carrier usually limited to aircraft of a maximum certificated takeoff weight. Regulated only by registration with the Civil Aeronautics Board and the filing of liability insurance. In 1969, 1500 air taxi operators. Usually are non-scheduled operators, though one class of taxi operator, the commuter air carriers, are scheduled.

AIR TRANSPORT BOARD The regulatory authority for Canadian air transportation carriers. The counterpart of the United States Civil Aeronautics Board.

AIR TRANSPORTATION ASSOCIATION OF AMERICA The ATA is the principal trade association for the certificated, common air transportation carriers of the United States. Headquarters at 1709 New York Avenue, New York. Assembles statistics, serves as the spokesman, provides research, and performs numerous other functions for member air carriers.

AIR WAYBILL The document used for the shipment for air freight by the national and international air carriers. It states the commodities shipped, shipping instructions, shipping costs, etc.

AIR WAYBILLS (OF LADING) A signed receipt and a contract to deliver goods by air. Such bills are non-negotiable and do not convey title to the goods as do "to order" bills of lading used by ocean and land carriers. The title passes to the party to whom the goods are consigned (the consignee).

AISLE Any passageway within a storage area.

ALIUNDE From another course.

ALL-CARGO CARRIER A class of air carrier operating for the movement of air freight as a common carrier. It carries air mail, express and freight, over specified routes on schedule. It may serve as a non-scheduled carrier and also carry passengers.

ALL-COMMODITY RATES A freight rate usually based on a carload quantity, applying to a shipment which may include any combination of commodities, but subject to stated exceptions and conditions, is called an all-commodity rate. It may also be called an all-freight rate.

ALL-CONTAINER SHIP A ship fitted for container carriage in all available space. In van-container stowage, the ship is fitted with vertical cells for container placement. Some vans are carried additionally on deck. Longer containers are deck stowed. No provisions are available for cargo other than in container form.

ALL-FIBER DRUM A cylindrical container in which both the cover and body are produced of paperboard.

ALLOCATE To distribute, assign, or allot.

ALLOCATION MODEL A group of mathematical tools that determine the optimum manner in which to allocate goods or movements across a set of demands; a common application is the assignment of shipments from various warehouses to many customers in the lowest freight cost possible.

ALLOCATION (OF EXPENSE) In transportation accounting, the apportionment of the expenditures and revenues to the respective divisions of the organizations, such as maintenance of way and structure costs being divided between freight and passenger service since they are used by both.

ALLOCATION (OF PURCHASES) Term that is used to imply that the vendor supply market is tight and customers are limited as to purchase quantities according to formulas established by vendors or government agencies.

ALLOCATION OF RESOURCES The use of the resources for different activities.

ALLONGE A paper attached to a bill of exchange, on which additional endorsements may be placed when the back of the bill has already been filled with named.

ALLOTMENT TICKET An order for payment of wages to seaman's family at set intervals during his absence on a voyage.

ALLOWANCE A deduction made from the gross weight or value of goods or services. The Revised Interstate Commerce Act requires the carriers to furnish the service of carriage (haul) and also such facilities as are necessary to make the service of transporting a shipment as safe and complete as possible under conditions existing at time of movement. If the necessary equipment, such as dunnage, elevation, or private cars, is furnished by the shipper and not by the carrier, the carrier may under proper tariff authority, allow such costs. *Mileage allowance* is an allowance, based on distance, made by the railroads to private owners of freight cars. *Lateral allowances* are allowances for services performed granted by large rail lines to smaller connecting lines.

ALL-PURPOSE AIR CARRIER A carrier of passengers and cargo by air carrier.

ALL-RAIL An act of carriage exclusively by railroad transportation. The term includes those lines or that service using car ferries or lighters.

ALL-RISK CLAUSE An insurance coverage in which all loss and damage to goods are insured unless caused by inherent deficiencies.

ALL-WATER An act of carriage exclusively by water transportation.

ALOFT Locations above the deck, such as an observer aloft, or cargo aloft on a derrick head.

ALONGSIDE By the side of.

ALPHANUMERIC This designates that the characters may be either letters or numeric symbols.

ALTERNATIVE OR OPPORTUNITY COSTS The cost of an option or commodity in terms of its alternative use. The value measured in terms of its foregone worth in an alternate usage.

ALTERNATIVE RATES Two or more rates, of which the lowest charge is applicable.

ALTERNATIVE ROUTE A motor carrier is authorized to perform regular service over a specified route under a permit or certificate. However, sometimes it is permitted to substitute an optional motor-carrier route instead of the specified route.

ALTERNATIVE TARIFF A tariff containing two or more rates, from and to the same points, on the same goods, with the authority to use the one which provides the lowest charge.

AMBIGUOUS Susceptible of several interpretations.

AMENDED ITEM An item that has been changed or modified by a succeeding publication, made necessary because of error or changed conditions, and showing item in its revised form.

AMENDMENT An alteration, change or correction.

AMENDMENT A written notice of change in the terms of a letter of credit, which becomes an integral part of the original letter of credit.

AMERICAN BUREAU OF SHIPPING This organization is committed to the classification, specification, and examination of vessels for seaworthiness.

AMERICAN FLAG CARRIER An air transportation common carrier involved in international transportation movements. They operate under a certificate of public convenience and necessity, and are approved for service by the President of the United States. Some also perform domestic air transportation service. Their operations are on specified routes according to schedule.

AMERICAN SOCIETY OF TRAFFIC AND TRANSPORTATION A professional society in the field of transportation and logistics; has as its main form of membership that of Certified Member; requires passing or waiving exams in transportation economics, traffic management, general management and either transportation law and regulation or logistics analysis; a final requirement is writing an original research paper. The AST&T is based at 1816 Norris Place, Louisville, KY; it has chapters throughout the U.S. and it publishes a journal called the *Transportation Journal*.

AMERICAN STANDARD ASSOCIATION MH-T COMMITTEE A committee dedicated to the standardization of containers, container procedures and handling systems. It represents all segments of transportation carrier and shipper groups.

AMERICAN TRUCKING ASSOCIATIONS The trade association serving the trucking industry. A composite of the state organizations of truckers operating in the United States. Headquarters at 1616 P Street, N.W., Washington, D.C. 20036.

AMERICAN WAREHOUSEMEN'S ASSOCIATION Voluntary organization of warehousemen established to assure high standards in the warehouse.

AMORTIZATION COST The annual payment for expiring a debt according to a contract or other agreement on a continuous basis is called the amortization cost. Therefore, amortization cost is established when something is purchased from borrowed funds, and the annual payment represents the gradual repayment of borrowed funds. In addition to the amortization cost, an interest on the unamortized investment is likewise involved in the payment.

ANALOGOUS ARTICLES Articles having similar characteristics.

ANALOGY, CLASSIFICATION BY A term indicating that a product not specifically named in a tariff will be classified for rate billing purposes according to its similarity in transportation characteristics and inherent nature with another product that is specifically named in the tariff.

ANCHORAGE A spot near shore where ships are in safety.

ANDERSON SCALE The name given the mileage basis formally used by New England carriers in a decision handed down by Commissioner Anderson.

ANGLE STACKING Placing stock in a storage area at a 45 degree angle to the aisle.

ANKER A common foreign liquid measure, varying from nine to ten gallons.

ANNOUNCEMENT A formal statement or notice given out by a commission or carrier with respect to its action or intent covering established practices or findings in some particular case.

ANNUAL REPORT TO THE INTERSTATE COMMERCE COMMISSION Yearly reports to the Commission, summarizing its activities during the year and offering recommendations for legislative changes affecting interstate commerce.

ANNUAL VOLUME RATE A rate that is tied to a minimum annual tonnage volume by a shipper; a form of contract rate.

ANNUS Year.

ANTE Before.

ANTI Against.

ANTI DUMPING DUTY A tariff imposed for the purpose of preventing the sale of foreign goods in the country at levels below their standard price in the country of origin.

ANTITRUST LAWS The legislation prohibiting acts that will cause or tend to cause monopolistic practices or price fixing; includes the Sherman Antitrust Act.

ANY-QUANTITY RATE A rate which is not qualified by any weight minimum, and therefore is applicable to any quantity of freight tendered. This is a single rate which is applied regardless of the quantity shipped. There is no minimum weight on these rates. AQ rates are commonly used in cotton goods. This permits the shipper of the commodity to move goods on a larger quantity basis without extra charge. Usually any quantity refers to a *rating* that applies to an article regardless of the weight.

APPARENT GOOD ORDER When freight appears to be free of damage and in proper condition so far as can be determined from a general survey, it is designated as apparent good order.

APPEAL The transfer of a case from an inferior to a superior court.

APPELLATE JURISDICTION Courts having power to review decisions of lower courts.

APPLICATION Of rates, the points to, from, or between which the rates and routes named in a tariff apply; of tariffs, the points to, from, or between which the provisions of a tariff apply.

APPLICATION FOR CHANGE IN CLASSIFICATION A form used in filing with a classification committee a request for change in the classification of a commodity.

APPORTIONMENT DISTRIBUTION When rolling stock is distributed on a predetermined basis, or when the tonnage of several carriers is distributed without preference on a predetermined basis, it is usually referred to as apportionment distribution. The term is also applicable to passenger service. When the fares of an interline operation are distributed between carriers on a predetermined basis this term is also applied.

APPRAISE To set a value on goods or property.

APPRAISEMENT Ascertaining the value of goods or property.

APPRAISER One who determines the value of goods.

APPRAISER'S STORES The warehouse or public stores to which at least ten percent of imported goods are taken to be inspected, analyzed, weighed, etc., by examiners or appraisers.

APPROPRIATION The allocation of funds for a specific purpose.

APPURTENANCES As used in shipping, the term embraces whatever belongs to the owner on board a vessel or ship used for the object of a voyage.

APRON An aircraft parking spot in front of a hangar or aircraft shelter which is used primarily for loading and unloading of aircraft.

APRON TRACK Railroad track along the apron of a pier designed for the direct transfer of cargo between the car and ship.

ARBITRAGE The profiteering from the exchange of one country's currency for that of another to acquire the advantages in the exchange rate.

ARBITRARY An added charge over a fixed rate to account for an added leg of a shipment. It amounts to the combination of a fixed rate with an added rate.

ARBITRATION A means of settling disputes (labor and loss and damage) with an objective outside party acting as a primary decision body.

ARBITRATION CLAUSE An arrangement for settling disputes which is inserted in the sales contract.

ARBITRATION OF EXCHANGE It is customary to calculate rates of exchange between two countries by a comparison of the currency of intermediate places to discover whether it is more profitable to forward money directly or indirectly. Simple arbitration involves the use of but one intermediate place and compound arbitration includes two or more intermediate places.

ARCH CONSTRUCTION The arch construction of a vessel eliminates the need for lower beams in the vessel by making the deck beams of exceptional strength.

ARMED GUARD SERVICE A service provided for in the tariffs which involves the surveillance of the shipment by armed guard. Extra charges are assessed for such service.

ARRIVED SHIP When the following conditions prevail, the vessel is considered to be an *arrived ship*: (1) the vessel is ready to load or discharge cargo; (2) the vessel has arrived at the unloading berth according to the charger; (3) the shippers or consignees have been notified in writing.

ARRIVAL NOTICE A notice, furnished to consignee, of the arrival of freight.

ARTICULATED CAR In railroad transportation, this is a rail car consisting of two or more full-sized units which can swivel.

ARTIFICIAL ADVANTAGE An advantage which a locality of shipper has over another because of an action on the part of some transportation company or other agency.

ARTIFICIAL PERSON A company, corporation or body, such as the New York Central Railroad and United States Steel Corporation, considered in law or in commercial transactions as an individual.

AS CUSTOMARY A shortened form of *"with all dispatch as customary."* In a contract of affreightment, this refers to the usual manner of performing service, without specifically stipulating the period of time in which the work is to be performed.

AS FAST AS A STEAMER CAN DELIVER A charter party clause providing for the discharge of a vessel's cargo with the utmost practical dispatch — port customs, facilities for delivery and other existing circumstances considered.

ASH PAN ACT An Act of Congress requiring ash pans of certain specifications on all locomotives engaged in interstate or international commerce.

AS PER ADVICE A term used on a bill of exchange to indicate that notice of the drawing of the bill has already been sent to the drawee.

ASSEMBLY AND DISTRIBUTION RATES When multiple shipments are assembled for shipment, or are terminated at a single point, they are less costly to handle than individual shipments originating from the business. Rates approximately 10% lower are provided on assembly and distribution rates. *A & D Tariffs* require these shipments be forwarded within five working days. These rates service the industrial shipper who maintains a regular consolidation operation.

ASSEMBLY SERVICE The process of a single carrier assembling many shipments enroute to the same consignee.

ASSENT An agreement between carriers for a publication by another carrier or agent relative to rates, etc.

ASSET A property of tangible or intangible value owned by the business or individual.

ASSIGN To transfer or make over to another party.

ASSIGNED RAILCAR A railcar that is only used by one shipper for a specific period of time. No other person may use this railcar without permission.

ASSIGNED SERVICE Equipment or vehicles that are reserved for the service of a certain shipper or consignee; specifically equipped rail cars and contract carriage trucks are often assigned for loading only by the specific shipper.

ASSIGNED SIDING A sidetrack owned by a transportation line, and assigned for the use of one or more firms, or individuals, in loading or unloading cars.

ASSIGNEE One to whom a right or property is transferred.

ASSIGNMENT A term commonly used in connection with a bill of lading which involves transfer of rights, title, and interest for the purpose of assigning goods by endorsement of the bill of lading.

ASSIGNMENT OF PROCEEDS A request by the beneficiary to pay all or part of the funds due to him to a third party. This instrument does not transfer the letter of credit nor the title to the goods. It authorizes the bank to pay the third party from the proceeds of the draft presented by the beneficiary.

ASSIGNOR One by whom a right or property is transferred.

ASSOCIATION The union of a number of individuals or companies for a common purpose.

ASSOCIATION OF AMERICAN RAILROADS The trade association of the railroads of the United States. It provides research, public relations, coordination, and numerous other functions. Headquarters in the American Railroads Building, 1920 L Street, N.W., Washington, D.C. 20036.

ASSOCIATION OF LOCAL TRANSPORT AIRLINES The trade association which services the interests of the local service, intra-Hawaiian and intra-Alaskan air carriers.

ASSOCIATION OF PRACTITIONERS BEFORE THE INTERSTATE COMMERCE COMMISSION An organization composed of persons admitted to practice before the I.C.C.

ASSUMPTION OF RISK An expression of the assuming of all or part of the liability for loss and damage to a shipment.

A.S.T.M. American Society for Testing and Materials.

ASTRAY FREIGHT When less-than-carload freight has been separated from the regular revenue waybill after it has been marked for destination, it is usually referred to as astray freight.

ATA—AMERICAN TRUCKING ASSOCIATIONS The nationwide association of trucking companies in the United States is called the American Trucking Associations. It has headquarters in Washington, D.C.

ATHWART OR ATHWARTSHIP At right angles to the keel of the vessel.

AT SIGHT A term used on a bill of exchange to indicate that the bill is payable on demand without any days grace.

AUDITING The review of freightbills to determine errors is called auditing. An outside auditor or an inside rate man performs the auditing operations. A shipper usually is given 48—120 hours to review bill of lading charges for payment. Motor, and freight forwarders may extend seven days credit.

AUDITOR An accountant who analyzes and passes upon the accuracy of accounts.

AUTHORITY OF LAW Where there is an exercise of the police powers of a state.

AUTHORITY TO NEGOTIATE The advise of a bank to a local exporter, based on instructions from its foreign correspondent, to negotiate the exporter's drafts on a foreign buyer if the drafts are accompanied by certain specific documents.

AUTHORITY TO PAY This document is not a letter of credit, but merely an advice of the place of payment which also specifies documents needed to obtain payment. It does not oblige any bank to pay. It is much less expensive than a letter of credit and has been largely superseded by "documents against payment" (D/P).

AUTHORITY TO PURCHASE An authorization extended by the buyer's bank to an American bank, permitting the American bank to purchase the seller's time draft drawn on the buyer and payable to the issuing bank. This authority can be issued in a revocable or an irrevocable form. An irrevocable authority may be confirmed by the advising or paying bank, while the revocable authority is never confirmed. It also stipulates whether drafts are to be drawn with or without recourse to the seller. At the time of processing, the seller receives the face amount of the draft, and the issuing bank's account is charged face value plus fees. An irrevocable authority without recourse offers the seller (the drawer) the same protection as an irrevocable letter of credit. It differs from an irrevocable letter of credit in that the draft is drawn on the buyer, and thus neither bank can create a banker's acceptance. If the draft is drawn with recourse to the seller and the buyer fails to pay at maturity, the seller could be held responsible for refund. "Authority to purchase" exists only in Far Eastern trade.

AUTO CARRIER In motor transportation, this is a low slung trainer with ramps for the carrying of automobiles. This single axle, tandem wheeled trailer can sometimes be converted to a light capacity flatbed trailer.

AUTOMOBILE CAR A car equipped with the facilities for the safe and proper handling of automobiles.

AUTO RACK CONTAINER A container designed to store automobiles for shipment. It may be open or closed sided.

AVAILABLE SEAT MILES The product of seats times miles flown in a transportation service. Applies primarily to air transportation, but seat miles could apply to any carrier mode.

AVAILABLE STOCK The amount of inventory on hand that can be sold or used.

AVAILABLE TON MILES The product of the tonnage capacity carried and miles flown or traveled.

AVERAGE This is a marine insurance term referring to the proportional distribution of a general loss. When a cargo must be jettisoned it is necessary to establish general average charges. The apportionment is usually prorated to the various cargo lots on the basis of value-in addition to the vessel itself and its freight earnings on the voyage. The shipment loss is collected from the insurance company and until this is paid the assessment of the loss constitutes a lien against the shipment. Even a shipper who is not protected by insurance can be made to pay a general contribution for a loss sustained from a jettison of other cargo. In order to validate general average it is necessary to establish the following: the action must be voluntary and for benefit of all; it must have come about as the result of the master's order; it must have been successful and necessary; and it must not have come about as a result of the fault of the party requesting the contribution.

AVERAGE BOND A document signed by contractors to a general average adjustment under which they receive delivery of cargo upon agreeing to pay their proportion of the general average contribution as soon as the amount is known.

AVERAGE CLAUSE A clause inserted in marine insurance policies which specifies certain goods as free from average unless general average applies, or unless the loss is above a certain percentage.

AVERAGE DEMURRAGE AGREEMENT An agreement made between a shipper and a railroad line whereby the shipper is debited for the time cars are held for loading and unloading beyond a certain period and credited for the time cars are released by him within a certain period. Demurrage charges are assessed by the transportation line at the end of the month, for any outstanding debits.

AVERAGE HAUL The average distance in miles traversed by each ton of an aggregate number of tons, determined by dividing the number of ton-miles by the total number of tons.

AVERAGE INVENTORY The average inventory level over a period of time; it is the average of the peak and base stock weighted for the amounts at the intermediate points in time.

AVERAGE WAREHOUSE COST A distinction must be made between the warehouse rate, or storage rate, and the average warehouse cost. The average warehouse cost is comparable to the warehouse rate. It is the cost of housing. When the industrial firm owns its own warehouse it computes the average warehouse cost by summing the cost of operation of the warehouse. This requires adding depreciation cost, warehouse utility cost, warehouse taxes, interest on investment in warehouse, and all other costs except for labor costs, obsolescence costs, stockout costs, and comparable thereto. Since labor costs is charged separately in the public warehouse, private warehouse labor is likewise treated separately.

AVOIDABLE COSTS The total set of costs that will disappear in the firm as a result of one unit reduction in output product or service; concept is applied in abandonment or plane discontinuance analyses.

AVOIRDUPOIS The commercial standard of weight in the United States and Great Britain.

AXLE LOAD This may refer either to an allowance or an existing weight carried on the axle of a motor vehicle. An axle limitation placed on a highway requires that the axle load weight cannot be exceeded by the heaviest axle.

AXLE WEIGHT The gross weight of the heaviest axle of the motor truck.

—B—

BACK DOOR SELLING A purchasing field term for the situation in which a salesman goes around the purchasing manager to have a company engineer or manufacturing manager specify his firm's goods for the purchasing manager to order.

BACK HAUL The traffic for the return movement of a vehicle which is providing a traffic service of known proportion in one direction. The term empty-back-haul infers that a payload has been achieved for the movement in one direction but a return is not available.

BACK HAUL RAIL CHARGES The back haul shipment normally occurs in instances of diversion or reconsignment. The railroad tariff specified the procedure for charging for the back haul service. One common procedure is to assess a charge on a through rate from the point of origin to the final destination, plus a reconsignment charge, in addition to a back haul charge based on the additional miles hauled. Back haul charges may also be figured as if there were a reshipment, with the lowest charges applying. The term out-of-line haul is applied synonymously with back haul shipment.

BACKING A cushion made of paper cloth as a surface sheet, for protection.

BACKING WIRE A piece of hardware (wire) used to take the strain of stopping and reversing of a barge when a towboat is backing. Located usually at the aft of the barge or towboat.

BACK LOG The volume of traffic left at a station after a scheduled flight, and which normally would have moved by that flight.

BACK ORDER PROCEDURE Procedure to be used when customer orders a quantity to be shipped which is in excess of what is on hand.

BAD ORDER CARS Freight cars awaiting repair, and therefore out of use, are termed bad order cars. A car which had been condemned and is awaiting dismantling or sale may likewise be referred to as a bad order car.

BAD ORDER FREIGHT A term applied to freight, the condition of which indicates that some of it may have been lost or damaged.

BAG A flexible material used as a container.

BAGGAGE Articles ordinarily carried by travelers.

BAGGAGE CHECK A receipt given to a passenger by a carrier for baggage transported by it.

BAG TRUCK A truck with two fixed wheels, having the framework of a pair of shafts and a shoe protection or blade.

BAIL A container handle.

BAILEE One to whom goods are entrusted.

BAILMENT (a) A delivery of goods by one party to another, to be held according to the purpose of the delivery and to be returned or delivered when that purpose is accomplished. (b) A transfer of possession without transfer of title.

BAILOR One who entrusts goods to another.

BAIT BOX Device with food inside to lure rodents and trap them.

BAIT STATION Area where poisoned food is placed to kill rodents.

BALANCE An equality between the debit and credit sides of an account, and designated *in balance*. This term also represents the amount remaining after a lesser quantity or sum has been deducted from a larger—and known as *balance due* or *balance on hand.*

BALANCE OF PAYMENTS A debit and credit system used by nations to account for payments made by residents to foreigners and payments made by foreigners to residents. When they're equal, there is a balance of payments.

BALANCE OF TRADE The difference in value between total imports and exports of a country.

BALESPACE Expressed in cubic feet, it is the cargo space under the deck.

BALLAST Increases stability by placing a quantity of weighty substances (iron, stone, gravel, etc.) in the lower hold of a vessel to lower the center of gravity.

BALLAST BONUS Denotes a way that a charter can receive more of a payload.

BALLAST CAR A special vehicle for carrying ballast and grading material for roadwork.

BALLOON FREIGHT Cargo that is light, bulky, and has low density.

BAND Strapping of metal.

BANDING Material used to wrap around the shipment to hold it in place. Material nailed to the sides of a car or trailer to hold merchandise in place.

BANK A facility where transactions of loans, exchange of money, extension of credit, and where reserve money is stored.

BANK CREDIT A term to denote the practice of a bank to increase the size of an account of a depositor to create credit; these purchases become assets of the bank.

BANK DRAFT This is a *negotiable instrument* made out by a seller against the purchaser which directs the payment of a given amount of money through an intermediary bank. They are very similar to checks made on bank accounts.

BANKERS ACCEPTANCE A term usually used in international trade; the bank pays specific bills for one of its customers.

BANKING SYSTEM A financial institution that encourages credit that will create economic growth. The system has three primary functions: (1) lending money; (2) acceptance of funds on deposit; (3) creating and lending of its own credit.

BANK RATE A control of credit.

BANKRUPTCY ACT An Act to accord relief to railroads and effect their reorganization, approved March 3, 1933; often referred to as Section 77 Bankruptcy.

BAR DRAFT Maximum clearance for a ship to pass over the sand bar.

BAREBACK The tractor alone—without its semi-trailer.

BARE BOAT CHARTER A ship without a crew that is chartered.

BARGE A flat-bottom boat used primarily in the transportation of such bulk cargo as coal, brick, gravel, sand and lumber, etc., and employed in inland and coastwise water transportation movements. It may be pulled or pushed by a tugboat, or it may be self-propelled.

BAR POLE CHARTER A ship without a crew that is chartered.

BARQUE (OR BARK) A three-masted vessel carrying no square sails on the mizzen mast.

BARRATRY The willful act of officers or other members of a ship's crew in destroying, injuring, stealing, or otherwise performing a harmful act on a vessel or its cargo.

BARREL Made of either wood, aluminum or steel, it is a container of cylindrical shape which is longer than it is wide and ends have equal diameters,

BARREL BARK In freight measurement, five cubic feet.

BARRIER A term to describe the separation of one element from another by an agent.

BARRIER MATERIAL Materials that can withstand water, oil, vapor and various other gases.

BARTER A direct exchange of one commodity or service for another.

BASE A term to denote either the container floor or home depot of container or equipment, or other transportation equipment.

BASILOAD Lift truck attachment designed to handle appliances with a handling flap on the carton.

BASIN A basin is a dock for the berthing of ships along side of quays.

BASING POINT RATE A designated geographic point which is the basis for constructing rates to or from the basing point to the designated destination is called a basing point rate. It is common practice to construct a rate by using the rate to the basing point plus a differential to a destination beyond.

BASING POINT In a general geographic area, a particular point or city may be identified as representing the general area for rate making purposes. It may also be the point used in constructing through rates between other points. Sometimes it is the location specified in the sales contract for the purpose of making price determination.

BASE STOCK Generally, base stock is synonymous with base inventory level. This is thought to equal the aggregate lot size inventory, plus safety stock. Under a "Q" System of inventory management, where order quantity is optimized, and ordering may occur whenever the stock level reaches the reorder point, the ELQ (most economic logistics qty.) plus the safety stock would equal the aggregate stock level. This would equal the base stock. Some writers equate the base stock with the lead stock, or the reorder quantity, but it actually equals the lead stock, plus the normal use stock, plus the safety stock.

BATCH PROCESSING PRODUCTION Production taking place in groups or lots rather than continuously.

BAY A designated area within a section of a storage area outlined by markings on columns, posts or floor. An inlet on the sea.

BAY STORAGE The use of a large designated area for storing merchandise.

BAZAAR An oriental term for a market or place of trade, and particularly applied to shops for sale of fancy articles known as Bazaar Goods.

BEACON A signal light for the guidance of mariners; usually erected and sustained by the government.

BEACONAGE Money paid for the maintenance of a beacon.

BEAM The greatest width of a ship.

BEAN HAULER A trucker of vegetables and fruit.

BEARER One who holds and presents for payment a bill, draft, note or check.

BEARINGS OF A VESSEL The water line at its widest part when in trim.

BED A trailer or truck floor.

BEDDING (CHARGE) At most of the large stock yards, straw, sand, hay or sawdust with which to cover the floor of live stock cars is furnished, and a charge, usually assessed per car, is made for the service in addition to the rate.

BELL BOOK A book to record the time and signal of engine orders.

BELLY A term applied to a jet aircraft which refers to its underfloor cargo area. Each aircraft usually has fore and aft compartments which are heated and pressurized.

BELT DRIVEN This applies to a tractor with tandem axles. Belts connected to powered front-axle transmit power to rear axle.

BELT LINE An interchange rail carrier circumventing the city often serves the purpose of switching for a commercial area. Belt railroads make it possible for a carrier approaching a major commercial area to circumvent the area. This provides a great saving of time by avoiding transportation to the city center for a complex switching process.

BENDING BOARD A term to denote a capability of withstanding a single fold through 180 degrees F. without damaging the plies in paperboard.

"B" END OF THE CAR The end of the car where handbrake is located.

BENEAPED The term to denote a vessel run aground by the spring tides. These are the highest tides of the year.

BENEFICIARY A person or a business entity to whom the money is payable. The entity in whose favor the letter of credit is issued. The seller and the drawer of the draft.

BENELUX The Belgium, Netherlands and Luxembourg custom union.

BERANEK The name of a guide used to determine the share of revenue for carriers in an interline.

BERTH The water area at the edge of a wharf or pier provided for a vessel for the purpose of discharging its passengers or cargo is called a berth. When a ship is *on the berth* it is in position to discharge its cargo.

BERTH CARGO Freight a steamship does not normally solicit due to its poor shipping characteristics or low freight rates, but is often carried at low rates rather than sail the ship with water ballast; the berth cargo itself serves as a sort of ballast.

BERTH CHARTER, PORT CHARTER A charter contract of affreightment for loading *on berth.*

BERTH RATES In maritime, rates charged by regularly operating water lines on general cargo as distinguished from rates on full cargoes and chartered vessels.

BERTH (SLEEPING CAR) The upper and lower beds in the space called a section is referred to as a berth.

BIBLE The *Golden Rule* safe driving book.

BIG HAT A state trooper.

BIG RIGGER A driver who refuses to drive anything but big trucks.

BILATERAL AIR-TRANSPORTER AGREEMENT Two nations exchanging air transport rights over specified routes in some type of an agreement.

BILATERALISM The act of two countries exchanging goods and services to protect each country's consumer from international specialization.

BILGE AND CANTLINE When barrels are stowed in a ship's hold, the bilge of the upper tier of the barrels fits into the cantline of the lower of the barrels to save space. The bilges of the lower tier are normally raised off the floor by beds. The bungs are placed up to prevent leakage.

BILGE KNUCKLE Denotes when the frame turns from the barge's vertical side to form the bottom of the barge.

BILL A name given to statements in writing; as goods, a draft, a note, etc. In another sense a law not enacted; also an exhibition of charges.

BILL AND NOTE BROKER One who negotiates the purchases and sales of bills of exchange and promissory notes.

BILL, ADVANCE A bill used with a correction notice to denote a transfer of charges due to an error in billing a shipment.

BILL BOOK A register of bills of exchange payable or receivable by a firm.

BILL DISCOUNTING The act of raising money on a bill of exchange at interest before it matures.

BILLED WEIGHT The weight shown in a waybill and freight bill for purposes of constructing the freight charges; may be different than actual weight in load.

BILLET CAR A gondola car built entirely of steel for the purposes of transporting steel billets is referred to as a billet car.

BILLING The process of sending a statement of charges to customers who have purchased on credit.

BILLING AND GUIDE BOOK A schedule containing instructions for a waybill or the making out of a waybill.

BILLING MINIMUM The smallest amount of money charged a customer regardless of activity.

BILL OF CREDIT A letter of instructions issued by one person to another authorizing or directing the latter to pay a sum of money or to give credit for a certain amount to a third person named therein and promising to reimburse the person making the advance requested.

BILL OF ENTRY The statement of the nature and value of goods entering a customs house is detailed on the bill of entry. It is employed for statistical reference.

BILL OF EXCHANGE When a signed order directs the addressee to pay a given amount of money to bearer on demand, or as of a given date, the document is called the bill of exchange. If it is payable in the country where made up, the bill of exchange is referred to as a domestic or inland bill of exchange. A foreign bill of exchange is often used to obtain payment for an export shipment.

BILL OF HEALTH The authorities of a port make out a bill of health to a vessel operator which designates the state of the port with respect to public health at the time of sailing. A clean bill of health states that no plague or other contagious diseases exist at the time of sailing. A foul or touched bill of health confirms that a contagious disease exists, or is suspected, or anticipated.

BILL OF LADING (B/L) Both the straight non-negotiable and the order negotiable bill of lading document are contracts for transportation between the shipper and the carrier. The contents of the bill of lading were outlined originally in an act effective January 1, 1917 which codified the preparation, handling and negotiability of bills of lading in interstate commerce. There are numerous types of bills of lading. Some are Clean Bills of Ladings, Onboard Bills of Lading, Optional Form Bills of Lading, Received for Shipment Bill of Lading, Short Form Bill of Lading, etc.

BILL OF LADING, CERTIFIED When the consular officer endorses an ocean bill of lading, and specifies that the shipment meets certain requirements of his country for importation, a certified bill of lading is provided.

BILL OF LADING, CLEAN (OR CLEAR) A clean bill of lading, or a carrier-receipted bill of lading, is provided when a shipment is in good condition with no apparent loss or damage. Under these circumstances the bill of lading contains no exceptions and is a readily negotiable instrument.

BILL OF LADING, EXPORT (THROUGH) In international joint land-water carrier movements, a through bill of lading is issued by the inland carrier to contract for the movement of goods from an interior point of origin to the ultimate foreign destination.

BILL OF LADING, NEGOTIABLE OR "TO ORDER" A bill of lading consigned directly to the order of a party, usually, the shipper or a bank, whose endorsement is required to transfer the title to the merchandise. Title thereafter passes to the holder or party to whom it is endorsed. The bill of lading must be surrendered to the steamship, railroad, or trucking company before the goods will be released.

BILL OF LADING, NON-NEGOTIABLE OR STRAIGHT A bill of lading consigned directly to the consignee and therefore not negotiable. Goods will usually be delivered by the steamship, air carrier, truck or railroad company without surrender of the bill of lading.

BILL OF LADING, "ORDER NOTIFY" The same as negotiable or to order, except that the bill of lading contains an additional clause to the effect that a specified party, usually at the port of destination, is to be notified upon arrival of the merchandise. The insertion of this clause does not give the party to be notified title to the goods.

BILL OF LADING, THROUGH A bill of lading issued by a shipping company or its agent covering more than one mode of transportation.

BILL OF MATERIALS A term in Materials Requirements Planning listing the components required in the manufacturing of an item.

BILL OF PARCELS A document containing a detailed account of goods sold and sometimes used for invoice; also known as a *Facture*.

BILL OF SALE A contract for the sale of goods.

BILL OF SIGHT A custom house document, allowing consignee to see goods before paying duties. Such inspection is made in the presence of a customs officer and is requested by an importer for the purpose of obtaining details which will enable him to prepare a correct Bill of Entry. This latter document must be completed within three days of Bill of Sight, otherwise goods are removed to government warehouses.

BILL OF STORES A license to re-import dutiable British goods free within five years of the original date of exportation.

BILL OF SUFFERENCE When coastal vessels are given the authority to carry goods in bond, a document known as a bill of sufference is provided.

BILLS OF LADING ACT The United States Congress passed the Bills of Lading Act, January 1, 1917, which provided for the requirements necessary in the preparation of a bill of lading, and the character of the negotiability of the bill of lading.

BILLS PAYABLE Bills and notes issued in favor of other parties.

BILLS RECEIVABLE Bills and notes made by others and payable to ourselves.

BINDERS Slang term for brakes.

BIN STORAGE Storage in bins so that an item may be withdrawn without breaking open a package containing a number of such items.

BIRDYBACK The intermodal operation of highway freight containers for a joint motor-air shipment.

BIT A term in short for a binary digit.

BITTS These are used for the purpose of securing mooring or working lines by the means of steel casts or wooden posts.

BLANK Shipping forms such as way bills, vouchers, bills of lading, export declarations and the like, are often referred to as blanks. In a more distinct sense a blank is a space left in form to be filled in with the insertion of words necessary to complete the sense or to adapt the same to one particular case.

BLANK BILL A bill of exchange from which the name of the payee is omitted.

BLANK CREDIT This term signifies permission to draw money on account, no particular sum being specified.

BLANK ENDORSEMENT The endorsement of a Bill of Exchange without specifying the name of the person or persons to whom it is given.

BLANKET BOND Coverage of a group of people or properties through a bond.

BLANKET ORDERING A system in which a firm agrees to buy a large quantity of goods from a vendor over time; each order in the blanket order is then handled in a simplified manner since the goods are part of the overall agreement.

BLANKET POLICY In marine insurance, a policy not on particular goods but on whatever there may be at a certain time or a varying quantity, such as on a stock of goods subject to sale and replenishing, or the cargo of a vessel on a particular voyage.

BLANKET RATES A blanket rate is the extension of the group rate principal to an extreme. Carrier and market competition may create the grouping of a geographic area that covers a large part of continental United States into a single group. Thus, a grouping of the area west of the Cascade range might be considered a blanket rate grouping. It is believed that the most significant single causal factor for transcontinental group rates is competition between rail carriers and inter-coastal water carriers. The establishment of blanket rates under these circumstances provides a means of avoiding violation of Section 10726 on inland points. A movement to or from any point in the blanket area to a given point takes the same rate.

BLANKET TARIFF SUPPLEMENT A single publication containing additions to or changes in two or more tariffs.

BLANKET WAYBILL A waybill covering two or more consignments of freight.

BLASTING AGENTS A material designed for blasting which has been tested in accordance with DOT regulations and found to be so insensitive that there is very little probability of accidental initiation to explosion or of transition from deflagration to detonation.

BLIND CHECK The tallying or checking of freight without access to records disclosing kind and amount of freight contained in the shipment.

BLIND CORNER Intersection of an aisle or storage area where vision is blocked.

BLIND SIDE The right side of a truck and trailer.

BLIND TALLY Counting and recording in bound goods without package list or manifest indicating what might be on the load.

BLOCKADE The act of besieging or blockading the passage of supplies by a hostile nation. The prevention of moving passengers or property to, through or from a specific point.

BLOCK DIRECTORY A list of the principal points in rate blocks with a code showing the belt and tier to be used in determining the scale and mileage in computing the rate.

BLOCKED SPACE A large volume shipper agreeing to ship a given minimum volume of freight between two cities over a given period of time. Provides the shipper a lower rate.

BLOCK (EXPRESS) Groups of points considered together for the purpose of rate making in connection with express transportation.

BLOCKING When pieces of wood or other material are used to prevent the movement of goods in a car it is referred to as blocking. It is used in the loading of rail shipments in order to prevent damage from breaking. Blocking regulations are established by the Interstate Commerce Commission and the Association of American Railroads. Bracing is a term which might be regarded as synonymous.

BLOCK RATE A rate applying between a point in one express block and a point in another.

BLOCK SYSTEM A system was devised for dividing railroad tracks into blocks of three or four miles in order to establish signal systems for safety purposes. Under the block system, a train cannot enter a block area until the preceding train has departed. Automatic brakes are supposed to prevent this happening.

BLOCK TIME A term to denote actual time the aircraft uses after it removes his blocks by his wheels until their replacement at the aircraft destination.

BLOCK TO BLOCK SPEED A term to denote speed from the time an aircraft engine starts to the time of shutting off the engine at the destination.

BLUE LABEL A term applied to radioactive cargo's warning label.

BOARD, FACE Face of the box material.

BOARD, GREASEPROOF Greaseproof paper or board made of such material as glassine, so it can be pasted to paperboard, making the paperboard grease and oil resistant.

BOARD, KRAFTLINEN Sulphate pulp material in the top liner of the paperboard, for exceptional strength.

BOARD, LAMINATED Two processes for paperboard: (1) combining two or more plies together; or (2) combining either side of a thin paper with specific properties.

BOARD OF TRADE An association of business men or firms to regulate matters of trade and further their mutual interest; also called Chamber of Commerce, Merchants' Association, and the like.

BOARD, STENCIL A product that is used to produce lettering and numbers. It is made of stiff oil kraft board.

BOARD, V. Fiberboard made by U.S. government specifications.

BOB TAIL Another term for a tractor driven without its trailer; it can also refer to a straight truck.

BODY TRACK Each of the parallel tracks of the yard, upon which cars are sorted or stored.

BOGEY A term to denote a chassis that has two axles.

BOGIE TRUCK Known as a restless dolly, it is a low skeleton platform mounted on two load carrying wheels, and fitted with either two or four stabilizing wheels.

BOILER INSPECTION ACT A federal act was passed in 1911 requiring the inspection of boilers and steam generating facilities on locomotives involved in interstate and international commerce.

BOLL WEEVIL An inexperienced truck driver.

BOLSTER To block or hold a container on a trailer or railcar by a special device.

BOMB HOAX False information of a bomb on the plane.

BONA FIDE In good faith.

BOND This term applies to a long term debt which is under contract, and has a specified interest rate and date due.

BONDED GOODS Goods in charge of officers of customs and on which bonds instead of cash have been given for export duties.

BONDED WAREHOUSE Goods which must be held until duties are paid or goods are otherwise properly released are normally put in a bonded warehouse. This warehouse must be approved by the U.S. Treasury Department, and it must be under bond or guarantee for compliance with the revenue laws.

BOND NOTE A customs certificate showing that the bond has been given with reference to the regular acceptance of dutiable goods from a government or bonded warehouse.

BOND OF INDEMNITY A bond of indemnity is a certificate filed with the carrier for the purpose of relieving it from liability or the payment of charges that might result from some action for which it might otherwise be liable a second time.

BONDSMAN One who gives security for the performance of an act, payment of money or integrity of nature.

BOOKING The act of recording arrangements for the movement of goods by vessels.

BOOKING NUMBER An identity reference on bills; it is usually the number placed on a contract of affreightment.

BOOKING REQUEST FORM The form often used by steamship companies on which shippers describe freight when seeking space on a certain sailing.

BOOKING SPACE The act of contracting space aboard a vessel for cargo which is to be transported.

BOOK INVENTORY A record of items on hand by type and number based on the paperwork recording of receipts and shipments during a given period.

BOOK INVESTMENT Recording in the accounts of carriers on how much their assets are worth.

BOOK VALUE Property carried in the investment account of the general ledger of a carrier is valued at book value. It is also the amount carried in the general ledgers to record investments in securities, which could be a very different figure from the par value of the securities.

BOOM ATTACHMENT Used to lift hollow objects, it is an attachment to a forklift truck.

BOOMERS Devices used to tighten the chains holding the truck shipment.

BOOM IT DOWN Tighten the chains holding the truck shipment.

BOOT-TOPPING Denoted usually by a red band of paint at the waterline.

BOTTLERS BODY A truck body designed for the movement of cased and bottled beverages.

BOTTOM DUMPS Trailer that unloads through the use of bottom gates.

BOTTOMRY The act of borrowing for the purposes of repair of a vessel, or the purchase of equipment for a vessel, is termed bottomry. When this is done the ship or its cargo is pledged as security for the loan.

BOTTOMRY BOND The instrument or obligation generally executed in a foreign port in repayment of or as security for sums advanced to supply necessities for the ship, together with such interest as may be agreed upon. The bond creates a lien upon the ship, enforceable in Admiralty in case of safe arrival in port of destination, but becoming absolutely void in the event the vessel is lost before arrival at port. In order to make valid a bottomry bond against a ship, the following requisites are necessary: the repairs or supplies must be necessary; the master must have no apparent funds or credit available in the port; and the repairs or supplies must be such as would have been ordered by a prudent owner, had they been present.

BOW FENDER A term to denote a device to protect the bow of a tugboat against damage; made of intertwined rope or rubber strips.

BOX Refers to a semi-trailer; also used to refer to the transmission of the tractor.

BOXBOARD DIMENSIONS Dimensions of a box, where width is given first, then length.

BOX CAR A closed railroad car with a roof and door in the sides and/or ends, which is used for general service in railroad transportation. It provides protection for the shipment from weather and pilferage as required under the responsibilities specified in the bill lading.

BOX, CLEATED FIBERBOARD A five or six cleated panel faces in a rigid container.

BOX, CLEATED WOOD A reinforced nailed wood box, inside or outside, with one or more sides and/or ends.

BOX, CORRUGATED AND SOLID FIBER A container made of either solid fiberboard or corrugated fiberboard. It is a rectangular and three dimensional shipping container.

BOX, FOLDING PAPER A carton made of bending grade paperboard having a thickness of .016 or .045 inches, and suitable for packaging; not weighing more than ten pounds.

BOX, LINERED END A wirebound box, reinforced with liners, stapled across the grain.

BOX, LOCK CORNER Side and end members of a wooden box that are joined together by locks which interlock and are held together by glue. The ends are fastened by nails.

BOX, PLAIN END An unreinforced box.

BOX, PLYWOOD Made of single piece plywood. A box with a top, bottom, ends and sides which are nailed to cleats.

BOX, SET-UP A box made of paper and paperboard that is three dimensional rigid in set up form, and has a specified class.

BOX, SET UP DROP-END A two part, set up paper box, where the side of the base is made in two parts, which can be hinged together or an end is hinged to the bottom.

BOX, SET UP FORM A piece of boxboard which is loose or attached and placed within a base or lid.

BOX, TELESCOPE A container of two sections. The lid fits over the base.

BRACING Protecting the contents of a car to prevent shifting and damage. Several methods of bracing are employed, such as center, crib, crosscar, diagonal, K, knee, side, and top bracing. Bracing used inside a car is called *bulkheading.* (See *blocking*)

BRANDING A method of putting addresses on wooden packages by means of hot irons; also used on cattle to denote ownership.

BREACH (OF CONTRACT) A violation or a breach of a contract or duty, either by acting or by failing to act, as in the case of a carrier not delivering goods, which it has contracted to transport.

BREADTH A term measured by the distance between the outer faces of the frames is called the molded breadth. The registered breadth is measured between the outside of the shell plating.

BREAK-AWAY Denotes the parts of a three piece trailer; the gooseneck, platform and rear axles.

BREAK BULK 1) When a large shipment is inbound to a distribution center, it is necessary to subdivide its many different component commodities for the purpose of scattered distribution. 2) Break bulk may also take the form of reducing a very large shipment of a single commodity to many small shipments to satisfy the need of dispersed buyers. 3) Term also applies to ocean shipping of packaged goods that are not containerized.

BREAK BULK BOAT A ship that carries packaged, crated, bagged, etc., freight.

BREAK BULK POINT A point at which a portion or all of the contents of a car are unloaded and distributed.

BREAKAGE An allowance made by a shipper for loss caused by the destruction of merchandise.

BREAKEVEN LOAD FACTOR The minimum percentage of airplane seats or freight capacity on a run that must be filled in order to avoid a loss on the flight; the percent of seats necessary to be filled in order to cover variable and direct fixed costs of the flight.

BREAK-EVEN POINT A point where total cost equals total revenue at a certain production level. The point where revenue equals the sum of fixed and variable costs.

BREAKING DOORWAY After the safe placement of the dock plate, unloading of the railcar can commence. If the load is deadpiled, it will be necessary to place an empty pallet load. It will be necessary to offload enough product by this method until enough space is clear inside the railcar to place a pallet on the floor of the car.

BREAKING POINT A point at which the rate is divided or at which rates are made.

BREAK THE UNIT The process of uncoupling, or unhitching, the tractor from the trailer.

BREAKWATER Denotes an enbankment or bulkhead that provides shelter from the sea.

BREAST WIRE The attachment between two barges, or a barge and towboat that leads directly athwartship at right angle to the reel.

BRIDGE PLATE A portable metal plate which is placed in the doorway of a railroad car to provide a ramp between two cars, or between a car and a platform.

BRIDGE TOLL A charge made for transporting traffic over a bridge.

BRIEF A written abstract of testimony and pleadings in a case and commentaries thereon.

BROACHING CARGO A term to denote breaking into the ships cargo and stealing food, drink, and other articles for individual use.

BROKEN STOWAGE Denotes when space for storage is interfered with by parts of the ship that extend into the hold. Odds and ends of freight are used to fill the spaces.

BROKER A person who owns equipment and leases it out, or a person who arranges buying and selling of marketable items. A ship agent who acts for the ship owner or charterers. He locates cargo and performs business for the ship.

BROKERAGE LICENSE Authority granted by Interstate Commerce Commission to persons engaged in the business of arranging for transportation of persons or property in interstate commerce.

BROWNIE An auxiliary transmission.

BUDGET A formal financial plan for future income and expenditures.

BUDGETARY CONTROL The actual performance under the planned budget of each department.

BUFFER STOCK A certain level of inventory maintained on account of sales demand and lead time variations so as not to incur an out of stock situation.

BULK DENSITY Stated in pounds per cubic foot, this is the weight of a unit of volume of a given substance.

BULK (FREIGHT) When a carload shipment is shipped loose or in mass, rather than being shipped in packages or containers, it is termed bulk-freight shipment. This commonly takes place in the movement of grain in a box car, sand in a hopper car, or in the transportation of sulfur in the hold of a ship.

BULKHEAD An upright partition in a car, vehicle, or vessel which separates one part of it from another.

BULK HEADING See *Bracing*.

BULK WAREHOUSES Public warehouses providing tank storage of liquids and open or sheltered storage of dry products such as coal, sand, stone and chemicals.

BULK WEIGHT This is the weight the carrier will show on a way bill or a freight bill for the purposes of assessing the charge.

BULKY A term applied to freight taking up considerable space in comparison to its weight.

BULLETIN A notice or an announcement officially published concerning matters of public importance.

BULL HAULER A livestock mover.

BULLION A commercial name for uncoined gold or silver.

BULL MARKET A condition of rising prices of the most traded items, such as a bond, stock, commodity, etc., in the market.

BUMBLE BEE A two cycle engine.

BUNCHING (CARS) When cars are accumulated in excess of those ordered for the purpose of loading or unloading, or when cars are gathered in quantities that exceed the capacity of the tracks and unloading facilities, it creates a condition known as bunching.

BUNKER CHARGE Coal loaded into the bunkers of a vessel for the use of the vessel is assessed a bunker charge for the loading operation. This does not include the cost of the coal itself.

BUNKER CLAUSE A clause that charterers must replace and pay for the fuel and coal in the vessel's bunkers at port of delivery.

BUNKERING The task of fueling a ship so that the greatest payload may be carried.

BUNKER (REFRIGERATOR) The place where ice is stored in a refrigerator car.

BUNKERS Denotes stowage space for coal in a vessel.

BUOYS Floats that give mariners information by their shape and color.

BURDEN OF PROOF Proving disputed facts which are at issue in a proceeding; viz. the Interstate Commerce Act provides that the burden of proof is upon the carriers to show that changes in rates, rules, etc., are reasonable.

BURDEN VESSEL A vessel that has to yield to an oncoming vessel.

BUREAU VERITAS Classifications of ships by the French Society.

BURTON FALL A rope, cable, or whip which passes through a block set which is outboard above the wharf and beyond the gunwhale of the vessel for the purpose of lowering or hoisting goods to or from the hatch to the wharf.

BUSH FLYING Flying in remote regions where there may be no airports or other navigable aids.

BUSHEL A dry measure containing eight gallons or four pecks, $18^{1/2}$ inches in diameter and 8 inches deep in size. Its capacity is 2,150.42 cubic inches.

BUSINESS Any activity where business transactions and operations take place.

BUSINESS CYCLE The combination of recession and expansion of business activities over considerable time. There are different types of cycles for different time periods.

BUSINESS FLYING A term to denote owner operated air transportation for the purpose of business.

BUSTING STRENGTH The actual strength (in weights) a package can withstand.

BUTTON HER UP The process of tying down the load on the trailer.

"BUY AMERICAN ACT" Legislation requiring that certain military and government purchased or financed goods be purchased from U.S suppliers only.

BUYER One who orders goods and agrees to pay them.

BUYER'S RIGHT TO ROUTE The right of the buyer to designate the route of his shipment, when the seller doesn't pay freight charges. The seller is held responsible for the buyer's instructions. Routing is permitted for rail shipments, but not for motor shipments beyond the first carrier.

BY-LAW Located in the constitution or in a fundamental law for the use of authority.

BY-PRODUCTS An accessory product of some value resulting from some specific process or manufacture.

BY THE STERN A term to denote that a vessel is deeper than normal at the stern, because of excess weight aft.

—C—

CAB The driver's operating compartment of a tractor on a truck or the locomotive of a rail engine.

C.A.B. The Civil Aeronautics Board, which is the economic regulatory authority for common carrier interstate air transportation. The Civil Aeronautics Board was established under the Civil Aeronautics Act of 1938, but was called the Civil Aeronautics Authority until 1960.

CABOOSE The car used by the brakeman and conductor which is placed at the rear of the freight train is called a caboose or a cabin car. Sometimes also referred to as the conductor's car, or the way-car.

CABOTAGE This water transportation term applies to shipments between ports of a nation. It commonly refers to coast-wide navigation or trade. Many nations, like the United States, have cabotage laws which require domestic owned vessels to perform domestic interport water transportation services.

CAB-OVER A truck tractor unit that has the engine under the driver's cab and the front of the vehicle is flat; cab overs allow for longer trailers within the overall tractor-trailer length limitation.

C & F NAMED PORT A selling term in international trade whereby the seller quotes a goods price that includes the freight charge to the named point of destination.

C.&L. Canal and lake.

CALL STATION The pickup and delivery station presented by a carrier. Warehouse and dock facilities are not available at the call station.

CANCELLING DATE The date agreed upon by the ship owner and charterer which the vessel must be ready for loading. Missing the loading date represents just cause for cancelling the charter contract.

CAPACITY The amount that can be carried in a vessel, truck, or car expressed in terms of weight or measurement, is its capacity.

CAPACITY AGREEMENT An agreement among airlines to limit flights in certain origin-destination markets in order to conserve fuel.

CAPACITY PLATE Plate affixed to a forklift truck or forklift truck attachment indicating the maximum weight which can be raised or moved.

CAPITAL CHARGE A budgetary charge made by a firm against assets employed in divisions, departments or subsidiaries; it reflects the opportunity cost of the firm's funds tied up in fixed assets; example, 15% of asset book value.

CAPITAL RATIONING The process of allocating funds to capital budget requests; consists of the basic project accept/reject decision.

CAPSTAN The capstan is a mechanism used to raise and lower heavy weights, move objects, assist in the mooring of a vessel, and sometimes to move dead engines in a terminal area.

CAPTAIN'S PROTEST A document prepared by the captain of a vessel on arriving at port, showing conditions encountered during voyage — generally for purpose of relieving ship owner of any loss to cargo, thus requiring cargo owners to look to the insurance company for reimbursement.

CAPTIVE SHIPPER Railroad industry term for a shipper that has no other railroad company option to ship to a destination other than the one serving the origin plant.

CAR DAY One freight car on a railroad line held for a 24-hour period is a car day.

CARDEX FILE System of cards used to report and keep track of inventory levels, inbound and outbound shipments.

CARETAKER A person accompanying a shipment requiring special attention while en route.

CARFLOAT A flat-bottomed boat used to ship rail cars. They are used primarily in harbor areas, and are equipped, of course, with track.

CARGO The lading (contents) of a railroad car or trailer.

CARGO TONNAGE The weight in U.S. is 2000 lbs. or 2240 pounds. In British countries it is in the English long or gross ton of 2240 pounds. In France and other countries having the metric system the weight ton is 2204.62 pounds. The usual measured ton is 40 cubic feet, but in some instances a larger number of cubic feet is taken as a weight ton.

CAR LINING Materials placed on the walls of a car for the protection of the goods.

CARLOAD The weight requirement necessary to qualify for a carload rate is a carload; or, a car loaded to its total capacity may also be called a carload.

CARLOAD MINIMUM WEIGHT The weight which must be transported or paid for to qualify for a carload rate.

CARLOAD, MIXED A shipment consisting of two or more commodities which meet the requirements of having a total weight equal or greater than the minimum weight of the highest minimum weight commodity, and which is charged the rate of the highest rate commodity in the mixed carload shipment, qualifies as a mixed carload.

CARLOAD RATE This is a rate that would apply to a quantity qualifying for a minimum carload weight. It is applicable to rail movements. It should be distinguished from a per car rate. The carload rate is applicable to class rates. The carload quantity referred to on a carload rate has nothing to do with the quantity of that commodity that will be required to fill a rail car. The minimum weight specified to qualify for a lower class rate permits a carload rate.

CARLOAD TRAFFIC For the purpose of reporting, a shipment of not less than 10,000 pounds of one commodity from one consignor to one consignee. Where mixed carload ratings are provided in classifications or tariffs a mixed carload is treated as a carload within the meaning of this paragraph, provided such shipment is from one consignor to one consignee at one destination or in the case of shipments upon which stopovers are permitted, from one consignor to two or more consignees each at a different destination; and provided the shipment is waybilled at and the charges are collected upon the basis of the carload rate applicable. In such cases, the shipment is treated as a carload of that commodity which forms the major portion of the shipment in weight.

CARMACK AMENDMENT An amendment to the Interstate Commerce Act that presents the liability of the carrier and the requirements relative to the bill of lading forms and provisions. This is presented in Section 11301 of the Revised Interstate Commerce Act.

CAR MILE The movement of a car a distance of one mile. It may be subdivided into *freight car miles, passenger car miles, loaded car miles,* and *empty car miles.*

CAR POOLING When car equipment is coordinated through the operation of a central control for the joint benefits of the owners and users of the cars, a pooling arrangement is established. This is performed for the benefit of the owners and users of all the cars controlled by the central agency involved in this type of service transportation.

CAR RENTAL An amount which is paid for the use of private cars by carriers and others.

CARRIAGE The actual movement of a consignment of goods from the point of destination after having been loaded and before being unloaded.

CARRIAGE OF GOODS AT SEA ACT U.S. legislation that covers to some degree ocean carrier loss and damage obligations.

CARRIER An individual, partnership or corporation engaged in the business of transporting goods.

CARRIER COMPETITION Competition between one carrier and another serving the same points of origin and destination.

CARRIER, DELIVERING (OR DESTINATION) The common carrier that makes delivery to the consignee in either a joint or single movement is the delivering carrier.

CARRIER, SETTLING The carrier that actually comes to terms with the claimant; in the case of interline settlements, the carrier having a debit balance.

CARRIER'S LIEN When a carrier is forced to retain the property it has transported for security for collection charges, the property becomes a carrier's lien.

CAR SEAL A device fastened to the locks of the doors of cars. Will indicate if door has been opened.

CAR SERVICE This is a general term which covers such services as car supply, handling and distribution. It usually becomes involved in matters of interchange, demurrage handling, settlements, per diem, allowances, etc.

CAR SERVICE RULE A rule imposed by the ICC so as to provide incentives or disincentives to certain practices in the national rail car fleet; includes powers over per diem, demurrage, car distribution and movement practices.

CARTAGE The charge made for the hauling and the transferring of goods by trucks, wagons, drays, etc. It is short haul and transfer in nature.

CARTAGE AGENT Firm engaged in hauling freight on trucks.

CARTAGE, LOCAL Service performed in local distribution by a common or contract carrier engaged in either local hauling or pickup and delivery service for over-the-road or line-haul carriers.

CARTAGE TO SHIPSIDE The charge made for carting, draying or trucking freight alongside a vessel.

CARTING The hauling of freight on carts, drays or trucks.

CARTON A container constructed of solid or corrugated fiberboard or paperboard.

CARTON CLAMP Attachment for a forklift truck which allows the movement of goods. Product normally not on pallets is squeezed between two flat surfaced, hydraulically operated plates. Designed to handle unitized loads of cartons much like holding a box in between the palms of your hands.

CAR UTILIZATION FACTOR 1. The number of revenue trips per year a rail car handles; 2. The number of days per year in which a car is loaded with revenue moves; 3. The percentage of a car that is loaded in relation to its weight or cubic capacity.

CAR YIELD A railroad management measure of rail car revenue producing experience; it is the total car revenue over a certain period divided by the number of loaded trips. If the car is in a consistent, assigned service, it is the carload revenue times the number of trips per month.

CASE The subject-matter of litigation.

CASH AGAINST DOCUMENTS Payment for goods upon presentation of documents evidencing shipment.

CASH IN ADVANCE A purchasing term that requires payment prior to shipping from seller's point of origin.

CASH WITH ORDER A purchasing term requiring payment with the initial order.

CASUAL LABOR Temporary workers used by the warehouse or office to meet the workload.

CASUAL (OR OCCASIONAL) OPERATIONS In freight or passenger train operations, seasonal service, maintenance, and/or operation, as distinguished from steady, or scheduled operations.

CASUS FORTUITUS Contract of affreightment to protect vessel owner's liability in case of inevitable accident such as lightning and similar perils of the sea.

CAVEAT EMPTOR Let the purchaser beware.

CE Consumption Entry.

CEASE AND DESIST A regulatory order to cease performance of a specific act which is usually in violation of the regulatory Act.

CELLULAR FLOW The term cellular flow is commonly applied in logistics to mean shipment volume. A cellular flow channel planning system involved the determination of the total logistics cost on the basis of the cost per shipment. In-bound and out-bound shipments to and from a factory take the form of single shipment of one or more commodities per shipment. Each shipment is a cell.

CENTERFLOW A type of covered hopper car that has loading hatches longitudinally on the center top of the car; likewise, the internal walls direct the outflow toward a small hatch at the bottom center of the car rather than spilling over the rails as with conventional hoppers and covered hoppers.

CENTRALIZED PRODUCTION When a manufacturer centralizes his production he locates all production facilities in the same general location. In its simplest form, this consists of a single large plant. Obviously, centralized production may consist of many plants located adjacent to one another that are complementary. Centralized production is to be distinguished from decentralized production only by the location of the production facilities, and not on the basis of the overall volume of output. The production of automobiles of the Detroit area is an example of both centralized production for firms as well as centralized production for the industry.

CERTIFICATE OF ADMEASUREMENT A document stating what portion of a vessel is excluded from gross tonnage.

CERTIFICATE OF DAMAGE A document or certificate issued by dock companies in regard to merchandise received or unloaded in a damaged condition.

CERTIFICATE OF INSURANCE A document or certificate taking the place of a marine insurance policy.

CERTIFICATE OF ORIGIN This document is required on shipments to many countries of foreign products that are granted preferential treatment in the trade agreements between the United States and the foreign country. It is a certificate which specifies the country of origin, number of packages, number of boxes or cases, marks and number, gross and net weight, and a description of the goods.

CERTIFICATE OF PUBLIC CONVENIENCE AND NECESSITY This is an operating right for a common carrier in the United States. It is a document which is issued by the regulatory agency of Congress which permits the applicant to operate as a common carrier for a particular mode, usually between specified points, for designated cargo, under established rates.

CERTIFICATE OF REGISTRY A document issued by maritime authorities stating that a ship has been legally registered.

CERTIFICATE OF WEIGHT An authoritative statement issued by the shipper as to the weight of a shipment.

CERTIFIED INVENTORY REPORT An inventory report signed by an officer of the company or designated responsible party to attest to the correctness of the report.

CERTIFIED CHECK A check that has been validated by an official upon which the check is drawn as evidence of payment.

CERTIORARI To be more fully informed. An original writ or action whereby a cause is removed from an inferior to a superior court for trial. The record of the proceedings is then transmitted to the superior court.

CESSER CLAUSE This clause relieves the charter of the responsibility of the shipment from the time the cargo is shipped. It provides the owner with a lien on the cargo and assures the shipper's liability to pay the freight instead of paying the charterer.

CHAIN-FALL This contrivance is used to take off a demountable body from a truck chassis in a sling-like machine.

CHAMFER BLOCK A wooden beam generally used on flat cars to prevent shifting. Short chamfer blocks are sometimes called chock blocks.

CHANNEL The means, in terms of ownership, by which product moves from the manufacturer to final user; includes brokers, wholesalers, company distribution centers, etc.; approximately ten such channels are possible.

CHANNEL JUMPING Situation when a firm by-passes a normal channel party to sell to a final user or buyer; example, large volume sales direct to user rather than through the regular wholesaler in the area.

CHANNEL OF DISTRIBUTION The means by which a manufacturer distributes products from the plant to the ultimate user; includes warehouses, brokers, wholesalers, retailers, etc. Approximately ten distinct channels of distribution are in common use.

CHARGE, CONTINUOUS A shipment made through to destination without an interruption in transit for breaking bulk, transfer, or rebilling.

CHARGES (PAYMENT OF TRANSPORTATION CHARGES) The specified amount of payment for transportation services rendered. Payment must precede the release of the goods. Credit may be extended up to specified days when adequate precautions for payment have been taken.

CHARTER The contracts for the use of a vessel involve numerous types of charters. 1) The Bare Boat Charter is a lease which establishes that the charterer pays all the voyage and cargo expenses, pays crew costs, and covers the marine risk and repair services. 2) The Time Charter provides that the lessee is provided with the provision of ship, supplied with deck and engine room stores for a stated period, for a service within specified limits, to be operated over a given period of time, for a stated amount of money. 3) Under the Net Form Charter the ship is hired for a voyage and the freight may be charged at a specified rate on the dead-weight capacity or on a rate per unit—or even on a lump-sum basis. Under this type of charter the owner pays the operating expenses and the voyage and cargo expenses. 4) The Gross Form Charter establishes the owner pays all the regular expenses involved in a voyage from the time the ship is berthed until the cargo is unloaded.

CHARTERED RATES Charterer agrees to pay a given price per tonnage on the cargo, when leasing a vessel or ship. Under a variety of conditions.

CHARTERED SHIP A ship leased by its owner or agent for a stated time, voyage or voyages.

CHARTERER One who leases a ship or part of its cargo space. A vessel may be hired or leased from its owners in whole or in part for a voyage, a single or round trip, or a stated period, under what is known as trip, or time, charter.

CHARTER PARTY A marine contract between the ship owner and the one leasing the ship. A principal clause of every charter party refers to *lay days*, the time allowed the charterer for loading and/or unloading. These *lay days* are usually calculated from 24 hours after charterers have been notified that vessel is ready to load. They may be either *running days*, i.e., consecutive days, or *working days*, i.e., those days usually devoted to work at the place where the vessel is loaded, omitting holidays and Sundays.

CHECK, BLIND The checking of freight in a given shipment without access to records which show the kind and amount of freight contained in the shipment.

CHECKING (RATES) Comparing rates assessed on a shipment with the tariff applicable or other authority to determine their correctness; considering rates in effect or proposed by representatives of the traffic department of carriers to determine their proper adjustment.

CHICANEUR One who is shrewd, and lays claim to secure rebates and discounts to which he is not entitled.

CHOCKS Blocks or stops which, when placed under the wheels of a railcar or trailer, prevent the vehicle from rolling.

CHUTE Inclined trough used in the movement of grain, livestock, etc.

CIF A selling term in international trade whereby the seller quotes a goods price that includes freight charges to a destination point and marine insurance enroute.

C.I.F.C.I. Cost, Insurance, Freight, Corrections Charges, and Interest. This is the basis of pricing commonly used in the Far East.

CIFI&E Cost, insurance, freight, interest and exchange.

CIRCUITOUS ROUTE This is an indirect route. The ICC gives carriers the right to meet the rates of *short-line* carriers, but it is necessary to limit the percentage of circuity—which is the percent which the long-haul movement exceeds that of the short-line carrier.

CIRCULAR NOTE An issue of the bank for the accommodation of a traveller, calling upon its correspondence at different places to pay money on demand; bill.

CIRCULARS Publications issued by the carriers containing provisions for the handling of freight, distinguished from tariffs in that their provisions are general in character. Circular carriers are carriers that file brief circulars, showing only mileages and a few other facts, with the Interstate Commerce Commission.

CITATION Decided case, statute, decision or book of authority, to establish and prove a point.

CITATION OF AN ADMINISTRATIVE REGULATION Citation form of a regulation found within agency's administrative rulings; for example; ICC's rulings are in Title 49 of the Code of Federal Regulations; loss and damage claim processes are in Part 1005 of that publication; citation is 49 C.F.R. 1005.

CITATION OF DECISION The reference made to the location of a decision or opinion rendered by a court or a commission. A citation such as 29 I.C.C., 161 would be to page 161 of the volume 29, the Interstate Commerce Commission's Report.

CIVIL PENALTIES A term to indicate that the legal penalty for a certain unlawful act includes fines and various decrees.

C.L.&R. Canal, lake and rail.

CLAIM When a document is submitted which shows evidence of a right to recover a loss by damage or overcharge it is referred to as a claim. It may require compensation to the owner for loss or damage of goods in transit. It may involve a request for refund by a carrier for charges in excess of the legal or tariff rate—which is called an overcharge claim. It may involve restitution for losses caused by applications of rates greater than the lawful rates. It may likewise involve a demand made by carriers on shippers for payment of undercharges.

CLAIM TRACER A document seeking to determine the status of a claim which has been made, but not finalized.

CLAMP, BARREL Lift truck attachment designed to handle drums and barrels.

CLAMP, PAPER ROLL Lift truck attachment designed to handle rolled paper products.

CLASS A FREIGHT FORWARDERS Freight forwarders with a gross annual revenue over $100,000 annually.

CLASS B FREIGHT FORWARDERS Freight forwarders with a gross revenue less than $100,000 annually.

CLASS AND COMMODITY TARIFF A tariff containing both class and commodity rates.

CLASSES The various divisions or groups, designated by numbers and/or letters, into which articles offered for shipment are classified and to which rate schedules are adjusted.

CLASSES OF LEGAL SERVICE Transportation carriers are classified in accordance with the character of the legal service offered in the following manner: (1) common carriers of property; (2) contract carriers of property; (3) private carriers of property; and (4) brokers of property.

CLASSES OF MOTOR CARRIERS Motor carriers are classified as Class I, Class II, and Class III. Class I have an average annual operating income of $5,000,000 or greater over a period of three years. Class II motor carriers have an average annual operating income equal to or greater than $1,000,000 but less than $5,000,000 for three successive years. Class III motor carriers have an average annual operating income of less than $1,000,000 for three successive years.

CLASSES OF RAIL CARRIERS Interstate common rail carriers are classified as Class I and Class II. Class I are those with operating revenues of $50,000,000 or more. In 1980 there were 40 Class I railroads.

CLASSIFICATION This publication assigns ratings to articles and commodities for rail, water, motor, freight forwarder class rates. The classification services class rates as contrasted to commodity rates. It is a book that groups commodities into classes for rate making purposes.

CLASSIFICATION OF CARRIERS BY COMMODITY Transportation carriers are classified on the basis of the character of the commodities carried in the following way: (1) carriers of general freight; (2) carriers of household goods; and (3) carriers of special commodities.

CLASSIFICATION OF CARS The designation of letters and the descriptive definitions adopted by the Association of American Railroads to cover various types of freight and passenger cars.

CLASSIFICATION (OF FREIGHT) The grouping of articles that have similar transportation characteristics, for the purpose of simplification. Such factors as weight, risk in handling, bulk, value of article, competition, and cost of handling are considered in determining the class to which any article belongs for the purpose of applying class rates. Also, the class to which articles are assigned for the purpose of applying class rates.

CLASSIFICATION OF SHIPS The process of gathering and correlating information concerning the seaworthiness of vessels which may be used by underwriters in providing an insurance. The registration assistants perform the operation of classification.

CLASSIFICATION RATING The class to which an article is assigned for the purpose of applying class rates.

CLASSIFICATION SCHEDULE A publication that contains the description and ratings of articles offered for shipment, together with the rules and regulations governing their preparation and handling.

CLASSIFICATION TERRITORY The Classification Territory is a geographic area within which the classification of given freight applies. In the United States there are three classification territories. The Official Classification Territory involves the area north of the Ohio and Potomac Rivers and east of Lake Michigan, and a line drawn between St. Louis and Chicago. The Southern Classification Territory is the area south of the Official Classification Territory and East of the Mississippi River. The Western Classification Territory is the rest of the United States west of the Mississippi.

CLASSIFICATION YARD The purpose of the railroad classification yard is to serve as a kind of break bulk station, but in this instance a break car station. A rail train will have its cars separated for movement in differing directions under separate trains in the classification yard. Trains approaching the Minot Burlington Northern Classification yard westbound, for example, would have their cars separated for new trains destined for varying points west, south, and north. One train may be made up for Seattle, another for Denver, and the third for a California destination. A transcontinental shipment may move through many classification yards.

CLASS RATE It is a rate resulting from a rating provided in a classification.

While commodity rates are available only on limited commodities, a class rate can be found on practically any commodity. The rate in the class rate tariff is normally on class 100 commodities. To determine the class rate it is necessary to multiply the first class rate by a percentage figure applicable on its rating. In the uniform freight classification, the percentage of first class is automatically provided in the classification. That is, a class 87 would mean 87% of first class. Class rates were created to simplify the preceding process providing a specific rate on each commodity moved.

CLASS TARIFF A tariff containing only class rates.

CLASS YARD The railroad yard that is used to sort railroad cars for grouping into trains for specific destinations.

CLAYTON ACT An anti-trust act of Congress making price discrimination unlawful. F.T.C. is empowered to enforce these prohibitions.

CLEAN BILL OF LADING A bill of lading which the carrier has accepted without making notations relative to the *Shippers Load and Count.* It represents a clean acceptance of the freight in accordance with the content of the bill of lading.

CLEAN CREDIT (See "Letters of credit").

CLEAN DRAFT A sight or time draft (bill of exchange) to which no additional documents are attached (See "Documentary draft").

CLEANING IN TRANSIT The stopping of articles, such as peanuts, etc., at a point located between the points of origin and destination to be cleaned.

CLEARANCE A customhouse certificate stating that a ship is free to leave and that all legal requirements have been met.

CLEARANCE INWARD A customhouse certificate stating the quantity of dutiable goods still remaining on a ship after the cargo has been discharged at a port and before taking on fresh cargo.

CLEARANCE LIMITS The dimensions beyond which the size of, or projections on a shipment may not extend in order to clear obstructions along railway tracks, such as switchstands, platforms, tunnels, mail cranes, water tanks, third rails, low bridges, signal stands, etc.

CLEARANCE OUTWARD A declaration made to the customs authorities by the ship's captain before proceeding to leave a port stating that all legal requirements have been met.

CLEAR DAYS Business days free from weather, interference, strikes, or government restraints.

CLEARING (1) Entering a ship at a custom house and obtaining clearance; and (2) Exchange of checks and settling balances at the clearing house.

CLEARING A BILL Receipt of money due on a bill of exchange.

CLEAR RECORD A record which shows that a shipment was handled without any loss or damage being sustained.

CLEAT A strip of wood or metal used to afford additional strength; to prevent warping; to hold in position.

COASTING (COASTWISE) TRADE Domestic maritime trade between points within a country as distinguished from trade between a point in one country and a point in another country.

COASTING VESSEL Ships trading between ports of the same country.

CODE OF FEDERAL REGULATIONS The U.S. Government Printing Office publications which contain the regulations various agencies have created and promulgated within their quasi-legislative powers; the DOT's and ICC's rules are contained within Title 49 of the Code of Federal Regulation series.

COD SHIPMENT One in which the carrier is used by the shipper to collect the invoice value of the goods from the consignee prior to or at delivery; the amount is then remitted to the shipper less a service fee.

C.O.F.C. Container-on-flatcar. Special C.O.F.C. tariffs were developed originally for a joint land/water movement for international shipments. Thus, a C.O.F.C. rate might be applicable on a movement between Salt Lake City and Seattle for a shipment destined for Japan. These rates were usually lower than other rail rates in order to encourage international shipments. This is a type of rail rate. Since trailers are a form of a container, some tariffs apply to both containers and trailers. Actually, the container car is a different type of car than a trailer flatcar.

COLLECTING BANK A bank which acts as an agent to the seller's bank (the presenting bank). The bank's function is to surrender documents to the buyer either upon payment or acceptance of the draft by the buyer. The collecting bank assumes no responsiblity either for the documents or the merchandise. The collecting bank's risk for letters of credit; therefore, the service is less costly to the trading parties.

COLLECTION A draft drawn on the buyer, usually accompanied by documents with complete instructions concerning processing for payment or acceptance (See "Trade acceptances").

COLLECTION ON DELIVERY (C.O.D.) The amount of the costs and charges on the shipment which are collected when the carrier delivers the goods to the consignee. The amount less a collection fee is then remitted by the carrier back to the shipper.

COLLECTION RATES Rates for inbound movement of many shipments that were consolidated at an intermediate point for long haul; it is the reverse of distribution rates.

COLLECTIVE RATEMAKING The activity of many carriers acting through the medium of a rate bureau to meet, discuss and establish rates.

COLLECTOR OF CUSTOMS A representative of the United States Treasury Department acting for the government in connection with foreign traffic.

COLLECT SHIPMENT A shipment on which freight charges are to be paid by the consignee.

COLUMNS Beams used to support a building. May be placed vertically or horizontally.

COMBINATION CARRIER An airline that carries passengers and freight.

COMBINATION (OR COMBINED) CAR A passenger train car divided into two or more compartments to accommodate different classes of traffic.

COMBINATION EQUIPMENT Aircraft which carries both passengers and cargo.

COMBINATION RATE A rate made by combining two rates published in different tariffs.

COMBINATION THROUGH RATES When more than one carrier is involved in providing through routes, but do not publish joint rates, a combination through rate would be effective. They are composed of any combination of local rates, joint rates, or a combination of local and joint proportional rates.

COMBUSTIBLE LIQUID Any liquid having a flash point above 100° and below 200° F as determined in DOT tests.

COME-A-LONG Chain and winch device used to open railcar doors.

COMMERCE CLAUSE Art. 1, Section 8, Clause 3 of the constitution which gives Congress the power to regulate commerce with foreign nations and between the several states.

COMMERCE COURT A court created by Act of Congress (1909) to have jurisdiction in all cases for the enforcement of orders of the Interstate Commerce Commission, other than the payment of money.

COMMERCE LAW Varying and rather indefinite signification, includes legal rules for the usage of trade.

COMMERCIAL ATTACHE A representative of the Bureau of Foreign and Domestic Commerce located in a foreign country for the purpose of assisting and fostering the foreign trade of the United States.

COMMERCIAL AVIATION Transportation of persons or property via air routes operated as a business enterprise.

COMMERCIAL INVOICE This is commonly referred to as the bill of statement. It specifies goods sold from one party to another. There are two forms of commercial invoices: (1) the Invoice and Certificate of Value;

and (2) the Invoice and Declaration of Value. The commercial invoice is a term commonly applying to international exchanges.

COMMERCIAL TREATIES Treaties between state regulating the commercial rights of the nationals of each in the territories of the other. They establish the condition under which debts due a foreign trader may be collected through the courts.

COMMERCIAL ZONE Specified area within a city in which a trucking company may operate.

COMMINGLING Whenever different shipments or goods are moved in one shipment; example is interstate goods moving along with others that are intrastate in a single movement.

COMMISSION The percentage granted an agent for transacting a business operation based on the value of a contract. This term is also used to apply to a person or persons who have been delegated the responsibility of performing an investigation of regulation process. The term also refers to the Interstate Commerce Commission.

COMMODITIES CLAUSE This was a clause in the Hepburn Act of June 29, 1906, now appearing as Section 10746 of the Revised Interstate Commerce Act, which provided that it was unlawful for a rail carrier to transport property for a company in which the carrier has ownership. Of course, this would not apply to commodities when the commodities are used for the common carrier's own purpose.

COMMODITY In transportation, a movable article, goods, or merchandise afforded special rates and service.

COMMODITY RATE A rate on a specific commodity, or article, moving between specific points, sometimes in a specific direction, and sometimes for a specific minimum quantity. The purpose of the commodity rate is generally to provide a lower rate to reflect lower costs resulting from large scale movement or otherwise. The commodity rate can be higher than a class rate, but it usually is not.

COMMODITY TARIFF A tariff containing only commodity rates.

COMMODITY WAREHOUSE Cotton warehouses, wool warehouses, tobacco warehouses, other agricultural product facilities and grain elevators.

COMMON CARRIER The most accepted characteristics of the common carrier are: (a) availability of service to anyone seeking a transportation movement; (b) the publication of rates; (c) provision of the service on schedule; (d) service to designated points or a designated area; (e) service of a given class of movement and commodity.

COMMON COST A cost for a function, activity or staff necessary for two or more separate products or services; common costs are such that they can not rationally be traced to either one of the functions on any sound basis.

COMMON LAW A legal finding which has long been accepted. The force of the law comes from consent, rather than written statute.

COMMON POINT A point reached by two or more transportation lines.

COMMON TARIFF A tariff published by or for the account of two or more transportation lines as issuing carriers.

COMMUNICATIONS ACT OF 1934 An act of Congress regulating communication by wire or radio. Approved June 19, 1934.

COMPANY CAR A car in operation on the line owned by the carrier. Sometimes the term is also applied to a car used by various departments of a carrier firm in the performance of construction work.

COMPARATIVE RATE SCHEDULE A table of rates showing the differences in charges existing via two routes or through different modes of transportation; rail, motor, water, etc.

COMPARTMENTIZED CAR A boxcar equipped with moveable bulkheads, which can be used to divide the car into separate compartments.

COMPARTMENT TANK CAR A tank car with compartments or separate tanks into which different kinds of grades of oil or other liquids may be transported.

COMPELLED RATES Rate which is established lower than the general adjustment of its related rates.

COMPETITION Rivalry between interests in the securing of business or business advantages.

COMPETITIVE POINT A point at which two or more transportation lines compete for the movement of traffic.

COMPETITIVE RATE May be established for purposes of either carrier or market competition. When a rate is set on a particular level to offer competition with another line it is referred to as carrier competition. When a competitive rate is set sufficiently low to permit one producing area to compete with another producing area in a given market, it is called market competition.

COMPETITIVE TRAFFIC Traffic in the movement of which two or more transportation lines compete.

COMPLAINANT A person or party who makes a complaint.

COMPLAINT A complaint filed with the Interstate Commerce Commission alleging violation of the statute and to be investigated and adjudicated under formal procedure provided by the rules of the Commission.

COMPRADORE A native advisor or agent, employed by foreign establishments in China, to have charge of its native employees and act as an intermediary in transactions with natives.

COMPRESSED GAS Any material or mixture having in the container a pressure *exceeding* 40 pounds per square inch at 70° F, or pressure exceeding 104 psi at 130° F; or any liquid flammable material having a vapor pressure exceeding 40 psi at 100° F.

COMPRESSION A term applying to cotton and meaning the compression of a bale of flat cotton to either standard density or high density.

COMPRESSION IN TRANSIT Shipment of uncompressed cotton tendered to the carrier and compressed by or at the expense of the carrier before delivery at destination. The cost of such compression in transit is included in the rate itself and is paid for by the carrier out of such rate.

COMPUTE (A BILL) Determine the maturity date for a bill of exchange.

CONCEALED DAMAGE When the consignee signs a Delivery Receipt indicating no damage, but later there is an alleged damage, it is referred to as concealed damage. It may be either concealed damage or loss.

CONCEALED DISCOUNTING A situation in which a posted price remains high, but the vendor will begin to pay freight or provide other services for that same price.

CONCEALED LOSS Alleged loss in spite of fact that consignee signed Delivery Receipt without exception.

CONCENTRATE To bring to a common center; to gather into one body or force.

CONCENTRATION POINT The geographical location where less-than-carload shipments are brought together to be combined for carload shipment.

CONCLUSIVE EVIDENCE Evidence that cannot be contradicted by other evidence.

CONCURRENCE When a carrier signs a document which verifies that it is participating in rates published in the tariff by a given agent, and when the document is filed with the I.C.C., it is called concurrence.

CONDITIONAL SALE A transaction in which the user is treated as the owner of the asset; the user acquires title to the asset upon payment of the final installment amount.

CONDITIONAL SALES CONTRACT A method of purchasing a capital item whereby a contract is signed to pay certain amounts on a periodic basis; upon the last payment, title passes from the seller to the buyer.

CONDUCTOR's TRAIN (OR WHEEL) REPORT The conductor of a train makes out a report of the train's movement showing the equipment handled, the points between which all units are moved, etc. The numbers and names of all equipment are identified and initialed by the conductor. When freight cars are involved, the type of car, its contents, the origin and destination, the gross and net weight, etc., are also shown on most rail lines.

CONFERENCE General term for a collective ratemaking body.

CONFERENCE RATE Rates arrived at by conference of carriers applicable to transportation, generally water transportation.

CONFERENCE RULINGS Rulings of the Interstate Commerce Commission which express its views on inquiries involving special facts or requiring an interpretation and construction of the law.

CONFIRMED CREDIT Credit that cannot be cancelled without mutual consent of the buyer and seller.

CONFIRMING BANK The bank that adds its confirmation to another bank's (the issuing bank's) letter of credit and promises to pay the beneficiary upon presentation of documents in compliance with the L/C. Confirmation is requested by the beneficiary when the issuing bank's ability to pay is in doubt.

CONNECTING CARRIER A carrier which has a direct physical connection with another carrier for a through movement is called a connecting carrier. It may also refer more specifically to a carrier that provides a link between two other carriers.

CONNECTING LINES All carriers which make up a through route are connecting lines.

CONSIDERATION (IN A CONTRACT) The benefit or service one party will provide for another; typically consideration is spelled out in terms of dollar payment.

CONSIGNED STOCK The finished goods inventories in the hands of agents, dealers, or customers which are still the property of the manufacturing source by agreement.

CONSIGNEE The receiver for a shipment of goods.

CONSIGNEE MARKS The use of such symbols as a square, diamond, triangle, circle, a cross, etc. which is placed on packages for export and is used for the purpose of identifying the shipment for the consignee are termed consignee marks. These symbols are used with designated letters and numbers for identification purposes.

CONSIGNMENT A movement of merchandise where the goods and the title remain with the shipper (the consignor) until the buyer (the consignee) sells the goods. Usually, the goods are stored in a warehouse by the shipper's agent until sold by the consignee.

CONSIGNMENT PURCHASING A method of purchasing in which a vendor maintains inventory on the premises of the buyer; the buyer's obligation to pay for the goods begins when he draws them from the stock for use.

CONSIGNOR The shipper of a transportation movement.

CONSOLIDATED CLASSIFICATION Unifying minimum carload weights, number of classes, assignment of articles to classes, as well as descriptions of articles, and rules and regulations governing their preparation and handling.

CONSOLIDATING Combining two or more small shipments in order to obtain reduced freight rates on higher volume shipments.

CONSOLIDATION Practice of consolidating many less-than-carload (L.C.L.) or less-than-truckload (L.T.L.) shipments in order to make carload or truckload movements is termed consolidation.

CONSOLIDATION POINT When many small shipments—L.C.L. or L.T.L.—are combined for reshipment at a chosen location, the point is referred to as a consolidation point. Sometimes this is referred to as an assembly point.

CONSOLIDATION OF SHIPMENT The process of combining a number of L.C.L. shipments into a carload shipment is consolidation. When L.C.L. shipments are so combined, it is customary to try to combine articles of the same rating and originating from the same point.

CONSOLIDATIONS (OR MERGERS) According to Sections 11343-11349 of the Revised Interstate Commerce Act, when two or more carriers consolidate or merge with the approval and authorization of the Interstate Commerce Commission, and form one corporation for the purpose of management and operation, a consolidation or merger takes place. This should be distinguished from a joint acquisition, a lease, an acquisition, or an acquisition of control since it results in the legal unionization of the separate entities into a single corporate entity.

CONSOLIDATOR A firm that combines separate shipments, usually piggy back, so as to realize cost savings and service improvement for what would otherwise be less than full load shipments.

CONSTANT COST Those logistics cost which remain constant with an increase in the volume of shipment are constant costs. Again, constant logistics costs refer to costs that remain constant with the volume of shipment; whereas constant economic costs normally refer to fixed costs which do not change with an increase in the volume of production. They represent a relatively small proportion of total logistics costs. Examples of constant logistics costs would be administrative costs, utility costs, depreciation on building and equipment, and inventory-in-transit. Most constant logistics costs do change with a change in the volume of shipment, but not sufficiently to justify measurement. For example, rate research, a traffic related functional cost, may or may not change with an increase in volume of shipment. However, if the difference is insufficient to justify considerable research it would be termed a constant increasing cost. Some may contend that large volume shipments would tend to move on commodity rates per car rates, sealed carload rates, TOFC rates, or even unit train rates, and therefore require a little rate research. This would seem to make them decreasing costs. Another industrial firm may believe there is insufficient justification for this and prefer to classify them as constant costs.

CONSTRUCTION DIFFERENTIAL SUBSIDY The subsidy paid by the U.S. Maritime Administration for the extra cost of building certain U.S. flag ships in American shipyards rather than overseas at lower construction cost.

CONSTRUCTIVE MILEAGE When a joint carrier movement is involved it is necessary to divide the joint rate. An arbitrary mileage is normally specified for each carrier on a mileage basis. This is termed constructive mileage.

CONSTRUCTIVE PLACEMENT When a car is placed for loading and unloading at an available point other than on an industry track, due to inability of consignor or consignee to receive it, carrier may, by giving customary notice, consider it as being placed at the point usually designated.

CONSTRUCTIVE PLACEMENT OF CARS When a carrier cannot place cars on an industrial or private track due to conditions attributable to the consignee or consignor, and it is forced to place the cars elsewhere, it is termed constructive placement. Under these circumstances, the cars so placed are subject to the usual demurrage rules and charges.

CONSUL A government official residing in a foreign country to care for the interests of his country.

CONSULAR INVOICE, THE This document is written in the language of the foreign country for which the goods are destined. It fully describes the goods to be exported and provides evidence of a shipper's Declaration of Value of the shipment. The Consular Invoice is required by foreign countries for customs and statistical purposes.

CONSULAR REPORTS Reports issued by consular officers regarding trade opportunities for specified classes of merchandise.

CONSULAR VISA An official signature or seal affixed to certain documents by the consul of the country of destination.

CONSULATE The office or position of a consul, also the premises occupied officially by a consul.

CONSUL FEES Charges certifying and translating invoices.

CONSUMER COMMODITY (With ORM-D) means a material that is packaged or distributed in a form intended and suitable for sale through retail sales agencies or instrumentalities for consumption by individuals for purposes of personal care or household use. This term also includes drugs and medicines.

CONTAINER Anything in which articles are packed.

CONTAINER CAR In railroad transportation, an open flat-bed car used for the purpose of transporting steel freight containers is called a container car. Sometimes, the term container-type car is used to denote a flat-car equipped with a number of removable containers.

CONTAINER-TYPE CAR A specially designed flat car equipped with a number of removal containers which may be lifted off and placed on another car or truck for transportation to any desired destination.

CONTAMINATION The spread of physical qualities of one item to another so as to lessen the value or useful function of the second item; examples are odor in textiles, exposure of food to toxins, etc.

CONTENTS INSURANCE RATES Rates assessed to the customer by his insurance company for protection of merchandise stored in a public warehouse. These rates vary according to the type of building and whether or not the building is sprinklered. The rates are expressed in terms of cents per one hundred dollars of inventory valuation.

CONTINUITY OF SUPPLY One of the primary objectives or missions of modern purchasing management as practiced; it recognizes that an out of stock raw materials situation is more in cost than that of a higher price but more reliable source.

CONTINUOUS CARRIAGE A shipment made through to destination without stoppage in transit for breaking bulk, transfer or rebilling.

CONTINUOUS SEALS A term denoting that the seals on a car remained intact during movement of the car from point of origin to destination; or, if broken in transit, that it was done by proper authority and without opportunity for loss to occur before new seals were applied.

CONTRA Against.

CONTRABAND Illegal or prohibited merchandise.

CONTRACT An agreement between parties to do or to abstain from doing certain acts.

CONTRACT CARRIER The contract, carrier, whatever the mode, provides a service according to contractual agreement. The contract specifies charges to be applied, the character of the service, and the time of performance. There are no specified rates under regulation, but the charges applied must be made public.

CONTRACT WAREHOUSE Warehouse operating under a formal agreement with a customer for a fixed amount of space.

CONVENTIONAL TARIFF A tariff to contain and represent all the concessions provided for by the commercial treaties concluded by the particular country.

CONVERSION The process of appropriating all or part of a shipment by a carrier is called conversion.

CONVEYANCE Common application to the instrument or vehicle of transfer.

CONVEYOR A mechanism which moves and transports freight by a revolving belt-like facility for short distances.

COOPERAGE The price paid for putting hoops on casks or barrels, or the process of reconditioning these types of facilities to make them suitable for safe transportation.

COORDINATED SERVICE A classification of transportation service whereby (1) one form of service assists another in extending service into areas without sufficient traffic to support one service alone; (2) one form of service is substituted for another for economical reasons; (3) two or more of the types of transportation are combined.

COPY A reproduction of an original work.

COPYRIGHT Exclusive rights of reproducing, by writing, printing or otherwise.

CORDAGE The products of twine, cord and rope industry. More specifically, the rope of which the running rigging of a ship is made.

CORNER GUARD Plate used to protect merchandise from being hit by equipment.

CORNER POST Upright guard post used to prevent equipment from hitting product or other equipment.

CORPORATE VOLUME RATE A lower than normal rate charged to a shipper that provides increasing discounts with increasing tonnage shipped from that firm to a particular carrier throughout specified time periods.

CORPORATION NAME A name under which a corporation is authorized to do business and which must be used in filing complaints.

CORPUS JURIS A body of law; Corpus Juris Secundum is a publication containing an encyclopedic treatment of the whole body of the law.

CORRECTION ACCOUNTS The destination carrier may correct or adjust differences in the freight accounts which have been initiated by the forwarding or intermediate carrier. This process of auditing and correcting the interline freight account comes under the term of correction accounts.

CORRECTION NOTICE In order to collect additional charges or to grant a refund, a form which presents a new billing, or which abstracts errors which have already been made on a carrier's record, may be made out. The correction notice is usually a copy of the freight bill as originally billed, with the refunds and corrections applied.

CORROSIVE MATERIAL Any liquid or solid that causes visible destruction of human skin tissue or a liquid that has a severe corrosion rate on steel.

COST AND FREIGHT (C. & F.) Under this term, the seller quotes a price, including the cost of transportation to the named point of destination.

COST BASED RATE INCREASE SYSTEM This is a system for changing railroad rates to meet changes in costs. According to this system the percent of change of cost in the terminal and line haul areas would be separately computed. The extent of the rate change in each of these areas would be applied to that part of each tariff rate which involved respectively terminal and line haul costs.

COST AND FREIGHT (C&F OR CAF) Same as CIF (Cost, insurance, and freight), except that the seller does not pay insurance costs.

COST, INSURANCE, AND FREIGHT (CIF) A basis for quotation by a seller which indicates that the seller will pay the insurance and freight charges to destination only.

COST, INSURANCE, FREIGHT, AND EXCHANGE (CIF&E) An expression used in trade with British colonies, Australia, and South Africa; the element of exchange is added to the items of cost, insurance, and freight.

COST, INSURANCE, FREIGHT, COLLECTION CHARGES, AND INTEREST (CIFCI) A basis of pricing used in the Far East.

COST PLUS INCENTIVE An extension of the cost plus fixed fee contract; the final payment will be for vendor costs incurred plus a fee that is greater for early completion or design improvement.

COURSE OF EXCHANGE The current price of bills of exchange existing between two places.

COVER NOTE The assurer's advice to the exporter stating that a shipment has been covered.

CRANAGE The price paid for the use of a wharf crane.

CREW LIST The names and description of each member of the crew, place of birth, and residence.

CRIMINAL PENALTIES As distinguished from civil penalties, criminal penalties include fines and prison terms; example, Elkins Act or hazardous materials violations.

CRITICAL MATERIALS It is common in recent years to specify steel, copper, brass, bronze, aluminum, etc., as representing critical materials for national defense purposes—or materials essential to the health and welfare of the people.

CRITICAL PATH METHOD An operations research tool that assists one in determining which sequence of tasks in a project will delay its completion if anyone of the individual components is delayed.

CROSS EXAMINATION The inquiry by an opposing party in a case into points made by a specified person or item of evidence.

CROSS TRADES Ocean trade term for a ship or traffic that is between nations other than the one in which the ship is domiciled.

CUBE OUT A situation in which freight fully fills a transportation vehicle but is less than the weight limit.

CUBE-PER-ORDER-INDEX A mathematical technique that considers orders-per-day and required-cubic-footage to determine a low cost stocking layout for a warehouse.

CUBE UTILIZATION The maximum use of vertical and horizontal space for storage.

CUBICAL CAPACITY The carrying capacity of a car according to measurement in cubic feet.

CUBIC CARGO Ocean shipping term for freight that is charged on the basis of its cubic size rather than on weight; usually light, bulky cargoes.

CUBIC CONTENTS Solid or cubical contents of any package. When cubic restrictions are used they involve the length, depth and breadth of the package. The product of these functions is a cubic dimension.

CUBIC FOOT A cubic foot is 1728 cubic inches. It involves a cubic content of 12 inches X 12 inches X 12 inches.

CUMMINS AMENDMENT An amendment to the Act to Regulate Commerce relating to liability of transportation lines for loss of or damage to freight.

CURRENCY Circulating medium by which debts are paid and business of the country transacted.

CURRENCY ADJUSTMENT FACTOR (CAF) Surcharges on shippers of ocean freight to make up for losses or gains resulting from U.S. dollar fluctuations in world currency.

CURRENT OF TRAFFIC Movement of trains on a main track, in one direction, specified by rules.

CURRENT RATIO An accounting term; current liabilities divided by the sum of cash, securities, near term investment, accounts receivables and notes receivables.

CURVE FITTING A mathematical process in which a series of data is described in terms of a formula that attempts to correspond to the actual data.

CUSHION UNDERFRAME The spring and shock absorbing mechanism built into some rail cars that act to reduce switching and train operating vibration and impacts upon the lading; a feature found mostly on specialized box cars.

CUSTOM CLEARANCE An act of obtaining permission for steamship companies to deliver merchandise inbound.

CUSTOMER PICKUP Merchandise picked up by a customer at the warehouse.

CUSTOMER RETURN Merchandise sent back to the warehouse (after shipment) by a customer, because of error, damage, etc.

CUSTOMER SERVICE An all-encompassing term for non-price and non-physical product features about a product; it usually consists of service leadtime, consistency of leadtime, etc.

CUSTOMER SERVICE RATIO A percentage figure that provides a measure of delivery performance. It measures the percentage of stock delivered when compared to the amount ordered.

CUSTOM HOUSE ENTRY Making out a statement and paying the fees in the process of clearing a ship.

CUSTOMS The taxes, tolls, or other duties imposed on goods as they pass a frontier. It usually involves imported goods.

CUSTOMS BROKER A person licensed by the U.S. Treasury department that acts on behalf of exporters and importers in clearing shipments for international moves.

CUSTOMS HOUSE BROKER An agent whose functions are to expedite shipments by preparing the necessary import documents at the port of entry for subsequent movement through U.S. Customs and other regulatory agencies.

CUSTOMS INVOICE (U.S.A.) A special invoice, prepared by the seller, on a form supplied by the U.S. Treasury, describing the imported goods. This invoice is presented to the U.S. Customs Bureau at the time import duties are paid. The customs invoice is not needed for shipments valued under $500 or for merchandise incoming via parcel post.

CUSTOMS OF THE PORT Charges, physical facilities, cargo transfer systems and methods, exchange, dues and general laws peculiar to a port.

CUSTOMS TARIFF The government published schedule of charges assessed on the importing or exporting of goods. This is in the customs tariff.

CYCLE COUNTING The counting of inventory frequently in order to maintain a close monitor on levels, instead of once a year purely for accounting valuation purposes; cycle counting is a valuable materials requirements planning element.

CYCLE STOCK That part of the inventory which is depleted through sale or use, and is replenished through an order. Safety stock, the other main component of inventory, is not so replenished, and is not a part of cycle stock.

CYCLE TIME The replenishment cycle represents a period of time required to order and make available the required stock. Consequently, cycle time is thought to be composed of two factors: (a) order cycle; and (b) replenishment cycle.

CYCLICAL INVENTORY COUNT A continuously performed inventory count, as contrasted to inventories taken periodically. A cycle inventory may be taken when the stock level reaches the reorder point, or when the stock ordered arrives.

—D—

DAMAGE CLAIM The formal claim for damaged freight made against the carrier by the shipper.

DAMAGE FREE RAIL CAR (DF) A rail car that has internal bulkheads and other features that reduce the need for shipper dunnage and other bracing efforts and expenses.

DATA BASE The data of a company's operations stored in raw form to permit flexibility for analysis by varying systems.

DATA TERMINAL Point for the sending and receiving of information via a computer.

DEAD AXLE Rear axle, tandem truck or trailer without power.

DEAD EYE AND BOLT An eye at the end of a rope or wire that is used instead of a shackle.

DEAD HAULING Without a load.

DEADHEAD The movement of an unloaded vehicle on the line haul. It also refers to a non-paying passenger.

DEADLINE VEHICLE When a vehicle is set aside for temporary repairs it is a deadline vehicle.

DEAD LOAD The orders ahead which have not been released by a manufacturing facility. They represent orders a departmental dispatcher has on hand. In air transportation, the term dead load applies to the power plant, fixed equipment, and structure of the aircraft.

DEAD PILE Products received and shipped in other than unitized loads; require hand stacking.

DEAD SPACE Unoccupied space.

DEAD STORAGE Product which does not move in or out once it has been received.

DEAD-WEIGHT TONNAGE, D-W The number of tons a vessel can transport of cargo, stores, and bunker fuel. In this concept, a ton equals 2,240 pounds. It is equal to the difference between the numbers of tons of water a vessel displaces when light, or empty, and the numbers of tons it displaces when submerged to the load line. The dead weight tonnage may also be termed the displacement tonnage.

DEBENTURE A debenture is a certificate which entitles an exporter a refund on duties paid. It is a custom house certificate.

DEBENTURE STOCK A form of preferred stock that provides for a specific return for a given period.

DECENTRALIZED PRODUCTION Under decentralized production, rather than producing all output for a given firm in a single general location, production facilities are divided and placed near the markets. Thus, regional production facilities for shoes might be geographically spread over several different locations. Shoe plants might be located in southwestern United States for the California and neighboring state areas, another production facility in the northwest area, a plant in the southeastern states in Atlanta, another plant in Chicago to serve the north-central market, and another production facility in the New England area. Decentralization of production is deemed feasible for circumstances in which savings in logistics and/or marketing costs are sufficiently great to offset dissavings in production costs on a per-unit basis. Total production under centralized and decentralized production circumstances are conceptually equal.

DECISION TREE Statistical tool useful in evaluating outcomes of any number of possible events given various probabilities of each one occurring.

DECK The floors of a vessel. A steamer will have a main deck and a raised forward section called a forecastle. The aft deck is called the poop deck. In larger vessels, the first deck above the tanks or hold is called the lower deck. Above this are the second, main, third, fourth and promenade decks.

DECLARATORY ORDER A decision made by a regulatory agency that hopefully resolves an issue prior to a party commiting a certain act rather than later it being found unlawful; a declaratory order is sought in advance of an act.

DECLARED VALUE The process of stating the value on an air bill or similar type of document by a shipper for the purpose of achieving a lower rate is referred to as a declared value.

DECOUPLING INVENTORY A stock retained to make possible the independent control of two operations. It is sometimes called line-balancing stock.

DECREASING LOGISTICS COSTS Those logistics costs which decrease with an increase in the volume of shipment are decreasing costs. It is the decrease in the per unit cost—as contrasted to total costs—which make these costs decreasing costs. Very few logistics costs are so classified. Examples of decreasing logistics costs are ordering costs, the cost of carrier payment, the cost of purchase payment (not including purchase price), etc. These examples of decreasing logistics costs decrease per cwt. inversely and proportionally to the increase in the volume of shipment. For example, a five dollar ordering cost would cost five dollars per cwt. for a one hundredweight shipment, fifty cents per cwt. for a thousand weight shipment, and five cents per cwt. for a ten thousand pound shipment. Few decreasing logistics costs exist that do not decrease inversely and proportionately with an increase in the volume of shipment. However, one cost that may *not* decrease inversely and proportionately with an increase in the volume of shipment would be shipping and receiving cost. It may be found, that increasing volumes of shipment involve such completely different packaging and equipment usage that the per unit costs would decrease in something other than inversely and proportionately with an increase in the volume of shipment.

DEDICATED SERVICE Transportation equipment and or crews that are assigned for the use of one particular shipper.

DEDICATED VEHICLE See dedicated service.

DEDICATED STORAGE SPACE That portion of occupiable storage space that is actually being used to store merchandise. Expressed as square footage.

DEEP TANK The ballast tank amidship used to increase a vessel's draft.

DEFECTIVE CAR When a car is in the condition which makes it defective, and therefore liable to injure the contents of the shipment, it is designated as a defective car.

DEFENDANT The party toward which a complaint is registered, or a legal action of some form is taken.

DEFERRED AIRFREIGHT A shipment received for transportation by an air carrier after all revenue traffic has been received. An accommodation shipment, in addition to the planned shipments.

DEFERRED RATE A rebate from carrier to shipper for having shipped a minimum volume or all tonnage via a certain carrier or set of carriers during a specified time period.

DEFERRED SHIPMENT RULE A rule permitting shipments of cotton from points of origin to certain ports, moving on a through bill of lading, under instructions from the shipper. To be stopped in transit for compression or for consolidation with other shipments in order to aggregate the carload minimum. The through rate to prevail from origin on the weight reshipped from the transit station plus transit charge.

DEFICIT WEIGHT When the actual weight of a shipment is less than the minimum weight, it is referred to as a deficit weight. The amount of the deficiency is the deficit weight.

DELAY The amount of time in excess of the scheduled time for a movement.

DELIVERING CARRIER The carrier that makes the delivery of the shipment to the consignee in a joint carrier movement is the delivering carrier.

DELIVERY The act of transferring possession, such as the transfer of property from consigner to carrier, one carrier to another, or carrier to consignee.

DELIVERY CYCLE The time from the receipt of an order to the time of the shipment of the product.

DELIVERY RECEIPT This term is commonly used in transportation to indicate a document which names the commodities, the number of pieces, etc. for the purpose of permitting acknowledgement of a receipt of a shipment. When the consignee signs the delivery receipt with no exceptions noted, it means that the shipment is *in good order,* and the contract of carriage has been executed.

DEMAND DRAFT A bill which requires payment on presentation.

DEMAND DURING LEAD TIME The amount of material required for sales or service during the lead time.

DEMAND SENSITIVE RATE A rate designed to smooth out the peaks and valleys of seasonal product transportation demands; generally higher in peak season, sometimes lower in low season.

DEMISE This term is applied to the transfer of a ship to a charter for a limited period of time. Under these circumstances, while the ship is in use, the rights and obligations relative to the ship remain with the owner since the title stays with the owner.

DEMOUNTABLE BODY The body or box of a motor truck or trailer especially designed to be inter-changeable on railroad flatcar equipment.

DEMURRAGE The detention of a shipment beyond its specified time resulting in the payment for detention is termed demurrage. Originating early in the 17th century, it applied to the detention of vessels beyond a specified time for sailing. Charges are published in the mastertariff for all United States railroads. The purpose is to prevent the use of freight cars for free storage. Since cars held by a nonowning railroad must pay a per diem charge, the demurrage charge aids the renting rail carrier in meeting this financial obligation. Two plans exist for settling demurrage charges between a rail carrier and shipper: (1) Straight Demurrage; (2) Average Demurrage. Under straight demurrage, a carrier is not charged for the first 48 hours measured from the first 7 A.M. after placement. After free time, the shipper must pay $10/day for the first four days, $20/day for the next two days, and $30/day for each day thereafter. Under the average demurrage plan, the shipper is permitted to receive credits for early release which may be used to counteract debits accumulated for time after free time.

DENSITY METER An instrument to measure the density of a mixture.

DENSITY OF COMMODITY The pounds per cubic foot, or other cubic measurement, represents the density of a commodity.

DENSITY RATE A transportation rate that is generally lower per hundredweight for products that are dense (heavy per cubic foot) and vice versa.

DENSITY (VOLUME) OF TRAFFIC The measurement of the volume of traffic per mile, or tons miles per period of time, indicates the density of the traffic.

DEPARTURE TRACKS (YARD) When cars leaving a classification yard from a receiving yard move to an arrangement of tracks for the purpose of switching, the connecting track is called a departure track.

DEPENDENT DEMAND Situation in which the demand for a certain product is dependent upon certain other products or decisions.

DEPOSITION A sworn statement of a witness taken down in writing to be used as evidence in lieu of the appearance of the witness.

DEPRECIATION COST The allocation of the value of a facility over its expected life period in the form of a cost for the purpose of determining allocated cost, per time period, is called depreciation cost. Under straight line depreciation costing systems, value or price is divided by years of life to determine depreciation cost per year.

DERELICT When a ship and its cargo are abandoned at sea the term derelict is applied.

DERRICK This is a cargo boom with its foot at the base of the mast, and supported by a topping-lift tackle. It is controlled by guys. It is employed to load and unload cargo.

DESPATCH (DISPATCH) LINES Two or more carriers that operate through fast-freight schedules.

DESPATCHING FOREIGN SHIPMENTS IN BOND Using the services of bonded carriers to avoid payment of internal-revenue tax on goods which would be subject to this tax if sold in the United States. Bonded carriers may forward unstamped goods and deliver aboard steamship in bond under customhouse inspection and certification. Goods imported into the United States are frequently carried in bonded warehouses without payment of dues until sold.

DESPATCH MONEY An agreement whereby the charterer received a fixed sum per day for each day saved in loading out of a number of lay days specified in the charter party.

DESTINATION The place to which a shipment is consigned.

DESTINATION CARRIER The line-haul carrier performing the delivery service at the destination. This does not include the destination local delivery service.

DESTRUCTIVE COMPETITION Primarily a transportation term indicating one firm pricing below its costs temporarily with the intent of driving a competing firm out of the market.

DETENTION The charge assessed on a motor vehicle held beyond the free time allowed. Assessed for the time required to load or unload beyond the free time.

DETENTION CHARGE (MOTOR CARRIER) In the motor carrier industry the penalty assessed against shippers for delaying in releasing carrier equipment beyond the allowed free time is referred to as detention charge. In rail transportation this is called demurrage.

DETERIORATION The value loss from spoilage during time in storage.

DETERIORATION COSTS The quality of an article or commodity held in storage frequently diminishes through its inherent characteristics. Deterioration may be magnified if conditions of temperature, moisture content of the air, etc. are not proper. Deterioration cost is a logistics cost because it is related to time in storage. When decreases in purchasing, price, and transport rate are acquired by increasing the volume of shipments, other logistics costs are affected. Deterioration costs is one such cost. It is classified as an increasing cost. It increases with an increase in the volume of shipment.

DETERMINISTIC MODEL A type of mathematical, computer or other analytical model that does not develop an optimal answer, rather provides an answer based upon information and data used within it; generally used to test "what if" type questions.

DETOURED FREIGHT Shipments which due to washouts, wrecks, etc., are rerouted over the rails of another carrier for the convenience of the carrier on which the disability occurred.

DEVIATION CLAUSE A clause inserted in a charter party which authorizes a vessel to stop at ports other than the original port of discharge.

DEWAR A tanker designed to transport gases in liquid form by holding them at low temperature. The temperature is kept under 100 degrees below zero by double-walled, vacuum-construction of the tank trailer. This was developed by a Scottish chemist named Sir John Dewar.

D.F. When these letters are printed on the side of a car it means that the car is *damage free.* This means special equipment is installed in the car to eliminate damage to the merchandise enroute.

D.F.B. CAR (DAMAGE FREE BULKHEAD CAR) Railcar which is equipped with a cushioned under-frame, special blocking or bracing, and moveable doors to hold merchandise in place.

DIFFERENTIAL The difference in rates serving given point, either on the same or different routes. The differential is also a part of the power unit of a vehicle.

DIFFERENTIAL RATES Differential rates are thought of as a reduced form of rate. The reduced rate is provided on an alternate routing which is less desirable. Frequently a combination of rail and water movements, in competition with an all rail rate, would receive a lower rate in order to encourage traffic. This lower rate is called a differential rate. The idea of the differential rate is to establish reduced rates for slower transportation and more handling of the freight. Sometimes differential rates are established in agreement between carriers to make rate concessions to less desirable ports.

DIFFERENTIAL ROUTE Route for which there exists no published rate. The rate is obtained through existing published rates.

DIMENSIONAL WEIGHT SHIPMENT When the charges for a shipment are computed on the basis of volume rather than weight it is referred to as dimensional weight shipment. If the tariff indicates a specific number of cubic inches per pound, and the shipment exceeds this, it will be charged on the basis of one pound for each of the specific number of cubic inches or fractions in excess.

DIRECT CONNECTOR A new term applying to joint line ratemaking now that some of the antitrust immunity of the rate bureaus has been repealed in the major legislative acts of 1980; only those railroads that directly connect on a through movement may jointly discuss rates on the through move.

DIRECT COSTS From the position of channel management planning, direct costs are those costs for which actual payments are made. They are distinguished from hidden costs, for which there are no payments made although the cost is actually sustained. Direct costs are identifiable on the profit and loss statement, while hidden costs are not. In logistics, examples of direct costs would be transport rate, purchase price, and warehouse costs.

DIRECT FLIGHT The transportation movement without transfer of a shipment, on one or more transportation carriers. It may have any number of enroute stops.

DIRECT FREIGHT CHARGES As applied to company material, specific freight charges paid to other railways and not included in the invoice.

DIRECTIONAL A term used to refer to rates which are reduced to encourage traffic in one direction to counter-balance traffic which is primarily in the other direction.

DISCRETE LOT SIZING A production, shipping, order processing term indicting that goods are handled in certain size lots rather than in any range of quantities.

DISCRIMINATION In transportation this involves differences in rates not justified by differences in costs. This occurs when two commodities moving under essentially the same circumstances have completely different rates which cannot be justified by the cost of service.

DISPATCHED LINES Sometimes this is spelled *dispatch.* When two or more carriers operate on a through fast-freight schedule they are referred to as dispatched lines.

DISPATCHING This is synonymous with expediting, or sending a shipment under a speeded up process. In the rail transport industry, the individual responsible for train movement is called a dispatcher.

DISPATCH MONEY The payment on completion of the loading and/or discharging to the charterer. It is a payment for time saved on allotted lay days.

DISPLACEMENT, ACTUAL In water transportation this refers to the loaded weight of the vessel for a particular voyage.

DISPLACEMENT, TONNAGE In water transportation, the amount of water displaced by a vessel when afloat is its displacement tonnage. A cubic foot of water is calculated to weigh 64 pounds, or 1/35th of a ton (2,240). One may divide the cubic foot content of the vessel by 35 to determine its displacement tonnage. The term *displacement light* means the weight of a merchant vessel when the crew and supplies are all on board. The term *displacement loaded* means the weight of the vessel when the full cargo, stores and passengers have also been taken on the vessel, and it is loaded to its maximum draft, or its deep load line.

DISPLACEMENT OF VESSEL The weight in tons of water displaced by the capacity of the vessel and its cargo in tons of 2240 lbs. Displacement light is the weight of the vessel without stores, while displacement loaded is the weight of the vessel, cargo and stores.

DISTANCE RATE The process of setting a rate on the basis of mileage. It is either a local or joint haul.

DISTRIBUTION The process of distributing the finished product through the post-production channel to the ultimate consumer. In economics, it amounts to the distribution of the returns of production to the participating factors of production.

DISTRIBUTION CENTER A warehouse of finished goods. Also applied to the facility from which wholesale and retail orders may be filled. A materials warehouse would also be a distribution center for the buyers of its stock.

DISTRIBUTION CHANNEL The post-production channel. Not to be confused with the pre-production, or materials flow, channel.

DISTURBANCE OF ADJUSTMENTS The situation that exists when the rate relationships or the authorized bases of rates are in jeopardy.

DITCH LIGHT A spotlight aimed at the right-hand side of the right-of-way.

DIVERSION Diversion is the process of changing the destination, but not the consignee, while the shipment is enroute. Both diversion and reconsignment must be done while the shipment is enroute and not after the shipment has arrived at its original destination. While the terms diversion and reconsignment are not synonymous, the same rules prevail for both, and are published in the same carrier tariffs. In a diversion act, it is necessary to instruct the point of diversion before the car leaves the point. Obviously, if you do not, you cannot effect a diversion or a reconsignment. The charge for either diversion or reconsignment is not great. It is established in the tariff provisions. Diversion can only be performed at the request of the owner of the goods. Under an FOB Destination, the seller must be asked to make the desired change. Diversion is primarily used in the lumber and perishable goods industries. It provides a means of shortening the period of time enroute.

DIVERSION OF TRAFFIC A shift of traffic from one carrier to another, or one carrier mode to another. This diversion usually takes place as a result of rate differentials.

DIVERT The process of changing the route of a shipment while it is in transit.

DIVISION 1. A managerial district on a railroad that is governed by a superintendent or general manager. 2. A division is a point at which crew changes take place. 3. The revenue split between carriers on joint rate moves.

DIVISIONAL NOTICE Under Plan I piggyback movements, the tariff-like contract specifies for motor carriers the amount payable to the rail carrier.

DIVISION RATE The proportion of a joint rate which is used to determine the revenue accruing to each carrier party to such rate for performing its part of the joint haul.

DOCK The sorting platform attached where shipments are loaded and unloaded.

DOCKAGE The charge assessed for the use of a dock.

DOCK AND WHARF BONDS Bonds issued to provide funds for the construction and equipment of docks and wharves.

DOCKET The official registration of a proceedings for a legal action.

DOCKET, INVESTIGATION AND SUSPENSION A record of the cases pending in connection with tariffs or other publications issued by the carriers the operation of which has been suspended by the Interstate Commerce Commission in order that the reasonableness of the suspended provisions may be determined.

DOCK PLATE A moveable ramp allowing access to a railcar or trailer.

DOCK RECEIPT A document given to a shipper when he delivers goods to a dock or pier for an international shipment.

DOCK-WALLOPER The person in charge of loading and unloading vehicles, also the handling of freight on the dock.

DOCTRINE OF THE LAST FAIR CHANCE A rule that a person will do all in his power to avert, or lessen, a disaster that seems imminent.

DOCUMENTARY CREDIT A letter of credit which requires the beneficiary to present a draft and specified documents. In practice, the documents must comply to the terms and conditions stated in the L/C before the draft can be paid (See "Clean credit").

DOCUMENTARY DRAFT When a draft or order to pay has attached to it various documents of title, such papers as insurance certificate, etc., the draft and documents are referred to jointly as a documentary draft. The documentary draft is used in connection with export credit, or it may be required for clearance from a port, or to obtain entry abroad.

DOCUMENT CHARGE The amount of money a customer pays for having a document (receipt or bill of lading) prepared.

DOCUMENTS AGAINST PAYMENT (D/P) An indication on a draft that the documents attached are to be released to the drawee only on payment.

DOG A truck which is not very powerful.

DOG TRACKS A unit or straight truck which has run out of line.

DOLLAR DENSITY A logistics term indicating the value of a product per pound; determined by dividing pounds into item value; generally used to indicate modal split potential of various freight markets; high dollar density products can stand higher rate, premium services.

DOLLAR-FILL, MEASURE OF A customer service term indicting how much, in terms of dollars of orders, a facility was able to process during a given time period.

DOLLY (a) A trailer converter dolly—an auxiliary axle assembly having a fifth wheel used for the purpose of converting a semi-trailer to a full trailer; (b) A device with small platforms on rollers or wheels used for the handling of freight in a warehouse.

DOMESTIC OPERATIONS Transportation operations within the territory of the United States. It includes intra-Hawaiian and intra-Alaskan carriers.

DOMESTIC SHIP When the owner of a ship resides in the country of reference, it is a domestic ship. Thus, when the owner of a vessel resides in the United States it would be a domestic ship for the United States. A ship may be called either domestic or foreign, depending on the residence of the owner, rather than the nature of its enrollment.

DOMESTIC TRUNKS Air transportation common carriers operating primarily in the United States, and serving the principal gateway cities of the nation.

DONUTS Truck tires.

DOODLE-BUG A small tractor used to pull two-axle dollies in a warehouse.

D.O.T. Department of Transportation.

DOUBLE BOTTOM A combination of two trailers pulled by the tractor.

DOUBLE-CLUTCHING The shifting of gears on a truck transmission without making them clash.

DOUBLE-DECK (STOCK CAR) When a second floor is placed on a stock car for the purpose of increasing the capacity for carrying small livestock, it is referred to as a double-deck stock car.

DOUBLE TRACK A two-way rail track system to handle traffic moving in both directions.

DOWN IN THE CORNER Creeper gear

DOWN TIME The amount of time an aircraft is not available for revenue service. This includes time required for maintenance, overhaul and other required services.

DOWNTIME The time when production is not underway.

DRAFT (VESSEL) The number of feet between the water line and the bottom of the vessel—or the depth beneath the water—is the draft.

DRAFT (BANK) The draft is a written order transferring a certain amount of money from one person to another to be paid on a certain date. It provides a means of settling accounts in foreign trade. It is a negotiable evidence of a relative amount of indebtedness. This instrument affirms a buyer's obligation. The draft is also referred to as a bill of exchange.

DRAFT An unconditional order in writing, addressed by one party (drawer) to another party (drawee), and requiring the drawee to pay at a fixed or determinable future date a specified sum in lawful currency (either in dollars or other currency) to the order of a specified person (the payee). A draft is a formal demand for payment. Also know as "bill of exchange."

DRAFT, CLEAN A draft to which no documents are attanched.

DRAFT, DATE A draft so drawn as to mature on fixed date, irrespective of the time of acceptance, for example, 90 days after date.

DRAFT, DISCOUNTED A time draft under a L/C which has been accepted and purchased by a bank at a discounted price. In practice, if the discount charges are payable by the beneficiary, the accepting bank pays a lesser amount than the face value to the beneficiary. If, on the other hand, the discount charges are payable by the buyer, the beneficiary receives the face amount of the draft.

DRAFT, DOCUMENTARY See Documentary draft.

DRAFT, SIGHT A draft so drawn as to be payable on demand upon presentation to the drawee.

DRAFT, TIME A draft so drawn as to mature at a certain fixed or determinable time after presentation or acceptance. For example, 90 days A/S means draft will mature 90 days "after sight" from the date of acceptance by a bank or the buyer.

DRAG The movement of one or several cars (usually without caboose or customary train make-up) within yard limits, or a transfer made at a junction or interchange point.

DRAG DOWN Shift too slowly to lower gears.

DRAGLINE A facility in a truck terminal which consists of carts drawn by a continuous cable, for transferring pickup to line haul operations or vice versa.

DRAWBACK When a payment is made by the government to exporters for goods assessed as an import duty, the refund is called drawback. The amount of the drawback is almost the total extent of the original duties paid. On the average it amounts to about 99% of the import duties paid.

DRAWEE Any party, such as an individual, a bank or a firm, on whom the draft is drawn and from whom the payment is expected. Under letters of credit the draft is drawn on a bank whose name usually appears on the left side of the draft.

DRAWEE BANK The bank on whom the draft is drawn, also known as the "paying bank."

DRAWER Any party who draws or signs the draft. Under an L/C, the beneficiary is the drawer of the draft, also called "the maker" of the draft.

DRAYAGE The rate for the transportation of freight in trucks, drays, or carts. It involves local cartage movement.

DRAYAGE TO SHIPSIDE The charge made for carting, draying or trucking freight to alongside a vessel.

DRILL A local freight train that acts to pick up and deliver cars to shippers and consignees along a line.

DRILLING The handling or switching of cars in freight yards or to and from industry tracks. *Drill engine* refers to the motive power used for such service.

DRIVE-IN RACK Storage rack which allows high stacking and easy access of the same product.

DRIVERS Drive wheels.

DRIVERS' DELIVERY TICKET A receipt retained by the driver of a motor carrier for delivery of the shipment. The charges will be billed at a later date.

DRIVE THROUGH RACK Storage rack which allows high stacking of products of the same kind, and easy access to the product.

DROMEDARY A special type of vehicle that combines the truck and, tractor, with a fifth wheel behind the body, and van at the rear of the unit.

DROP FRAME TRAILER A low level trailer with minimum highway clearance.

DROP IT ON THE NOSE Uncoupling the semi-trailer without lowering the landing gear to support the trailer.

DROP THE BODY The process of unhooking the tractor from the semi-trailer.

DRUM A shipping container of cylindrical shape and flat ends. They may be stored without crating or boxing.

DRUM FORKS The forks used to lift drums, barrels or other cylindrical types of loads.

DRY DOCKAGE A charge against a vessel that is placed in a dry dock for inspection and repair.

DRY LEASE An aircraft leasing arrangement which provides for the lessor to lease only the aircraft. The lessee provides the personnel, provisions, and fuel required in the operations.

DUAL RATE SYSTEM Ocean conference rate practice in which a lower rate is charged to shippers that agree to move all of their breakbulk freight via member lines of the conference.

DUALS A pair of tires mounted together.

DUE BILL The balance due, which usually involves additional charges as a result of error or otherwise, is the balance due bill. The due bill frequently has another meaning associated with a receipt signed for ocean bills of lading delivered with specific credit privileges.

DUE DATE The date at which an order, part or otherwise should be completed.

DUMP BODY A truck body that can be tilted to dump its load.

DUMP CAR An open car that is equipped with automatic dumping devices for discharging its contents either through the doors or by tipping the total car body.

DUMPER A mechanism for transferring bulk materials from open-top cars into the cargo space of vessels, used also at industrial plants for unloading materials into storage bins or onto piles, and at terminals for transferring materials from such equipment into other cars.

DUMPING When a sale is made at a lower price in a foreign national market it is referred to as *dumping.*

DUNNAGE This is lumber, wiring, or other material used for the purpose of stabilizing a shipment that has been placed on freight cars, vehicles, vessels, or other conveyances. It does not include the packaging.

DUPLICATE BILLING Freight bill covering shipment(s) that has already been billed previously.

DUPLICATE PAYMENT A double payment for the same shipment.

DUSTING Driving on the shoulders of the road, creating dust.

DUTY The charge assessed by the government on shipments imported or exported.

DYNAMITE ON THE BRAKES Using every brake on the vehicle.

DYNAMOMETER CAR A car specially equipped to measure the horsepower, drawbar pull, and other performance capabilities of a locomotive and the cars under operating circumstances.

—E—

EASTBOUND OR EASTWARD The direction of train movement in which the distance by rail from San Francisco is increasing. A few exceptions have been established on branch lines where this rule would result in confusion because of so-called *eastbound* trains actually operating *westbound.*

ECONOMIC REGULATION Refers to the control given regulatory authorities over the economic activities of the carrier—including entry, rates, abandonment, the record system, financial requirements, service obligations, etc.

ECHELON CHANNEL The post-production channel may be structured in many ways. The most complicated structure for the channel could take the form of moving goods from a manufacturer's facility through a series of echelon service facilities to the ultimate retailer. Under the echelon system, each echelon node would service the echelon node beyond it. Thus, a shipment from a manufacturing plant could consist of a truckload of kitchen ranges which would move to multi-regional warehouses. At the multi-regional warehouse a break-bulk operation would take place in which combinations of kitchen ranges, refrigerators, etc., would be made up for a regional echelon warehouse at a point beyond.

EIGHTY-TWENTY RULE See Pareto's Law.

ELASTICITY OF DEMAND The ratio of change in demand for a change in price.

ELECTRONIC PROTECTION A security system using electronic detection to notify a monitoring station if the building is broken into.

ELEVATING CHARGE (VESSEL) A charge for services performed in connection with floating elevators; also charges for using grain elevators.

ELEVATOR A hydraulic end-gate.

ELKINS ACT An act of Congress (1903), supplementing the Interstate Commerce Act, which makes the giving of rebates unlawful and provides penalties for this and other violations of the Act.

ELQ The most economic logistics quantity. Represents that quantity which will minimize total logistics costs in the shipment, or in the Cellular Flow. This means it must minimize whatever combination of purchasing costs, traffic costs and storage costs exist in the shipment.

EMBARGO A denial of entry of freight, particularly in foreign trade. It is usually brought about by a unique set of circumstances.

EMBARK To board a vessel about to sail.

EMBAYED Incapacity to enter a bay due to wind, current or sea.

EMERGENCY RATE A rate established to meet some immediate and pressing need, and without due regard to the usual rate factors.

EMERGENCY TEMPORARY AUTHORITY ICC granted permission for motor carrier operations for short periods due to strikes, fires or other sudden problems. ETA usually to begin on one day notice.

EMINENT DOMAIN The right of a governmental power to take property required for a public use.

EMPTY BACK HAUL A condition of low load factor which results from a greater volume of shipment in one direction than in the reverse direction is called empty back haul. Private carriage commonly results in empty back haul when deliveries are made and no return shipment is available.

A general condition of a greater amount of volume moving regionally, or transcontinentally, than is true of the reverse direction, creates a general condition of empty back haul to some degree.

EMPTY BACK-HAUL RATES Rates that are set unusually low in order to provide some carriage for facilities that normally would move empty back to a required origin are called empty-backhaul rates. Thus, the movement of industrial goods from the Chicago area toward the West Coast may create an abnormally large availability of shipping space for the return of the cars to the Chicago area. In order to encourage some utilization of these cars when returning, a low rate on bulk commodities may be offered.

EMPTY CAR MILES Freight car miles in the movement of empty cars.

ENDORSEMENT Signature making the document a legal transfer of possession.

ENPLANEMENTS Number of passengers boarding planes at certain points or on certain runs.

EN ROUTE A shipment on its way, or involved on the route of movement is en route.

ENTERED When the vessel has entered the port, and the master has gone to the customs authorities to declare the contents of the cargo.

ENTITY CHARTER A charter specifying that the transportation costs will be borne by the chartering organization, rather than the individual passengers.

ENTREPRENEUR A business man. Engaged in a business of making, or trading products, or presenting a service for sale.

ENTREPOT This is a place where goods are deposited without payment of duties while awaiting transportation elsewhere.

ENTRY This term has two meanings. On one hand it refers to a right to operate. For example, the regulatory authorities control entry, or the right to operate. It also means the customs document required to clear a shipment which has been imported into the country.

ENTRY (CUSTOMS) The process of registration of the ship's papers or goods with the customs authority is customs entry. The term *entry inwards* is used to apply to the statement filed on incoming ships or imported goods. When the shipment is outgoing, the statement made on goods under export is *entry* outward.

EOQ A concept developed by Ford Harris of Westinghouse in 1915 which determines the most *economic order quantity* on the basis of ordering costs and carrying costs. When incremental ordering costs equal incremental carrying costs, the most economic order quantity exists. It does not optimize the order quantity, and thus the shipment quantity, on the basis of total logistics costs, but only ordering and carrying costs. The equation for the EOQ is:

U Annual usage
A Ordering costs
i Cost of carrying a unit of inventory
Q The order quantity under computation
V Value of unit

$$Q = \sqrt{\frac{2UA}{Vi}}$$

EPA Environmental Protection Agency; federal agency responsible for pollution control enforcement.

EQUALIZING RATE A rate adjustment to reflect the costs of shippers and localities.

EQUIPMENT The rolling stock of a railroad or motor carrier, the ships of a steamship line and the planes of an airline.

EQUIPMENT BOND A loan secured by the carrier's equipment.

EQUITY The net balance of a firm's assets over its liabilities.

ERROR RATE, MEASURE OF A percentage of total items picked and/or shipped in a distribution facility that are not specifically what were ordered by customers.

ESCALATION CLAUSE A part of a purchase or rate contract that permits price increases during the term of the contract for cost factors beyond control of the vendor or carrier; usually for materials and fuel.

ESCORT SERVICE Found in high, wide and heavy shipments; owners or others having interest in shipment travel with it on train or in convoy.

ESTIMATED WEIGHT When a weight is prescribed in a tariff for a commodity shipped in specific containers or in a specific manner, the prescribed weight is referred to as the estimated weight.

ESTOPPEL A legal document that establishes liability for facts and obligations before a court of law.

E.T.A. Estimated time of arrival.

ET CETERA And other things; and so forth.

ETIOLOGIC AGENT A viable micro-organism, or its toxin which causes or may cause human disease.

EUROPEAN ECONOMIC COMMUNITY The Common Market nations in Europe.

EX or X Out of. The designation of a car whose contents have been transferred to another car.

EXAMINER (I.C.C.) The examiner is a representative of the Interstate Commerce Commission. His powers are extensive. He examines witnesses, administers oaths, takes testimony, and conducts hearings as a representative of the Interstate Commerce Commission throughout the country. Title has been changed in late 1970's to Administrative Law Judge (ALJ).

EXCELSIOR A material made of shredded wood for cushioning.

EXCEPTIONS TO THE CLASSIFICATION Ratings on class rates that differ and take precedence over those shipments known in the normally governing classification are called exceptions to the classification. While a commodity rate will give a reduced rate on a specific commodity moving between specific points, an exception to the class rating will give a reduced rate on a given commodity throughout the system covered by the classification. The exceptions rating may be thought of as a change in the rating on a given commodity. The *exceptions to the class rate* are made available to all classification and tariff holders as they occur. The exceptions rating is frequently provided to distinguish one item in a general classification in order to provide a lower rating. Thus, a lower rating might be provided on men's jeans as compared to men's dress trousers.

EXCESS FREIGHT When the amount of a shipment exceeds that shown on the original carrier's bill of lading, the amount in excess is referred to as excess freight.

EXCHANGE BILL OF LADING One bill of lading exchanged for another bill of lading usually for a stop off operation.

EXCLUSIVE USE OF TRUCK A provision in the bill of lading presenting a request of the shipper for exclusive use of the truck.

EXCURSION FARE A reduced fare intended to encourage traffic in certain types of movements, at certain periods of time, or under other specified circumstances.

EX DOCK An F.O.B. term that specifies that the title to the goods, and the responsibility for the transportation movement, will change when the shipment is placed on the dock for shipment at the originating point of purchase.

EXEMPT CARRIERS Trucks which carry certain products that are exempt from Interstate Commerce Commission economic regulation. Most exempt carriers haul agricultural products or seafood.

EXEMPT COMMODITY Specific commodities which can be transported exempt of regulation by the commission. No rates or operating authority is required.

EXEMPTIONS In order to encourage the importation of certain articles, duties are modified as they appear in the tariff. The articles for which the modification takes place are termed exempt articles.

EXEMPT TRANSPORTATION A transportation service exempt from economic regulation by a regulatory authority.

EX-FACTORY Under the F.O.B., Ex-Factory, both title and transportation cost responsibility transfer at the same point, which is at the factory. The price quoted involves making the goods available for possession and transportation at the factory at a given date. In an international shipment, all export taxes, documents, etc., are the responsibility of the buyer.

EXHIBIT A document or physical object introduced in evidence.

EX-LAKE A term used to describe a commodity reaching the carrier by boat line plying on a lake.

EXPANDABLE A flatbed trailer that is expandable for larger shipments.

EX PARTE This term was applied to investigations by the Interstate Commerce Commission, undertaken on its own initiative, for the purpose of determining general rate changes. While this should involve a necessary change in rates either up or down, historically it involves increasing rates to meet changes in increasing costs of operations. The *ex parte* rate changes began as early as 1911. To this date the most common system of implementing changes in rates to meet changes in costs is through the flat percentage increase system. This is also called the horizontal rate increase system.

EXPEDITER Refers to a personal tracer placed on goods or freight usually moving in carloads.

EXPEDITING The process of making arrangements for the transport of goods either prior to shipment or prior to arrival at a junction or transfer point in order to speed up the transportation movement is called expediting. The consignor should confirm that a shipment is properly started and the carrier has complete instructions for forwarding. At that time, the consignor should wire, phone, or write the consignee and instruct him concerning full routing, date of shipment, the intended date of delivery, etc. This permits the consignee to contract the delivering carrier to make arrangements for shortcutting the delivery of the destination. The loss of documents sometimes requires an expediting act.

EXPENSE BILL A freight bill.

EXPENSES PER LOADED FREIGHT CAR MILE The freight car total expense divided by the number of loaded freight car miles.

EXPIRATION NOTICE A date specified in a tariff for the expiration of the tariff, or some part of it.

EXPIRY DATE The final date on which the draft and documents must be presented to the negotiating, accepting, paying, or issuing bank in order to effect payment. The issuing bank's obligation ceases on that date if the L/C is a "straight credit." If the L/C is a negotiable credit," the issuing bank must honor the credit, provided the documents were submitted to the negotiating bank prior to the expiration (or expiry) date.

EXPLOSION CHART A pictorial illustration of an item with all its parts shown separately but in general relation with each other.

EXPLOSIVE Any chemical compound, mixture, or device the primary or common purpose of which is to function by explosion, i.e. with substantially instantaneous release of gas and heat.

EXPLOSIVE, CLASS A A detonating or otherwise of maximum hazard.

EXPLOSIVE, CLASS B In general, function by rapid combustion rather than detonation and include some explosive devices such as special fireworks, flash powders.

EXPLOSIVE, CLASS C Certain tyypes of manufactured articles containing Class A or Class B explosives, or both, as components but in restricted quantities, and certain types of fireworks.

EXPORT To send goods to a foreign country.

EXPORT COMMISSION HOUSE An agent for a foreign buyer in international trade.

EXPORT DECLARATION This document is required by the United States government for all shipments destined to foreign countries. It is filed with the Customs House at the port of export. It provides a means for compiling statistics on international trade, and trade to territories of possession. The export declaration is approved by the Collector of Customs at the port, and is given a serial number and a validation stamp.

EXPORT INVOICE A written account or itemized list, usually made out in triplicate, given to a foreign buyer. In addition to the customary commercial (domestic) invoice items, it contains such significant facts for the buyer's information as steamer's name, insurance, marks, code words, and statement of inland freight, storage, cartage, and other charges.

EXPORT LICENSES The Department of Commerce export licenses are of two categories: (1) general; and (2) validated. No application is required for the general license and no document is granted or issued. It is a document that is available to all persons and permits exportation within the provisions that are prescribed in the Export Regulations. The validated license specifies limitations for exportation of commodities. It is issued only on formal application accordant with procedures set forth in *Schedule B*. The export is presented to the Collector of Customs by the shipper before commodities are placed on the dock for loading on the carrier.

EXPORT RATES Rates which reflect an export movement which are established on a lower basis than domestic traffic. These rates take precedence over other rates between the same points via the same route on export traffic.

EX POST FACTO After that fact.

EXPRESS Air transportation by the air express tariff.

EXPRESS BODY An open box truck body.

EXPRESS TRAIN A train that does not stop at all stations on the route, carrying express freight.

EXTENSION FORKS Attachment placed on the forks of a forklift truck which lengthens the forks for moving larger items.

EXTENSION OF PROTEST Made out to support a Note of Protest. Endorsed by the officer, petty officer and two seamen. Reveals the circumstances of the voyage and actions taken to protect the shipment.

EXTRA BOARD The spot from which employees are called for work when they do not have sufficient seniority to bid for specific jobs.

EYE WIRE A device used in barge operations, consisting of a rope or wire with a large eye or spliced loop on end.

—F—

F.A.A. Free all average.

FABRICATION-IN-TRANSIT RATE A through rate plus an additional charge applied to a shipment stopped at some point between origin and destination for the purpose of fabrication.

FACILITATION A system to increase the speed of international commerce through modernizing customs procedures, duty collection, agriculture inspection and other procedures.

FACTOR An agent appointed to sell goods on commission.

FACTORING A business operation which provides professional services for collection and credit.

FACTOR OF PRODUCTION Land, labor or capital required for production.

FALSE BILLING When the shipping papers contain descriptions of commodities which fail to reflect the true contents of a shipment, it is referred to as a false billing.

FAMILY GROUPING A term used in materials handling and stock layout indicating that different products of the same manufacturer or product lines are stored together.

FAR EAST Western Coast of Pacific Ocean in vicinity of Japan, China, and Philippine Islands.

FAS (FREE ALONG SIDE) A selling term in international trade whereby the selling party quotes a goods price including delivery of the goods along side the overseas vessel at the exporting port.

FAST-FREIGHT LINE An organization of the carriers to promote dispatch of freight between certain points for specified traffic.

FAST FREIGHT TRAIN A freight train which does not stop at all of the stations on its route.

FDA Food and Drug Administration.

FEDERAL AVIATION ACT The federal legislation by the United States Congress which superseded the Civil Aeronautics Act of 1938 regulating air transportation. It was termed the Federal Aviation Act of 1958.

FEDERAL AVIATION ADMINISTRATION The successor to the old Civil Aeronautics Administration. A federal agency which initiates and executes policy relative to the promotion of safety and efficiency in flight operations. It is now in the Department of Transportation (DOT) under a 1967 order.

FEDERAL MARITIME COMMISSION Regulatory agency responsible for rates and practices of ocean traffic to and from U.S.

FEDERAL REGISTER A publication produced by the U.S. government that provides information concerning notices and rules of the federal regulatory agencies. This was provided for under the Federal Register Act.

FEDERAL TRADE COMMISSION Government body created for the purpose of overseeing business practices and verifying their loyalty.

FEEDER 1. Another term for air commuter company. 2. A pick up and delivery vehicle or ship.

FEEDER LINES Branches or short-line railroads traversing territory untouched by the trunk lines and interchanging traffic at connecting points.

FEEDER SERVICE In motor transportation, short truck routes involved primarily in the collection and distribution of freight to and from main truck lines (for long hauls), usually from terminals.

FEEDING IN TRANSIT The stopping of shipments of livestock, etc., at a point located between the points of origin and destination to be fed and watered.

FERRY CAR When a freight car is loaded with several L.C.L. shipments by a shipper to a railroad, or by a railroad to a receiver, it is termed a ferry car. It may also be called a trap car.

FERRY CHARTER RATE The portion of the charter charged by the carrier to cover the necessary miles or hours of the aircraft to the point of origin of the charter, and the return of the charter aircraft to the destination of the carrier.

FERRY OPERATION Operation of equipment from one point to another in non-revenue service for the purpose of positioning it for another revenue run.

FIBERBOARD A shipping container material of heavy board—3 to 4 plies.

FIELD WAREHOUSE A warehouse provided by a public warehouse firm, located on the premises of a business.

FIFO Inventory rotation, first in, first out.

FIFTH WHEEL The device used to connect the semi-trailer and the tractor.

FIGHTING SHIP When a shipping conference designates a particular ship to combat nonconference competition, it is given the term fighting ship. This is executed by making the rates on the fighting ship so low that competition is forced out of business or required to reduce the rates to acceptable proportions. Fighting ships were declared illegal under the Shipping Act of 1916.

FINANCE DOCKET The dockets of the Interstate Commerce Commission on which are listed for consideration and decision, questions relating to financing, extensions, abandonments, and consolidations of common carriers.

FINANCIAL ACCOUNTING STANDARDS BOARD, BULLETIN #13 A statement from the accounting profession as to how leases are to be treated for accounting purposes; difference between handling them as leases or capitalizing them on the company balance sheet.

FINANCIAL STATEMENT A report of the liquidity, profitability, and solvency of a firm.

FINGER PIER A long, enclosed walkway extending from airport terminal to the loading gate. Also a water carrier pier.

FINGER TERMINAL The standard air terminal which has a central ticketing and general operations section, with projecting corridors for passenger facilitation.

FINK AWARD A report issued in 1880 as to freight rate differential at Atlantic ports, when goods were, in addition to rail movement, water-borne. Albert Fink was chairman.

FIRE, CLASS A A fire involving combustible materials such as wood, packing materials, paper and cloth.

FIRE, CLASS B Fires involving oil, gasoline, paint or grease.

FIRE, CLASS C Fires involving wiring, fuse boxes, energized electrical equipment.

FIRE, CLASS D Fires involving combustible metals.

FIRE CURTAIN Large curtain made of a fire resistant material to prevent a fire from one side of the curtain to the other.

FIRE PALLET Portable platform on which sits fire extinguishers and fire fighting equipment, to be moved to the scene of a fire.

FIRE WALL A wall made of fire resistant material to prevent the spreading of fire.

FIRING POINT The temperature required for the vapor from a liquid to be in sufficient quantity to provide a continuous flame. It is higher than the flash point.

FIRKIN A capacity measurement equal to one-fourth of a barrel.

FIRM A commercial establishment that provides goods or services.

FIRST CLASS SERVICE Transport service for passengers where standard or premium quality service are provided.

FIRST MAIN TRACK As applied to line-haul roads, a single track extending the entire distance between terminals, upon which the length of the road is based, used to effect a line-haul and therefore kept clear for the passage of trains.

FIRST REFUSAL RIGHTS An operating right situation in which a carrier has prior rights on charter or other special services in international transportation operations by air.

FISHYBACK When highway trailers are transported aboard ships through a process of demounting the trailers, the shipment is referred to as fishyback.

FITNESS A transportation regulation term pertaining to motor, water and forwarder financial stature.

FIVE FREEDOMS (1) Right to cross the territory of another country (by air); (2) right to land for technical, fueling or comparable necessities; (3) right to deplane traffic that was enplaned in the home country of the carrier; (4) right to enplane traffic bound for the home country of the carrier; and (5) right to enplane in one foreign country, enroute to another foreign country.

FIXED ASSETS Non-consumable production facilities.

FIXED BASED OPERATOR The selling of transportation and/or servicing of an aircraft, giving flying instructions, making charter flights, etc., all at an airport.

FIXED CHARGES Those transportation costs which do not vary with the volume of transportation.

FIXED COSTS Costs that do not change with a change in the volume of operations.

FIXED IMPROVEMENTS Structures of permanent character.

FIXED INTERVAL SYSTEM An inventory reordering rule in which goods are reordered at specified fixed time intervals, the size of the lot varies.

FIXED LOCATION SYSTEM Location of a product in the warehouse—is in a specific place as indicated by a floor marking.

FIXED ORDER QUANTITY An inventory reordering rule in which the lot size ordered each time remains the same, the length of time between orders varies.

FIXED PRICE When price is not affected by demand.

FIXED REORDER POINT SYSTEM An inventory rule that calls for reordering at fixed time intervals.

FIXED WING AIRCRAFT Aircraft having wings that are fixed to the airplane body.

FIXING LETTER A document drawn to establish the conditions for a charter.

FIXTURE A report of vessel charters that explains the basic elements of the charter.

FLAG STATION A station at which trains stop only when signaled.

FLAMMABLE GAS Any compressed gas meeting the requirements for lower flammability limit, flammability limit range, flame projection, or flame propagation criteria as specified in DOT regulations.

FLAMMABLE GOODS Goods that give off vapors which become combustible at a certain temperature.

FLAMMABLE LIQUID Any liquid having a flash point below 100° F as determined in DOT tests.

FLAMMABLE SOLID Any solid material, other than an explosive, which is liable to cause fires through friction, retained heat from manufacturing or processing, or which can be ignited readily and when ignited burns so vigorously and persistently as to create a serious transportation hazard.

FLANGE In rail transportation, the steel edge inside the rim of the wheels to provide guidance on the track.

FLASH POINT The minimum temperature at which a substance gives off flammable vapors which in contact with spark or flame will ignite.

FLAT BED CAR An open railroad car without sides or top.

FLAT BOTTOM A flatbed truck or trailer without sides.

FLATCAR A freight car without ends, sides, or top, used principally for the transportation of lumber, machinery, and unusually bulky articles; often called a *platform car*.

FLAT FACE A cab over engine type of vehicle.

FLAT PERCENTAGE RATE INCREASES This is a system of changing rates to meet changes in costs of operations by means of changing all existing tariffs by a given flat percentage. This system may be criticized because it fails to take into consideration the difference in changes of costs of operations in the line-haul and terminal areas, respectively. It would be a coincidence if terminal and line-haul costs increased at the same rate, yet the flat percentage system assumes they do. The most common criticism applied to this method of rate increase has been that it results in a greater absolute increase to the long haul shipper. This is an erroneous criticism if the objective is to change rates to meet changes in costs. If the costs of transportation increase, it should be expected that long haul shipments will sustain a greater absolute increase in rates, since the distance is greater.

FLAT RATE A local or joint rate applicable to all circumstances of shipment.

FLEXI-VAN Truck trailers or containers that are loaded on specially constructed flat cars equipped with two turntables.

FLIGHT EQUIPMENT The equipment facilities required for flight.

FLIGHT EQUIPMENT INTERCHANGE Circumstances in which a single plane is used by more than one carrier on a route, and where the crew is changed to fly the routes of the carrier.

FLIGHT STAGE The time from take-off to landing.

FLIMSEY A train order to the crew indicating that certain action will be required by them or will otherwise affect their train.

FLOAT A flatbed semi-trailer.

FLOATAGE A charge for floating or transferring cars across water.

FLOAT BRIDGE A drawbridge completing a connection between land, railroad tracks, and car floats, and affording an interchange of rolling stock.

FLOAT, CAR A flat-bottomed craft without power, equipped with tracks, and accommodating from ten to twenty cars at a time. The cars are run from the land by means of a flat bridge.

FLOATER A driver who skips from job to job.

FLOATING THE GEARS Changing gears without using the clutch.

FLOATS Large single tires that are used instead of duals.

FLOOR LOAD The range or maximum capacity of a car, in pounds per square foot.

FLOTSAM Cargo swept from a vessel and found floating in the water. Since ownership of such property is not lost, flotsam is liable for salvage.

FLOWCHART A diagram depicting the sequence of events that should take place in a complex set of tasks.

FLOW PROCESS CHART Similar to a flow chart.

FLOW RACK Metal rack which allows the stacking of product and easy access to product.

FLUTE A zig zag rib, usually on the inside portion of corrugated fiberboard.

FLYER A round trip run involving a trip to a distant terminal and the return trip without stop.

FLYING ORDERS The instruction given the driver on the trip.

F.O.B. This means free on board. The F.O.B. terms go far beyond this concept and establish the contractual arrangements in which (1) title is transferred between seller and buyer; and (2) the point where transportation responsibility is shifted from seller to buyer. The F.O.B. abbreviation implies loading on a conveyance at the designated point. After these letters, it is usually designated where title and control of the goods pass to the buyer.

F.O.B. DESTINATION Free on board to the point of destination. Freight cost is paid to the point of destination. Title transfers at destination.

F.O.B. FACTORY Under this term, cartage from the factory to the railroad head will be paid by the buyer. Both title to the goods and carrier responsibility terminates with the seller at the factory. If the factory has a railroad siding, the goods will be made available at the railroad siding.

F.O.B. (NAMED INLAND CARRIER AT NAMED INLAND POINT OF DEPARTURE) Under this contractual term, the seller makes the goods available at an inland shipping point. Both title to the goods and responsibility for transportation are transferred at the named inland point for shipment. All transportation costs, export taxes, document costs, and responsibility for loss and damage transfer when possession of the goods is taken at the inland point of transfer. The seller places the goods in or on the conveyance for delivery to the inland carrier. The seller arranges for the loading of the goods on rail cars, trucks, etc. for transportation.

F.O.B. (NAMED INLAND CARRIER AT NAMED INLAND POINT OF DEPARTURE; FREIGHT ALLOWED TO NAMED POINT.) Under this term, title transfers when the goods are placed on the inland carrier. A price is quoted which includes transportation charges from the factory in the country of sales to the destination. Thus, price is the manufacturer's price, plus transportation costs to the consignee. The goods are sent freight collect, but the buyer is billed by the seller for the manufacturer's sales price, not including transportation. The seller arranges transportation, but he does not pay for it. The buyer has an opportunity to directly compare the total costs inclusive of transportation of all competing sellers. The buyer is responsible for all costs, including export costs, document expenses, etc. from the factory of the seller to the destination.

F.O.B. (NAMED INLAND CARRIER AT NAMED INLAND POINT OF DEPARTURE; FREIGHT PREPAID TO NAMED POINT OF EXPORTATION.) Under this term, title transfers at the named inland point of departure for the initial inland carrier, but transportation is included in the seller's price all the way to the named point of exportation. The named inland point of departure obviously is not the same as the named point of exportation. The buyer is responsible for all export taxes, document costs, etc. necessary in the event of an export shipment.

F.O.B. (NAMED INLAND CARRIER TO NAMED INLAND POINT OF EXPORTATION.) Under this F.O.B. term, a foreign buyer requests a price which includes invoice price, and the transport cost, to a common export point. Therefore, under the quoted price, purchase price and transportation cost may be directly compared. It permits the foreign buyer to control the international water routing, but puts the domestic routing from the named inland point to the export point in the hands of the seller.

F.O.B. VESSEL (NAMED PORT OF SHIPMENT) Both title and transportation costs transfer after the goods are delivered on the vessel. Since they have not left the harbor, all export taxes and costs involved in documents for overseas shipments would be assessed to the buyer.

FOOD AND DRUG ADMINISTRATION Agency of the federal government regulating all activity concerning food and drugs. Inspects warehouses and sanitary conditions.

FORBIDDEN (HAZARDOUS MATERIAL) One that must not be offered or accepted for transportation.

FORCED BILLING When no bill can be located, the forced billing provides a means for delivery of freight. This is most common when the traffic is moving partly in the U.S. and partly in a foreign country, or involves an international movement.

FORCE MAJEURE A condition typically found in rail, motor, and water rate contracts that relieves either party from contract obligation if major unforeseen events beyond their control prevent compliance; typically the obligation is suspended for resumption at a later time.

FORECASTLE HEAD The foremost part of the spar deck. It is the raised deck of most merchant ships, in the front of the vessel.

FOREIGN AIR CARRIER PERMIT A right to operate, issued by the C.A.B. to the foreign carrier, authorizing it to operate between a foreign country and U.S. cities.

FOREIGN CAR In the railroad transportation business, rail cars move between lines and between nations. The car of one railroad used by another railroad line is termed a foreign car. It usually does not involve a foreign national car, but it can.

FOREIGN-FLAG AIR CARRIER Foreign registered air carriers.

FOREIGN FREIGHT FORWARDER A party that acts to arrange for foreign movement for shippers and consignees; distinct from domestic forwarders; foreign forwarders do not take on the same obligations.

FOREIGN TRADE ZONE A site sanctioned by the Customs Service in which imported goods are exempted from customs duties until withdrawn for domestic sale or use; such zones are used for commercial warehouse or production plants.

FOR-HIRE AIR CARRIER A common or contract transportation carrier.

FORKLIFT TRUCK A machine which can raise and lower freight for stacking and move freight to different locations.

FORK POCKETS Space under containers to facilitate the forks of a forklift truck.

FORMAL COMPLAINT A complaint filed with the Interstate Commerce Commission alleging violation of the statute and to be investigated and adjudicated under formal procedure provided by the rules of the Commission.

FORWARD BUYING A practice in purchasing whereby goods required in future periods are ordered in the present one; common reasons are favorable deals, pending price increases or future product shortages.

FORWARDER, FREIGHT One who accepts LCL shipments from shippers and combines them for forwarding in CL lots. A foreign freight-forwarder attends to custom procedures and documents in connection with foreign shipments.

FOUL BILL OF LADING A lading receipted by the agent of the carrier, indicating damage or a shortage when goods were shipped.

FOUND Equipped, provided, or supplied; as, a ship was well found.

FOUNDER To fill with water and sink; to cause (a ship) to founder.

FOUR BANGER Four cycle engines.

FOUR BY FOUR A vehicle with four speed transmission and four speed auxilliary transmission.

FOURTH SECTION APPLICATION When a carrier wishes to publish rates which are in violation of Section 10726, it submits an application. The "Fourth Section" provides that one cannot charge a higher rate for a shorter than a longer haul over the same route. If the I.C.C. goes along with this application, an order is issued. "Fourth Section" is the name still used because it involved section four of the original Interstate Commerce Act; it was recodified in 1978 to Section 10726 of the Revised Interstate Commerce Act.

FOURTH SECTION ORDER A Federal Commission order which grants authority to publish charges not in conformity with Section 10726 of the Interstate Commerce Act. See "Fourth Section Application."

FOURTH SECTION RATES Under Section 10726 of the Act, one cannot charge more for a shorter than a longer haul on the same commodity moving between the same points. Traffic managers may achieve reductions in rates by finding a lower commodity rate to a more extended distance, and applying the lower commodity rate rather than the shorter class rate. See "Fourth Section Application."

FOURTH SECTION RELIEF Permission granted by the Interstate Commerce Commission to carriers, under certain conditions, to publish and charge higher rates for a short haul than for a long haul over the same route. See "Fourth Section Application."

FRANCO (DELIVERY) When a delivery is made to the consignee's door, all charges have been paid, and all circumstances completed, it is called a franco delivery.

FRANK To exempt mail express matter or telegraph messages from the usual charge.

FREE ALONG SIDE (F.A.S.) VESSEL Under this F.A.S. term, the seller agrees to deliver the goods in proper condition along side the vessel. It may be delivered on a lighter or on a receiving pier. The buyer assumes all subsequent risk and expenses after delivery.

FREE ASTRAY A term applied to freight which has been unloaded at the wrong terminal. It will be transferred to the correct terminal free of charge.

FREE BAGGAGE ALLOWANCE The amount of baggage allowed to the passengers before an additional charge is made.

FREE ENTERPRISE A national ownership system for production facilities. Prices are established through the supply and demand of the consumer and producer.

FREE (____) HARBOR The delivery of goods to the port of entry named. The exporter assumes all expense connected with the movement of the goods, even to transshipment costs, should a vessel be forced, by accident or unseaworthiness, to discharge cargo at a port other than that named.

FREE LIGHTERAGE When carlots are unloaded from cars, transferred to lighters, and transported to a restricted territory within a harbor with no additional charges attached beyond the rail head, this is referred to as free lighterage.

FREE MARKET An economic situation in which price is the result of the supply of goods or services at different prices, and the demand for each price level.

FREE OF PARTICULAR AVERAGE (F.P.A.) In maritime insurance, when goods are damaged by an accident of the vessel in which they are being conveyed, but are not covered to the extent of minor damages, the term free of particular average is applied. If a shipment is free of particular average under 5%, it means that the insurance company will not allow a claim for partial loss or damage under F.P.A. conditions unless the actual damage and loss amounts to 5% or more of the amount for which the shipment had been insured. This is set forth in the policy.

FREE OF PARTICULAR AVERAGE UNDER 5 PERCENT A term denoting that no claim under F.P.A. conditions will be allowed unless the actual damage or loss amounts to or exceeds 5% of the amount of the insurance policy.

FREE ON BOARD (F.O.B.) In domestic trade, and when this term is used with no further attachments, it means delivery of the goods with all charges paid onboard the cars at the point of manufacture.

FREE OVERSIDE (OVERBOARD) Sold at a price to the buyer which does not include charges up to and including the unloading of a vessel.

FREE PORT A port which permits the loading and unloading of ships without the payment of a duty.

FREEPORT LAW A state law that exempts inventories held within the state from state inventory taxes as long as the inventory will eventually move on to customers or users out of that state; used as an industry attraction policy device; prime examples are Nevada and Georgia.

FREE TIME The time allowed the shipper to load, or the receiver of the freight to unload before demurrage charges begin, is called free time. In LCL freight, free time is the time which would be allowed the consignee before storage charges begin to accrue. These conditions are spelled out in the Code of Car Demurrage Rules which govern rail carload freight.

FREE TRANSPORTATION In Chapter 107 of the R.I.C.A., carriers are permitted to issue free passes only to their employees and persons engaged in certain pursuits.

FREEZABLE FREIGHT Freight that cannot be frozen for shipment without damage.

FREIGHT Goods being moved by transportation lines from one place to another; also, the transportation charge.

FREIGHT ALLOWED This means that shipments will move freight collect and the extent of the transportation cost will be deducted from the total cost of the goods when the invoice is paid. This permits the seller to quote a price that does not include transportation charges, thus avoiding tying up his capital.

FREIGHT, ASTRAY (FREE ASTRAY) When less-than-carload shipments become separated from the regular revenue waybill, even though it is marked for destination, it is termed freight astray.

FREIGHT BILL The freight bill is the carrier's invoice. At the destination it is prepared from waybills or collect shipments, while at the point of origin it is prepared on the basis of prepaid shipments. An original and four copies of the freight bill are made out. While the original is known as the freight bill, the other copies are the arrival notice, delivery receipt, cashier's memorandum, and the station record.

FREIGHT CHARGE The rate established for transporting freight.

FREIGHT CLAIM A demand on a carrier for reimbursement as to over-charges, or loss, damage, delay, or other act of omission connected with the handling of freight.

FREIGHT CLAIM RATIO, FOR CARRIER The percentage of revenues paid out in claims.

FREIGHT CLAIM RATIO, FOR SHIPPER The percentage of shipments or value of shipments involved in claims.

FREIGHT CONSOLIDATION PLAN Pool distribution in reverse. Con-solidation of small orders at the warehouses into truckloads or carload quantities and thus gaining lower freight rates.

FREIGHT CONTRACT (STEAMSHIP) The ocean carrier books cargo in advance of sailing. This permits the most efficient and maximum loading of the vessel. A contract is written which authorizes a shipper to deliver according to specific requirements. The freight contract contains the name of the ship, vessel, port, time for loading, cargo descriptions, etc. The carrier can cancel any part of the contract for circumstances such as strikes which are beyond the carrier's control. Freight contract bookings are entered on a booking sheet. Freight contracts are currently limited to bulk cargo.

FREIGHT, DEAD When a charterer fails to provide a full cargo for the vessel he has engaged, the loss sustained by the ship owner must be made up by the shipper. The unused space is called dead freight. The term also ap-plies to the unused space itself.

FREIGHT EQUALIZATION Practice by sellers of paying some or all of the freight to some customers in order to have the various customers pay the same amounts for freight.

FREIGHTER A vessel built and equipped for, and deriving its principal revenue from, the carriage of cargo.

FREIGHT FORWARDER Designated as a common carrier under the Interstate Commerce Act, the freight forwarder is an individual or a company that accepts LCL shipments or LTL shipments from shippers and combines them into carload lots. Generally speaking, the freight forwarder charges the shipper on the basis of LCL size shipments, but pays the carrier on the basis of CL shipments and covers his costs, inclusive of fair return, on the difference between these rates.

FREIGHT FORWARDER An agent whose functions are to help expedite shipments by preparing the necessary documents and making other arrangements for the outward movement of merchandise.

FREIGHT FORWARDER ACT Originally Interstate Commerce Act, Part IV; now a Subchapter IV carrier in the Revised Interstate Commerce Act.

FREIGHT FORWARDER RATES Freight forwarder tariffs are predominantly governed by the motor classification, since freight forwarders try to maintain rate levels that do not exceed those of motor carriers. Freight forwarder class and commodity tariffs present rates on both less than volume and volume shipments. It is because a freight forwarder pays carload or truckload charges that he is able to publish rates of his own to the public on any volume less than these quantities. Forwarder class rates are competitive with motor carrier rates down to Class 50 on less than volume shipments, and down to Class 35 on volume shipments.

FREIGHT HOUSE The station facility of a transportation line for receiving and delivering freight.

FREIGHT, LUMP Payment in one sum for the hire of a ship for a complete voyage or other purpose.

FREIGHT, MISROUTED Freight which, through the carrier's error, is forwarded to the correct destination via a route with a higher rate than that applicable via the route specified by the shipper; also, freight for which the shipper has not specified route but which is forwarded via a route with a rate higher than is applicable *via the cheapest available route.*

FREIGHT PAK A term applied to air freight customers.

FREIGHT RATE Charge assessed for transporting freight.

FREIGHT REVENUE The revenue received from freight, transit, stop, reconsignment and any other source required by the tariff.

FREIGHT TRAIN A unit or a combination of units of equipment (exclusive of light locomotives) moving over tracks by self-contained motor equipment in connection with the transportation of revenue and company freight, whether loaded or empty.

FREIGHT TRAIN CAR A freight-carrying car, caboose, or other train service equipment required in the operation of a freight train.

FROG The section of a rail track which permits a cross-over to another track at an intersection.

FTC Federal Trade Commission; regulatory agency responsible for administering a large part of the Robinson-Patman Act.

FUEL SURCHARGE An extra charge on transportation movements to account for the increased fuel cost since the base rate was put into effect.

FUEL TAXES Excise taxes on gasoline and other fuels.

FULL EMPLOYMENT A situation in which unemployment is less than 4%.

FULL FREIGHT A trailer with wheels on all corners, as contrasted to a semi-trailer which requires the tractor to hold the front end.

FULL PAYMENT LEASE One in which the lessor shall receive the full cost plus financing, overhead, and accepts a return on his investment.

FULL REACH AND BURDEN Cargo space normally available, including deck.

FULL-SERVICE LEASE The lessor can provide everything such as maintenance, insurance, taxes and other incidentals; this lease can be tailored to provide or eliminate any type of service or expense by the lessee.

FULL TRAILER A trailer with wheels at both ends, rather than requiring a fifth wheel for support by the tractor.

FULLY ALLOCATED COST A cost consisting of the variable cost per unit plus a prorata share of fixed costs; the latter term typically being total fixed costs divided by the expected number of units to be handled in the lot.

FURNITURE CAR A car equipped with facilities for safe and proper handling of furniture.

FUTURES MARKET A sales opportunity for future delivery of commodities, which may be bought and sold. This is an insurance against price fluctuations and avoids risks.

—G—

GAGE (GAUGE) OF TRACK The distance between the heads of the rails on a railroad measured at right angles thereto at a point $5/8$ inches below the top of the rail. The standard gage is 4 feet $8\frac{1}{2}$ inches. Narrow gage is generally 3 feet.

GALE A wind of from 35 to 65 miles per hour, of varying intensity.

GANGPLANK A bridge of some sort from ship to shore.

GANGWAY A platform used in conveying shipments from dock to vessel, platform to car, or car to car; also, the passageway by which passengers enter or depart from a ship.

GANTRY CRANE A crane placed on track with the capacity to lift weights by a tackle.

GANTT CHART A control chart which shows the relationship between planned performance and actual performance. It was named after Henry L. Gantt. One use is to measure loading performance, with one horizontal line representing capacity, and another to illustrate load compared to the capacity. Sometimes it is used to measure progress, with one horizontal line showing production schedule, and another showing performed progress.

GATEWAY A point at which freight is interchanged between territories is normally thought of as a gateway. The term is commonly applied in air transportation to air terminals at which passengers may be transferred to other carriers.

GAUNTLET A railroad track set off from a regular high speed track that is used to bring trains close to an adjoining train platform for loading/unloading.

G.B.L. Government bill of lading.

GEAR BONGER Slang name applied to a driver who does not know how to shift gears.

GEAR JAMMER Same as gear bonger—a driver who grinds the gears when shifting.

GENERAL AVERAGE A contribution made by the owners of a ship and its cargo toward a loss sustained by one or more of their number whose property has been thrown overboard or sacrificed necessarily in order to save the ship and a part of its cargo.

GENERAL AVIATION All civil aviation except common carrier service. It does not include the certificated common carriers, supplemental carriers, intrastate carriers or military movements. Business aircraft flights and contract flights represent the most common types.

GENERAL COMMODITIES An operating right to carry all commodities except those specifically listed—such as iron and steel, brick, dry or liquid bulk materials, etc.

GENERAL COMMODITY AIR RATE An air rate that applies to all commodities except special commodity rates. These rates are based on weight and distance. They are published for each combination of cities and air carrier serves.

GENERAL LICENSE (EXPORT) Right to export without specific approval.

GENERAL RATE INCREASE A term for a rate increase that applies generally to all or a broad set of commodities and traffic by a carrier; often called exparte increase.

GENERAL SHIP A vessel, navigated by its owner, that receives and carries freight impartially for all who apply.

GLAD HAND A system to couple the braking system of the tractor with the brakes of the trailer.

GOAT'N SHOAT MAN A farm livestock truck driver.

GODOWN A waterfront storehouse in far eastern ports.

GOING CONCERN VALUE A ratemaking term indicating that a rate that is over out of pocket costs will contribute to the overhead and profit of a firm; the covering of out of pocket costs and an addition to the firm's overhead is seen as contributing to what is needed for the firm to continue.

GONDOLA CAR An open car, with sides and ends but no top, used for hauling sand, gravel, coal, and similar commodities, and referred to as a *gon.*

GONDOLA CAR, DROP-BOTTOM A gondola car having a level floor equipped with several drop doors for discharging the load.

GONDOLA CAR, DROP-END A gondola car with the ends in the form of doors, which can be dropped to accommodate material whose length exceeds the length of one car.

GOODS Merchandise in transportation.

GOVERNMENT BILL OF LADING Special form of bill of lading used for U.S. Government and military traffic.

GOVERNMENT LICENSE A document permitting goods to be shipped out of the country. Although basically a wartime measure, it is still required on some commodities shipped to certain foreign countries.

GRAB-ONE The process of shifting to lower gears on a high grade.

GRAIN BODY In highway transportation, an open flat body used to haul grain and other loose shipments. Low sides.

GRAIN DOOR The partition across the door of a boxcar which prevents grain from leaking.

GRAIN ELEVATOR A storehouse into which grain in bulk is carried upward by elevators and placed into bins arranged for the different grades of grain.

GRAIN TANKER In motor transportation, a specialized grain carrying tank trailer. It is a low slung tank with grain trailer sides. The grain used in molasses production is carried on the top of the tank.

GRANDFATHER CLAUSE When a carrier has been operating for some period of time and seeks an operating permit on the basis of his vested interest, it may be given a Grandfather Clause operating right. The Grandfather Clause of the Motor Carrier Act of 1935 permitted carriers to continue their operations by simply establishing the extent of the operation.

GRANDMA Has the same meaning as a creeper gear.

GRASS The term for a rope used by a bargeman.

GRAVITY CHUTE A chute or trough used to load bulky commodities by gravity.

GRAY AREA A transportation service which borders between the legal and illegal. These services are most subject to legal dispute.

GREAT CIRCLE SAILING Sailing along the great circle routes between ports.

GREEN SEA Name applied to solid water carried aboard.

GRID TECHNIQUE A simple mathematical tool utilizing longitude and latitude scales with market and source tonnages to determine an ideal minimum total transportation cost location point for production or distribution.

GROCERY MANUFACTURERS ASSOCIATION Provides a suggested set of regulations for pallet sizes; often referred to as "GMA."

GROCERY PALLET COUNCIL Provides a suggested set of regulations for pallet size and manufacture. Controls manufacture through licensing and stamps, which must be burned onto a pallet.

GROSS REQUIREMENT The requirement for a particular component—not including any inventory of the component on hand.

GROSS TON (G.T.) A *long ton*; the gross ton is 2,240 pounds.

GROSS TONNAGE The term gross tonnage applies to the vessel and not to the cargo. The gross tonnage is determined by dividing the cubic feet of the vessel's closed in space by 100. Therefore, a vessel ton is 100 cubic feet.

GROSS TON-MILE The movement of a ton of transportation equipment and contents a distance of one mile.

GROSS TON-MILES PER TRAIN-MILE The total gross ton-miles divided by the total train-miles, not including gross ton-miles of locomotive and tender unless so specified.

GROSS WAREHOUSE SPACE Length times width of building—measured from outside wall to outside wall. Expressed as square footage.

GROSS WEIGHT This is the weight of both the container and its contents, as well as the material that might be used for packing.

GROUND EFFECT MACHINE This is more commonly known as air-cushion vehicle, levapads, hovercraft, etc. It travels on a cushion of air over land, water, swamp, mud, sand, etc., with only a few inches of elevation.

GROUNDING A general order to stop flying. It may be a voluntary move, or an order from the Federal Aviation Agency. Usually the result of conviction of malfunctioning aircraft.

GROUND LEADER Leader of a group or crew while working with them. Responsible for the details of assignments received from proper authority.

GROUND LEVEL DOOR Overhead door which leads from the warehouse to the ground level outside the warehouse.

GROUND STORAGE The storing of shipments on the ground. More commonly called outside storage.

GROUND SWELL Undulations following the passage over shoaling water and proximity to the bottom.

GROUP Several points considered together for rate-making purposes.

GROUPAGE A consolidation service, putting small shipments into containers for shipment.

GROUP FARE A reduced or promotional fare offered to a group of people that will fly together under certain conditions.

GROUP RATES Group rates are established on two different patterns: (1) through the use of base points with distance scales determining different rate groups; and (2) under the commodity rate structures which group competitive producers and manufacturers in a geographic area which will receive the same rate. Under the second system, all salt fields throughout the country may be grouped together geographically, and a shipment from any salt mine to a destination would receive the same rate. Group rates tend to encourage dispersion of manufacturing facilities, and thus have long range beneficial environmental impact.

GUARANTEED LOAN An aircraft purchase loan guaranteed by the Federal Government under the Department of Commerce. It is provided by helicopter lines, local service carriers, Intra-Alaskan carriers, Intra-Hawaiian carriers and others to obtain the necessary capital to buy aircraft. Many other applications.

GUARANTEED RATE 1) a contract carriage rate; 2) an annual volume rate.

GUIDE BOOK A tariff containing instructions for waybilling and routing shipments and bases for rates to certain point.

GUM BALL MACHINE The rotating emergency light on a vehicle.

GUNTER'S SCALE A two-foot ruler with logarithmic scale on one side and trigonometric functions on the other.

GUNWALE The deck space between the outboard side of the hold and outside of the barge.

GYPSY An unregulated trucking operation which consists of a self-owned vehicle, operated wherever traffic is available. It may take the form of a lease of the tractor, or tractor and trailer for single trips. Sometimes it takes the form of a buy and sell operation, under prearranged contracting.

—H—

HAND CAR The small maintenance car which is moved by hand power and employed in track inspection and repair work.

HANDLING AISLE An aisle used to gain access from one area of the warehouse to another.

HANDLING CHARGE A charge for ordinary labor and duties incidental to the final point, but not including unloading or loading of the cars, vehicles, etc.

HANDLING COSTS The cost involved in transferring, preparing and otherwise contacting inventory.

HAND TO MOUTH BUYING Purchasing term indicating that current purchase lots are less than those required for current needs; generally used in period when company wishes to reduce inventory.

HARBOR A place of security or haven for vessels.

HARBOR MASTER An officer having charge of the berthing of ships.

HARDWARE The computer system machine equipment.

HARTER LAW The Harter Law was passed in 1893 and established the rules for governing vehicles and their cargos for clearing ports of the United States.

HATCH The opening in the vessel's deck to enable merchandise to be lowered in the hold, or the opening through which grain may be placed in hopper cars or ice in refrigerator cars of railroads.

HAULING POST-HAULS Driving an empty truck or trailer.

HAVEN A place of shelter and safety. A sheltered anchorage for ships.

HAZARDOUS COMMODITY Material that may be dangerous to move or to store. It may be subject to explosion, burning, or have damaging fumes. These commodities are subject to safety regulations while being transported; regulations may be found in Title 49, Code of Federal Regulations, Parts 100-199.

HAZARDOUS MATERIALS Means a substance or material which has been determined by the Secretary of Transportation to be capable of posing an unreasonable risk to health, safety, and property when transported in commerce, and which has been so designated.

HEADACHE RACK An extension of a holding rack over the cab from the trailer. Normally used for holding pipe or such freight.

HEADER BAR A protective device placed at the front end of the flat bottom trailer which stops freight from inching forward.

HEADER RECORD A record of constant, common, identifying or other information for data which will follow.

HEAP SYSTEM A method of filing tariffs whereby schedules issued by various agents or carriers are segregated and kept in labeled boxes, drawers, or pigeonholes.

HEARING The regulatory authority (for example, the Interstate Commerce Commission) which provides an opportunity for interested parties to present evidence concerning a particular case. This meeting and presentation is referred to as a hearing. A carrier rate conference may also conduct a hearing to receive evidence of interested parties. The regulatory authority will designate a time and a place for the hearing which will provide the sufficiency of evidence necessary for rendering a decision.

HEATED CAR SERVICE Warming a cart to keep perishable freight from freezing and usually performed by caretakers.

HEAVY LIFTS When freight is too heavy to be handled by the ship's regular tackle, special equipment is used and a *heavy-lift charge* is assessed.

HEURISTIC The process of solving problems by evaluating each step in the progress. A search for satisfactory, rather than optimal solutions. It restricts the number of alternatives to be considered by trial and error considerations.

HIDDEN COSTS Those costs in logistics which are almost impossible to determine without a cost allocation process from the data available in conventional financial statements are commonly referred to as hidden costs. They are hidden because they are usually a part of a more general cost. Thus, for example, inventory in-transit costs are part of interest costs that may cover many different interest costs over the period covered by the financial statement.

HIGH CUBE A truck body with greater than average cubic space. It is usually constructed with thin walls and low floors.

HIGH CUBE CAR A railcar with dimensions larger than a regular box car; such cars are either longer or higher enabling them to carry light bulky products or one more tier of palletized goods.

HIGH IRON Mainline track.

HIGH SEAS The unenclosed waters of the ocean outside the boundaries of any country.

HIGHWAYS A public road; a course or path on land or sea which everyone has the right to use.

HOBO Tractor that is transferred from one terminal to another.

HOG LAW A federal law requiring train crews to leave the train after a maximum of 16 hours.

HOLD-DOWNS Those rates on commodities that are not increased in a general rate increase.

HOLDER One in whose possession a bill or note may be.

HOLD ORDER A directive to interrupt or terminate certain operations, pending a change in the process.

HOLD POINTS A term applied to stocking points for semi-finished inventory.

HOLD TRACK It is common practice to place rail cars on a side track pending disposition. When orders are received from shippers or receivers, the car is moved from the hold track toward its destination.

HOLE A siding into which one train enters so that another may pass.

HOME CAR As contrasted to a foreign car, a home car is a car operating on the track of its owner.

HOME LINE This term is used in connection with cars and has reference to the line owning the car.

HOME ROAD Used in connection with car service to denote the road that is owner or lessee of a car, or upon which the home of a private car is located.

HOME ROUTE Road from which foreign freight car was originally received.

HONEYCOMBING An aspect of storage which from partial depletion of a lot results in the inability to utilize the entire cubic capacity of a given amount of floor area.

HOOD LIFTER A mechanic.

HOPPER BODY A truck body that discharges through the bottom without need for tilting.

HOPPER CAR A car which moves bulk dry freight and usually unloads through gravity by vents on the underside is termed a hopper car. Some hopper cars have an open top while others have closed tops.

HOPPER CAR, COVERED A hopper car with a permanent roof and roof hatches, which has a bottom opening for unloading for the purpose of carrying cement or other bulky commodities.

HORIZONTAL INTEGRATION The ownership under a single corporate entity of competing industrial operations on the same channel level. Usually this is thought of as involving ownership under a single company of competing producers. It may involve product or service producers. It is to be distinguished from vertical integration since it is common ownership of comparable business operations. The purpose of horizontal integration is control of the market, while the purpose of vertical integration is independence through control of service institutions serving inbound and outbound movements.

HORSE A power unit—one horse-power.

HORSE LIGHT A spot light placed on the hood or otherwise. It may be used to find open range livestock.

HORSEPOWER The process of raising 33,000 pounds one foot per minute is one horsepower. Horsepower may also be measured by raising 550 pounds one foot per second. This is equivalent to 746 watts.

HORSE VAN BODY A special vehicle used for transporting valuable horses or other livestock.

HOSE REEL A portable carriage on which to store a fire hose.

HOSTLER Truck terminal yard vehicle used to move trailers from one spot to another.

HOT LOAD A rush shipment.

HOUSEHOLD GOODS Furniture and house furnishings. When transported by transportation companies does not include such articles as silverware, valuable paintings, etc., except upon special contracts.

HOUSE TRACK A track alongside or entering a freight house, and used for cars receiving or delivering freight at the house.

HUB A central transfer point in a transportation company's route structure; hubs are served by and serve spoke routes to outlying points.

HULL POLICY An insurance policy covering the main hull and structure of a ship.

HUMP This is a term applicable to the railroad classification yard. As cars approach the junction point in the tracks for making up varying trains heading for different destinations, they must go over the hump for gravity purposes. At the hump the cars are uncoupled from the original train and roll by gravity to the desired classification track.

HUMP YARD A switching yard with an elevated track or hump over which cars are pushed by a switching locomotive to travel by gravity to classification tracks or other designated points. See Retarder Yard.

HUNDRED MILE COFFEE Strong coffee.

HUNDREDWEIGHT (CWT.) In ocean-freight parlance the hundredweight is equivalent to 112 pounds, or 1/20th of a ship's (long) ton of 2,240 pounds. In rail transportation, however, it is 100 pounds in the United States.

HUSBANDAGE The charge for attending the ship by an owner or agent for a commission is called husbandage.

HYPOTHECATE In the shipping industry, the process of borrowing from the bank on the value of a consignment of goods by pledging the shipping documents as security.

—I—

ICE ALLOWANCE Found in pulpwood rail moves and some coal, an allowance for the weihgt of ice/snow on the lading so that it is not counted as part of the product weight when computing freight charges.

ICING This was a practice more commonly used in years gone by in which ice was placed in bunkers of a refrigerator car either prior to shipment or while in transit for the purpose of preserving the commodities.

IDLE-HOUR SYSTEM A method of furnishing empty cars to coal mines whereby the allotment is reduced or increased depending on the state of idleness existing in comparison with other mines.

IDLER This term is applied to a flat car which is used for the movement of commodities of a bulky nature that extend beyond the limits of the car. The article or shipment does not rest on the car but overhangs it.

IMMUNITY Exemption from any duty, office or tax; freedom from natural or usual liability. Exempt from punishment for evidence rendered.

IMPORTANT MARINE RISKS The possibility of loss in ocean trade from these possible contingencies: (a) Loss of vessel through standing, sinking, fire or collision; (b) loss or damage caused by shifting cargo, by seawater from bad weather, by fire or flood on shore before loading or after discharging; (c) theft or pilferage on board or while loading, or awaiting loading; (d) breakage from any cause; (e) war risks afloat or ashore.

IMPORT CREDIT A foreign buyer establishes credit in the country where a purchase is to be made in a bank in the country of purchase. The bank issues a letter of credit to the foreign shipper.

IMPORT RATE A specific domestic inland rate for traffic that has been imported.

IMPORT TRUST RECEIPT An instrument executed by an importer, who wishes to dispose or use the goods during the interval of their arrival and maturity of the draft. It gives the bank direct control of the goods or their proceeds, and enables the importer to effect final release of the consignment from the steamship company and custom house.

IMPOST A tax on imported goods.

IMPUTED COSTS Similar to opportunity costs; often a charge levied in budgets against the fixed assets used by a division.

IN APPARENT GOOD ORDER A shipment not showing any loss or damage, though subsequent examination might find some.

INCENTIVE RATE A general term for any low rate on lots heavier than the normal truckload or carload weight bracket so as to induce heavier loadings by shippers.

INCIDENTAL DAMAGES Damages incurred other than to the physical loss or damage to goods involved; examples are overhead, lost cash opportunity, employee time, and filing costs that are not generally recouped in the claims process.

INCIDENTAL TO AIRCRAFT EXEMPTION A motor carrier term signifying that pick up and/or delivery moves prior or subsequent to air line haul is exempt from ICC operating regulation; by 1980 all air freight moved in this manner is exempt while some passenger transportation prior or subsequent to air moves is subject to ICC jurisdiction.

INCLINE An inland tract on a river bank at a protected landing place, with adjustable apron and cradle for connecting to the track on a car float for transfer of cars.

INCREASING COST The term increasing cost does not have exactly the same meaning as its usual economic definition. Whereas it usually is closely associated, if not synonymous with, variable cost, it has a slightly different meaning when used in logistics management. Those costs which increase with an increase in the volume of shipment (as contrasted to volume of production) are increasing logistics costs. It is important to observe that increasing costs increase per unit—meaning per hundredweight. Obviously, practically all logistics costs increase with an increase in the volume of shipment, but only the increasing costs increase per hundredweight with the volume of shipment. The overwhelming proportion of contrived logistics costs that increase with an increase in the volume of shipment (commonly referred to as the cellular flow) are inventory-in-storage and average warehouse costs. These costs increase directly and proportionately with an increase in the volume of shipment.

Demurrage is also an increasing cost but it does not increase in a linear pattern, since the demurrage rate increases at an increasing rate for all time after 48 hours of free time.

INCREMENTAL COST The extra costs incurred by the firm from additional units of output or service.

INDEMNITY An indemnity is a guarantee against loss. It represents a compensation for the loss for damage which has been sustained.

INDENT An indent is a comprehensive order transferred from a foreign buyer to a shipper, buying agent, commission house, etc. for the purpose of making a purchase. An open indent provides for the choice of the seller at the discretion of the house that handles the order. However, a closed indent would identify the firm with which the business must be transacted.

INDEPENDENT ACTION A rate publication action by a carrier in rate bureau tariffs that takes place without the vote or discussion of the entire rate bureau; until 1980 independent action typically only occurred when a carrier rate proposal was turned down by the bureau membership and the carrier still wished to publish a rate on its own behalf.

INDEPENDENT DEMAND An experience in sales or other demands in which one customer is independent of any other.

INDEPENDENT LINE A line not dependent or supported by or governed by other lines.

INDIFFERENCE VOLUME Wherever a reduction in price is quoted for a minimum volume of purchase, transportation, or otherwise, an indifference volume may be computed. The indifference volume is that volume at which it is indifferent so far as total costs are concerned whether the total charge was computed on the basis of the less than quantity volume at the less than minimum volume price or at the volume price times the minimum volume. The computed indifference volume is the initial volume in the indifference volume zone.

INDIRECT COMPETITION Rivalry between carriers, localities, commodities, etc. For example: A direct route between points in competition for a circuitous route.

INDORSEE One to whom a negotiable instrument is transferred by being indorsed or guaranteed by the signature of a third party.

INDORSEMENT A writing on the back of a negotiable instrument.

INDUSTRIAL Pertains to a productive industry. In transportation matters it signifies the difference between transportation companies and manufacturing industries.

INDUSTRIAL CARRIER When a short railroad is owned or operated by one or more companies for their exclusive use, and does not serve as a common carrier, it is known as an industrial carrier. The industrial carrier has been known to serve likewise as a common carrier however.

INDUSTRIAL TRACKS Rail tracks which service mines, mills, or specific industries, and are not classified as branch lines, are called industrial tracks. The industrial track belongs to the industry and no rent can be charged for its use by a carrier.

INFESTATION The spoilage of merchandise through the presence of rodents, birds or animal remains.

INFORMAL COMPLAINT A complaint made by letter or other writing to the I.C.C. protesting a violation of the Act.

INHERENT NATURE OF THE GOODS A freight claim related term indicating that the goods involved have a potential problem of deteriorating while enroute, particularly a problem with vegetables and fruits.

INITIAL CARRIER The carrier which receives the shipment and is first in a joint carrier operation is identified as the initial carrier.

INJUNCTION A formal prohibition of an act by a court.

INLAND BILL A bill of exchange or draft drawn upon a person in the same country.

INLAND CARRIER The carrier performing the act of carriage on the domestic, export and import traffic between ports and inland points.

INLAND WATERWAYS CORPORATION ACT This act was passed by the United States Congress on June 3, 1924. It provided for the creation of an inland waterway corporation. The purpose of the corporation was to operate government owned domestic waterway services. These services might involve canals, rivers, or coastal movements.

INSPECTION AND RATING OF A VESSEL When marine insurance is placed on a vessel, the extent of the risk must be assessed. The American Bureau of Shipping rates the vessel through inspection. *A-1 for twenty years* or *A-1 for sixteen years*, would be examples of a rating placed by the U.S. Steamship Bureau.

INSPECTION BUREAU An organization maintained by the carriers for the purpose of seeing that commodities presented for shipment are properly packed and meet the requirements and rules of the governing classification or schedule.

INSPECTION CERTIFICATE When the Department of Agriculture issues a document to exporters of meat products or livestock destined to various countries, it is called an inspection certificate. This is required by the customs regulations of the United States as well as by the foreign counselor's rules.

INSPECTION CERTIFICATE A certificate issued by an independent agent or firm attesting the quality and/or quantity of the merchandise being shipped. Such a certificate is usually required in a L/C for commodity shipments.

INSTALLMENT SHIPMENTS Successive shipments are permitted under letters of credit. Usually, they must take place within a given period of time. If not shipped within that period, the credit ceases to be available automatically unless otherwise authorized in the L/C.

INSTRUMENTALITIES Implements to carry out an activity. In transportation same includes boats, barges, cranes, elevators, etc.

INSULATED VAN BODY A van body designed to protect from temperature changes and thereby used for moving commodities under controlled temperature.

INSURANCE An insurance policy or certificate normally covers the shipments of merchandise from the time they leave the warehouse at the shipping point until they reach the destination point named in the policy or certificate. This type of coverage is called "warehouse to warehouse" and includes all modes of transportation necessary to deliver the goods to the point of destination. The insurance policy or certificate should be dated prior to, or on the same day as, the date shown on the shipping documents.

INSURANCE, ALL RISK This type of insurance offers the shipper the broadest coverage available, covering against all losses that may occur in transit. To establish a claim, it is not necessary for the assured to prove what caused the loss, but merely that goods were in proper condition and properly shipped and that the loss was not due to any inherent vice of the goods. Exclusions: Losses arising from war; civil disturbances; and spoilage.

INSURANCE BROKER One who negotiates insurance contracts between the insurer and the insured.

INSURANCE, FREE OF PATICULAR OF AVERAGE This type of insurance covers losses or damages arising only from marine perils: sinking, stranding, fire, or collision. It is the most limiting clause and is, thus, least expensive.

INSURANCE FREIGHT Insurance that covers a shipment for damage en route.

INSURANCE, GENERAL AVERAGE This clause covers damages or losses arising from maritime ventures for all parties shipping or owning. It covers partial losses resulting from voluntary sacrifice made on the part of ship or cargo to prevent the loss of lives, whole ship, or cargo. The voluntary sacrifice includes jettisoning, cutting away, or partial flooding of the holds. In one event, the master beached a sinking ship thinking it was sand but, in reality, it was mud. The loss incurred far exceeded the master's expectations and thus it was covered and shared by all parties.

INSURANCE POLICY A contract between the insurer and the insured, to cover loss of life, injury to person or damage to property.

INSURANCE, WITH AVERAGE CLAUSE This type of clause covers merchandise if the damage amounts to three percent or more of the insured value of the package or cargo. However, if the vessel burns, sinks, collides, or gets sunk, all losses, partial or otherwise, are fully covered. The word "average" in marine insurance is used to describe partial damage or partial loss.

INTACT SEALS Seals that have not been broken or tampered with. (Car Seals)

INTER (Latin) Between.

INTERCHANGE The process of passing freight from one carrier to another between lines is called interchange.

INTERCHANGE POINT When a joint movement involves more than one carrier, the location where transfer of freight between carriers takes place is known as the interchange point.

INTERCHANGE TRACK A track on which cars are delivered or received as between railways.

INTERCOASTAL As contrasted to coastal water operations, intercoastal refers to water transportation serviced between coasts, such as between the Atlantic and Pacific coasts.

INTERCORPORATE HAULING Private truck operation whereby fleet handles movements for other subsidiaries of a parent company.

INTEREST CLAUSE A clause in the face of a draft instructing a foreign bank to collect interest at a designated rate.

INTEREST ON UNAMORTIZED INVESTMENT The investment cost on the unpaid balance is the interest on unamortized investment. It is a contract debt that requires payment. It is computed on the basis of the contractual interest rate times the unpaid balance. It is not to be confused with the prorated payment off on the loan.

INTERLINE Between two or more transportation lines.

INTERLINE ACCOUNT The process of reporting a settlement of a shipment and apportioning the revenue by the destination carrier to the other participating carriers on the basis of a published division of rates is referred to as an interline account.

INTERLINE DIVISIONS The basis upon which the revenue derived from a through rate from origin-to-destination is divided between two or more carriers participating in the haul.

INTERLINE FORWARD Railroad term for traffic that is originated by one railroad, interchanged to another for ultimate delivery to the consignee.

INTERLINE FREIGHT Tonnage passing over the lines of two or more carriers. The interchange is termed an interline movement. Freight moving from point of origin to destination over the lines of two or more transportation lines.

INTERLINE RECEIVED Term for shipments that are received by a railroad from another carrier for delivery to the consignee.

INTERLINE WAYBILL A waybill covering the movement of freight over two or more transportation lines.

INTERMEDIATE CARRIER The carrier that serves to bridge between two other carriers in a three carrier movement would be the intermediate carrier.

INTERMEDIATE CLAUSE A provisional clause in a tariff for rates to points not listed therein but en route and intermediate to points that are listed.

INTERMEDIATE COMMERCE The commerce of a country which passes through it.

INTERMEDIATE POINT Any point that is located on the line of a carrier that is intermediate to the point of origin and destination would be an intermediate point.

INTERMEDIATE RATE One of the factors used in making up a through .combination rate.

INTERMODAL CONTAINERS Containers designed to be carried by more than one mode of transportation.

INTERMODAL SERVICE Through transportation movement involving more than one mode, e.g., rail-motor, motor-air, or rail-water.

INTER-PLANT SWITCHING Industrial switching which involves rail carrier switching services within a plant or industry.

INTERNAL REVENUE Government revenue derived from domestic sources.

INTERNATIONAL COMMERCE The exchange of objects between buyers and sellers in two different countries.

INTERSTATE COMMERCE ACT, NOW REVISED INTERSTATE COMMERCE ACT An act of Congress (1877) which regulates the rates, rules, and practices of rail transportation lines engaged in interstate traffic (Part I); regulates motor vehicles for hire (Part II—referred to as the Motor Carrier Act of 1935); regulates common and contract water carriers operating in domestic trade (Part III); and regulates freight-forwarding companies (Part IV—referred to as the Freight Forwarders Act). It was recodified in 1978 to the Revised Interstate Commerce Act.

INTERSTATE COMMERCE COMMISSION The agent of Congress designated to implement the Interstate Commerce Act. Consists of eleven members. The I.C.C. has considerable control over the economic actions of the common carriers under its jurisdiction.

INTERSTATE TRAFFIC Traffic which moves across state lines in the course of a transportation movement from origin to destination is usually referred to as interstate traffic. By contrast, intrastate traffic has origin and destination within the same state.

INTER-TERMINAL (SWITCHING) An interchange of cars, the movement of which is confined to the switching limits of the same station or switching district.

INTER-URBAN The uniting of or belonging to two cities.

INTERVENE To participate and take action in proceedings started by others. This takes the form of an intervening petition, and the one participating is an intervener.

IN THE ROUGH A term stating that an article is not in a state of complete manufacture. It is an unfinished product.

IN TRANSIT En route between point of origin and destination.

INTRANSIT PRIVILEGES Changes in degree of manufacture, treatment and other accessional services provided for in the tariffs on commodities between points of origin and destination. Involves cleaning, dipping, elevation, fabrication, creosoting and milling.

IN TRANSIT RATES Frequently these are referred to as transit rates. Ordinarily a local rate into the transit point is charged and the finished or semi-finished product which is forwarded to the ultimate destination is charged on the basis of the balance of the through rate applicable on the finished product from the point of origin to the point of destination. It is particularly significant that the rate charged on the raw materials from the point of origin to the destination of the finished product is based on the finished product rate computed from the original origin of the raw material to the ultimate destination. The rate which had been paid on the raw material moving to the transit point is deducted from the total charge on the finished product from raw material origin to ultimate destination. The balance remaining after payment between point of origin of raw material to the transit point is paid at the transit joint at the time of reshipment or when the processed product arrives at the final destination. The terms of the sale determine this. This method of transit settlement is generally known as the revenue method. If the commodity moved from the transit point to the ultimate destination is not recognizable as having originated from certain raw materials, the transit privilege is usually not allowed. An example of this would be a transit rate that is not allowed on alcohol made from grain. Some of the leading examples of the use of transit privileges include: barreling, stopoff for compression, stopoff for creosoting, stopoff for fabrication, stopoff for livestock feeding, and stopoff for sacking, grading, and cleaning of agricultural products.

INTRALINE TRANSFER Transfer of freight or passenger between two vehicles, runs or routes on the same carrier.

INTRAMODAL COMPETITION Competition faced by a carrier from carriers of the same mode; e.g., motor-motor.

INTRA-PLANT SWITCHING Switching performed within a plant of any industry.

INTRASTATE TRAFFIC Traffic originating and terminating within a given state and not moving out of the state at any point is intrastate traffic.

INTRINSIC VALUE The real genuine value of an article. The same regardless of place or person.

INVENTORIED COST PER UNIT This term is not to be confused with inventory-in-storage costs, which is the interest on the value of the goods stored for the time period they are in storage. Inventoried cost per unit represents the determination of the value for the products. Normally it includes the purchase price and the cost of inbound transportation. For products produced within the company, the standard manufacturing costs are used to establish the value of inventoried products. Since inventoried costs include transportation, the value for a given product at distribution centers will be greater than those at plants. In rare instances, inventoried costs are measured by the incremental value added to the product by moving it from a plant warehouse to a distribution center—but this is a rare interpretation of the term.

INVENTORY The merchandise a customer has on hand at a warehouse, or a production process has on hand at one end or other of the production line.

INVENTORY CARRYING COSTS There are great variations in the definitions of carrying costs. Generally speaking, carrying costs involve all costs associated with holding goods in storage. As a minimum it should include inventory-in-storage, warehousing, obsolescence, deterioration or spoilage, and labor costs. The computation of the warehousing costs would also include property taxes, warehouse administrative costs, warehouse utility costs, depreciation on warehouse, and operating equipment depreciation, etc.

INVENTORY-IN-PRODUCTION The capital costs of materials and parts in production (in assembly or manufacturing). Computed by applying the interest rate, times value, times the period of time (percentage of a year) in production.

INVENTORY-IN-STORAGE The capital costs of materials, parts, supplies and finished products held in inventory for storage purposes in the pre-production, post-production, or in-production channels. Computed by multiplying the interest rate, times the value, times the period of time (percentage of a year) the goods are held in storage.

INVENTORY-IN-TRANSIT The capital costs of materials, parts, supplies or finished goods en route aboard a transportation carrier (common, contract, or private). Computed by multiplying the interest rate, times the value, times the period of time (percentage of a year) the shipment is en route.

INVENTORY TAX A tax imposed by some state and local governments upon the value of inventory held on hand; usually consists of a determination of the value of the inventory held on hand and a tax paid which is a percentage of the total value.

INVENTORY TO SALES RATIO The total inventory on hand divided by one month sales dollars.

INVENTORY VALUATION The accounting field treatment of inventory value for purposes of determining the cost of goods sold in income statements; most are first-in-first-out, last-in-last-out, and weighted average.

INVESTIGATION AND SUSPENSION DOCKET (I.C.C.) A record containing a list of investigations pending in connection with tariffs or other publications that have been issued by the carriers.

INVESTMENT TAX CREDIT A tax credit that is obtained when acquiring new capital investments; a percentage of asset acquisition cost is credited against the firm's tax liability.

INVOICE The itemized listing of merchandise shipped or sent to the consignee with the quantity, charges, and values or prices attached is the invoice.

INVOICE VALUE The value of a shipment which is the same as the invoice billed to the customer of the shipper.

IRON An old model truck.

IRON LUNGER The standard 220 or 250 horsepower engine.

IRREGULAR ROUTE CARRIER When a common carrier serves points within a given area, but the routes and usually the schedules are not specifically defined, it is referred to as an irregular route carrier.

IRRITATING MATERIAL A liquid or solid substance which upon contact with fire or when exposed to air gives off dangerous or intensely irritating fumes, but not including any poisonous material, Class A.

ISSUING BANK A bank that opens a straight or a negotiable letter of credit. This bank assumes the obligation to pay the beneficiary or a bank if the documents presented are in accordance with the terms of the L/C.

ISSUING CARRIER The carrier by which a tariff is published or bill of lading or other documents are issued.

ISSUING DATE As applied to a tariff or other transportation schedule, the date it was issued, and shown on the title page.

ITEM POPULARITY Materials handling term indicating how many times each stockkeepoing unit is demanded in a period.

ITEM SIZE Materials handling term for cubic dimensions of each stockkeeping unit.

—J—

JACKET A cover placed over containers in the form of cans and bottles.

JACKING IT AROUND The process of backing a semi-trailer around a sharp corner.

JETSAM Goods thrown overboard which have sunk.

JETTISON The process of throwing cargo overboard when the ship is in danger is an act of jettison. The division of the responsibility among the shippers for an act of jettison which is done for the good of all shipments aboard is provided for in the law.

JETWAY A telescope-type structure that extends to connect an airline passenger terminal with airplanes; acts to protect passengers from weather as well as speed up loading and unloading.

JOBBER A middleman who buys and sells merchandise for others.

JOINT AGENCY TARIFF A tariff that is published on behalf of two or more rate bureaus on traffic moving between the respective geographic jurisdictions.

JOINT AGENT An official who acts as agent for two or more carriers.

JOINT BOARDS When a case involves three or a lesser number of states, a joint board may be established with representatives of each of the states to hear the case and make the decision. The joint boards have essentially the same powers of that of the regulatory authority—like the Interstate Commerce Commission. The joint board usually reviews motor carrier operating requests and other motor carrier issues. The joint board was created under the Interstate Commerce Act, Motor Carrier Act of 1935, now RICA section 10341.

JOINT COST A cost in one area or function that arises because another activity or function took place; the difficulty comes in that the cost of either can not be rationally allocated to each; example: cost of backhaul in relation to cost of fronthaul.

JOINT RATE A rate applicable from a point located on one transportation line to a point located on another transportation line. Such rates are made by agreement or arrangement between, and published in a single tariff under proper concurrence of all transportation lines over which the rate applies.

JOINT TARIFF A tariff containing joint rates.

JOINT TRAFFIC Freight that is transported by two or more carriers between origin and destination.

JOINT THROUGH RATES When a transportation movement requires two or more carriers, the ICC may require the carriers to agree on a joint through rate. A single rate is published to cover the interline movement. A distinction should be made between a joint rate and a through rate, however. A joint rate requires a specific written agreement between the carriers to be effective. A through rate is the result of an expressed or implied agreement. A through rate may be a joint rate or a combination of local or joint rates. It is a well established principle that a joint through rate is the only legal rate between the points where it is unconditionally established. It will take precedence over any combination of intermediate rates between the given points. However, the tariff may provide that the aggregate of the intermediate rate is applicable. Under these circumstances, if a combination of several intermediate rates is lower than a through rate, it is applicable.

JUMBO (BOOK) A car record kept on sheets in binders large enough for posting the daily movements of fifty cars for thirty-one days (one month).

JUMPED THE PIN The loss of the fifth wheel pin on the trailer that is used to couple the tractor to the trailer.

JUNCTION POINT The connecting point where lines of two or more railroads meet; or where lines of the same company meet, including the connection of a main line and a branch line.

JURISDICTION The extent or power of exercising judicial authority.

JURISPRUDENCE The system of laws of a country.

JUSTIFICATION The act of showing certain acts or deeds to be just or right.

—K—

KAFFIR TRUCK Cheap goods, such as glass-beads, suitable for the native markets in some foreign countries.

KDF CARTONS Knocked down (flat) carton—unassembled.

KEEL The chief and lowest support of the whole frame of vessel, extending from stem to stern.

KEELAGE The toll or charge that is placed on a vessel entering a port.

KEG A small barrel.

KENTLEDGE Ballast along the keelson in the form of metal pegs.

KETCH A two masted, fore and aft rigged vessel, strongly built.

K FACTOR An order point calculation wherein some of the values apply to a group of items, and thus are calculated once and expressed thereafter as a K value.

KICKBACK Rebate usually given to person who is in position to purchase or order transportation service for his/her firm.

KICK DOWN Shift down to lower gears.

KICK THE DONUTS Check the tires.

KIDNEY BUSTER Hard riding truck.

KILO-BYTES A cluster package of about a thousand bytes of core.

KILOGRAM The French measure of weight equal to 2.2046 lbs.

KITTING AREA An accumulation bin.

KNOCK DOWN (K.D.) When articles are taken apart for the purpose of reducing the cubic space of the shipment it is referred to as a knock down shipment. This is simply a process of disassembling.

KNOT This represents a nautical mile of 6,082.66 feet. A measurement of speed in sea travel amounting to a nautical mile per hour. It may be used to measure the speed of a vessel or the current.

KNOWN DAMAGE Damage discovered at the time of delivery, or known before delivery.

KNOWN LOSS Loss, or the absence of part of the shipment, discovered on delivery, or known before delivery.

KORT NOZZLE A funnel shaped structure built around the propellers of tow-boats to concentrate the waterflow to and from the propellers.

KUROSHIWO The term applied to the Gulf Stream of the Pacific Ocean. It moves northeast along the coast of China, and passes Alaska, Canada and the Pacific coast of the United States. It provides warm waters of beneficial effect.

—L—

LABOR Heavy working of a vessel at sea due to sea conditions.

LACHES Neglect to do a thing at the proper time.

LADING The contents of a vessel, car, truck, etc. is the freight lading.

LAKER Vessels that navigate on the lakes, as contrasted to those that move on the high seas, are called lakers.

LAKE TYPE STEAMER A steamer whose engines are located at the aft.

LAND BRIDGE The movement of containers with a ship movement preceding and following the land haul. The land bridge movement is executed to shorten an all water haul.

LANDED COST The total cost of producing, storing and transporting a product to the site of consumption or transfer to another part.

LANDED WEIGHT The weight at the point of lading.

LANDFALL The first sighting of land when coming from the open sea.

LAND GRANT Land granted or given by the government to a transportation line.

LAND GRANT DEDUCTION A deduction made from freight charges on government traffic in consideration of a land grant.

LAND-GRANT RATES Reductions from the published tariffs for government movements on account of promotional land grants made to railroads many decades ago were called land-grant rates. It was estimated that total transportation costs reductions resulting from land-grant rates up to June 30, 1943, amounted to approximately $530 million. This was several times larger than the value of the land-grants at the time they were made.

LANDING CERTIFICATE A document in which the foreign consignee takes an oath before an American consul or merchant, or *two respectable foreign merchants,* stating that merchandise described therein has actually been delivered to him.

LANDING GEAR The device that supports the semi-trailer when it is not attached to the tractor.

L & R Lake and rail.

LASH The process of binding tightly by rope or otherwise.

LASH Acronym for Lighter Aboard Ship, a system of loaded barges that can be carried on board ocean ships; avoids port handling of freight.

LASHING A rope or wire that is used to secure two barges together.

LASHING EYES Loops at the end of ropes which are used to secure.

LATENT DEFECTS Faults that are not readily apparent through normal diligence. In accordance with the Hague Rules, the owner of a ship is not responsible for latent defects of a vessel which cause loss and damage.

LATITUDE The angular distance measured from the equator to the North Pole or South Pole. The latitude is measured along the meridian that runs north-south. The latitude lines run parallel to the equator. Distance is measured in latitude from the equator in degrees.

LAWFUL RATE If a published rate, which is the legal rate, is unreasonable and must be replaced with a reasonable rate, it is unlawful. A lawful rate is reasonable, non-discriminatory, and it is not prejudicial or preferential in violation of the Interstate Commerce Act. Consequently, the legal rate may or may not be lawful and the lawful rate likewise may or may not be legal. However, any legal rate which is reasonable, non-discriminatory, non-prejudicial, non-preferential, etc. is both legal and lawful.

LAWFUL TRADE A restriction against contraband aboard in a time-charter party.

LAY DAY The allotted time for discharging a vessel (unloading), before demurrage charges begin.

LAYER One complete row of boxes or product on an pallet or unitized stack,

LAYOUT The design and planning of the storage areas and aisles of a warehouse.

LAYOVER Eight hours or more rest before continuing the trip, or any off-duty period away from home.

LAY ON THE AIR Apply the brakes.

LAZARETTO (Italian) A place set apart in quarantine for fumigating goods.

L-C Letter of credit.

L. & D. Loss and damage. This term is usually applied when a loss or damage is discovered when the package is delivered. The term located loss or damage is used when the damage to goods, property, or persons occurs at a specific and identifiable time en route.

LEADMAN Another name for a group leader. A working crew member who is responsible for the crew.

LEAD TIME The period of time elapsing between when an order is placed and the order is received in storage. In a fixed order interval system, this is often called replenishment time. Processing lead time is the time required to process the order. Delivery lead time is the time required for an order to be delivered.

LEAD TRACK A track that connects either end of a yard with a main track.

LEAKAGE An allowance made for waste due to leaking of casks and barrels.

LEAKER A damaged container with contents coming out.

LEARNING CURVE A common phenomenon that is found in most production activities; in basic form: the number of man-hours required to perform a task decreases with each successive unit of production.

LEASE, DIRECT Can be almost any type of lease but the lessor holds title to the asset.

LEASE, FINANCE (CAPITAL) Lessee makes payments over the useful life of the asset and meets the requirements of Financial Accounting Standards Board Bulletin #13; similar to full payment lease.

LEASE, LEVERAGED A group of investors provide a portion of the purchase price for the assets and the balance is borrowed from banks and/or institutional investors; the asset is then leased to a using party.

LEASE, MASTER An agreement for the leasing of certain equipment with options for the lessee to lease additional equipment as necessary at a predetermined rate without a new contract.

LEASE, NET Similar to a finance (capital) lease except that all other payments such as taxes, maintenance, insurance, and others are paid by the lessee.

LEASE, NON-FULL PAYMENT A contract in which the lessor depends upon an unguaranteed portion of the residual value of the asset to recover costs plus a return on his investment.

LEASE, OPERATING Lessor provides maintenance or some other service in addition to the use of the asset at a price that fills the requirements of the Financial Accounting Standards Board Bulletin #13; similar to non-full payment and a true lease.

LEASE/PURCHASE AGREEMENT Similar to a conditional sale, but the lessee has the option to purchase the asset at a bargain price at the end of the term.

LEAST SQUARES METHOD A statistical method of smoothing a curve to minimize the sum of squares deviations of the given points.

LEG A term applying to each origin-destination hop on an airplane trip; A New York-Chicago-Seattle run consists of two legs.

LEGAL RATES The legal rate is the properly published rate filed with the Interstate Commerce Commission in compliance with the *Publicity Section* of the Act. A carrier is required to charge in accordance with the published rate even if the published rate is in error and obviously incorrect. The carrier cannot change the published freight rate on its own volition. This is to be contrasted with the lawful rate, which is a reasonable rate in keeping with the Interstate Commerce Act.

LEGAL WEIGHT The weight of the goods and interior packing but not the container. (used in foreign trade)

LENGTH BLOCK A pallet pattern in which package lengths are loaded parallel to the pallet length.

LESS THAN CARLOAD RATE (LCL) If a class rate shipment does not qualify for a carload rate it will be required to pay the higher less than carload rate. It is applicable to rail shipments. As contrasted to years gone by, there are very few less than carload shipments initiated by rail carriers. Most small quantity shipments move by motor carrier or are consolidated by freight forwarders.

LESS-THAN-CONTAINERLOAD A shipment by container consisting of less than the weight or cubic capacity of the container.

LESS THAN TRUCKLOAD (LTL) A quantity of freight weighing less than the amount required for the application of a truckload rate.

LESS THAN TRUCKLOAD RATE Rate that is applied to a less than truckload shipment.

LETTER OF CREDIT (L/C) The letter of credit may be revocable of irrevocable. If it is revocable, the bank reserves the right to withdraw from the operations. If it is irrevocable, the bank cannot withdraw its credit prior to the specified expiration date. Under the arrangements of the letter of credit, the bank guarantees that if the shipment is made and all the terms of the letter of credit filled or payment will be made soon. The importer normally makes the necessary arrangements with his bank to establish credit for a particular sum of money which would cover the arrangements of the letter of credit. The solvency of the buyer is of no concern under these circumstances to the seller since the bank stands back of the contract. The exporter normally has his own bank, called correspondent or confirming bank, which confirms the letter of credit arrangements. The purpose of the letter of credit is to provide a means for the bank to substitute its credit for that of the individual firm in order to make possible a foreign trade shipment. The buyer and exporter agree on the amount of the letter of credit. The buyer then applies to his bank for the letter of credit. The application lists the value of the merchandise to be shipped and describes the shipment in full detail. The exporter is named as the beneficiary of the credit and a time period is designated for the credit to be enforced.

LETTER OF CREDIT, BACK-TO-BACK A secondary letter of credit issued to a beneficiary on the strength of a primary credit. In this instance, the beneficiary of the primary credit (the middleman) becomes the applicant of the secondary, but smaller credit. The issuing bank of the secondary credit does not have to rely on the creditworthiness of the applicant (the middleman) since it relies on the credit of the bank, who issued the primary credit. Secondary credits are usually issued for lesser amounts allowing the middleman a profit margin for handling the business transaction. This type of credit is usually issued for parties who have fully utilized credit lines, are not well established, or are unable to obtain a credit line from their banks. The issuance of secondary credits is always contingent upon the terms and conditions stipulated in the primary credit. Caution must be exercised prior to issuing back-to-back credits by very carefully determining their workability.

LETTER OF CREDIT, CLEAN A letter of credit which requires the beneficiary to present only a draft or a receipt for specified funds before he receives payment.

LETTER OF CREDIT, CONFIRMED A letter of credit issued by one bank to which another bank added its irrevocable confirmation to pay, thereby obligating itself in the same manner as the opening bank. Example: "We hereby undertake to pay drafts drawn in accordance with the terms and conditions of the letter of credit."

LETTER OF CREDIT, CUMULATIVE A revolving letter of credit which permits any amount not utilized during any of the specified periods to be carried over and added to the amounts available in subsequent periods (See "Revolving").

LETTER OF CREDIT, DEFERRED PAYMENT A letter of credit issued for the purchase and financing of merchandise, similar to acceptance type letter of credit, except that it requires presentation of sight drafts which are payable on installment basis usually for periods of one year or more.

LETTER OF CREDIT, IRREVOCABLE An instrument, once established, which cannot be modified or cancelled without the agreement of all parties concerned.

LETTER OF CREDIT, NON-CUMULATIVE A revolving letter of credit which prohibits the amount not used during the specific period to be available in the subsequent periods (See "Revolving").

LETTER OF CREDIT, RESTRICTED A condition within the L/C which restricts its negotiation to a named bank.

LETTER OF CREDIT, REVOCABLE An instrument which can be modified or cancelled at any moment without notice to and agreement of the beneficiary, but customarily includes a clause in the credit to the effect that any draft negotiated by a bank prior to the receipt of a notice of revocation or amendment will be honored by the issuing bank. Its negotiability is always restriced to the advising bank.

LETTER OF CREDIT, REVOLVING An irrevocable letter of credit issued for a specific amount which renews itself for the same amount over a given period. Usually the unused portion of each period is non-cumulative and cannot be carried over to the next period. The contingent liability amount for such a credit is the amount of the credit multiplied by the number of periods the credit is to revolve. The amount in a revolving L/C is either cumulative or non-cumulative.

LETTER OF CREDIT, STRAIGHT A letter of credit which contains a limited engagement clause addressed to the beneficiary stating that the issuing bank promises to pay upon presentation of the required documents at its counters or the counters of the named bank. In this instance, the issuing or the named bank verifies all documents and thus functions as the negotiating bank. The main difference between a negotiable and a straight credit is that a straight credit is payable only at the counters of the issuing or the named bank. A negotiable credit can be negotiated by any bank. This authority is given by the engagement clause which permits the credit to be negotiated by drawers, endorsers, or bona-fide holders.

LETTER OF CREDIT, TRANSFERABLE A letter of credit that allows the beneficiary to transfer in whole or in part any amount of the credit to one or more third parties (second beneficiaries) provided that the aggregate of such transfers does not exceed the amount of the credit. Under this type of L/C partial shipments must be allowed when affecting partial transfers.

LETTER OF CREDIT, UNCONFIRMED A letter of credit forwarded to the beneficiary by the advising bank "without engagement" on the part of the advising bank. In international transactions, the beneficiary must depend on the foreign bank for his payment. Thus, this type of L/C offers less protection to the seller than the confirmed type.

LETTER OF HYPOTHECATION When a shipper authorizes a lien on certain goods in return for money advanced on them, he submits a letter of hypothecation.

LETTER OF INDEMNITY When the consignor submits a guarantee to a consignee against any loss or damage arising out of a faulty or defective shipment of merchandise, he submits a letter of indemnity. This letter makes it unnecessary to add any statement to the bill of lading concerning the shortage or fault as noted on the ship's receipt.

LIABILITY, JOINT AND SEVERAL An obligation undertaken by two or more carriers to carry out a contract or a claim or to assume an obligation.

LIABILITY, LIMITATIONS OF DAMAGES Damages may be limited by a term in the warehouse receipt or storage agreement limiting the amount of liability in case of loss or damage, and setting forth a specific liability per article or item, or value per unit of weight beyond which warehouseman shall not be liable; provided, however, that such liability may on written request of the bailor at the time of signing such storage agreement or within a reasonable time after receipt of the warehouse receipt be increased on part or all of the goods thereunder, in which event increased rates may be charged based on such increased valuation, limitation of liability contained in the warehouseman's tariff, if any. No such limitation is effective with respect to the warehouseman's liability for conversion to his own use.

LIABILITY, WAREHOUSEMAN'S LEGAL A warehouseman is liable for damages for loss or injury to the goods caused by his failure to exercise such care in regard to them as a reasonably careful man would exercise under like circumstances, but unless otherwise agreed he is not liable for damages which would not have been avoided by the exercise of such care.

LIEN When a claim is made on goods to the satisfaction of a debt of duty, it carries the legal name of a lien.

LIE SHEET The driver's log book.

LIFE CYCLE COSTING An analysis of the total acquisition, operating, maintenance and opportunity costs of a capital asset over its entire life; tool reduces chances of selecting an inexpensive to purchase asset that in the long run is more costly than another that has a more expensive initial cost but is economical to operate.

LIFELINE Lines that are stretched fore and aft along the decks so that the crew won't be washed overboard.

LIFT TAIL GATE A tail gate that is power operated and capable of lifting freight from street level.

LIFO Last in, first out. A method of inventory control.

LIGHT AIRCRAFT A fixed wing aircraft having a maximum gross weight less than 12,500 pounds.

LIGHTER This is an open or covered barge normally towed by a tugboat and used primarily in the harbor areas. This flat-boat is used for the transportation of freight between cars, vessels, and piers, and usually is towed by the tugboat.

LIGHTERAGE The duty or charge assessed for transferring, unloading, loading, etc. cargo by means of barges or lighters is called lighterage.

LIGHTERING The hauling of freight on lighters or barges.

LIGHTERAGE LIMITS The area within which, under certain rules, regulations, and charges, freight is regularly handled by means of lighters and barges.

LIGHT WEIGHT This refers to the weight of an empty car.

LIMIT An inventory management interpolation technique based on lot size. It looks at the lot sizes for groups of products to determine the effects of lot sizes on total inventory and set up costs.

LIMITED QUANTITY Means the maximum amount of a hazardous material; as specified in the DOT regulations, for which there are specific exceptions from the requirements of the regulations.

LINEAR PROGRAMMING This is a method of mathematically allocating scarce sources between options to achieve a given objective when both the environmental constraints and the objective which limit the degree of achievement of the objective can be stated in terms of linear equations and equalities. Linear implies unchanging and definable relationships between the variables of the problem. The term programming only brings out the concept of an orderly process by which this type of problem can be solved. It is generally concurred that linear programming may be solved in any of the following ways: (1) through the graphical method; (2) through the algebraic method; and (3) through the simplex method. The transportation linear programming problem employs only one form of the simplex method.

LINE DECK Deck spaces of a barge between the bow and the forward cargo hold of the barge, and between the cargo hold coaming and the stern.

LINE-FUNCTIONAL AREAS These areas of the organizational table of an industrial firm which are involved in the actual creation of the utilities — the direct functions performed on the commodity as it moves through the vertical stream—are the line functional areas. Production, marketing, and logistics are the line functional areas of the industrial firm. Obviously, the line-functional areas of a service firm would be somewhat different. At one time it was thought that all economic activities performed in our society could be identified within the scope of the four utilities involving the creation of (1) time utility, (2) possession utility, (3) form utility, and (4) place utility. A more perceptive analysis of this subject matter reveals that most of the staff functional areas of the firm could hardly be identified with the creation of any of these four utilities. The provision of such staff services as credit, personnel hiring and terminating, etc. represent examples of staff areas of the industrial firm which do not create time, form, place, or possession utility. The line functions of the firm are directly involved in establishing the options, costing the options, and managing the execution of decisions throughout the vertical stream.

LINE HAUL The movement of freight over the tracks of a transportation line from one town or city to another town or city (not a switching service).

LINE HAUL COSTS Those fixed and variable costs of performing the intercity segment of the total transportation operation. It may be contrasted to the terminal costs, or it is sometimes contrasted to the local pickup and delivery costs.

LINE HAUL SWITCHING The moving of cars within yard or switching limits of a station, preceding or following a line haul.

LINES A transportation agency or carrier known as a rail line, water line, etc. Where a number of carriers are united by ownership, they are termed lines. Some forms of lines are, belt, branch, connecting, family, independent, industrial, lateral, main, number, short, tap and trunk.

LINE STEAMER A vessel operating between certain points on time schedule.

LINK In the post-production channel, there may be several nodes, or stopoff storage and handling points. This would require several movements, rather than a single movement, to move through the channel from the manufacturing plant to the ultimate retailer. The transportation movement and the subsequent storage point represents a link. In the computation of the total logistics costs within a link, in order to eliminate duplication of costing, only the subsequent, or following, storage operation is added to the transport movement to involve the link. However, in the initial movement from the plant to the first node, it is necessary to compute both plant storage and initial mode storage with the transport cost to determine the total logistics costs in the first link. Beyond the first link, only the transport operation and the following node storage cost represent the link.

LIQUIDATE To settle the accounts and distribute the assets of a business in bringing it to an end.

LIST OF STORES A document submitted to the customs authorities, containing a list of provisions and similar articles remaining on board a vessel at the end of a voyage.

LITIGATION A judicial contest. The act or process of carrying on a lawsuit.

LIVE AXLE A powered axle.

LIVE CHARTER RATE Actual aircraft miles or hours of the charter passengers or cargo, which is proportional to that of the total charter rate charged by the carrier.

LIVESTOCK CONTRACT A document taking the place of the bill of lading on shipments of livestock, due to unusual conditions surrounding their movement.

LIVESTOCK WAYBILL A waybill used for shipments of livestock.

LLOYD'S The internationally known association of marine underwriters.

LLOYD'S REGISTER A yearly register issued by Lloyd's, containing the tonnage, age, build, character and condition of ships.

LOAD The amount of scheduled work confronting the manufacturing facility, usually expressed in terms of hours of work.

LOAD CHART A chart showing the weight of shipments loaded in a trailer and the position in the trailer of larger items.

LOAD FACTOR The percentage of seats occupied by revenue passengers in an airplane in relation to the total seats available for loading.

LOADING AND UNLOADING In domestic shipping a service usually performed by the shipper and consignee in carload lots and by the carrier in less-than-carload quantities. In marine shipping, a service performed by stevedores and called stevedoring (on vessel).

LOADING GATE A passage in an airport finger where passengers are enplaned or deplaned.

LOADING PLATFORM A flat surface to facilitate loading, usually erected alongside a warehouse at the approximate level of a car or truck floor, sometimes of the portable type.

LOADING SEALS Seals applied to the doors of cars when cars are loaded, i.e. when the freight is checked from the freight house platform to the cars. They reveal break in.

LOADING SYSTEM Some of the most common loading systems are: (1) Unit loading (strap loading); (2) Unitization (topping and strapping many packages); (3) Bonded Blocking (loading like bricks); (4) Cube Loading (on pallets or unitized for grab trucks); (5) Glued Loading (applying glue in strips on each side of the box to tie as many as 20 cartons together, usually on a pallet); (6) Bulk Packing (loose and in bundles to permit one large fiberboard box as a substitute for smaller boxes).

LOAD LEVELING A production scheduling term for the practice of assigning each job to manpower and machinery so as to smooth out flow to fully occupy each resource with a minimum of backlog and idle time.

LOAD LIMIT The maximum allowable weight for a vehicle on a road or bridge.

LOCAL A train which serves the principal function of stopping to deliver or pickup freight at each station between division points is called a local.

LOCAL CARTAGE The service of display or delivery from a municipal terminal to particular commercial sites is called local cartage. It may be performed by a common or a contract carrier. It involves both pickup and delivery services in conjunction with line-haul operations. The rates charged by local cartage operators are regulated by the state regulatory commission if it is a common carrier.

LOCAL RATES The local rate is applicable on a single carrier line. It's a movement between two points on a single carrier. It's to be contrasted with a joint movement which involves a movement between two points involving more than one carrier. Any additional switching service or pickup and delivery service performed by another carrier would have no effect on the structure of the rate.

LOCAL SERVICE CARRIERS Domestic route air carriers operating between smaller traffic centers and principal centers or regional centers.

LOCAL STATION A station located only on one transportation line.

LOCAL TARIFF A tariff which lists the rates applicable between points on the same transportation line.

LOCAL TRAFFIC All traffic that terminates or originates on the same railway line is referred to as local traffic. It does not involve any intermediate movement by a connecting railway. Sometimes it is limited to a given classification territory.

LOCAL WAYBILL A waybill covering the movement of freight over a single transportation line.

LOCATION The exact spot in a warehouse where a particular product can be found.

LOCATION SYSTEM Provides an efficient way to locate stock and increase handling and storage efficiency.

LOCATOR FILE A record system that records where the product is stored. It is necessary where stock may be stored in varying, unpredictable locations.

LOCK The water passage process which permits a vessel to move from one level of water to another between enclosed gates which lower and raise the water is referred to as a lock. This is necessary for all canals connecting water bodies of different levels.

LOCKING PADS The mechanical device used to lock the container to the chassis of the ship hold or railcar.

LOCO A term signifying that a quotation covers only the cost of goods as they stand, without packing cartage, or other charges which may accrue.

LOGAIR Logistic air lift, which is an Air Force contract freight air lift service similar to that of the Navy's QUICKTRANS.

LOG BODY A trailer or truck built to transport logs or other loads which may be boomed or chained in place.

LOG BOOK This water transportation term refers to the official register kept by the master of a ship which spells out the daily record of events while at sea such as deaths, weather, births, accidents, or any other instance of significance.

LOGISTICS Logistics is the management of all inbound and outbound materials, parts, supplies, and finished goods. Logistics consists of the integrated management of purchasing, transportation, and storage on a functional basis. On a channel basis, logistics consists of the management of the pre-production, in-production, and post-production channels. The term logistics should be distinguished from physical distribution in that the latter normally applies to only the post-production channel.

LOGISTIC TRAILER A truck trailer capable of carrying double deck freight, thus creating a bigger payload.

LONG-AND-SHORT HAUL CLAUSES Section 10726 of the Revised Interstate Commerce Act prevents carriers from charging a higher rate for a short haul than the rate on the longer haul, when the short haul is a part of the long haul. Special exceptions by the I.C.C. are sometimes attained.

LONG DATED BILL A bill of exchange with a long period to run before maturity.

LONGER A row of barrels stowed fore-and-aft.

LONG HAUL Distances of 1000 miles or more. (Air freight.)

LONG PRICE Price after duties are paid.

LONG RANGE AIRCRAFT Aircraft that will fly 1000 miles or more non-stop without refueling.

LONGSHOREMEN The harbor employees who load and unload vessels.

LONG TON A long or gross ton consisting of 2,240 pounds.

LOOP STATION A through station in which the station track layout forms a loop or part of a circle, enabling trains to move in one direction only.

LOOSE Not packed.

LORRY In years gone by, the term lorry was applied to a low four-wheeled wagon without sides, of considerable length.

LOSS AND DAMAGE (L&D) CLAIMS—GENERAL The terms of the Uniform Straight Domestic Bill of Lading reads that the carrier in possession of property shall be liable at common law for any loss or damage thereto. This makes the carrier practically an insurer against all losses except for Acts of God. A time limit of nine months for notification, and two years and one day for filing suit, is specified. The document entitled Standard Form for Presentation of Loss and Damage Claims is filled out.

LOSS AND DAMAGE CLAIMS PAPERS The papers normally included in submitting a claim are: (1) standard form of small L&D for presentation; (2) proof of value (certified copy of invoice); (3) statement of claim (itemized listing); (4) transportation companies inspection report; (5) paid freight bill or express receipt; (6) original bill of lading; and (7) copies of correspondence.

LOSS CLAIM (FREIGHT) Expressive of injury to shipment of goods and generally referring to non-delivery.

LOSS, TOTAL When there are no salvageable parts of the shipment remaining, and the destruction is complete, the term total loss is applied.

LOST SALE A sale that could have been made but did not because of a stockout.

LOT The units of goods for which a separate accounting is to be kept by the warehouseman.

LOT NUMBER Identifying number or numbers used to keep a separate accounting for specific merchandise.

LOT SHIPMENT If a shipment consists of only one piece, it is called a *single-lot shipment.* If the shipment consists of more than one piece, it is given the term *lot shipment.*

LOT SIZE The amount of a product ordered. It is equal to ELQ. It may be less than a purchase quantity if the purchase quantity is to be transported in several shipments. It does not include safety stock.

LOW BOY A trailer built low to facilitate hauling equipment and other heavy machinery

LUMPER Term applied to independent contractor who assists owner-operator in loading or unloading of freight usually at food distribution centers; often coercive form of intimidation which adds to total cost of transportation; need for this service often arises because of food facility refusing to perform truck loading or unloading and requesting a trucker to do so.

LUMBER BODY A trailer body or platform truck with traverse rollers that was built to transport lumber.

LUMP FREIGHT Payment in one sum to cover the hire of a vessel for a complete voyage or purpose.

—M—

MAIN LINE That part of a transportation system (railway), exclusive of switch tracks, branches, yards and terminals.

MAIN TRACK All track of a rail carrier kept clear for the passage of trains is termed the main track for a line-haul railway. The term first main track is used.

MANDAMUS The action of a court requiring a specific action to be taken is commonly referred to as a writ of mandamus.

MANDATORY A proceeding or action containing a command or order.

MANIAC Shop mechanic.

MANIFEST The document which lists the particulars of a shipment aboard a vessel or car is termed a manifest.

MANUFACTURER'S AGENT An individual or firm who acts in the capacity of agent and is usually located at a port, in international movements.

MANUFACTURES Articles which have been made or fabricated from raw material (not crude or raw), into a form suitable for use.

MARGINAL COSTS The increase in total costs that result from the movement or production of one more unit.

MARINE INSURANCE Insurance against loss or damage to property while in transit by water.

MARINE INSURANCE CERTIFICATE A document certifying that a shipment is covered by insurance under an open cargo policy, issued by a merchant and duly countersigned for evidence. It is a negotiable document.

MARINE INSURANCE POLICY The contract whereby the assurer (insurance company) agrees to pay the assured (one insured), for loss or damage incurred to ship or cargo to the extent of risk and to the amount of value expressly stipulated therein.

MARITIME Business pertaining to commerce or navigation transacted upon the sea or in seaports in such matters as the court of admiralty have jurisdiction over, concurrently with the courts of common law.

MARITIME ADMINISTRATION Federal agency responsible for subsidy administration of the U.S. flag steamship industry that receives construction and operation differential subsidies; agency also studies and proposes efficient port design and practices.

MARITIME LAW Legislation relating to ships, seamen and harbors.

MARITIME PERIL Under the Marine Insurance Act of 1906, "Maritime perils mean the perils consequent on, or incidental to, the navigation of the sea; that is to say, perils of the sea, fire, war, pirates, robbers, thieves captures, seizures, restraints and detainments of princes and peiole, jettisons, barratry, and any other perils, either of the like kind or which may be designated by policy." Only fortuitous accidents of the sea, not including actions of wind and waves, are included.

MARITIME POSITIONS The location of sea related circumstances on the basis of longitude and latitude.

MARK A letter, figure or device by which goods are distinguished.

MARKED CAPACITY The stenciled or marked weight on a car denoting its carrying capacity.

MARKER Rear train red light.

MARKET A public place where provisions or other wares are sold.

MARKET COMPETITION This is a term generally used in the making of rates. It is the competition of one market against another.

MARKET DOMINANCE A railroad regulation concept that must be proved in order to challenge the lawfulness of a railroad rate as being too high; interpreted variously by the ICC since 1976, market dominance applies to situations in which a railroad or group of railroads experience a lack of competition that would otherwise place a ceiling on rates.

MARKET VALUE As used in the adjustment of freight claims it denotes the value of a shipment at destination after freight charges (if uncollected) are deducted.

MARKING (FREIGHT) Addressing packages for shipment and applying marks.

MARKING MACHINE A machine that imprints or embosses a mark on a label, ticket, tape, package or tag; power driven or package-operated.

MARRIAGE RULE A carrier has an option of stopping a car for completion of loading, or placing a separate car at a stopoff point to receive the transfer of a shipment. The marriage rule involves the process of placing a separate car at a stopoff point.

MART A commercial center; same as *market*.

MARU A name attached to all Japanese vessels which implies perfection or completeness. The original meaning was derived from sphere or circle.

MASTER CARTON A single large carton that is used as a uniform shipping carton for many smaller packages of different products.

MASTER FILE A file of major data on some aspect of business—like accounts receivable.

MASTER OF A SHIP The commander or captain, who has chief charge of the government and navigation of a vessel, as well as the general command of crew and control of cargo.

MASTER PACK A larger box made of fiberboard that is used to pack a number of smaller boxes or containers. A protection system to aid in handling and self packaging.

MASTER SCALE Test cars are weighed and verified as to weight on a master scale.

MATERIALS AND SUPPLIES Goods on hand required for repairs or replacements and for use in the general business of operations of carriers.

MATERIALS REQUIREMENTS PLANNING An inventory and purchasing planning system that integrates product components, lead times and ultimate deadline to plan acquisition timings; called MRP.

MATE'S RECEIPT A cargo receipt signed by the chief officer.

MATRIX Arrangement of numbers in rectangular array for mathematical operations. It provides for solving rows of equations with certain column variables. Actually, any table of data is a matrix.

MATURITY The time fixed for payment of a note, bill or draft.

MATURITY DATE The date on which negotiable instruments become due for payment. Acceptances maturing on a non-business day are payable either before or after such date.

MAX. Maximum.

MAXIMUM The highest, or greatest; (sum, quantity, price, etc.)

MAXIMUM AND MINIMUM RATES A maximum rate may be set by a regulatory authority to represent the highest rate a carrier may charge. The minimum rate represents the lowest rate that may be charged on any movement between given points for a given commodity. The maximum rate is to protect the public from excessive rates. The minimum rate is intended to restrain individual carriers from excessive competition. When no maximum rate is in effect, the ICC has held that the class rates are to be considered the maximum rates which a commodity can bear.

MEASUREMENT The measurement of the tonnage according to well defined rules, in maritime transportation.

MEASUREMENT GOODS (CARGO) That class of merchandise on which the freight assessment is based on measurement.

MEASUREMENT TON Forty cubic feet or 2,240 pounds on the Atlantic, and forty-two cubic feet or 2,000 lbs. on the Pacific coast.

MEASURE OF DAMAGES Rule or rules exercising the control in adjusting or apportioning the extent of damages to be compensated in actions at law for injury.

MEASURES MORE THAN IT WEIGHS When the weight of a shipment is less than 56 pounds per cubic foot, the term *measures more than it weighs* is applied. It is not common for commodities to conform to these specifications. When this does occur, the assessment is made on the basis of the measurement rather than the weight.

MEMBER LINE A line connected with an association.

MEMORANDUM BILL OF LADING The third copy of the bill of lading is called the memorandum bill of lading.

MEMO WAYBILL An internal railroad document usually used to route empty cars to a particular destination.

MERCANTILE AGENCY A concern which procures and furnishes information on the financial standing and credit of business firms.

MERCANTILE LAW Law pertaining to trade and commerce.

MERCANTILE PAPER Notes or bills issued by merchants for goods consigned or bought.

MERCANTILE REGISTRY An institution existing in most foreign countries for the purpose of insuring publicity of the essential facts as to the ownership or organization of business houses.

MERCATOR CHART A charting methodology originated by Gerardus Mercator, 1512-1594. The earth charting was on the basis of the earth being a cylinder, being parallel and tangent to the equator. Distance per unit would increase as one moved toward the poles. Thus, an island at the poles would be larger than if near the equator.

MERCHANDISE That which is bought or sold in trade other than real estate, bullion and negotiable paper.

MERCHANDISE BROKER He who negotiates the sale of merchandise for another without having possession of the goods.

MERCHANDISE CAR A rail car containing several less-than-carload shipments. Thus, containing several shipments from different consignors.

MERCHANDISE WAREHOUSE A public warehouse for the storage and distribution of products, in great variety, that do not require refrigeration for their preservation. Some public merchandise warehouses provide air conditioned and humidity controlled facilities and may provide both refrigerated and merchandise warehousing services.

MERCHANT One who buys and sells goods.

MERCHANTABLE In salable condition; fit for market.

MERCHANTMAN A commercial vessel.

MERCHANT MARINE The commercial steamship fleet of a country.

MERCHANT MARINE ACT An Act of Congress (1920), intended for the promotion, operation and maintenance of an American Merchant Marine and providing for a final adjustment of matters developing in connection with the construction and employment of ships built during World War I.

MERCHANT MIDDLEMEN The merchant middlemen consist of the general classes: (1) service wholesalers; and (2) limited function wholesalers. The service wholesalers may be called regular wholesalers, jobbers, service wholesalers, and full function wholesalers. The term semi-jobber is applied to a wholesaler who serves the wholesale merchant and the retail merchant. Most service wholesalers service businesses within 100 miles of their establishment. Some operate regionally or nationally. Usually they sell to small retailers. They take title, assume ownership risk, and are independent. Among the services rendered are carrying stock, extending credit, making deliveries, and maintaining the sales force. Most wholesalers have a limited line of stock. That is, a grocery service wholesaler would service the grocery line for the retailers he services. The service wholesaler may be (1) a general merchandise service wholesaler, or (2) a specialty wholesaler.

The limited function wholesalers do not provide the extensive services normally rendered by the service wholesalers. They are classified as follows: (1) drop shippers; (2) mail order wholesalers; (3) cash-and-carry wholesalers; (4) truck distributors; and (5) converters.

METACENTER Relates to ships. A point on a vertical line that marks the intersection between the center of gravity of the vessel when it is upright and the vertical line passing through the center of gravity of the displaced water of the vessel when it is listed or heeled.

METALLIC CURRENCY Gold, silver and copper coins, forming the circulating medium of a country.

METER (METRE) A meter is equivalent to 39.368 United States inches.

METRIC SYSTEM The system which uses the meter as the unit of measurement of length is called the metric system. The liter and the gram are cubic and weight measurements, respectively, of this system. The other units of the metric system are decimal subdivisions of the liter and gram. Extensions of the metric system use milli-gram as 1/1000th of a gram, the centi-gram as 1/100th of a gram, and the deci-gram as 1/10th of a gram. The deca-gram is 10 grams, the hecto-gram is 100 grams, and the kilo-gram is 1000 grams.

METRIC TON A ton of 2204.6 pounds.

MICRO-BRIDGE Intermodal transportation from internal cities to seaports for through movement transfer of container freight on overseas ships.

MIDSHIPS The center of the fore-and-aft line of the vessel. The middle of the fore and aft length. Also called amidships.

MILE 5,280 feet.

MILEAGE Length or distance in miles; the number of miles of a single railroad or a combination of railroads.

MILEAGE ALLOWANCE An allowance made by carriers to owners of private freight cars, and based on distance.

MILEAGE, CONSTRUCTIVE An arbitrary mileage allowed a carrier in dividing joint rates based on a mileage prorate and not on the actual mileage.

MILEAGE GUIDE A form of tariff that either states the distance between points, or prescribes how to compute the distance.

MILEAGE RATE The division of the through charge to participating carriers on the basis of mileage.

MILEAGE TARIFF When the rates of a tariff are based on mileage rather than involving a point to point rate, the tariff is normally referred to as a mileage tariff. Its value lies in the fact that it is possible to construct the total rate between any combination of points on the basis of the mileage tariff.

MILK CONTAINER CAR A specially designed car, consisting of removable containers, each of which encases a glass-lined, heavily insulated tank, capable of carrying milk. Each container unit can be hoisted to and from motor trucks and platforms.

MILLING-IN-TRANSIT While this term seems to imply only a milling process, it is more general. Whenever a stopover is allowed under the tariff to permit a finishing process, or something comparable thereto, the term milling-in-transit is applied.

MINI-BRIDGE Ocean-rail container movement that replaces all water movement; example: Europe to Charleston ocean movement with rail move to New Orleans consignees in place of a Europe to New Orleans water haul.

MINIMUM The least, or lowest (sum, quantity, price, etc.)

MINIMUM BILL OF LADING Many ocean bills of lading are known as *minimum* because they contain a clause which specifies the least charge that the carrier will make for the issuance of a lading. This charge may be a definite sum varying from five to ten dollars, or it may be the current charge per ton or for any specified quantity of cargo.

MINIMUM CARLOAD WEIGHT The minimum weight, as provided for in a tariff, classification, and exception thereto, shows the least amount of an article that will be accepted for shipment, in order that it may be classed as a carload.

MINIMUM CHARGE Applied to a commodity shipment, it establishes the minimum rate, regardless of weight of the shipment, that will be assessed against the movement. It is expressed in terms of a total charge rather than a charge per hundredweight.

MINIMUM RATE As contrasted to the minimum charge, the minimum rate is the lowest rate per hundredweight that will be charged for a movement.

MINIMUM TRUCKLOAD WEIGHT The weight at which a shipment is handled at a truckload rate.

MIMIMUM WEIGHT When a given rate is based on a minimum weight of shipment, this is referred to as the minimum weight for the rate.

MINNIE Less than 100 lbs. in the shipment.

MINI MAX The upper and lower bounds —or high and low limits. Used for auditing and rejecting.

MIN. WT. The minimum weight.

MISDELIVERY A shipment that is delivered to the wrong consignee or the wrong location of the correct consignee.

MISDEMEANOR A crime less than a felony; a crime of a minor degree.

MISDESCRIPTION BY SHIPPER Situation in which shipper's description of goods on bill of lading is not correct in relation to what is actually being shipped.

MISROUTE When a carrier errs by violating the routing instruction, or sends a shipment via a route with a higher rate, this class of a mistake is termed a misroute.

MISROUTED FREIGHT Freight that is sent to the correct destination, but by a route that results in too great a rate, or results in a rate higher than that specified by the shipper's routing.

MISROUTING CLAIM When an unreasonable utilization of high rated routes is used, the shipper has a right to file a claim for misrouting. Even though a legal rate has been assessed, another lower rate may be applicable. The failure of the carrier to move by the route with the lowest rate will create a condition which authorizes the shipper to file a claim for misrouting. Both the misrouting claim and the overcharge claim may be settled without first obtaining authority from the Commission. The misrouting claim must be filed within two years —as contrasted to three years for overcharge —from the date of delivery.

MISSHIPMENT Shipping the wrong product, quantity, or to the wrong destination.

MISSIONARY RATES When a rate is established at an unusually low level to aid in the development of a particular industry, it is called a missionary rate. Missionary rates cannot be used in measuring the reasonableness of rates.

MIXED CARLOAD Two or more different commodities in the same car.

MIXED CARLOAD RATE The rate on a shipment of many less-than-carload shipments combined into a carload shipment. Either the highest rating and minimum weight will be needed to qualify for the mixed carload status, or under the Modified Rule, each shipment (commodity) will take its own carload rating times its actual weight.

MIXED LOAD A load of different articles in a single consignment.

MIXED SHIPMENT Two or more different articles in the same container or shipment.

MIXED TRAIN A railroad train composed of both freight and passenger cars is a mixed train. The mixed train was most common during its earliest operations in Western United States.

MIXED TRUCKLOAD RATES Rated applicable on a single shipment composed of numerous small shipments, all moving from like origin to destination.

MIXING PRIVILEGES The authorization to mix truckload freight in accordance with various combinations and alternatives. The rate applicable to each article is its truckload rate—as though its weight justified a truckload rate.

MODE Mode is the vehicles system used for intransportation. It is normally classified by the system for propulsion and the methodology of right of way. Carriers moving on highways are referred to as motor transportation mode or highway mode. Mode is a general term that covers all of the carrier classifications based on right of way, propulsion system, etc.

MODIFIED PROCEDURE When a complaint has been served under this procedure, the parties in the case are requested to submit and exchange memoranda and exhibits giving the facts upon which they rely. The case then proceeds to hearing solely on the points on which agreement has not been reached. To conserve time and delay in the service of a proposed report, parties are requested to be prepared at the close of the hearing to orally argue the case before the examiner, and to waive the filing of briefs. After the proposed report has been served its procedure is the same as all other cases handled under the proposed report plan.

MO 4 (AGREEMENT) A managing and operating agency agreement No. 4, under which Government Shipping Board vessels are being operated; whereby the operator under bond, mans, equips and supplies the vessel as the Emergency Fleet Corporation directs, closing freight contracts, issuing bills of lading and collecting moneys due the Corporation. For these services the operator receives commissions up to 5 percent, on outward voyages and 2½ percent, on inward voyages, plus a managing agent's fee.

MOLDED DEPTH The measurement from top to keel of one, two and three deck vessels. Length from the top of the keel to the top of the upper deck beams at the side of the vessel.

MONEY ORDER A non-negotiable order requesting one person to pay money to anothr. The most commonly used of post office and express orders.

MONOPOLY Sole permission or appropriated power to deal in any species of goods or perform a service.

MOORSOM'S RULE A mathematical formula worked out for measurement of the cubical content of a vessel. It uses 11 cubic feet as a gross ton. Proposed and adopted in Britain in 1949. Suggested by a commission. Adopted by U.S. in 1864.

MORE-THAN-ONE-CONSIGNMENT WAYBILL A waybill used for more than one consignment of freight.

MOTIVE POWER A term relating to the self-propelling equipment of a railroad.

MOTOR CARRIER A transportation service company that transports in a motor vehicle over the highways.

MOTOR CARRIER ACT OF 1935. Part II of the Interstate Commerce Act, which brought motor carriers under the regulatory jurisdiction of the I.C.C. It involves regulation of common and contract carriers. It is incorporated into the Revised Interstate Commerce Act in 1978; motor carriers are referred to there as Subchapter II carriers.

MOTOR FREIGHT ASSOCIATION An association of motor carriers for any legitimate purpose, like issuing tariffs, lobbying, etc.

MOTOR TRANSPORT A term used to signify transportation by auto truck.

MOTOR VEHICLE Any vehicle, machine, tractor, trailer, or semi-trailer propelled or drawn by mechanical power and used upon the highways in the transportation of passengers or property.

MOUNTAIN-PACIFIC GROUP The rate territory which is west of a line between North Dakota and Montana, between South Dakota and Montana, between Wyoming and South Dakota, until it comes to the main line of the Union Pacific, then extends west to Cheyenne, Wyoming, then south to Denver, and on through to Colorado Springs, Pueblo, Trinidad, and then follows the track of the AT&SF through Raton, Las Vegas, Albuquerque, and on to El Paso.

MULE A small tractor used about the warehouse to move two-axle dollies. Also a yard tractor.

MULLEN TEST Fiberboard and similar material is tested in strength by a device through what's called the mullen test.

MULTI-CITY-WAREHOUSE COMPANY A firm operating warehouses in more than one city.

MULTI-MODAL INDIFFERENCE VOLUME It is possible to determine the optimum carrier mode on the basis of transport rates alone. While this is incomplete logistics planning, under some circumstances it is helpful. Two competitive carriers will probably have different less than volume and volume rates, as well as different minimum volumes, to qualify for the volume rate. That volume at which the continuous per unit transport cost curves of the different modes cross is known as the multi-modal-indifference volume. At that volume it would be feasible to change carrier modes on the basis of transport rates alone.

MULTIPLE HAZARDS A material meeting the definitions of more than one hazard class.

MULTIPLE CAR AND MULTIPLE TRAILER LOAD RATES In recent years the ICC has shifted its policy to permit multiple-car and multiple-trailer load rates. They must be compensatory, that is, above out of pocket costs. Likewise they must be competitively necessary, and properly related, to single car rates. In years gone by the ICC would not authorize these rates because it was believed that only large shippers could take advantage of them.

MULTIPLE CLASSES Classes which have a fixed multiple of a lower class. For example, three times the first class rate.

MULTIPLE LOADING When two or more carload shipments are loaded on one car at the same origin for different destinations, or at different origins for the same destination, or at different origins for different destinations, any of these processes are referred to as multiple loading.

MULTI-SERVICE CARS When hopper-type or gondola cars are adapted for carrying bulk commodities, and are equipped for discharge of content to the center of both sides of the track, the multiple use of cars is referred to as multi-service cars.

MULTIPLE SHIPMENT RATE A transportation rate for freight whereby a lower rate applies on each shipment when many are tendered at the same time.

MULTIPLE UNITS Railroad engines or powered passenger cars that operate simultaneously from one set of controls by one engineer.

MULTI STOP BODY A fully enclosed truck body with a quick and easy driver's compartment entry.

MULTI-STORY WAREHOUSE A warehouse with more than one major floor level on which goods can be stored.

MULTI-TINE FORK Attachment to a forklift truck that allows the movement of two pallets side-by-side, rather than the usual one pallet on the forks.

MUSHROOM LINE A transportation company operating mushroom steamers.

MUSHROOM STEAMER When a ship is put into effect on short notice, and has no specific operating policy but moves to and from advantageous ports, it is called a mushroom steamer.

MUSTER A collection of samples.

—N—

NANO-SECOND One billionth of a second. A term used in data processing to a greater extent. Often used in reference to computer speeds.

NATIONAL AIR CARRIER ASSOCIATION A trade association made up of air carriers performing as supplemental carriers, and originally incorporated as the Military Air Carrier Association.

NATIONAL TRANSPORTATION POLICY A congressional statement in the Revised Interstate Commerce Act that presents the overall policy of the congressional branch with regard to ICC regulation of the various modes.

NATURAL ADVANTAGE A benefit one locality possesses over another, due to its geographical location, its proximity to the seaboard and navigable rivers and general transportation facilities.

NATURAL DIFFERENCE A disparity between a shipper or dispute of a locality because of the presence or absence of natural advantages or disadvantages such as rivers and waterways, highways and mountains.

NATURAL SHRINKAGE The ordinary loss of weight of livestock; loss in weight because of evaporation of liquids and loss within tariff allowance on grain and seeds.

NAUTICAL That which pertains to ships, sailors or navigation; maritime.

NAUTICAL ASTRONOMY The use of astronomy to guide ships at sea by identifying points in the heavens and guiding on them.

NAVICERT When it is desirable to exempt noncontraband shipments from seizure or search by patrols maintaining a blockade, a certificate called a navicert is issued.

NAVIGABLE A term applying to waters that can be navigated by freight and passenger carrying vessels.

NAVIGATION The science of conducting ships.

NEAPED When the draft of the vessel exceeds the depth at high water neaps, the vessel cannot move until the high spring tides.

NECK-IN A means of reforming a portion of a container to a smaller size than the rest of the container.

NEGLIGENCE Any general process of failure to exercise the degree of care required by law results in a verdict of negligence.

NEGOTIABILITY Credits are classified "negotiable" or "straight." Negotiability authorizes third parties to negotiate the beneficiary's drafts.

NEGOTIABLE INSTRUMENTS An instrument such a draft, promissory note, check or bill of exchange which is transferable from one person to another in good faith for a consideration. To be legal, the instrument must be in writing, signed by the drawer, must promise to pay a certain sum in money on demand or at a future date, and must be payable to order or to the bearer who must be named.

NEGOTIABLE PAPER Bills, drafts, and notes, which may be transferred with all their rights by endorsement or assignment.

NEGOTIATING BANK A bank named in the credit (or the credit freely negotiable) which examines the documents and certifies to the issuing bank that the terms are complied with. The bank may be authorized to purchase the draft and/or create an acceptance. In practice, the negotiating bank is usually the seller's bank and mails the documents to the issuing bank for payment or acceptance. When the discount charges are for the account of the seller, the seller has a choice of having drafts discounted by the negotiating bank.

NEGOTIATIONS Making a bargain or agreeing upon a mercantile transaction.

N.E.S. Not elsewhere specified. A term used in an air freight tariff that means the rate specified applies to all commodities in the group not elsewhere appearing under their own name.

NESTED The process of packing articles so that they rest partially or entirely within one another, thereby reducing the total cubic foot displacement, is referred to as nesting or nested articles.

NESTED SOLID Articles nested so that the bottom of one rests on the bottom of the one lower.

NET The amount of revenue remaining after deductions, charges, expenses, losses, etc. Of course, this term also applies to a knotted rope or twine contrivance for the purpose of lowering or lifting cargo.

NET EARNINGS Earnings remaining after the deduction of operating costs and necessary deductions pertaining to the carrying of passengers and property.

NET OPERATING INCOME The balance left after deducting all operating expenses from all income received from operation.

NET TON 2,000 pounds.

NET-TON-MILE The movement of a ton of freight one mile.

NET TONNAGE Represents the total cubic contents of those parts of a vessel closed in and devoted to the carrying of cargo and passengers; the weight measure being one gross ton for each 100 cubic feet of capacity. Net tonnage of vessel is ascertained by deducting from its gross tonnage, the cubic contents of certain spaces that are specified in the measurement laws and rules of the various maritime nations or in the measurement rules applicable at the Suez and Panama Canals. Net tonnage may be about 2/3 of gross tonnage, although not so with fast trans-Atlantic liners, which have large coal bunkers, machinery and housing quarters.

NET WEIGHT The weight of the contents of a shipment, without respect to the weight of the container or the car, is the net weight.

NEWSBOARD In materials handling, it is a cheap board made from waste newspaper by means of a cylinder machine.

NODE All institutions which receive and hold goods moving in a channel are referred to as nodes. They may or may not take title to the goods. They are receiving and shipping points. The number of nodes in the channel has a significant effect on the length of haul, and therefore the volume of shipment, and the systems for logistics control.

N.O.I. Not otherwise indexed.

NOIBIN Not otherwise indexed by name.

NON-AGENCY STATION A station at which a carrier has no agent.

NON-COMPETITIVE TRAFFIC Where no competition exists between carriers in the movement of traffic, it is said to be non-competitive.

NONCONTIGUOUS COMMERCE When the territory of a nation is not directly connected to the mainland, commerce between the mainland and the territory is referred to as noncontiguous commerce. Consequently, movements between continental United States to such areas as Puerto Rico, Alaska, etc. would be so regarded.

NONDUMPING CERTIFICATE In order to prevent the whole market from being flooded by foreign exporters, many nations, notably Canada, require a *value* certificate. This certificate must stipulate the cost of the goods to the foreign buyer and the fair market value for home consumption.

NONFLAMMABLE GAS Any compressed gas other than a flammable compressed gas.

NON-POWERED AXLE An axle used to support the load, but no driving power is used on the axle.

NON-PRIORITY MAIL Mail bearing a surface carrier postage, that will go by air on a space available basis.

NONSCHEDULED SERVICE Flights for revenue not performed under schedule, and including all non-revenue flights incidental to such operations.

NONSTOP Performance of a movement without stopping enroute.

NORMAL CRUISING SPEED The standard cruising speed in statute miles per hour for an aircraft at flight altitude.

NORTH ATLANTIC TREATY ORGANIZATION Military defense agreement among the United States, Belgium, Canada, Denmark, German Federal Republic, Greece, Iceland, Italy, Turkey, Portugal, Netherlands, Norway, Luxembourg, and the United Kingdom.

NOS Not otherwise specified.

NOSE DIVE Trailer tipped forward on its nose.

NO-SHOW A flight reservationist who fails to appear or cancel the flight.

NO-SUSPEND ZONE A band or zone within which rates may vary and not be subject to regulatory protest before the ICC.

NOTARY (NOTARY PUBLIC) A public officer who attests or certifies to acknowledgement of bills, notes, protests and other papers.

NOTE A written or printed paper acknowledging a debt and promising payment.

NOTE OF HAND A written undertaking to pay money at a certain time.

NOTICE The notification that an act has been performed —such as delivery of freight. It may involve an act to be performed.

NOTICE OF READINESS The notice sent by the master of the vessel to the charter when the vessel is ready to load or unload.

NOZZLE, CAMELBACK In materials handling, it is a unit with a control valve for regulating air intake.

NOZZLE, SUCTION In materials handling, a device to lead materials into a suction line.

NUMBER BASE Refers to the number of digit symbols used in performance of arithmetic manipulations and computations.

—O—

OATH OF ENTRY In foreign trade, this term applies to a form which is required for the importation of goods into the country.

OBSOLESCENCE COST The decrease in finished goods inventory value resulting from the charge in market value, usually associated with time, is obsolescence cost. This cost results primarily in high-fashion goods, and industries of highly technical equipment with a high rate of innovation.

O/C Overcharge.

OCCUPIABLE STORAGE SPACE Warehouse net piling space. It includes the inside dimensions of the warehouse excluding interior walls, permanent aisles, elevator shafts, stairways, offices, receiving and shipping platforms or other areas where goods are not usually piled. It is measured in square footage.

OCEAN AND RAIL Transportation partly by ocean and partly by rail.

OCEAN BILL OF LADING Under the Carriage of Goods by Sea Act of 1936, the conditions to be printed in the ocean bill of lading were specified. This bill of lading serves the same purpose as the domestic bill of lading. It is a contract for carriage and a receipt of goods shipped. The ocean bill covers only an ocean movement. It is not intended to cover a combination of land and water movements.

OCEANOGRAPHY The science of the oceans, tides, currents, temperatures, waves, salinity and other ocean matters.

OFFICIAL AIR CARGO TARIFF CIRCULARS A circular put out by the Air Tariff Publishers, Inc., specifying the requirement by state and federal governments for accepting and transporting special commodities. Used for the movement of livestock, human remains, gambling equipment, etc.

OFFICIAL AIRLINE GUIDE (OAG) A bimonthly airline timetable guide published for services throughout the world.

OFFICIAL LOG BOOK The log of events happening at sea on the vessel; includes deaths, births, marriages, accidents, fines, sickness, etc. The log book is provided by the Department of Commerce and used by the Shipping Commissioner in compensating the crew.

OFFICIAL RAILWAY GUIDE A publication containing train timetables (passenger), distances between stations and named of officials and their addresses.

OFF-LINE Facilities and installations used by certificated air carriers for other than scheduled service.

OFF LOADING To unload.

OFF-ROUTE POINTS Points located off the regular route highways of line-haul carriers and served either on irregular schedules on deliveries of LTL freight or on truckloads only, whenever freight is available.

OFF-SEASON Refers to periods of low traffic of which special fares, etc., are directed.

OILFIELD BODY A heavily constructed truck body equipped with a bullnose or rear end roller for winch loading. Used primarily in the oil fields.

OILFIELD HAULER A motor carrier authorized to transport oil field equipment.

OLERON, LAWS OF The code of the sea created by Richard Coeur de Lion from the Rhodian laws. All modern maritime law has emerged from these laws. They were very strict laws. For example, a master who cast away his vessel through ignorance could be beheaded without accountability.

ON CONSIGNMENT Goods sent for sale at the best prices that the consignee can realize on behalf of the consignor.

ON-LINE Facilities and installations used in serving scheduled operations by the air carriers.

ON SOUNDING Within the 100 fathom curve.

"ON THE BELL" A railroad term for a train that has entered a block section of the road; arises from a bell that is rung automatically at a downline point from the train passing a specific spot.

ON THE BERTH A term denoting that a ship is ready to load or discharge cargo.

OPEN ACCOUNT A running or unsettled account.

OPEN AND PREPAY STATIONS An official list of freight stations in the United States with information as to whether goods may be consigned collect or whether charges must be prepaid.

OPEN CHARTER A charter in which neither the destination or nature of the cargo is specified.

OPENINGS The openings in the bottom deck of a double decked pallet that allow the finger wheels of a pallet truck to rest on the ground.

OPEN JAW TRIP A round air trip that generally has different points for terminating the outbound trip and initiating the return trip.

OPEN POLICY Insurance contracts which cover shipments throughout a specified period of time, or for all shipments of a certain value, but not limited to a single shipment, are referred to as open policy insurance contracts. The character of this contract specifies that the shipments insurance is automatic on each lot of merchandise, covering undefined risks and specifying that its terms should become definite by subsequent additions or endorsements to the contracts.

OPEN ROUTING Situation in which a rate between two points applies over more than one route, any of which are not specifically named.

OPEN STATION Any station at which an agent of a carrier is located and to which freight may be shipped collect.

OPEN TOP Trailer with sides but without permanent top; frequently used when heavy equipment is transported, which is lowered in to the trailer with a crane.

OPERATING AUTHORITY Routes, points and other traffic that may be served by a carrier as granted by a regulatory agency.

OPERATING DIFFERENTIAL SUBSIDY A subsidy paid by the U.S. Maritime Administration to U.S. flag steamship operators to somewhat equalize the firm's cost structures with those of lower cost foreign competitors on the same routes.

OPERATING EXPENSE The cost of handling traffic.

OPERATING RATIO Operating costs divided by total costs (or total revenue).

OPERATING REVENUE Total money received by a carrier, from transportation and from operations incident thereto.

OPPORTUNITY COST An implicit or explicit cost that exists whenever one alternative is chosen over another; the foregone benefit from choosing other than the best alternative.

OPTICAL SCANNERS Reading devices usually used in material handling to automatically record and/or affect sortation, stocking, picking, etc.

OPTIMIZING MODEL A model or formula that results in an optimum (maximum or minimum) answer of the entire function.

OPTION The permission to choose, or privilege of taking or delivering something at a given day and price.

OPTIONAL CARGO Cargo not yet sold when delivered at a port are termed optional cargo.

OR Owner's risk.

ORAL ARGUMENT In person presentation of evidence and other material before a court or regulatory body.

ORAL CONTRACT A contract that was made orally and not reduced to writing.

ORDER A commission to purchase; directions to deliver goods or to pay money.

ORDER AND COMMISSION DEPARTMENT (Express) One of the non-transportational divisions of the Express service embracing the purchase of supplies, payment of taxes, execution of legal papers, analyzing commercial conditions and locating new markets for shippers of fish, poultry, fruits and vegetables.

ORDER BILL OF LADING A form of bill of lading that can be used to sell (by the shipper) or affect payment (by the buyer) for the goods enroute in the care of the carrier.

ORDER CYCLE This includes the time and processes involved from the placement of the order to the receipt of the shipment. It includes the following processes: (1) communicating the order; (2) order processing; and (3) transporting the shipment. These are the functions performed in the lead time.

ORDER FILL, MEASURE OF A warehouse productivity measure that represents the total number of orders that were picked complete and/or shipped without stockouts or backorders in a given time period.

ORDER POINT SYSTEM OF INVENTORY CONTROL An inventory control mechanism that causes a reorder when the level drops to a certain quantity of goods on hand.

ORDERING COSTS All of the costs associated with the clerical work of preparing an order, transmitting the order, following up the order, and recording receipt of the order. It does not include machine set-up costs for manufacturing, since that is a part of purchase price. It does not include the costs of physically handling the inbound order, since that is accounted for in: (1) storage in-and-out costs, or labor costs; and (2) transportation shipping and receiving costs.

ORDER-NOTIFY (BILL OF LADING) A document which is used for goods consigned or destined to the order of a person or company named on the lading.

ORDER PICKER Mobile lift type equipment which allows the warehouseman to ride the pallet up and down to pick from various levels.

ORDER PICKING The preparation of an order by the packer involving the packing according to the written order.

ORDINARY A vessel in the harbor is known as in *ordinary*.

ORDINARY FREIGHT TRAIN A train consisting of a locomotive, with or without a caboose, with other freight train cars.

ORDINARY LIVESTOCK Defined in the Interstate Commerce Act as "all cattle, swine, goats, sheep, horses and mules, except such as are chiefly valuable for breeding, racing, show purposes and other special uses."

ORGANIC PEROXIDE An organic compund containing the bivalent $-O-O$ structure and which may be considered a derivative of hydrogen peroxide where one or more of the hydrogen atoms have been replaced by organic radicals must be classed as an organic peroxide unless otherwise specified in the DOT regulations.

ORGANIZATION The working structure of a company, corporation, association, etc., to handle efficiently various branches of work. Transportation organizations are divided into departments such as the executive, financial, operating, traffic, etc.

ORIGINAL First in order; that from which anything is copied. In Commerce, the original bill of lading, original invoice, etc.

ORIGINAL BILL OF LADING The one actually signed by the carrier and retained by the shipper; distinct from any of the copies or a facsimile copy.

ORIGIN OF TRAFFIC A point from which the traffic begins. The point or place which originates the traffic.

ORLOP DECK The lowest deck in the vessel. The beams may or may not have the deck laid. It may not run the length of the vessel.

ORM-A A material which has an anesthetic, irritating, noxious, toxic, or other similar property and which can cause extreme annoyance or discomfort to passengers and crew in the event of leakage during transportation.

ORM-B A material (including a solid when wet with water) capable of causing significant damage to a transport vehicle or vessel from leakage during transportation.

ORM-C A material which has other inherent characteristics not described as an ORM-A or ORM-B but which make it unsuitable for shipment, unless properly identified and prepared for transportation.

ORM-D A material such as a consumer commodity which, though otherwise subject to the regulations of the DOT, presents a limited hazard during transportation due to its form, quantity and packaging.

OSCILLATION, PERIOD OF The time of the roll, or oscillation, from port to starboard. If it includes the return roll to port, it is a double roll. The time required for a complete roll is the same regardless of the angle of the roll if there is no change in the trim. The swinging of the compass needle before coming to rest indicates a roll underway, and provides a means of timing the roll.

O.S.&D. Over short and damaged.

OSHA Occupational Safety and Health Act — a federal law.

OUNCE A weight of 1/16 of a pound avoirdupois; 1/12 of a pound, troy.

OUTBOARD Away from the center fore-and-aft line of the vessel.

OUT OF POCKET COST Those carrier costs directly attributable to the movement of the traffic.

OUTPORT A port or harbor located some distance from the chief port.

OUTPORT ARBITRARY An extra charge in steamship tariffs for picking up or dropping off freight at a port that is not a regular stop along a liner's route.

OUTRAGE The empty space in a container or drum to accommodate expansion, density change, etc., due to temperature change.

OUTRIGGERS Equipment used to increase the width of the trailer.

OUTSIDE DIMENSIONS (O.D.) The outside dimensions of a container or package. In drums it is measured by the diameter over the rolling hoops.

OUTSIDE STORAGE Storing products outside of the building on the ground.

OVERAGE The extent that the freight exceeds that on the shipping document, or the quantity to have been believed shipped.

OVER-AND SHORT-LANDED REPORT A report that shows missing packages, or *short-landed* shipments.

OVER-BOOKING The act of selling more tickets than there are seats available. It is synonymous with over-selling.

OVERCHARGES As used in the Interstate Commerce Act, charges for transportation services in excess of those applicable thereto under the tariffs lawfully on file with the Commission.

OVERCHARGE CLAIMS When the shipper or consignee pays charges for a transportation service which exceed those applicable under the tariff, a condition of overcharge claim exists. A carrier may make an error and create an overcharge in any of the following ways: (1) assessment of an incorrect rate; (2) errors in description on the bill of lading of the commodities being shipped; (3) errors in weight in which the weight designated on the bill of lading is incorrect, or an incorrect minimum weight is applied; (4) mistakes in tariff interpretation; and (5) clerical errors. Application for an overcharge claim must be filed in writing with the carrier within three years of time of delivery of the shipment. Normally, the claim is filed, the period is then extended six months from the time the claim would be disallowed. This permits the applicant to bring suit in the event application for an overcharge claim was disallowed by the carrier.

OVERDUE As applied to a draft or note, the specified time for payment of which has passed or matured.

OVER FREIGHT When freight is in the possession of a carrier without waybill or identifying marks it is normally referred to as over freight.

OVERHANG To project or extend beyond. It could refer to the overhand of products on a pallet.

OVERHEAD GUARD A protection overhead to protect the driver of a lift truck.

OVERHEAD RUNWAY SYSTEM The overhead tracks which carry the lifting blocks and trolleys in warehouse operations. They operate in one plane, but may go straight or have curves.

OVERHEAD TRAFFIC When traffic moves over a line which is a bridge in character, that is it is received by another carrier and delivered to a third carrier, it is called overhead traffic.

OVERHEAD WAYBILL A document used to cover shipments by a carrier on whose line neither the point of origin nor the destination is located.

OVERLAND COMMON POINT (O.C.P.) A term stated on the bills of lading offering lower shipping rates to importers east of the Rockies provided merchandise from the Far East comes in through West Coast ports.

OVERLOAD A vehicle that exceeds the regulation maximum in total weight or axle weight. Refers to motor transport vehicles.

OVER-SALE Selling more tickets than there are seats available. It results in a confirmed reservation without a seat.

OVER, SHORT, AND DAMAGE (OS&D) REPORT When a freight agent submits a report showing discrepancies between the bill of lading and the freight on hand, this type of report is issued. Excessive freight is called *over,* absent freight is called *short,* and bad condition freight is referred to as *damaged.* In freight stations, a room is frequently set aside for unclaimed, shortweight, damaged items, etc. and is called OS&D room.

OVER-THE-ROAD (CARRIER) A term denoting a motor carrier performing intercity service.

OVER WITHOUT BILL Freight without its bill of lading or freight bill.

OWNER-OPERATOR A driver who owns the vehicle he operates, and has leased it to a carrier.

OWNER'S RISK Indicates that shipper relieves carrier from part of transportation risk.

OXIDIZER A substance such as chlorate, permanganate, inorganic peroxide, or a nitrate, that yields oxygen readily to stimulate the combustion of organic matter.

—P—

PACKAGE A bundle, parcel or bale.

PACKAGE CAR A freight car holding two or more less-than-carload shipments which are moved jointly from a point of origin to a principal break-bulk point.

PACKAGE FREIGHT Packages making up less-than-carload shipments which are billed on the basis of the number of pieces or packages and are subject to check and inspection.

PACKAGING ENGINEER A professional trained in managing the packing operations of a firm.

PACKED A term describing an article protected by, or wih partitions, wrappers, excelsior, straw, or other packing and lining material, affording adequate protection against breakage or damage from handling or weather.

PACKING LIST The purpose of the packing list is to show the merchandise packed and all particulars. It is normally prepared by the shipper. It is not necessarily required by carriers. A copy is usually sent to the consignee to assist in verifying the shipment received.

PAS-CONTACT (PART OF SECURITY SYSTEM) Plate completing electrical circuit affixed to a door or window. If door or window is opened the circuit is broken, resulting in a security alarm.

PADDY Rice without the husks removed. A mixture of clean rice and paddy rice is called *cargo rice.*

PAJAMA WAGON A tractor with sleeper facilities.

PALLET The pallet is a device used for moving and storing freight. Commonly it is about four feet square and is so constructed to facilitate placement of a lift truck between the levels of a platform to move it on a freight car or into a warehouse.

PALLET, DOUBLE WING A pallet that has the top platform extending out on opposite sides.

PALLET, EXCHANGE PROGRAM An agreement between two firms that makes each responsible for the other's pallets. This is usually done on a one-for-one basis. Records are maintained on all pallet movements between the two parties. This alleviates the requirement of having to off load products from one point to another and delivering empty pallets each time a product exchange takes place.

PALLET, FIRE Safety platform that has emergency and fire fighting equipment stowed on it.

PALLET, FOUR-WAY Permits forks to enter at any of its four sides.

PALLET, GMA 48" X 40" hardwood, four-way (4) entry pallet.

PALLET HOOK A hook attached to a rope and used for lifting pallets.

PALLETIER RACK Frame and pallet which stack on top of one another for higher stacking.

PALLETIZE Placing specific size material on a specific size pallet in a prescribed arrangement.

PALLETIZER A type of materials handling equipment that acts to palletize units in place of or in assistance with personnel performing same.

PALLET LOAD UTILIZATION The percentage of total pallet square inches that are occupied by packages loaded upon it.

PALLET, ONE WAY A pallet that can only be accessed by a forklift from its front or back.

PALLET PATTERN The pattern of cases placed on each layer of a pallet or unit of merchandise.

PALLET, SAFETY WORK PLATFORM 48" X 40" pallet that has four sides 3' high constructed on it. It is used in conjunction with a lift truck to safely raise personnel for maintenance or other duties.

PALLET, THROW AWAY Designed to transport products one way and then disposed of. Usually two-way entry constructed of soft wood.

PALLET, TWO-WAY Permits forks to enter at only two of its four sides.

PANAMA CANAL ACT An act of Congress (1912) prohibiting the ownership by railroads of water lines with which they compete.

PAN-AMERICAN UNION An institution, with headquarters in Washington, D.C. very active in supplying information regarding South American countries. This institution is supported by the United States and the twenty Latin-American Republics.

PANCAKE Brake diaphragm housing.

PANEL BODY A delivery truck with a fully enclosed body commonly used for small package movements.

PAPER, GUMMED A dextrin coating on paper—or a coating of fish-animal glue. It is activated by moisture.

PAPER JACK In ocean transportation, a master who secures command through influence and depends on his mate for professional assistance.

PAPER RATE A published rate under which no traffic moves.

PAPER ROLL CLAMP F/L attachment which permits grasping and rotating large paper rolls.

PAPER, VCI Paper prepared with a volatile corrosion inhibitor.

PARCEL POST A part of the U.S. mail service providing for the carrying of merchandise and matter, up to and including certain dimensions and weights at zone rates.

PARCEL POST AIR FREIGHT Air parcel post package shipment as air freight to the postmaster at the destination city for delivery within that postal zone or beyond. The destination postage is affixed by the shipper.

PARCEL RECEIPT Receipt given by a steamship company for a parcel shipment.

PARCEL SHIPMENT A small package restricted as to value, generally samples of goods or advertising matter.

PARETO'S LAW A phenomenon found in many situations in which a relatively small number of products, sales or most activity comprise a large percentage of the total; see also eighty-twenty rule.

PAR OF EXCHANGE The actual value of a sum of money, as distinguished from theoretical value, of a similar sum in the currency of another country.

PARTIAL LOSS Damage to property, but not such as to make it totally valueless or useless.

PARTIAL SHIPMENTS Under letters of credit, one or more shipments are allowed by the phrase "partial shipments permitted." In bulk shipments (commodities, etc.), a tolerance of three percent is allowed.

PARTICIPATING CARRIER (TARIFF) Each transportation line which is a participant in a tariff is referred to as a participating carrier. The tariff may be issued by the transportation line, or by a tariff publishing agent.

PARTICULAR AVERAGE In marine insurance, particular average refers to partial loss on an individual shipment from one of the perils insured against, irrespective of the balance of the cargo, and so differs from *general average.* Such insurance can usually be obtained, but the loss must be in excess of a certain percentage of the insured value of the shipment, usually three to five percent, before a claim will be allowed by the company.

PARTITION A wall or panel used to separate sections or units. A means of separating commodities by slotted pieces for protection and packing.

PART OWNER In marine shipping, one of several owners of a ship.

PAR VALUE The face or nominal value of a commercial paper.

PAR WEIGHT The steamship par between weight and measurement goods, determined by dividing a long ton (2,240 lbs.) by 40 cubic feet, and equal to 56 pounds.

PASS An order providing for free transportation over specified lines or routes; known as *annual* or *trip.*

PASSENGER CAR A car employed for the transportation of passengers; also known as a *coach.*

PASSENGER/CARGO AIR CARRIER A certificated air carrier holding right (certificate of public convenience and necessity) to transport scheduled passengers and freight over specified routes. It may be distinguished from an all-cargo or all-passenger carrier. They are commonly called *all-purpose air carriers.*

PASSENGER LIST A list of the passengers of a vessel which is shown to custom house officials when entering port, either in the United States or abroad.

PASSENGER MILE A term denoting the transportation of one passenger for a distance of one mile.

PASSENGER RATE A carrier's charge or *fare* for transportation of a person from one point to another.

PASSENGER REVENUE Revenue derived from passenger business of a railway company.

PASSENGER TARIFF A schedule containing passenger rates (fares), excess baggage charges, routing, rules and privileges.

PASSENGER TRAFFIC The handling of passengers which also includes baggage, express, mail and other traffic handled by passenger trains.

PASSING REPORT The cars which are received or delivered in interchange between yards are identified on a passing report. This document is required by the traffic department to assure information on car movements which can be passed along to the shippers and consignees, or to the auditor's office. The passing report, obviously, becomes significant for bridge or overhead traffic.

PASSPORT A document which certifies the nationality for a person or vessel. It assures safe conduct for the person identified.

PAVED RAIL PIT Railroad track inside the building and area under and around tracks are paved, for ease of cleaning.

PAYBACK PERIOD, DISCOUNTED The time period in which the initial investment cost of an asset is recouped from earnings inflows that are discounted with a present value factor to reflect the changing time value of money.

PAYBACK PERIOD, SIMPLE The time period in which the initial investment cost of an asset is recouped in terms of earnings inflows in cash terms.

PAYEE A party named in an instrument as the beneficiary (the recipient) of the funds. Under letters of credit the payee (the beneficiary) is either the drawer of the draft or a bank.

PAYEE One to whose order a bill, draft, or note is to be paid.

PAYER A party that is responsible for the payment as evidenced by the given instrument. Under L/C's, the payer is the party on whom the draft is drawn—usually the drawee bank.

PAYMENT That which discharges a debt.

P.&D. Pick-up and delivery of freight.

P.D. CAR Permanent dunnage car—a boxcar equipped with dunnage.

PEAK TANK A tank used to trim ship, located in the fore or aft sections of the ship.

PEANUT WAGON A large trailer pulled by a small tractor.

PEDDLER CAR When a shipment is discharged to various consignees, or is peddled to various consignees, the car containing the less-than-carload shipments is referred to as a peddler car. Each shipment takes the less-than-carload rate, subject to a car minimum charge. Peddler car deliveries are commonly made to branch houses of shippers.

PEDDLE RUN A pickup and delivery operation over given routes involving frequent stops. It usually involves operations from one terminal, in one radial area.

PEG LEG A tandem tractor with only one power axle.

PENALTY Legal punishment either on the person or goods, or by a fine imposed for misrepresentation, false billing, or non-compliance with domestic and foreign tariff rules and regulations.

PENDENTE LITE While suit is in progress.

PER By; by means of; according to.

PER ANNUM By the year.

PER-CAR RATES The setting of a price or a rate per car on specific commodities is a per-car rate. This is commonly done with vegetables, fresh fruits, etc. Southeastern railroads use per-car rates as a means of competition against exempt motor carriers hauling into the east.

PER CENT By the hundred; rates of interest, discount, commission, etc.

PERCENTAGE An allowance figured by hundredth parts; also commission.

PERCENTAGE CLASSES These are classes which have a stated percentage, relationship to an existing class, such as 27% of 1st, 85% of 5th, 90% of 6th, etc.

PERCENTAGE GROUPS The related points considered as units in rate making; the same percentage applying to or from points within a group.

PERCENTAGE SYSTEM The name given a method of rate making between Trunk Line and New England territories on the one hand and Central Freight Association territory on the other; these areas being divided into Eastbound and Westbound *percentage groups;* the same being determined in accordance with their relation to New York or Chicago.

The commodity rates, New York and Chicago, are taken as a basis and rates between other points in the territories above named are made on a percentage of these rates.

PERCENTAGE TERRITORY Area within which the percentage system applies.

PER CENTUM By the hundred.

PER CONTRA On the contrary.

PER DIEM (P.D.) This implies for *one day.* It is a charge made by rail carriers against other rail carriers for the use of rail cars while on another line.

PERDIEM CHARGE The amount paid by one carrier to another from each day it keeps a car belonging to the other and generally in the form of a certain sum per car per day.

PER DIEM RULES, CODE OF The Association of American Railroads establishes per diem rules which govern the amount of the rate to be paid for the use of railroad rolling stock owned by another carrier. This is applicable to a common carrier railroad. The low per diem rates have been a matter of considerable contention over many years.

PERFORMANCE (CAR) The performance of a car is the number of miles travelled by the car in a given period—loaded or empty. The performance also refers to the amount of freight carried, the average daily movement, the transportation receipts and any other information relative thereto.

PERIOD COSTS Costs that are incurred over a time span rather than from activity volume; examples are leases, interest, property taxes.

PERIODIC ORDER SYSTEM OF INVENTORIES A system in which orders for good lots are placed in fixed time intervals; usually the lot size varies.

PERISHABLE FREIGHT Commodities subject to rapid deterioration or decay, such as fresh fruits and vegetables, dairy products, and meats, which require special protective services in transit, such as refrigeration, heating, and ventilation.

PERMEABILITY A characteristic of a film which permits liquids and gases to filter through.

PERMISSIVE OPERATING RIGHTS Operating authority that may be utilized by a carrier and not required to serve.

PERMITS Authority or permit granted by the I.C.C. to contract carriers by motor vehicle or water and freight forwarders to operate in interstate commerce.

PERMIT (WATER TRANS.) A written authority to remove dutiable goods.

PERPETUAL INVENTORY RECORD An inventory system that keeps constant track of all inflows, outflows and stock levels.

PERPETUAL INVENTORY SYSTEM A stock control system that maintains a constant monitor of the level of goods.

PER SE By and of itself.

PERT Program evaluation review technique; a planning tool for projects, construction, etc. in which many tasks are to be performed in parallel with others while some must be completed in sequence; system determines the critical path that can not incur any delay without causing a delay in the overall project completion time.

PERTURBATION Procedure in data processing in which a variable at a time is changed to observe its effect on the overall system.

PETITIONS Applications, protests or other statements presented to a regulatory body which calls for some action by that agency.

PETTY AVERAGE Small charges, such as pilotage, port charges, etc., borne in part by both ship and cargo.

PHANTOM FREIGHT The deficit weight placed on a freight bill for goods not actually in a shipment for purposes of qualifying the shipment for a higher weight break; lower rate that provides for lower total charges.

PHYSICAL CONNECTION Indicative of a switching connection between two carriers, allowing from interchange of cars.

PHYSICAL DISTRIBUTION The National Council of Physical Distribution Management adopted the following definition of physical distribution. "Physical Distribution is the term employed in manufacturing and commerce to describe the broad range of activities concerned with efficient movement of finished products from the end of the production line to the consumer, and in some cases includes the movement of raw materials from the source of supply to the beginning of the production line. These activities include freight transportation, warehousing, material handling, protective packaging, inventory control, plant and warehouse site selection, order processing, marketing forecasting and customer service." Physical distribution normally refers to post production logistics. This distinction comes from the fact that distribution is a marketing term. It involves the processes of distributing finished goods. The American Marketing Association defines physical distribution as: "The movement and handling of goods from the point of production to the point of consumption or use."

PHYSICAL INVENTORY A physical count of designated items located within the warehouse.

PHYSICAL VALUATION OF CARRIER A Federal Act of 1913, to find the value of the actual property, equipment and vested rights of the carrier for the purpose of securing a figure upon which to base, at a reasonable return to such carrier for services it might perform, a certain interest allowance.

PICKING ERROR Removing wrong product or quantity from the warehouse inventory.

PICK RACK Storage rack used for assembly (order).

PICKUP Those cars added to a train enroute between dispatching and the receiving yards are generally referred to as pickup. Sometimes they are added at the dispatching yard to a train operating over several divisions on a continuous wheel report.

PICKUP ALLOWANCE An allowance granted the consignor by the carrier for delivery of freight to the carrier terminal. It also means an allowance to the consignee for picking up freight at the terminal and taking to his business site when the rate called for carrier delivery.

PICKUP AND DELIVERY A service involving the collection of freight from door of consignor and delivery to door of consignee.

PICK-UP SERVICE The collecting of shipments by a transportation company from places of business, or residences, of the goods to be transported by said company. Formerly this service was principally performed by the express companies but is now extended to motor truck, air lines, and in some cases railroad and steamship companies.

PICK-UP TRUCK A small truck with low sides and small carrying area behind the cab.

PIER The projecting wharf, which may be either at an angle or perpendicular, which permits the side placement of ships for loading and unloading operations.

PIER HEADING The United States engineers establish a fixed line beyond which a pier may not be extended.

PIG A trailer transported on a rail flat car.

PIGGYBACK The transportation of highway trailers or removable trailer bodies on rail cars specifically equipped for the service is called piggyback. It is essentially a joint carrier movement in which the motor carrier forms a pickup and delivery operation to a rail terminal, as well as a delivery operation at the terminating rail head.

PIGGYBACK, PLAN I Through motor carrier service, shipper charged motor carrier rate, motor carrier performs pick up and delivery, line haul performed by railroad, motor carrier rate and liabilities apply for the shipper.

PIGGYBACK, PLAN II Through railroad service from door to door, railroad provides pick up and delivery, railroad rate and obligations apply.

PIGGYBACK, PLAN III Ramp to ramp service with railroad performing line haul; shipper and consignee must arrange for pick up and delivery; railroad rate and liabilities apply for linehaul.

PIGGYBACK, PLAN IV Railroad ramp to ramp service; shipper providing rail car and containers as well as arranging pick up; consignee arranges delivery; railroad rate for hauling equipment.

PIGGYBACK, PLAN V Through railroad-motor carrier service in which offer joint service beyond their lines; railroad provides rail car and the road or motor carrier provide containers as well as pick up and delivery; both responsible for obligations; each divides rate on division basis.

PIGGYBACK, PLAN V½ Innovation since deregulation of piggyback service in 1981; railroad provides through service of rail and motor links in railroad owned motor carriage service extending from its rail line territory.

PIGTAIL The cable used to transmit power to the trailer.

PIKE A turnpike.

PILFERAGE Felonious breaking into containers and taking and removing property of others.

PILOT In rail transportation this involves an employee who is assigned to a train when the engineer or conductor isn't acquainted with the rules. In water transportation the pilot is in charge of the vessel from the open seas through whatever channels may be involved to the proper dock.

PILOTAGE The charge for piloting a vessel, based on the draft or tonnage of the vessel; also, the navigation of a vessel by a pilot.

PINWHEEL PATTERN A type of package on pallet loading pattern that appears in a spiral like form from the outside inward to the center.

PIPE LINE A line of pipe used for transporting liquids, principally crude oil, or gas.

PIPE LINE CARRIER A company owning and transporting liquids, principally crude oil, through pipes and treated as a common carrier.

P.I.V. VALVE Post indicator valve, indicates water pressure in that particular post (hydrant).

PLACEMENT, ACTUAL When a rail car is placed in an accessible position for loading or unloading on a private or public delivery track or at a point designated by the shipper or consignee, it constitutes actual placement.

PLACEMENT, CONSTRUCTIVE When it is necessary to place a car as near as possible to the point of destination or the point promised by the carrier for the purpose of loading or unloading, or in circumstances in which the consignee's track or tracks are full, the approximation of optimum location involves constructive placement.

PLAINTIFF One who commences action in court to obtain redress for injury sustained.

PLATE B (RAILCAR) A railcar of standard length, width and height measurements that can travel over most lines in the nation.

PLATE C (RAILCAR) A rail car that is larger in length, width or height than the normal cars and must be carefully routed due to limitations on some rail lines; many of the larger, modern rail cars that have been built since the 1960s are Plate C cars.

PLATFORM BODY A truck or trailer with no sides or top, but only the floor.

PLATFORM COSTS The terminal freight handling costs.

PLATFORM HANDLING The transfer of a load from one truck to another in the motor carrier business, regardless of whether or not the load touchs the platform, is platform handling.

PLATFORM SLING A platform used in place of a sling in water transportation, to which tackle is attached by bridles to the corners.

PLEADINGS The written or oral position in a legal case, or in a hearing before the regulatory authority.

PLIMSOLL MARK The depth to which a vessel may safely load is identified by a horizontal line painted on the outside of the ship. In British merchant vessels this is normally referred to as the plimsoll mark. This mark must remain above the surface of the water.

PLUG DOOR A special tight sealing type of door often found on box, insulated and refrigerator rail cars.

PLY To beat to windward. Steamers also ply between ports to load and unload. Also a layer or fold.

PLYWOOD A laminated wood veneer, glued together.

POINT A word used synonymously with city, town or place and usually indicating some important traffic characteristic.

POINT OF ORIGIN The station at which a shipment is received by a transportation line from the shipper.

POINTS The tapered ends of rails in a railroad switch that separate from or join other rails in order to change train course.

POISON A Extremely dangerous poisons; poisonous gases or liquids of such nature that a very small amount of the gas, or vapor of the liquid, mixed with air is dangerous to life.

POISON B Less dangerous poisons; substances, liquids, or other solids (including pastes and semi-pastes), other than Class A or irritating materials, which are known to be so toxic to man as to afford a hazard to health during transportation; or which, in the absence of adequate data on human toxicity, are presumed to be toxic to man.

POLE TRAILER A form of truck trailer consisting of the axle unit and a rigid pole that attaches to the truck pulling it.

POLICY The written contract of insurance.

POOL An assembly of equipment to be drawn on by those creating the pool.

POOL DISTRIBUTION Technique of combining small orders to get truckload (TL) or carload (CL) rates.

POOLING AGREEMENT The process of agreeing on the divisions of revenues, or the divisions of tonnage business, between several carriers in accordance with a contract or agreement.

POOLING (CAR) When individual carrier equipment is managed through a central agency which serves several railroads for the joint benefit of the carriers and the shippers, a pooling action is involved.

POOLING EQUIPMENT The joint or common use of the station facilities, rolling stock and motive power, of and by two or more carriers.

POLYETHYLENE A synthetic material attained by polymerization of ethylene under great pressure.

POLYSTYRENE FOAM A plastic foam used for packing and protection. It is composed of open or closed cells.

POOP (DECK) A light deck, raised above the main or upper deck and extending a short distance forward from the stern.

POROSITY A condition of being permeable or of loose texture that permits the passage of liquids or gases.

PORT This may refer to either the left side of the ship or the harbor for ships.

PORT CHARGES The general assessment for pilotage, lighterage, towage, wharf services, etc. compose port charges.

PORT DIFFERENTIALS When a rate is added to the port-to-port rate for the continuous movement from a port to the interior, a port differential is applied. Interestingly enough, along the North Atlantic ports, New York uses it as a basing point for rates and the differential is the added charge from New York to whatever North Atlantic interior point is involved. Baltimore has also been used as a basing point for such rates.

PORT EQUALIZATION In order to assure a shipper the lowest possible charge from an interior point to a given port, it is common to have the steamship line absorb the differential between the cost of shipping freight from the interior point to the steamship's port for all excess charges beyond the movement to a rival port which might be shorter.

PORTERAGE The charge made by dock companies for the numerous services rendered by the porters.

PORT, FREE When a port is provided for the landing and holding of shipments for re-export without the imposition of the usual custom procedures and charges, this is termed a free port.

PORT MARK In international water movements, the final destination is the port mark. It need not necessarily be the port of entry if the port of entry is not the final destination.

PORT OF CALL A port in which vessels may load or discharge their cargo is a port of call. When it is necessary to provide extra transportation service to points beyond the port of call the process is normally referred to as *beyond port of call.*

PORT OF DEPARTURE The port from which a ship clears or sails and known as *Port of Exit.*

PORT OF DISTRESS Any port to which a vessel may turn in the event of trouble.

PORT OF ENTRY That port which provides the custom house services for the collection of duties on imports is the port of entry.

PORT OF ORIGIN AIR CARGO CLEARANCE PROCEDURE A procedure designed to expedite international transportation of goods. It permits the performance of customs formalities at non-gateway cities, rather than holding up the customs operations until the shipment is at the gateway city.

PORT-TO-PORT From one port to another port.

PORT WARDEN An official whose activities embrace the valuation, measurement, etc., of cargo or ship.

PORT WARDEN'S FEE A charge made at a port for a survey of cargo, hull, valuation, measurement, etc., of goods or ship.

POSSOM BELLY A livestock trailer with a drop frame that permits hauling small livestock and chickens under heavy livestock.

POSTAGE STAMP RATE A rate which is uniform throughout a large territory is referred to as *Postage Stamp Rate* because of its semblance to postage charges.

POST AUDIT A study conducted of a new warehouse, fleet, etc. to ascertain how well it is performing in relation to the proposal and financial analyses used to originally justify it.

POST ENTRY A statement of goods made after they have been unloaded and the particulars ascertained.

POSTING (TARIFFS) The filing of tariffs and other schedules for public use in compliance with the law at local and general offices of the carrier and to which the carrier is a party.

POTATO CAR An especially designed car for the transportation of potatoes.

POTENTIAL COMPETITION A competition existing in possibility and not in reality. For example: A river or other waterway paralleling a railroad and upon which no boats or steamships operate is considered potential competition.

POTS Warning flares that indicate an obstruction, breakdown, or other hazard.

POUCH CHECK When a check is made by the American Association of Railroads through its Car Service Division at certain points to determine the transit of freight in selected cars at the station at a given rate for the purpose of trying to locate delayed freight, it is referred to as a pouch check.

POULTRY CAR Car usually triple or quadruple decked, and constructed specially for the transportation of poultry.

POWER BRAKE Applying the brake with an open throttle.

POWER OF ATTORNEY Authority to do or forbear derived by one person from another. Also, authority granted by a transportation line to an agent to issue tariffs, etc., for its account.

PRACTICE That which has become customary through frequent action; the exercise of any profession.

PRATIQUE The temporary quarantine of a vessel is raised by granting the master of the vessel a pratique certificate. When granted pratique, the vessel is unrestricted. It is granted by the health officer.

PRECEDENT A former court or regulatory agency decision that acts as the basis of subsequent decisions involving similar circumstances.

PRECOOLING A process employed in the shipment of citrus fruits and other perishable commodities. The fruit is packed and placed in a cold room and the heat gradually extracted. The boxes of fruit are packed in a solid mass in cars that have been thoroughly cooled. The bunkers are completely filled with large cakes of ice, and the car is hauled through to destination without unsealing or opening bunkers.

PREDATORY PRICING A temporary pricing action by one firm to a point below variable costs that has the effect of removing competing firm from the market.

PREJUDICE Failure to give one shipper the same treatment as another shipper, under similar circumstances and conditions.

PREMIUM A sum beyond par value.

PREPAID Payment in advance of freight and/or other charges prior to delivery of shipment at destination, usually by shipper at point of origin,

PREPAY Pay before, or in advance.

PREPAY STATION When a station is identified for the purpose of requiring prepayment, it is referred to as the prepay station. Normally this is a non-agency station.

PRESENTING A DRAFT FOR COLLECTION Means that the bank accepts the documents from a shipper and effects collection through their branch or correspondent at foreign destination and credits the shipper's account upon receipt of advice that the draft has been paid by the consignee.

PRICE LIST A list of articles with prices attached.

PRICE, LONG The price of goods after all duties have been paid.

PRIMA FACIE At first view or on the face of it.

PRIMAGE An allowance of 5 to 10 percent added to ocean freight rates in the early days of shipping to be given to ship's officers and crew for the safe handling, stowage, and delivery of cargo consigned to their ship; now usually included in the tariff and quotation.

PRIMAGE AND AVERAGE ACCUSTOMED A prorate levy assessed by the steamship companies on consignors to cover the cost of wharfage, pilotage, and other port charges.

PRIME ENTRY A statement of goods based on details given in the bill of lading.

PRINCIPAL BILL The first of a set comprising a foreign bill of exchange to be presented and therefore the one which is accepted and paid.

PRINTER-SLOTTER A machine that prints, slots, creases and trims solid and corrugated box materials.

PRIORITY That which is first in rank, time or place; first claim.

PRIORITY MAIL Mail bearing air mail service rates for transportation by air on a priority basis.

PRIOR TRANSPORTATION A term found in some regulatory areas for a situation in which the leg of movement under examination had been preceded by movement by another mode.

PRIVATE AIR CARRIAGE Also called proprietary air transportation and business flying. It involves the use of company owned planes, or leased planes, to carry passengers, property, or freight for business purposes. It is not usually used to refer to personal private transportation.

PRIVATE CAR LINE A private concern owning its own rolling equipment, or leasing cars to or from railroads and operating them as private cars.

PRIVATE CARRIER Without becoming involved in the borderline distinctions between private and common carriers, suffice it to say that the private carrier provides a service for the movement of goods owned by the vehicle operator. It might be added that under circumstances in which a private carrier is receiving a larger compensation through the movement of his own goods than from the profits of a commercial buy and sell operation or manufacturing operation, he would not be classified as a private carrier but a common carrier.

PRIVATE LINE CAR A freight car not owned or leased by a railway company.

PRIVATE SIDING The rail track which serves a particular industrial plant is referred to as a private siding. The track may be owned or rented by the plant.

PRIVATE WAREHOUSE A warehouse operated by the owner of the goods stored there. A small stockroom at a manufacturing plant is a private warehouse, as is the huge order picking facility of the catalog mail order house.

PROCEDURE (I.C.C.) The rules and principles established for the conduct of cases before the Interstate Commerce Commission; found in 49 CFR 1100.

PROCURATION A general letter or power of attorney.

PROCUREMENT Overall activity of inbound logistics including purchasing, value analysis, cost analysis, inventory control, etc.

PRODUCE Farm products of all kinds.

PRODUCT AVAILABILITY Measure of the number of products available for use or shipping in relation to the total possible number manufactured or marketed by the firm at any point in time.

PRODUCT CODE Identification number or letter.

PRODUCT IDENTIFICATION Any number or marking clearly showing the type or lot numbers on freight bills, etc.

PRODUCTION COSTS The actual costs of producing a thing. This does not include profit or capital investment.

PRODUCTIVITY A work effectiveness measure that is, in general terms, the sum of outputs divided by the sum of inputs.

PRODUCT LIFE CYCLE A cycle that products experience throughout their life that consists of a conception stage, growth, maturity and decline; each part of the cycle calls for different materials management and distribution strategies; product life cycle can be as short as a few months as with fad items or as long as several decades.

PRODUCT MANAGEMENT PROBLEM The determination of the product mix resulting from the production activities of the industrial firm would represent its product management problems. The introduction of a new line for production requires the comparison of the total effect of one option product with another. This would necessitate anticipating the changes in production, marketing, and logistics costs with revenue for each product option.

PRODUCT PROLIFERATION A common phenomenon in most firms; indicates that over the years the number of products or stockkeeping units a firm produces or distributes has greatly increased.

PRODUCT RECALL The seeking out and arranging for product that has been sold or distributed by the firm to be brought back to it; usually for defective goods or health problem items.

PROFIT CENTER An accounting approach to internal operations in which all or most related revenues and expenses are assigned to specific functions, product lines or managers.

PRO FORMA For the sake of form.

PROGRAM A set of instructions to perform a computer operation. It performs a phase of a job or algorithm usually.

PROGRESSION OF CLASSES A series of classes increasing in relation to a basic class. For example: The first class being a basic class, all classes higher bear a relation to it.

PROHIBITED ARTICLES Goods which the carriers will generally not handle at all, or if so, only in accordance with separate and special set of rules and regulations.

PROMOTION OPTIONS Since the close of World War II, there has been a growing recognition of the need for determining public demand, and influencing that demand. Promotional activities are involved in each of these two classes of activities. The optional promotional plans of a firm may be regarded as involving different plans for promotion. Each plan would involve its own projected change in market demand, its own combination of media required, the uniquely different time of positive effect for each media, the allocated cost involved in the given plan for expenditure in each media, etc. Consequently, when two promotional plans are compared, the change in anticipated demand resulting from the promotion activity must be measured against the changes in total cost — production, logistics, and marketing costs. It cannot be measured against promotional costs alone.

PRO NUMBER The number placed on its freight bill by a carrier. The prefix *pro* is derived from the word *progressive*, i.e., *consecutive.*

PROOF OF DELIVERY The freight bill receipt signed by the consignee on delivery.

PROPORTIONAL RATES The proportional rate may be used only in constructing through rates on shipments which begin or terminate at points beyond the points from or to which the proportional rate applies. Sometimes they provide a means of establishing a competitive through rate where one of the carriers refuses to be a party to a competitive joint rate. The I.C.C. defined proportional rate as "one which applies to a part of a through transportation which is entirely within the jurisdiction of the Act to Regulate Commerce." The proportional rate is used to equalize rates via one gateway to rates that are available via another gateway. Sometimes they induce the movement of through traffic from origin to a destination when the traffic is similar to the intermediate local traffic between the points covered by the proportional rates. Export and import rates are illustrations of proportional rates. If export rates through Boston were made similar to export rates through New York, it would be an example.

PROPOPORTIONAL TARIFF A tariff containing only proportional rates.

PROPOSAL An act on the part of a shipper to change the rates, rules or regulations in the tariff. Action taken with the publishing agency or rate bureaus.

PROPOSAL The document with summarized technical information used to justify the acquisition of a capital asset.

PROPRIETARY AIR TRANSPORTATION See Private Air Transportation. The use of company owned or controlled aircraft for business flights.

PRO RATA In proportion.

PRO-RATA CHARTER A charter for an aircraft on a flat fee basis in which the passengers share the flat charter rate, on an equal basis. This form of charter is more common than the entity charter.

PRORATE A proportional distribution; according to a certain rate.

PRORATE, COMBINATION MILEAGE AND RATE In interline traffic, an average of the percentages determined between given points, by use of mileage prorates and rate prorates.

PRORATE, MILEAGE A division of revenue on interline shipments based on the ration of each carrier's miles to the total miles.

PRORATE, RATE On interline shipments, a division of revenue on the basis of the percentage of each carrier's local rate to or from the interchange point to the total combination rate from origin to destination.

PRORATING POINT A traffic point upon which a rate is prorated.

PRO-RATING TERRITORY Indicative of a territory to which shipments by several carriers in a joint shipment would divide the transportation rate on a prearranged percentage basis. In other words, the through rates constructed to such territory will be prorated, or divided, on an established basis of divisions between the carriers handling the traffic.

PROTECTIVE SERVICES Such services as refrigeration, icing, salting, and heating rendered en route, for which the tariff authority makes specific charges and allowances.

PROTECTIVE TARIFF Duties imposed on imports to encourage local manufacturing.

PROTEST A document filed by a party in an attempt to prevent a rate from going into effect or an application being approved.

PROTEST A legal means of proving presentation and default of a negotiable instrument, as well as providing notice to interested parties that the instrument was not paid.

PROTEST (CAPTAIN'S) A document prepared by the master of a ship on arrival at port concerning accidents or damage to ship or cargo during a certain voyage, generally for the purpose of relieving the shipowner of liability. In instances of jettison, the ship's master must *note* his protest before the consul of the country from which his vessel sails within 24 hours of his arrival at the first port he reaches, reporting the circumstances of danger, etc., attested to by two or more members of the crew. *Extending the protest* is a process whereby a more complete statement giving all details is drawn up after the expiration of the 24-hour period.

PROTESTING A BILL Attestation by a notary public, for the purpose of taking legal action, that a bill of exchange has been presented and refused acceptance or payment.

PROXIMO In the next month.

P-SYSTEM The system for managing inventory which involves ordering on a specific date each order, for the quantity required until the next fixed reorder date—plus the amount of the lead time stock. Thus, it involves a fixed review period, but a variable order quantity.

PUBLICATION Making public in the manner required by the Act, of tariffs, circulars, billing, instructions, guide books, territorial directories, classifications, exception sheets, etc., which in any way affect the handling of traffic.

PUBLIC SERVICE COMMISSION A name given to a State body having control of or regulating public utilities.

PUBLIC UTILITY That which is made use of by the general public, and the operation and conduct of which is vital to everyone.

PUBLIC WAREHOUSE A warehouse operated by a warehouseman engaged in the business of storing goods for hire. The word *public* refers to the fact that the warehouse provides a service to the public, and does not indicate public ownership.

PUBLISHING AGENT A person authorized by transportation lines to publish tariffs of rates, rules and regulations for their account.

PU&D Pickup and delivery. This operation involves the door-to-door pickup of freight from the consignor and the delivery operation to the consignee.

PULL DISTRIBUTION Situation in which demand at the retail or final level acts to stimulate inventory and transportation flows at preceding points in warehousing, etc., back to the factory and purchasing.

PULL THE PIN The process of releasing the fifth wheel lock.

PUL-PAC Another name for a Push/Pull attachment for a lift truck.

PULPBOARD A form of paperboard without sizing, with crude formation and low finish. It is composed of ground wood pulp mixed with sulphite or sulphate pulp to add strength.

PUNCH (CAR IDENTIFICATION) A small device on the outside of a freight car containing a punching die representing the car number. Cards are inserted into the punch by means of a paddle which transfers car number to the card by marginal punching.

PUNCHED TAPE In data processing, it is a paper tape perforated to represent data.

PUP A short semi-trailer used jointly with a dolly and another semi-trailer to create a twin trailer.

PURCHASE ORDER DRAFT A purchasing technique that utilizes a separate document in the placement of each order.

PURCHASE QUANTITY DISCOUNT If a reduction in purchase price per unit is made for buying in larger quantities, it represents a purchase quantity discount. Thus, a standard price per unit may be charged but reduced to a lower per unit price based on a minimum volume of purchase. The existence of purchase quantity discounts creates the need for computing the indifference volume just as it is computed in transportation logistics costing. At some volume less than the specified minimum volume for a purchase discount, the total cost of the purchase would be exactly the same when computed at the regular price times the indifference volume or at the minimum volume times the discount price.

PURCHASE PAYMENT DISCOUNTS Whenever a reduction in purchase price is made as a result of payment within a specific period of time, the extent of the reduction in purchase price for early payment is called a payment discount. If a purchase agreement should specify "2 per cent—10 days—30 days net," it offers an opportunity to reduce the price 2% by payment within 10 days. This is a 2% discount on the contract price.

PURE MATERIAL One that experiences little or no weight or cubic loss from extraction or other raw form through to being a finished product; has implications for optimal plant location.

PUSH DISTRIBUTION A distribution strategy that consists of stocking distribution centers, retail and sometimes use points in anticipation of an increase in future demand.

PUSHER-AXLE A non-powered axle on a trailer.

PUT ON THE AIR Apply brakes.

PUT ON THE IRON Put on chains.

PYROFORIC LIQUID Any liquid that ignites spontaneously in dry or moist air at or below 130° F.

—Q—

QUALITY The grade established by a standard.

QUANTITY Anything that can be increased, diminished, divided or measured as to bulk, weight or number.

QUANTITY DISCOUNT In purchasing, this is a reduction in the purchase price contingent on a quantity minimum for a particular commodity.

QUARANTINE A control process placed on an operation to protect against a health hazard. A ship may be quarantined so that it cannot leave a protected point. The Q flag is hoisted during the quarantine period.

QUARTER The fourth part; 28 pounds, avoirdupois; 8 bushels.

QUARTER DECK That part of a ship which is abaft the mainmast.

QUASI Almost. As if. That which resembles.

QUAY A term for a wharf, usually of solid as distinguished from open-pile construction, accommodating vessels on only one side, and parallel with the shore line.

QUAY DUES (QUAYAGE) A charge for berthing at a quay.

QUAY-PIER A structure either extending from the mainland or lying between two docks or basins of sufficient size to permit all the necessary elements of terminal facilities to be arranged parallel with the ship and serving ships on both sides.

QUEUE The lining up of messages or otherwise for processing.

QUICK-CHANGE (QC) This term is applied to the Boeing procedure for transforming a 727QC passenger aircraft into a cargo carrying plane. It has passenger seats and galleys set up on pallets for quick removal and conversion from passenger to cargo aircraft.

QUICK DISCONNECT (QDC) A system for expediting the change of the lift truck.

QUICK RATIO The division of cash, accounts receivable and marketable securities by the amount of current liabilities.

QUONDAM Former.

QUOTAS A system of controlling imports by specifying the limitation on the amount that can enter the country.

QUOTATION Current prices of commodities; etc., also the act of quoting or that which is quoted.

QUOTE To give the current price (or rate) of something.

Q-SYSTEM This management inventory system involves the optimization of the order quantity, and the standardization of the order quantity. It involves a variable review time, and a fixed order quantity. However, under ELQ (economic logistics quantity) logistics planning, the most economic logistics quantity may change—if the volume of sales or production changes. The carrier mode, and the source of purchase is shifted, container system may change. Changes in rates, purchase price, minimum purchase or transport requirements, etc., could result in such mode, source, and container decisions as to change the ELQ.

QTAM Queued telecommunications access method. In data processing, this is a micro-oriented BAL base programming language. It is applicable to message switching processes in traffic control in terms of terminals. It permits handling messages even though the data is random and unpredictable.

—R—

RACK CAR A freight car equipped with racks at both ends and used for the movement of pulp wood. It is a term used for rail flat cars with racks for handling automobiles. The 85 foot flatcar may have two or three levels of cars.

RACKING Hooks, racks, stilts and stripping placed in a refrigerator car on which meats and other perishable commodities are arranged for proper transportation.

RACK, PIT Storage rack located in the warehouse where a small supply of each item is stored specifically for efficient picking.

RACK, SHIPPING Rack designed to transport a specific product.

RADIOACTIVE MATERIAL Any material, or combination of materials, that spontaneously emits ionizing radiation, and having a specific activity greater than 0.002 microcuries per gram.

RADIUS Besides its standard meaning in geometry, in materials handling it means the horizontal distance between the centerline of a hook and the perpendicular going through the center of the rotation of the hook.

RAGS Bad tires.

RAG TOP An open top trailer with a tarpaulin cover.

RAIL AND WATER TERMINAL A terminal where freight is transferred between railway cars and boats.

RAIL BUMPER Metal device affixed to the rail track, designed to stop a railcar.

RAIL DOCK The platform which runs along the railroad track.

RAIL DOOR Large overhead door where rail enters building for entering and exiting of railcars.

RAIL-LAKE RAIL (RL&R) The carrier modes participate in that order in a movement.

RAIL PIT Area where inside rail track is located.

RAILROAD BOND A bond issued by a railroad for the purpose of financing improvements, extensions, etc., and generally secured by mortgages on tracks, rolling stock and other property.

RAILROAD RETIREMENT ACT An act of Congress, passed on August 29, 1935, and amended in 1937, establishing a retirement system for employees, subject to the Interstate Commerce Act.

RAILROAD STORAGE CHARGES In addition to the demurrage rules, hazardous shipments are also subject to charges for storage on railroad tracks. These charges vary from $8 to $20 per day, depending on the rate territory and the material. Storage charges are assessed as penalties, since railroads are not in the warehousing business. The charges are specified in the demurrage and storage tariff of the contract terms and conditions of the carrier's bill of lading.

RAILROAD UNEMPLOYMENT INSURANCE ACT An act of Congress (June 25, 1938) establishing an unemployment-insurance system for employees of certain firms engaged in interstate commerce.

RAILROAD WAYBILL This is normally called the historical record of the shipment. It is prepared for each carload and less-than-carload shipment from the shipping order. The shipping order is the carrier's copy of the bill of lading. The railroad waybill moves with the shipment from point of origin to destination regardless of the number of carriers over which the shipment is transported. The waybill consists of a list of added information such as the weights, the carton numbers if transferred en route, special services performed, etc. The original waybill will eventually be forwarded to the auditor's office. The Interstate Commerce Commission requires that the original waybill be retained for three years before destruction.

RAILS In materials handling, it means the fixed or removable horizontal members of the post pallets.

RAIL TRAFFIC That which pertains to the movement of goods and persons on rails.

RAILWAY FINANCE ACCOUNTING The keeping or examining of the revenues accruing from and expenses chargeable in the operation of the railways.

RAILWAY LABOR ACT An act of Congress (May 20, 1926) providing for the disposition of disputes between carrier and employees. An amendment (June 21, 1934) created the National Railroad Adjustment Board and the National Mediation Board.

RAILWAY LINE CLEARANCE The weight and size limitations for movements on a railroad line; published in an unofficial tariff.

RAILWAYS Synonymous with railroads and signifies the collective rail transportation lines of a country.

RAMP An inclined roadway or passage used to facilitate a loading or unloading operation. It is used, for example, to load semi-trailers on flatcars.

RANDOM ACCESS A form of computer storage system in which access is directly available to any storage location. Examples would be core, disc and drum storage.

RANDOM NOISE In data processing, it represents a procedure for simulating unpredictable events.

RANGE A term used with reference to a provision in *Cork for orders* Charter Party, by which the *loading port* is not specified when charter is signed but limited to ports within a certain *range* of coast line.

RATE The price of a carrier for providing transportation and related services.

RATE, ALL-COMMODITY A rate, usually based on a carload, applied to an assortment of merchandise or shipments which move at one time in one vehicle from one consignor to one consignee.

RATE, ALTERNATIVE A rate employed when the tariff provides for the use of more than one rate on particular kinds of traffic.

RATE, ANY-QUANTITY A rate applied regardless of quantity shipped.

RATE BASIS The economic factors which are involved in the making of a transportation rate.

RATE, BERTH In maritime traffic, the rate charged on general cargo by regularly operating water lines as distinguished from the rates charged on full cargoes and chartered vessels.

RATE, BLANKET A special rate covering several different articles in a single shipment.

RATE-BREAK POINT When two independent movements are added to provide a lower rate than the through rate, the point at which they connect is called the rate-breaking point. For example, if the rate from New York to Chicago was added to the rate from Chicago to Peoria, and this provided a lower combination than the through rate from New York to Peoria, the rate would be said to have Chicago as the rate-breaking point—or the rate is said to be made "over" Chicago.

RATE BUREAU An organization of carriers legalized under the Reed Bulwinkle Bill for the purpose of establishing agreement on rates. The bureau also publishes the tariffs for the participating carriers.

RATE CARD (SYSTEM) A card file system of keeping rates, showing article, commodity or class rates, I.C.C. authority, routing, marks, and classification governing.

RATE, CARGO A rate applying to a consignment which takes up all the freight carrying space in a vessel.

RATE, CHARTER A rate which applies when a charterer leases or hires a vessel for a trip, usually based on the weight of the cargo. The ship owners usually pay all charges agreed upon. Since this form of charter eliminates the element of risk from calculation of shipper, it is the form used most commonly. When a ship is hired for a period of time rather than by the trip, the rate is based on the net tonnage of register of the vessel, calculated monthly. The owners of the ship usually supply food and maintenance of crew and keep the ship in repair; the charterer furnishes fuel, passport and terminal charges.

RATE CHECK A freight bill audit for the purpose of discovering errors and overcharges.

RATE, CLASS A rate applied to an article not assigned a special or commodity rate and not covered by an exception. Class rates apply to the numbered or lettered groups or classes of articles that are contained in the territorial rating column in the classification schedule.

RATE, COMBINATION A through rate from point of origin to destination, made up of two or more rates added together.

RATE, COMPELLED A rate between points adjacent to rivers, lakes, and so forth.

RATE CONSTRUCTION The science, method or factors employed in the making of rates.

RATE, DECLARED (VALUATION) A transportation charge based upon the declared value of an article or articles. (See valuation, declared.)

RATE, DISTANCE A rate constructed on a mileage basis, usually local or joint, and applicable to a specified distance only. As the length of the haul increases, the per-ton-mile factor decreases.

RATE, EQUALIZING The rate that results from a voluntary adjustment of rates on a basis that equalizes natural disadvantages of shippers and localities as regards transportation facilities and costs.

RATE FACTORS The component rates which make up a through rate.

RATE MAKING Calculations used to determine charges for handling and clerical—plus any additional expenses.

RATE-MAKING LINES The transportation companies in a geographic area that control the rates established.

RATE, PAPER A published rate that is never assessed because no traffic moves under it.

RATE, POSTAGE-STAMP When a rate is uniform throughout a large territory, it is termed a *postage-stamp rate* because of its similarity to fixed postage charges.

RATE QUOTATION A rate provided by a carrier.

RATE, RELEASED A rate that applies when responsibility for the full value of the freight is not assumed by the carrier.

RATE, RETURNED-SHIPMENT A rate applied to mineral-water carriers; packages, drums, or cylinders used for transporting acids, ammonia, and gas; and to bags and sacks which are returned to the original shipper after their contents have been emptied.

RATE SCALE A table of rates graduated according to distance or zones.

RATE STRUCTURE Is that foundation upon which a series of related rates are based.

RATE TERRITORY The geographic division of the country to establish the jurisdiction for rate making purposes, establishing rate bureaus, or forming associations.

RATE, THROUGH A rate applicable from point of origin to destination.

RATE, VOLUME (VR) In motor-carrier tariffs, a term used to denote rates at quantities heavier than LTL lots (6,000 pounds) and lighter than TL lots (10,000 pounds).

RATE WAR The name given the action when carriers cut rates in an effort to secure tonnage; at the present time not so frequent among rail carriers as water lines.

RATING 1) A class to which an article is assigned; 2) Computation of proper charges for shipment.

RATING, VOLUME The rating established for high-density freight.

REACH TRUCK A form of fork truck with forward mounted load wheels that permit the fork carriage to extend forward for picking up or dropping a load.

REAL TIME A data processing with computations and results so immediately available that the results can be used for decision making immediately. Feedback on the problem is available with seconds—and at most a few hours.

REASONABLE CARE & DILIGENCE See liability, warehouseman's legal.

REASONABLE DISPATCH A transit time concept in claims.

REASONABLENESS (I.C.C.) A requirement under law (common) and by statute that a rate shall not be higher than is necessary to reimburse the carrier for the actual cost of transporting the traffic and allow a fair return.

REBATE That part of the transportation charge, returned by a carrier to a shipper, and now unlawful.

REBILLING Issuing a new waybill at the junction point to which the connecting line has billed the cargo.

RECEIPT A written acknowledgement of payment.

RECEIVE Inbound movement of goods.

RECEIVER Document listing the goods received on a particular shipment—quantity and description.

RECEIVER (OF FREIGHT) One to whom a shipment is consigned; the consignee.

RECEIVER'S CERTIFICATE When a receiver acts for a carrier by acknowledging an indebtedness under court authority to provide funds for equipment, supplies, fuel, and other requirements for the carrier's operation, a receiver's certificate is the term applied to the written acknowledgement.

RECEIVER WITH INTERNAL CYCLONE A vertical cylinder used in materials handling that enables the material to fall into the hopper by air being forced into the base of the cylinder.

RECEIVING PAYMENT (FOREIGN) The manner of receiving payment for goods sold in foreign countries can be divided into three principal methods, (1) Cash in advance, (2) Open Credit, and (3) Payment against Draft, (a) documents deliverable on acceptance of draft (D.A.), and (b) documents deliverable on payment of draft, (D.P.).

RECEIVING TALLY An independent listing of goods on a shipment which is prepared by receiving personnel at the warehouse.

RECHARGE BILL Authorized notice to charge freight or trucking fees to the shipping point.

RECIPROCAL SWITCHING When two rail carriers serve the same point and agree to absorb one another's local switching charges, a reciprocal switching agreement is in effect. Under these circumstances an industry that is located on one railroad and wishes to route its shipment via another railroad may do so without paying extra charges for the switching performed by the rail carrier on whose line the industry is located.

RECIPROCAL TREATY A commercial treaty between two nations, providing mutual advantages.

RECIPROCITY An exchange of rights. In motor transportation it may involve the granting of equal rights to vehicles of several states in which reciprocity agreements are in effect.

RECIPROCITY, CARRIER-SHIPPER A purchasing and carrier selection practice that consists of a carrier purchasing products needed in the company in effective exchange for the manufacturer selecting the carrier for shipments.

RECLAMATION In shipping, a claim made against the seller of goods which prove deficient or defective.

RECONSIGN To change the name of consignee and/or the destination while shipment is still in transit.

RECONSIGNMENT (R/C) The process of changing the consignee while a shipment is en route through a change in the bill of lading is called reconsignment. Reconsignment can only take place before the shipment is delivered to its original destination. A charge is made for reconsignment. The charge varies with the tariff provisions and depends upon the extent of change in destination. Reconsignment can take place only at the request of the owner of the goods. It is not available on LCL shipments. It is not practiced to any significant extent by motor carriers, airplanes, freight forwarders, or water carriers. Normally diversion will not change the name of the consignee while reconsignment will change it. This practice is indispensable to the lumber, perishable goods, and comparable industries. It permits reconsignment to the most advantageous market. Reconsignment is a change in the name of the consignee while en route, as contrasted to diversion which does not change the consignee, but is also made while the shipment is en route.

RECONSIGNING CHARGE Charge for re-billing a shipment enroute to other than original destination.

RECOOP Inspection of damaged goods, repacking, returning good stock to storage and disposing of the bad stock.

RECOOPERING Cooperage repair on wooden containers. It is often used to refer to the repair of all containers and packages used in shipping.

RECOUPER AREA Area set aside in warehouse for recartoning, etc., of damaged products.

RECURRING MANAGEMENT PROBLEMS Each business operation is confronted with a series of management problems of a general class that occur over and over again. While recurring management problems may be of a major or minor nature, it is possible to classify major management problems facing the industrial firm into a relatively few significant classes of problems. One classification of recurring management problems may be on the basis of whether they occur before or after the operations of the firm. Those occurring before the operations of the firm, for example, would be illustrated by location management problems and product determination management problems. It is necessary to determine what will be produced and where it will be produced before operations begin. Operational management problems can be divided into pre-production, in-production, and post-production recurring management problems. An example of a pre-production management problem would be planning the pre-production logistics channel. An example of a production management problem would be determining the optimum equipment for production. A post-production management problem might involve optimizing the post-production channel. On this classification basis, recurring management problems may be rather limited in number.

RED LABEL A label required on shipments of articles of an inflammable character.

REDUCED RATE A rate that has been reduced since some specified time.

REEFER This is a broad term covering refrigeration equipment in general. It may be more specific such as a reefer car, referring to a rail car with refrigeration equipment.

REFERENCE INQUIRY A form used by manufacturers when asking for references regarding the experiences of other manufacturers with foreign firms.

REFINING IN TRANSIT The stopping of shipments of sugar, oil, etc., at a point located between the points of origin and destination to be refined.

REFRIGERATED WAREHOUSE A public warehouse providing temperature control at 0 degrees F for the freezer space, 60 degrees F for the cooler space, and 25 to 60 degrees F in the atmospheric controlled space—where the humidity is held to 50-70 percent.

REFRIGERATION The process of keeping freight in a low temperature state. Usually performed by ice, liquid nitrogen or by mechanical refrigeration.

REFRIGERATION CHARGES The charge made for icing a refrigerator car, in some cases on per 100 pounds basis, and in other instances, per car.

REFRIGERATOR CAR A specially constructed car, insulated and equipped with ice bunkers or baskets, or a cooling system; and usually adapted for the installation of heating units, used primarily for the movement of commodities that need protection from heat or cold.

REFUND The term refund applies in circumstances of an overcharge collected by a carrier for charges billed or paid.

REFUSE BODY A truck body built for the movement of refuse—garbage.

REFUSED FREIGHT Freight which the consignee or owner refuses to accept; freight which, for any reason, cannot be accommodated on the flight of intended departure.

REGIONAL CARRIER Local service carriers that provide air transport services between smaller cities, or between principal cities and smaller cities.

REGISTER A specific storage location in the computer; or a document submitted by the custom officers which permit a vessel to pursue foreign trade. It specifies the major characteristics of the vessel.

REGISTER (OF SHIPS) A list, kept by the collector of customs, containing the names, ownership, and other facts relative to vessels registered in the merchant marine of a country. Three terms are used in the United States to designate the admittance of a self-propelled or sailing vessel to American nationality and privileges: *Registered* refers to vessels in a foreign trade. *Enrolled* refers to vessels in coastal and Great Lakes trade. *Licensed* refers to vessels of weights under 20 tons. All are referred to as *Documented*.

REGISTERED TRADE MARKS A trade mark is known as registered when certain requirements have been set and proper filing made in Washington, D.C.

REGULAR COMMON CARRIER A carrier authorized to serve the public in general, by set rates, over set routes, between given points, hauling general commodities.

REGULAR ROUTE CARRIER A carrier with an operating right that defines specific points on specific routes.

REGULAR ROUTE COMMON CARRIER A carrier offering a service to the public in general over a given route, on schedule, between specific points.

REGULAR TRAIN A train represented on the time-table and may consist of *sections.*

REGULATION The supervision by federal and state regulatory commissions of the affairs of the various transportation agencies.

REHEARING Second hearing. Is the opening of a complaint, case or discussion already concluded.

RE-INSURANCE The transfer of part of the contract of insurance from one insurer to another.

RELATED POINTS OF DESTINATION A group of points the rates to which are made the same as or with relation to rates to other points in the group.

RELATED POINTS (ORIGIN) A number of points the rates from which are made the same as or with relation to rates from other points in the same group.

RELAY In motor carriage it involves a line-haul movement that involves a change of driver and vehicle.

RELEASED RATE A rate based on a limitation of the carrier's liability for loss and damage, and therefore less than a rate applying without such limitation.

RELEASED VALUATION The value of a shipment set by the shipper which establishes the maximum liability of the carrier.

RELEASED VALUE RATES When a shipper declares in writing the value of a product being shipped, a choice of rates is made available. Under a higher rate, unlimited liability is placed on the carrier for the full value of the shipment. Under lower rates, the shipper is given a reduced rate but agrees that a claim in the event of loss and damage would not exceed a given dollar amount of the declared value. Authorization by the ICC must be obtained before the carrier can publish rates based on released value. This is specified in 10730 of the Act. It is usually necessary for a carrier to prove to the ICC that movement of this commodity has been highly susceptible to L & D and that variations in commodity values make claim settlements difficult.

RELIEF CLAIM A claim filed by the freight agent with the auditor of a carrier asking that a particular uncollectible item be taken out of his account.

RELIEF TRACK An extended siding long enough to allow an inferior train to continue running.

REMITTANCE The transfer of funds from one party to another.

REMOTE CONTROL A means of operating a crane from a point outside of the cab.

RENEWAL (OF NOTE) Extension of time or giving a new note for an old one.

RENEWAL STORAGE This is the rebilling on a monthly basis for products stored in the warehouse.

RENEWING A BILL Accepting a new bill of exchange in place of one which has become overdue.

RENTAL CONTRACT A short-term contract for the use of assets, including maintenance and insurance.

REORDER POINT QUANTITY In inventory management, this term is synonymous with the lead time inventory. It is the average quantity required to service production of sales for the time required to order, process and transport the new order.

REPACKING To put in new container.

REPARATION This is a compensation presented to a shipper to atone excess payments by the shipper. Reparations are awarded for discrimination, unreasonableness under RICA Chapter 107, departures for the long and short haul rule, etc. Proceedings may be formal or informal. A refund ordered by the ICC as an award for damages under circumstances when a charge which has been paid as judged to be unlawful is called a reparation payment. Payment in excess of legally applicable charges result in overcharge claims, but if the legally applicable charge is in fact unlawful, a reparations claim rather than an overcharge claim should be filed.

REPARATION CLAIMS A reparation claim is a request for damages by a shipper against a carrier through an action of law or an action before the Interstate Commerce Commission. Reparation payments may be due when the Commission finds that legally published charges were unlawful on past shipments because they violated some provision of the law. A distinction must be made between overcharge claims and reparation claims. If a payment exceeds the legally applicable charge, an overcharge exists. However, if the charges paid are the legally applicable charge, but are found to be unlawful, reparation payments should result.

REPARATION (ORDER) Redress in the form of adjustment or reimbursement on account of an assessed charge proved to the Interstate Commerce Commission to be unjust or unreasonable.

REPLEVIN The action to regain possession of goods which have been wrongfully taken from a party complaining.

REPORT (I.C.C.) An official statement of facts; description, an account of a meeting or a report of the Interstate Commerce Commission, expressive of its findings.

REPOSITORY In shipping, a warehouse or storehouse.

REPRISAL The seizure of ships or property to indemnify for unlawful seizure or detention.

RESERVE BUOYANCY The buoyancy created by all enclosed and watertight space above the waterline.

RESERVED FREIGHT SPACE An agreement between some airlines and shippers permitting them to reserve freight space for certain flights.

RESERVED MATERIAL Products that are still in a distribution center but are earmarked for outbound shipment to a particular customer.

RESERVE INVENTORY Inventory that is being held for future use.

RESHIPMENT The carrier has a responsibility of placing the car on a private siding under an original bill of lading. Any subsequent movement would involve a new contract or reshipment. However, in diversion and reconsignment, the through rate is from the origin through the point of diversion and on to the final destination. Under these circumstances, the diversion or reconsignment charge is not an additional charge.

RE-SHIPPING RATE Almost synonymous with proportional rate and usually applicable to commodities that are stopped in transit for some treatment or manufacturing process, and eventually forwarded to a final destination.

RESPONDENTIA BONDS A bond placed on a vessel by the master for emergency repair operations. Usually performed in a location distant from the owner and involving a lien on the vessel.

RESTORATION In shipping, the placing in effect again of a rate or service after once having been removed, cancelled or suspended.

RESTRAINT OF PRINCES, RULERS OF PEOPLE Under the Hague Rules, the common water carrier is relieved of any liability that results from restraints imposed by rulers of a people.

RESTRAINT OF TRADE Contracts in restraint of trade are those hald to interfere unjustly with competition and therefore illegal. A number of laws have been enacted to prevent illegal restraint of trade, foremost among them the Sherman Anti-Trust Law.

RESTRICTED ARTICLES Articles which are handled only under certain conditions.

RESTRICTIVE ENDORSEMENT An indorsement on a bill of exchange which restricts the right of further transfer of its ownership or which stipulates conditions for dealing with it.

RETARDER YARD A large freight yard where certain tracks are constructed over a hump so that cars can be pushed by a locomotive on to the hump and then released to roll down the incline by gravity. As the cars move downhill, a towerman, by remote control means (a series of mechanical devices known as car retarders and switches) can divert each car to appropriate track so that they can be readily made into a freight train in the proper order to best facilitate their delivery to destination. See hump yard.

RETIRE A BILL To pay a bill at maturity or under discount.

RETROACTIVE When a tariff, or a rule in a tariff, is applied to a date prior to the date of the publication of the tariff or rule, it is normally termed retroactive.

RETROFIT A process of modifying an aircraft after production, or even after some service, to install changes put on later models. For example, many 707-120 turbojet aircraft were retrofitted with turbofan engines, as well as changes in wing leading edges and leading-edge flaps. They were identified as 707-120B turbofans.

RETURNED SHIPMENT RATE A rate applicable to mineral water carriers, packages, drums, or cylinders used in the transportation of acids, ammonia and gas, also bags and sacks which are returned to the original shipper after being emptied of their contents.

RETURN ON ASSETS A profitability measure of asset investment in a firm; basically, net profit divided by assets; often referred to as ROA.

RETURN ON EQUITY A profitability measure of funds invested in the firm by stockholders; net profit divided by common stock, paid in capital and retained earnings.

RETURN ON INVESTMENT Usually the same as return on assets (ROI).

RETURNS Merchandise sent back to the warehouse.

REVENUE The income of a state; taxes and duties received.

REVENUE CARS LOADED In rail transportation, the number of cars loaded with revenue paying freight.

REVENUE CUTTER A small government vessel used in collecting taxes and preventing smuggling.

REVENUE FREIGHT A local or interline shipment from which earnings accrue to the carrier upon the basis of tariff rate.

REVENUE FREIGHT CARRIED Shipments of revenue freight originated on the line, or received from connecting carrier.

REVENUE FREIGHT ORIGINATED Shipments not identified as having had previous line-haul transportation by other rail carriers, including import traffic and traffic from outlying possessions of the United States received from water carriers at the port of entry, finished products from transit points, and shipments rerouted from concentration points.

REVENUE FREIGHT RECEIVED FROM CONNECTING CARRIERS Shipment received directly or indirectly from connecting line-haul rail carriers.

REVENUE FREIGHT TERMINATED Shipments delivered directly or indirectly to consignees, not identified as subject to further rail line-haul transportation, and including export traffic and traffic destined to outlying possessions of the United States delivered to water carriers at the port of clearance, and products delivered at transit points for finishing processes.

REVENUE LOAD A load placed on a vehicle for which freight charges are assessed is given the term revenue load. It may apply to any mode.

REVENUE-PASSENGER MILE (RPM) One paying revenue passenger traveling one mile; corresponding measure to ton-mile.

REVENUE TO COST RATIO The variable cost of a move divided by the revenue the carrier receives for moving it. In the context of market dominance, etc., the revenue is divided by variable cost to arrive at a percent figure that is a key to the analysis.

REVENUE TO FOLLOW A statement indicating that a shipment has been billed without the revenue being specified in order to speed up the movement. The charges to be specified at the time of receiving the bill of lading.

REVENUE TON-MILE Two thousand pound movement of revenue freight for a distance of one mile.

REVENUE WAYBILL A waybill showing the amount of charges due on a shipment.

REVENUE YIELD A carrier management term for the revenue generated by each rail car, trailer or airplane seat in a given period.

REVERSE DISTRIBUTION Product recall.

REVISED INTERSTATE COMMERCE ACT (RICA) The Interstate Commerce Act was recodified in 1978 into its current form; it is now referred to as the Revised Interstate Commerce Act. Old section numbers are no longer appropriate to use in citations; however, several sections, such as section 4 and section 22, are still heard in conversation.

REVISION The corrections made on freight bills following an audit.

REWAREHOUSING The re-arrangement of goods from one storage area to another.

RHUMB LINE Refers to a straight course followed by a vessel. It may not be a straight line of sight course, but a straight line on a Mercator chart which cuts each meridian at the same angle. On a sphere, it is a straight line.

RIDER (INSURANCE) Insurance coverage on goods that extends from when they are in the factory or warehouse to when they are delivered from a transportation shipment.

RIDE SHOT GUN The assistant driver, riding on the right of the cab, not driving.

RIG Any combination of truck and trailers or semitrailers.

RIGHTING LEVER The distance between those vertical lines which would pass through the center of gravity and the center of buoyancy. It is said that when the vertical line of the center of buoyancy meets the central line of the ship above the center of gravity, the lever is a righting one. If it is below, it is an upsetting one.

RIGHTING MOVEMENT An action to right a listing vessel.

RIGHT OF EMINENT DOMAIN The right of the sovereign power to appropriate property for public use.

RISER Water pipe that supplies water to a section of the sprinkler system.

RISK The probability of loss.

R&L Rail and lake.

RL&R Rail, lake and rail.

R&O Rail and ocean.

ROAD-BED The foundation on which the track of a railroad is placed.

ROAD HOG One who takes more than his share of the road.

ROADRAILER Innovation in late 1970's; piggyback trailer that has wheels for movement on rails and highway; transfer from one to the other takes place in minutes; does not require separate rail car.

ROADSTEAD A tract of water, not necessarily enclosed in any way, but usually near the shore line, where ships at anchor may ride with protection from the heavy seas afforded by the headland.

ROBINSON-PATMAN ACT An act that prohibits product sales in discriminatory ways (pricing, availability, etc.)

ROCK IT The process of freeing a vehicle from mud or snow by forward and reverse action.

ROLL The undulation of the sea that oscillates the vessel from one side to the other.

ROLL AND REST The process of stopping to rest at regular intervals by a long-haul driver.

ROLLER TRAILER A trailer with rollers on the floor. Product will slide easily on the rollers to aid in loading or unloading.

ROLLING STOCK The freight and passenger cars owned by a rail carrier, not including motive power equipment; also buses, trucks and trailers owned by motor carriers.

ROLLTOP A trailer with a sliding roof to facilitate crane loading.

ROOT MODULES In data processing, it is a technique for solving very comples problems that cannot be algebraically resolved.

ROSE BOX A strainer located at the base of the suction pipe of a bilge pump.

ROTARY, SEAL AIR LOCK OR FEEDER A multiple blade rotor in a casing that delivers materials into hoppers continuously without permitting the passage of gas.

ROTARY VAN FEEDER OR STAR VALVE Three or more rotary vans in a housing that permits materials to be discharged from a hopper at a controlled rate. It is not suitable for use as a gas seal.

ROTATING FORKS Forklift attachments.

ROTATING HEAD A clamp attachment or fork on a lifting carriage of the fork truck that permits the rotation of the load.

ROUGH MATERIAL RATES AND RATIO Shipments of rough lumber or unfinished article of forest products, shipped into a mill point at a local rate, with the privilege of reshipment of finished products from mill point via the inbound carrier, provided the outbound weight is a specified percentage of the inbound weight of the rough material, on basis of the local rate on the finished product from the mill point. The inbound charges are then reduced to basis of the rough material rate, which averages approximately 50% of the local rate assessed.

ROUNDHOUSE A building, usually semicircular, at a terminal, terminus, or division point into which locomotives are sent at the end of a *run* for cleaning and overhauling.

ROUND TRIP A journey that starts and ends at the same point. In origin and destination statistics it involves going and returning by the same route and the same class of service.

ROUTE (RTE.) The combination of carriers transporting a shipment, and the points through which they travel.

ROUTE CLASSIFICATION OF CARRIERS Transportation carriers are classified by the character of the routes they service in the following manner: (1) regular routes scheduled service; (2) regular route non-schedule service; (3) irregular route radial service; (4) irregular route non-radial service; and (5) local cartage service.

ROUTINE A set of computer instructions devised to perform an algorithm.

ROUTING The process of determining how a shipment will move between an origin and destination is referred to as routing. This requires the designation of the carrier, the route of the carrier, and directly or in-directly, the time enroute. The party holding title to the goods enroute should retain the right to route to protect his interests. Specific right routing is published either in a rate tariff or a routing tariff that might be referred to by the rate tariff. Commodity rates are more restrictive on the routing options than are class rates. If the shipper shows a rate lower than the rate applicable on the route specified, it is the legal obligation of the railroad agent to so inform the shipper and ask for instructions as to routing. According to Section 10763 of the Interstate Commerce Act, the shipper may prescribe the rail route. Routing by motor carrier is different since RICA does not confer on the shipper the right to route shipment when two or more motor carriers are required. However, most reliable motor carriers respect the wishes of the shipper. When the initial motor carriers select a joint motor carrier, it must protect the shipper by selecting one with the lowest through charges.

R&T Rail and truck.

RUDDER A contrivance hung vertically on the after side of the sternpost that serves as hinges for lateral motion of the vessel. The stock of the rudder enters the hull through the rudder port. The rudder is swung by a rudder head. The orders to the quartermaster are given in terms of the rudder rather than the helm by international agreement.

RUDDER CHAINS Chains used to control the rudder in the case of accident. They are secured to the horn of the rudder and lead to each quarter.

RULE 40 A rule in the Consolidated Freight Classification that specifies container construction requirements.

RULE 41 A rule in the Consolidated Freight Classification that establishes policy on bursting strength, dimensions, and the requirements for solid and corrugated fiberboard cartons and fiber drums.

RULE MAKING PROCEEDING A process in which a regulatory agency develops and implements administrative regulations.

RULES OF PRACTICE (I.C.C.) Rules governing the procedure to follow by parties to proceedings before the Commission. Parties to proceedings are complainants, defendants, interveners, protestants, respondents, applicants and petitioners, according to the nature of the proceeding and their relation thereto. Proceedings before the Commission consist of complaints, general investigations, investigation and suspension cases, valuation and finance cases. Found in 49 CFR 1100.

RUNNING DAYS Every day, including Sundays and holidays.

RUNNING DOWN OR COLLISION CLAUSE An agreement whereby if a vessel is to blame for a collision with another vessel, the underwriters pay for three-fourths of the damage to the other vessel, up to three-fourths of the value of the insured vessel. Provided for under the Institute Time Clauses.

RUNNING TRACK A track reserved for traffic movement through a yard.

RUN-THROUGH TRAIN A train that operates over two more railroads without change of engines and caboose.

RUNWAY DROP SECTION Facilities for raising or lowering the runway track so they can line up with other levels.

R&W Rail and water.

—S—

SADDLE TANK The fuel storage area that is located on the tractor.

SAFE BERTH, SAFE PORT A berth is safe for a vessel if it can be reached. To be safe while at berth, the vessel should not touch the bottom at low tide.

SAFETY ANGLE That stage in the roll of a vessel beyond which the righting power of the vessel is in danger.

SAFETY APPLIANCE ACT An act of Congress (1893) requiring the railroads to provide safety devices, such as air brakes, couplers, hand guard rails, and so forth, for their equipment.

SAFETY STOCK The averae amount of stock on hand when the new order is received. This will vary with the no-stock-out safety assurance level established. The safety stock would be greater for a 90 per cent assurance safety stock requirement than for an 80 per cent. The safety stock level depends on the deviations in: (1) delivery time for the carrier, (2) order fulfillment time required for the vendor, and (3) sales or production requirements which are serviced by the storage operation. Safety stock costs, which are the costs of retaining stock to meet deviations of an unpredictable nature, may be added to the other direct and hidden logistics costs in computing an optimum economic logistics quantity (ELQ) in logistics channel planning. Safety stock would be classed as a constant cost, since it does not vary per cwt. with changes in the volume of shipment.

SAGGED When a vessel has settled structurally amidship, it is said to have sagged.

SAID TO WEIGH According to the Hague Rules, the water carrier should issue bills of lading which show the weight or the quantity of the shipment as provided by the shipper. The carrier need not show a quantity or weight which he believes to be incorrect.

SAILING Within the meaning of a charter party, a stipulation that the vessel has her cargo on board and is ready to proceed at once on the voyage.

SAILING DAY The specified time that water carriers will receive cargo for a certain vessel and destination.

SAILING TRIM A vessel loaded to the proper draft fore and aft.

SALE/LEASEBACK CONTRACT A company sells some or all of its assets to a firm and leases some or all of them back under a direct lease; usually done by a company needing cash.

SALE AND LEASEBACK A common terminal financing method in the motor carrier industry in which the firm constructs the facility, sells it to recapture the initial cash outlays, then leases it for a long term period.

SALINITY The amount of salt in the sea water. Usually it ranges from 33 to 37 parts salt in 1,000 parts water. A salinometer is a hydrometer that measures the salinity of boiler water. The normal content of seawater in parts per 1,ppp is as follows: Sodium Chloride 27.213; Magnesium Chloride 3.807; Magnesium Sulphate 1,658; Calcium Sulphate 1,280; Potassium Sulphate 0.863; Calcium Carbonate & Residue 0.123; and Magnesium Bromide 0.076.

SALTING (IN TRANSIT) A service correlative with the services of refrigeration and ventilation, and imperative for the preservation and protection of certain commodities.

SALTY A Great Lakes area term for an ocean ship.

SALVAGE An award allowed those who voluntarily rescue ships, passengers, crew, or cargo from loss and peril; also, the goods or vessel saved.

SALVOR One who voluntarily engages in rescue at sea.

SAME AS A term meaning that the classified ratings for such articles are identical.

SAMPLE A small portion of merchandise taken as a specimen of quality.

SANITATION The formulation and application of measures designed to maintain clean and healthy surroundings.

SANITATION LINE An 18' wide, painted line completed around the inside warehousewalls so that any signs of rodents can be easily seen and to mark the area so that no merchandise will be stored there. Traps are placed in this area.

SANS RECOURS Without recourse.

SATELLITE TERMINAL The use of a separate ticketing and loading facility by one or more airlines at a large airport complex. Sometimes it is called a satellite terminal.

SCALE NUMBER (MERCHANDISE TRAFFIC REPORT) A number arrived at by deducting the smaller belt number from the larger belt number, the smaller tier number from the larger tier number named in the *Equi-Graphic Rate Blocks* and adding to the larger difference-tier or belt one-half the smaller (counting any fraction as the next whole number). The approximate mileage can then be obtained by multiplying the *Scale Number* by 60 which is the mileage of each block.

Block		Difference		Scale No.	Approximate Mileage
Belt	Tier	Belt	Tier		
21	55				
22	43	1	12	12 (12 plus ½ of 1) x 60	780

SCALES OF RATES Numerous rates adjusted with relation to each other.

SCALE TICKET Axle weights of a vehicle on a form.

SCANTLINGS The dimensions of the various parts of the ship's structure. It involves frames, stringers, plating, girders, etc. Rules concerning these dimensions are printed by the American Bureau of Shipping.

SCEND OF THE SEA The lifting of a vessel to the leeward as a result of the waves.

SCHEDULE (1) Designated time consumed or which is supposed to be required (and usually presented in tabular form) for a movement between two points. (2) The term also applies to a tariff or other publication containing a list of prices for services rendered or other kinds of specific information. (3) In a time-table, the schedule is that part prescribing the class, direction, number and movement of a regular train.

SCHEDULE, COMPARATIVE-RATE A table of rates that shows the differences, if any, in charges via two or more routes or via two or more of the several forms of carriage, such as rail, water, express, and parcel post.

SCHEDULES AIR TAXI A third level air carrier that offers passenger service from outlying suburbs and minor airports to the large municipal airports. These are also called nonscheduled carriers, though some nonscheduled carriers also carry cargo. Supplemental air carriers were granted restricted operating certificates under a 1961 amendment to the Federal Aviation Act.

SCHEDULED SERVICE A transportation service over the carrier's certificated routes on scheduled flights.

SCOOP CAR A car, constructed for use in railway service, having a scoop which is pushed along on top of the track, for removing snow, rock, or earth slides.

SCORE To cut or indent a piece of flat material to facilitate bending, creasing, tearing, or folding.

SCORING MACHINE A machine to make a cut or indentation to facilitate folding, creasing, etc.

SCOW A light draft vessel shaped like a box used in local transportation of bulk shipments—like coal, sand, gravel, etc.

SCRATCHED Non-available items that are taken off a customer order with the intent that they be reordered at a later date.

SCRIPT A term applied to bridge and tunnel toll tickets.

SCRIPT SHEET A document carried by the truck driver showing the details of the shipment on the truck. It is a manifest.

SCUPPERS The vessel drains running from the waterways of the weather deck and spar.

SCUTTLEBUT STORY A rumor.

SEADOCK Liquid petroleum loading or unloading facility at sea which very large ships can serve; product is then shipped via pipeline to and from dock on land.

SEA KINDLY A general condition of good trim of a vessel that results in comfortable movement.

SEAL A device used for locking a freight-car or motor-vehicle door. An unbroken seal serves as evidence that the door fastening has not been tampered with since the time of applying the seal.

SEAL LOG Document used to record seal numbers.

SEAL RECORD A record of the number, condition and marks of identification of seals made at various times and places in connection with movement of car between points of origin and destination.

SEALS, CONTINUOUS Car seals successively applied, without a check of the freight being made at the time they are applied. This means that when cars are stopped in transit to unload part of the freight, the seal is removed; when part of the contents have been unloaded, a new seal is applied with no check of the remaining contents of the cars.

SEALS, LOADING Seals applied to a freight-car or motor-vehicle door when the freight is checked from the freight-house platform to the car or in transit.

SEALS WITH EXCEPTIONS Seals that do not agree (either showing a different number or signs of having been tampered with), with record previously taken or reported by someone else.

SEA ROOM In water transportation, offshore a good, safe distance from shoals.

SEASONAL RATE A rate instituted for specified articles or commodities and effective only certain periods of the year.

SEASONAL TARIFF A tariff containing seasonal rates.

SEAWAY Sea motion when clear of the shoal water.

SEAWORTHY A vessel properly constructed to go into service. It is properly designed, equipped, manned and constructed.

SECOND, THIRD, AND OTHER MAIN TRACKS Main tracks laid parallel to the first main track.

SECOND VIA Copy of a bill of exchange forwarded by different ship, route or mail, from the first or *principal bill.*

SECTIONAL TARIFF A unique tariff which presents several different rates between the same pairs of points by putting them in different sections of the tariff. The provisions for different application of the sections are in the tariff.

SECTION-22 RATES, NOW SECTION 10721 (RICA) Reduced rates for shipments made by federal, state, and local government agencies were originally referred to as Section-22 rates. These rates may be established on short notice—30 days. The federal government makes extensive use of these rates for the movement of military traffic.

SECURE FOR SEA The process of preparing for sea movement by lashing all movable objects, placing grips on the boats, tying down the furniture, etc.

SELF UNLOADER A ship capable of unloading its own cargo rather than rely upon dockside assistance; usually found on coal, grain and other bulk ships.

SECURITY AREA Part of a warehouse protected by fence, electric eye, etc.

SEEL The action of the vessel to roll in a seaway.

SELF INSURANCE The process of providing for the assumption of risk under some self organized provisional insurance fund, rather than taking outside insurance coverage.

SEMI A semitrailer, although it usually means both the trailer and tractor.

SEMI CONTAINERSHIP Vertical cells to accommodate containers on a cargo ship.

SEMITRAILER A freight-carrying vehicle without its own motor power, attached to a tractor by means of a *fifth wheel*; sometimes called a *box.*

SEPARATION CLOTHS Fabric used to ward off moisture in certain cargo, such as sugar. Sheets of the cloth are spread over and under the cargo.

SERIES (OR SERIAL) NUMBER A number used principally by tariff publishing agents and transportation companies to identify a tariff or other publication. For example, if the first issue of a tariff is designated Series Number *100*, the first reissue would be called *100A.*

SET The direction of the current. It also refers to the direction the vessel moves as a result of the tide, wind, etc. The drift is the extent of influence of the current on the vessel. Drift is often confused with set.

SET IT DOWN Slang. To stop quickly.

SET-OFF A claim which one party has against another who has a claim against him; a counter claim.

SET-UP (S.U.) When articles are shipped ready for use, as contrasted to being knocked down, it is referred to as a set-up shipment. It is a completely assembled shipment.

SET-UP COSTS The variable costs involved in a machine set-up operation to produce for an order, or to change the rate of production to meet an order. It is a manufacturer's cost, which should be included in purchase (sales) price. It is an added production adjustment cost.

SHAFT ALLEY The extended alley in which the shaft operates.

SHAG A small city trailer.

SHAKE THE LIGHTS Blinking the headlights as a warning signal.

SHAPING A COURSE In water transportation, the process of calculating a course by taking it from the chart with parallel rulers, making allowance for deviation and presenting the course to the quartermaster for steering.

SHARED DISTRIBUTION A new concept for two or more firms cooperatively utilizing transportation, warehousing, etc.

SHEEP HERDER A slang phrase meaning a truck driver of questionable ability.

SHEER The upward curve of the deck. The term also applies to a change in the course of the ship due to shoaling or from another vessel in close proximity which displaces the water. A very sharp action of this form is called a rank sheer.

SHEER STRAKE The upper line of plates and/or planking.

SHELF LIFE The length of time a product can remain in storage or available for sale before it is necessary or desirable to remove it for quality reasons.

SHELL PLATING The outside skin of a steel or iron vessel.

SHERMAN ANTITRUST ACT Legislation that prohibits practices that will cause or tend to cause monopolistic situations.

SHIFTING BEAM This refers to a portable support for the tach covers.

SHIFTING BOARDS Temporary partitions placed in the hold of a ship to prevent bulk cargo from shifting.

SHIP In proper terminology, this term should apply only to a vessel that is square rigged on all masts from three up. However, it is used to apply to all vessels, When sea water comes aboard, it is said to be shipped. Also, anything put in place is said to be shipped.

SHIPBOARD, ON On a vessel, or within it.

SHIP BROKER An individual who makes contracts for the employment of vessels; or one who negotiates the purchase and sale of ships.

SHIPCHANDLER A person who deals in cordage, sail cloth, and other supplies for ships.

SHIP DEMURRAGE A charge for a delay to a steamer beyond a stipulated period.

SHIPMENT A single consignment of one or more pieces from one consignor at one time at one origin address receipted for in one lot and moving on airbill (or waybill) to one consignee at one destination address.

SHIPOWNERS The person or company under which a vessel is officially registered is the owner.

SHIPPED Goods which have undergone transportation.

SHIPPER Slang for the bill of lading. Also the consignor.

SHIPPER'S ASSOCIATION A non-profit cooperative that serves to consolidate shipments for member firms.

SHIPPER'S CERTIFICATE A form filled out by the shipper and presented to the outbound carrier at the transit point, along with instructions and the inbound carrier's freight bill, requesting reshipping privilege and transit rate on a commodity previously brought into the transit point.

SHIPPER'S EXPORT DECLARATION The declaration of the merchandise and its value for purposes of shipment to a foreign country, or to non-contiguous territories of the United States involves making out of the Shipper's Export Declaration. This is filed with the United States Collector of Customs, and a copy is left with the port or border point of exit. This is required on all shipments, whether they are foreign or domestic, except for some shipments which only move in transit through the United States from one country to another.

SHIPPER'S INTEREST INSURANCE Amount for which the shipment is insured, as declared in appropriate box on the Air Waybill. In no event can such value exceed actual value of the property at destination plus 10%.

SHIPPER'S LOAD AND COUNT (SL&C) OR SHIPPER'S LOAD AND TALLY (SL&T) A notation made on a bill of lading that the loading and counting was performed by the shipper without the carrier's supervision or verification, is referred to as the shipper's load and count.

SHIPPER'S ORDERS The official document which authorizes that a shipment travelling under an order bill of lading is released for pickup.

SHIPPER'S ROUTING The directions concerning the carrier or carriers that will perform the transportation operation.

SHIPPING A collective term for a number of ships or vessels; also the act of loading, unloading and transporting goods.

SHIPPING ACT An act of Congress (1916) which created the United States Shipping Board for the purpose of developing water transportation, operating the merchant ships owned by the government, and regulating the water carriers engaged in commerce under the United States flag.

SHIPPING ARTICLES The contract which is entered into by the officers and crew of the ship. The contract specifies the voyage, wages, etc. The articles are a contract between the master and crew.

SHIPPING CLERK One having charge of the packing and forwarding of goods.

SHIPPING COMMISSIONER An officer, appointed to a port of entry by the circuit court having jurisdiction over it, whose duties are to supervise seamen's contracts and enforce laws made for their protection and relief.

SHIPPING DAY A term used by carriers to specify the time they will accept freight for certain points.

SHIPPING ERROR Shipment of wrong product, quantity or to wrong destination.

SHIPPING INSTRUCTIONS In general usage, the instructions given the transportation company by the shipper relative to the movement of his goods. Freight forwarders sometimes provide shippers with a shipping instruction form, which is filled out and accompanies bill of lading. It contains instructions as to the name of consignee, class of steamer, kind of insurance, and any special information as may be required for the proper and expeditious handling of the shipment.

SHIPPING LAWS The laws of shipping related to vessels, their construction, ownership, inspection, registration, nationality, tonnage — in fact covering everything that has to do with the rights and duties of those engaged in shipping, as well as the contracts and general movement of merchandise.

SHIPPING ORDER (SO) Usually the triplicate copy of the bill of lading containing instructions from the shipper to the carrier for forwarding of goods.

SHIPPING POUND The gross weight of a package of silk, including the spool, bobbin, warp beam or cone on which it is wound.

SHIPPING PERMIT When the exporter of goods arranges for space, the steamship company issues a shipping permit to either the shipper or its agent. This document provides instructions to the receiving clerk at the pier concerning the quantity and character of the shipment. It is a common practice for the dock receipt to be attached with the shipping permit for signatures by the receiving clerk when the goods are delivered to the dock. When several shipments are made by truck, it is a common practice to provide a memorandum receipt to the truckmen. When the shipment is complete and all deliveries have been made, the memorandum receipts are exchanged for a dock receipt.

SHIPPING SUBSIDIES Financial aid to shipping by public grant. The terms *bounty* and *subvention* may be employed in the same sense.

SHIP'S (SHIPPING) ARTICLES The official written agreement between master and crew, specifying such matters as the voyage, name and position of each crew member, wages, time of service, and provisions agreed upon.

SHIP'S BILL The copy of the vessel's bill of lading retained by the ship's master.

SHIP'S BUSINESS The standard paperwork of the ship. This includes records, surveys and all documents.

SHIP'S DOCUMENT Papers issued by a water carrier in its dealings with government authorities and in the operation of its vessels. Among these are the shipping permit, shipper's export declaration, consular invoice, certificate of origin, non-dumping certificate, exporters' invoice, and ocean bill of lading.

SHIP'S HUSBAND The owner of a vessel, or an agent who acts for him in obtaining cargo and attending to whatever is essential to the due prosecution of the voyage.

SHIP'S MANIFEST A statement listing all the consignments on board a vessel, together with the quantity, marks, and destination of each. A copy of the manifest must be filed with the collector of the port before a vessel clears or enters. This copy, together with individual manifests filed by shippers, becomes the basis of the government's official foreign-trade statistics and, in the case of imports, serves as a check upon import duties. One or more copies are carried with the vessel to serve as means of cargo identification in case of search or detention. A ship's manifest is also used as a basis for freight accounting in the same way that a railroad waybill underlies railroad-freight accounts.

SHIP'S MASTER The commander of a merchant vessel. He has complete control of navigation and over all on board and represents the owners on a voyage and in foreign ports. He has authority to bind the ship by contracts for necessary supplies and repairs and may even pledge the cargo, if necessary.

SHIP'S OPTION The choice of a vessel to accept freight by weight or measurement tons.

SHIP'S PAPERS Documents which a merchant ship is required to carry, consisting of (1) register; (2) log book; (3) charter party, if ship is under charter; (4) muster roll; (5) ship's articles; (6) bill of health; (7) bills of lading, or duplicate receipts of cargo from master to shipper; (8) manifest, or general statement of cargo; (9) invoices, or statements of costs of goods; (10) clearnance, or permission from port authorities to sail; (11) certificate of inspection; (12) passenger list, if passengers are carried; (13) bill of sale, if ship has been sold by citizens of one country to those of another, together with consular certificate; (14) officers' licenses; and (15) license to carry on a port trade. Sometimes the ship's register is replaced or accompanied by a sea letter, issued by the local authorities of the port of departure; a passport, issued by the sovereign authority; and/or a certificate of enrollment, if the ship is employed in the United States coastal trade.

SHIPSIDE Alongside a vessel.

SHIP'S TACKLE All blocks, rigging, and other working gear utilized on a ship to load or unload cargo.

SHOO-FLY A temporary track constructed around a tunnel, bridge, or washout for purpose of detouring traffic during course of performing repairs and renewals to tracks, bridges and tunnels. This reduces delays to freight and passenger trains while the railroad is being repaired.

SHORE To support. To set blocking under an overloaded deck to shore it up. Also refers to a coastline or land near a body of water.

SHORTAGE A deficiency in the quantity of goods shipped; also, that part of a shipment that remains undelivered.

SHORT CAUSE ACTION An action to provide prompt trial for cases in chancery, which includes admiralty, providing documentary evidence is provided. There is no appeal on the decision. This is an action by England and others to save time.

SHORTENED PROCEDURE A procedure inaugurated by the Interstate Commerce Commission with a view towards simplifying, shortening and making less expensive complaints filed with it. Briefly, this procedure, upon consent of all parties to formal complaints, permits the presentation of evidence and argument by sworn statements of fact and dispenses with oral hearings. The case is assigned to an examiner for preparation of a proposed report to be served upon the parties and thereafter the procedure is the same as proceedings in which oral hearing is had.

SHORT EXCHANGE Payable on sight, demand, or within ten days.

SHORT FORM BILL OF LADING A deviation from the regular straight bill of lading which only refers to the contract terms but fails to include them.

SHORT-HAULING A term applied when a railroad accepts a shipment of goods to be hauled for a short distance over its own line and then transfers it to another, to be hauled to a point which the initial carrier also services. According to Section 10726 of the Interstate Commerce Act, "no common carrier may be compelled to short-haul itself;" a carrier may refuse such a shipment if, by accepting the short haul, it would lose business which it otherwise might have hauled to its ultimate destination by a noncircuitous route and without causing an extra freight rate to be charged the shipper.

SHORT LINE That carrier or combination of carriers having shortest mileage between two points.

SHORT NOTICE The process of filing a tariff in less than the required thirty days under approval of the Interstate Commerce Commission.

SHORT OF DESTINATION Before reaching final destination.

SHORT TON 2,000 lbs.

SHOTGUN CHANNEL The shotgun channel is the single warehouse channel, or single node channel. Under the shotgun channel system, goods flow from the manufacturing plant directly to a wholesaler or warehouse which services the retail facilities. With the exception of direct shipments from the manufacturing plant to the retailer, this represents the most simplified form of a post-production channel. (See Single Warehouse Channels)

SHOW-CAUSE ORDER A directive to respondents issued by a regulatory authority, such as the Civil Aeronautics Board, requiring the respondent to show cause why the Board should not implement its findings.

SHOVELING Slang reference to hasty loading or unloading of freight.

SHREVEPORT CASE A case decided by the United States Supreme Court in which it held that the Interstate Commerce Commission had the power to decide that intrastate rates might not be used for any undue or unreasonable or unjust discrimination against interstate traffic moving under like conditions.

SHRINKAGE Reduction in bulk of measurement. Natural shrinkage is the ordinary loss of weight of livestock, or reduction in weight because of evaporation of liquids, and reduction in bulk within the tariff allowance on grain and seeds.

SHRINK WRAPPING A packaging process that releases the strains in a plastic film by raising the temperature of the film. The package is wrapped while the film is still hot. As it cools, it shrinks and more closely fits the content of the package.

SHROUD A waterproofing process by means of covering the top and sides, while permitting air to circulate from the bottom.

SHUNTING (CARS) Switching, moving, or turning a car from the mainline to a side track.

SICK HORSE Slang—a tractor in poor mechanical condition.

SIDE TRACK (SIDING) A short track running parallel with another track, usually the main line, and connecting with it at both ends. An assigned siding is a side or team track owned by a carrier and assigned to one or more industrial concerns for the purpose of loading or unloading.

SIDE-TRACK AGREEMENT When a rail carrier and a shipper or receiver complete a contract covering the mutual responsibilities for the use and operation of a rail siding, it is referred to as a side-track agreement.

SIDING A track auxiliary to the main track for meeting or passing trains, or a track for industrial purposes.

SIGHT The time when a bill is presented to the drawee.

SIGHT DRAFT One payable at sight, i.e., when presented.

SIGHT ENTRY A procedure that must be put through to release goods from Customs, occasioned by the use of incorrect invoice form, and particularly applicable to traffic into Canada.

SIGNATURE SERVICE A system for safeguarding a shipment by having each person who passes on a shipment to the next carrier receive a signature of transfer.

SIGNED UNDER PROTEST The master of a vessel may sign bills of lading under protest if the charters object to the insertion of a certain clause in the bill. This forbids his signature being placed in evidence.

SILICA GEL A drying agent, or a desiccant, commonly placed inside containers to prevent moisture drainage. It is a colloidal silica possessing fine pores and is highly absorbent.

SILK SCREEN PROCESS A process for decorating containers by using a silk-screen stencil rather than metal plates. It is applicable to any shaped container.

SIMPSON'S RULES Rules used to find the areas of figures such as a parabola bounded by a curve on one side and a straight line on the other side.

SIMULATION One of the most powerful planning tools available to management is simulation. It consists of representing an operational procedure on the basis of its cost. The simulation of an operation is a model run-through of the operation as represented by cost and revenue figures. Simulation could take an infinite number of forms. It may be better understood in football. Preparation for a game frequently takes the form of one practice team simulating the plays of the coming opponent to help prepare the defense for the specific plays.

SINE DIE Without a day appointed.

SINGLE-CITY WAREHOUSE A firm operating a warehouse in one city.

SINGLE CONSIGNMENT WAYBILL A waybill involving only one shipment.

SINGLE PLANE SERVICE A transport service from origin to destination without need for changing planes, even though several stops may be required.

SINGLE-STORY WAREHOUSE A warehouse with one major floor level on which goods can be stored.

SINGLE TRACK A main track upon which trains are operated in both directions.

SINGLE WAREHOUSE CHANNELS In the single warehouse channel, the manufacturer would transport directly to a single warehouse in the post-production channel, and each warehouse would service only the retail requirements within the area. The single warehouse channel is often referred to as the *shotgun* channel and involves a direct *shot* of the goods from the plant to the wholesaler who then services the retail need without the involvement of a more complex echelon system.

SINKING FUND A fund set apart from revenue to pay a government or corporation debt.

SISTER SHIP CLAUSE A clause that specifies that if an insured vessel collides with another, or receives salvage services by another which belongs wholly or in part to the same owner, or are under the same management, the injured will have the same rights under the policy as they would have were the vessel entirely the property of parties with no interest in the vessel involved.

SIX BANGER Slang. A six cylinder engine.

SIXTEENTH SECTION ORDER An old term for an order issued by the Interstate Commerce Commission in pursuance of Section 16 of the Interstate Commerce Act; now Chapter 11, RICA.

SIXTH-FREEDOM TRAFFIC Air service that originates in one foreign country, stops in the home country of the airline, and then terminates in a third country. The stop in the home country may or may not involve a stop over for the passengers or a change of planes. The so-called freedoms involve rights of an airline relative to flying over, stopping off, picking up and dropping off traffic in other countries.

SKID Set of legs or planks used alone or in combination with wheels and platform to elevate and to transport articles. Also a slang for pallet.

SKINNIE AXLE Slang for a single axle trailer.

SKINS Tires.

S.L.&C. This refers to the shipper's load and count.

SLEEPER A tractor having sleeping compartments.

SLIDING FIFTH WHEEL A fifth wheel that can be moved forward or backward on the tractor to obtain the desired distribution of weight between the trailer axles and the tractor.

SLIDING TANDEM A two axle arrangement that can be moved forward and backward on the trailer body to provide the optimum weight distribution.

SLING A net of rope or chain in which goods are hoisted from ship to dock and vice versa.

SLIP A waterspace between two piers or wharves, or the slot in a dock in which a vessel lies.

SLIP OF THE WHEEL The percentage of distance lost through the mobility of water for a vessel. To get the slip, determine the distance run by the engines (or the pitch) times the minutes run, and divide by 6080 feet.

SLIP SHEET Piece of cardboard used to handle unitized loads with a push/pull attachment.

SLITTER A machine used to cut roll stock according to desired directions.

S.L.&T. This refers to the shipper's load and tally.

SMALL SHIPMENTS A relative term for shipments that are often mentioned in a negative sense as being close to marginal or unprofitable for carriers due to small weight and low freight charges.

SMOKE HIM Slang phrase for passing another vehicle.

SMOKER A term applied to a tractor emitting too much gas fumes.

SMOKESTACK The vertical exhaust tube on the side of the tractor cab.

SMOKE VENTS Vents in the roof of a building allowing smoke to leave the building during a fire.

SMOOTHING A procedure for evening out data that inevitably is variable. The use of averaging and multiple exponents helps accomplish this.

SMUGGLER One who avoids the payment of duties by secretly bringing (importing) goods into a country; also a name given a vessel engaged in *smuggling.*

SMUGGLING Bringing goods into a country without paying duties.

SNOW PLOW A work equipment unit moved by, but not attached to, locomotive to clear away snow from the right of way.

SNUB NOSE A cab over tractor.

SOFTWARE The programs and routines used in computer processing. It may include compilers, sub-routines, general purpose utility programs, etc.

SOLA In case that only one copy of a bill of exchange is in circulation.

SOLICITUDE Given to avoid a fine by promising to produce shipping documents that have missed carrying steamer, within thirty days.

SORT The taking of random data sampling and arraying them in an increasing or decreasing sequence.

SORTING TRACKS (YARD) A system of yard tracks where cars are classified in greater detail after having passed through classification tracks.

SOUNDINGS A vessel is said to be on or off soundings, depending on whether the bottom can be reached by deep-sea lead. The 100 fathom curve is the dividing line depth.

SPACE In marine shipping, space is generally considered as a unit for occupation of goods.

SPACER Short noticed metal bar used to connect storage rack uprights together in a parallel line.

SPACE WEIGHT RATE A rate that applies to weight or cubic measure, usually whichever is greater, to determine total freight charges, common in the ocean steamship industry.

SPAR AND BOOM GEAR This is a cargo handling set up. A boom is placed over the hatch and another over the side. The hatch tackle hoists the cargo, while the boom tackle carries the sling across the deck.

SPECIAL AGENT One authorized to act only on a specific matter or on one occasion.

SPECIAL CARGO Cargo with high value per unit weight or measurement. Precious metals and specie are examples. An extra charge is made for handling.

SPECIAL COMMODITIES DIVISION A division of a motor carrier that carries freight requiring specialized equipment such as for steel hauling, heavy loads, bulk liquids, etc.; usually handled with owner-operators on trip leases.

SPECIAL DAMAGES A carrier obligation term for damages in which goods have lost their value due to delay.

SPECIAL RATES The air special rates are special freight rates for transportation between specific cities. It involves movements by container, deferred air freight, import rates and surface air rates.

SPECIAL REPARATION DOCKET That part of the record of the Interstate Commerce Commission whereby application of the carriers for permission to refund unlawfully collected transportation charges are passed upon.

SPECIAL SERVICE TALLY Document prepared for any extra charges over and beyond standard charges.

SPECIAL SERVICE TARIFF A tariff containing switching, storage, demurrage, etc. charges, rules and regulations.

SPECIAL TRACKS In a typical yard there will be several tracks devoted to special purposes, varying with local conditions. Some of these are: caboose, scale, coaling, ashpit, bad order, repair, icing, feed, stock, transfer, sand, and depressed.

SPECIFIC COMMODITY RATE As contrasted with a general commodity rate, this is set upon individual commodities.

SPECIFICATION (PACKAGING) A summary of a packaging component, in great detail.

SPEDITEURS Forwarding agents.

SPLIT DELIVERY In addition to stopping-in-transit, specified carriers sometimes offer a split-delivery service on carload freight. The rules are published in the agency tariffs. Delivery may be made to one or more parties. Multiple deliveries at more than one siding requires a switching service. Additional charges are made for added switching services and the unloading of cars.

SPLIT LOAD A loaded trailer that is moved to two or more destination terminals. The multiple terminals may be close.

SPLIT MONTH BILLING Merchandise received before the 15th is assessed one month storage charge. Merchandise received after the 15th is assessed ½ month storage charge.

SPLIT MONTH STORAGE A full month's charge for goods received from the 1st of the month through the 15th. One-half month's charges assessed to all goods received from the 16th through the last day of the month. A full month's charges assessed to all goods on hand on the first day of the next month.

SPLIT PICKUP OR DELIVERY Multiple pickup and/or deliveries, involving one or more places of business.

SPLIT SHIPMENT Situation in which an entire shipment is separated for movement; done either by initial shipper or carrier.

SPLIT SHIFTING The process of shifting the main and auxiliary transmission gears simultaneously.

SPOILAGE One form of deterioration cost. A sub-set of deterioration. The reduction in consumption value resulting from inadequate facilities or opportunity for preservation.

SPONTANEOUSLY COMBUSTIBLE MATERIAL (SOLID) A solid substance (including sludges and pastes) which may undergo spontaneous heating or self-ignition under conditions normally incident to transportation or which may upon contact with the atmosphere undergo an increase in temperature and ignite.

SPOON DRIFT (SPINDRIFT) The sea mist blown from the waves.

SPOT A vessel at her loading port and ready to load or unload.

SPOTTER A terminal yard driver who parks vehicles brought in by regular drivers. The term is also applied to a supervisor who checks on line haul driver.

SPOT THE BODY Slang for parking a trailer.

SPOTTING The process of placing freight cars or trucks at a particular dock for loading is referred to as spotting the cars.

SPOTTING CARS Switching to a specified location.

SPREAD The gap between maximum allowable load and actual load carried.

SPREADER A device used to spread lifting cables, so it lifts straight up from the container corners.

SPREAD TANDEM A two axle arrangement on a trailer with the axles spread more than usual.

SPRINKLER Fire protection water outlets that automatically spray water if the temperature rises above a certain degree.

SPUR-TRACK A track which extends a short distance from a regular railroad track is a spur track. It may serve one or more industries.

SQUARE FOOT STORAGE Contractual agreement for a specific amount of square footage. Charge is determined by multiplying square foot rate by number of square feet contracted for.

SQUEALER A slang phrase for a tachograph.

SQUEEZE Slang for carton clamp.

STABILITY The degree of force which holds a vessel upright, or returns it to upright if keeled over. Weights on the lower hold will increase the stability. A vessel is stiff if it has high stability, and tender if low stability.

STACK The exhaust pipe on a diesel.

STACKER An individual who loads the freight on the truck, or unloads it.

STACKER CRANE Crane installed within a rack enabling the stack to be as high as 100 feet.

STACKING Placing of merchandise on top of other merchandise.

STACKING HEIGHT The distance as measured from the floor to a point 24" or more below the lowest overhead obstruction. Stacking height is usually controlled to coming into contact with overhead obstructions and to maintain clearances required by local fire regulations and ordinances.

STACKS Refers to product which is stacked up in the warehouse. Storage area.

STAFF FUNCTIONS Those functions in the industrial firm which service the line functional areas by providing them legal services, credit services, finance availability, personnel services (hiring and terminating), etc. are termed staff areas. The staff areas do not provide a time, place, form, or possession utility service in the firm.

STAGING AREA A temporary storage area in a warehouse or terminal where goods are accumulated for final loading at one time.

STAKE BODY A trailer platform body with removable stakes, which are usually joined by chains, panels or slats.

STAKING Stakes used on open cars to prevent the lading, such as poles, lumber and structural iron from shifting and rolling off cars.

STALE DATED BILLS OF LADING Shipping documents which are present to the negotiating bank after 21 days from the day of issuance. The L/C may stipulate a shorter or a longer period for presentation.

STANCHIONS The pillars used to support the deck. Stanchions are also used on deck to support awnings.

STANDARD BILL OF LADING A form of lading used to some extent in the Southeast, the conditions of which differ with those of the uniform bill of lading.

STANDARD CLASSES Those which are established as a fixed rule and are complete in themselves.

STANDARD DENSITY The compression of a flat bale of cotton to standard density of approximately 22½ pounds per cubic foot.

STANDARD FORMS Forms adopted for general use with a view to uniformity.

STANDARD GAUGE The distance between the rails of practically all North American railroads is 4 feet 8½ inches. This is standard gauge distance between the rails.

STANDARD INTERNATIONAL TRADE CLASSIFICATION A numerical identification of commodities moving by air. Adopted by the U.S. scheduled air carriers and developed by the United Nations.

STANDARD METROPOLITAN STATISTICAL AREA (SMSA) A designated zone for major population centers in the U.S.; useful in population, marketing and other analyses.

STANDARD RATE A rate established via direct routes from one point to another in relation to which the rates via other routes between the same points are made.

STANDARD ROUTE The carrier or carriers having the direct route between two points.

STANDARD TRAFFIC FORMS Forms that have become standard through continued use or which have been prescribed for use by the Interstate Commerce Commission.

STANDING ORDER An agreement whereby a customer agrees to purchase a certain quantity of specified goods at certain intervals, and vendor agrees to ship at those times.

STAPLE Principal commodity of a country or district; a commodity in everyday use.

STAPLING MACHINE, STRAP A machine that staples over-trap on cases requiring strong binding.

STARBOARD The right side of the vessel, looking forward. At one time a steering board was used on the right side of the vessel.

STATED REFRIGERATION CHARGE A freight refrigeration charge for service enroute based on a cwt., package, truck or other method of quoting the charge.

STATEMENT OF BILLING Brief of a waybill without names of consignors and consignees.

STATEMENT OF CHARGES An itemized list often submitted separate from the commercial invoice (the price or bill of goods), and embracing inland and ocean freights, cartage to steamer, insurance premiums, consular fees, and cooperage charges.

STATE TOLL A charge made by a State for the use of its highways or other facilities for handling traffic.

STATION A place designated on the timetable by name, at which a train may stop for traffic, or to enter or to leave the main track, or from which fixed signals are operated.

STATION COSTS Costs of rating, billing and routing a rail shipment.

STATION INDEX A list of points to, from and between which rates apply, and appearing in a tariff or other traffic schedule.

STATION ORDER CAR A car loaded by shipper with several less-than-carload shipments in destination order, for different points along the same route. Unlike the *Trap* or *Ferry*, this car is placed into a train without its contents being rehandled at the carrier's terminal at point of shipment.

STATION PIER A pier having no rail connections; where freight is received and delivered by car-floats.

STATUS QUO The existing conditions or state of things.

STATUTE OF LIMITATION A statute law limiting the time in which claims or suits may be instituted.

STATUTORY NOTICE The length of time required by law for carriers to give notice of changes in tariffs, rates, rules, and regulations—usually thirty days, unless otherwise permitted by authority from the Interstate Commerce Commission.

STAVE The breaking of the boat planking. Thes s say stove.

STEAM RAILWAY A carrier whose principal motive power is steam.

STEAMSHIP A vessel whose principal motive power is steam and not sails. There are three classes of steamships: (1) Freight carrying vessels (liners and tramps); (2) Combination vessels, (freight and passenger); and (3) Passenger carrying vessels.

STEAMSHIP AGENT A firm that represents the owner of a vessel in ports for purposes of handling port clearances, arranging dock space, stevedores, etc.

STEAMSHIP FREIGHT CONTRACT Sometimes the shippers in a steamship line contract for space and rates relative to future sailings.

STEAMSHIP GUARANTEE An indemnity issued to the carrier by a bank, which protects the carrier against any possible losses or damages arising from release of the merchandise to the receiving party. This instrument is usually issued when the bill of lading is lost or not available.

STEERING AXLE An axle which has the directional control of the vehicle attached. There may be more than one steering axle on a single unit.

ST. ELMO'S FIRE When the air is supercharged with electricity, a luminous brush-like appearance is seen on the ends of the yardarms, stays, or mastheads, on the vessel. The electrical discharge represents the relieving of the difference in the electrical potential between the atmosphere and the earth.

STEM The leg of a transportation vehicle trip to reach the first pick up or delivery site in an area.

STEM WINDER A slang phrase for a vehicle with a crank starter.

STENCIL Applies to any paper, board, metal, etc., that makes lettering by passing ink over a sheet with letters perforated.

STENCILLING Required on all orders under 5000 lbs. It provides positive identification of each shipment and can often prevent claims.

STENCIL WEIGHTS Weights stenciled on a car or container showing the capacity, light weight of car or container and the maximum weight to be loaded in car or container.

STET Let it stand.

STEVEDORE A person having charge of the loading and unloading of the boats.

STIFF The quality of a vessel to be stable, or to return to an upright position.

STITCHER A procedure for stapling box bottoms, tops, joints, etc., in solid fibers or corrugated containers.

STOCK CAR A car designed for the transportation of livestock.

STOCK LOCATOR SYSTEM A system whereby all spots within the warehouse are lettered or numbered.

STOCK MIXING When a marketing firm buys from different manufacturers and keeps a full line of products at the warehouse for shipments to customers.

STOCKOUT The condition of running out of the materials, parts, supplies or finished products required for production or sale. A deficiency of stock in storage.

STOCKOUT COST When the supply of an article or commodity runs out, losses are sustained. If the immediate effect of a loss is to shut down manufacturing or processing operations, the extent of the loss may be the combination of profits lost as well as production costs incurred during the period of shut down that could not be forestalled. If the stockout eliminates the availability of goods for sale in the post-production channel, the stockout cost may be measured by the combination of lost profits from potential sales, and marketing costs that could not be forestalled, and that will result in marketing facilities operating at less than full capacity. Stockout occurs when safety stock is gone. It is a safety stock cost.

STOCK REPORT A record of items on hand by type and number, based on the paper work recording of receipts and shipments during a given period.

STOCK ROTATION First in, first out.

STOCK SPOTTING A distribution method whereby goods are moved to forward storage points for fast, short replenishment order cycle times to customers; primary rationale for stock spotting is for customer service needs.

STOL Short takeoff and landing aircraft. Aircraft capable of landing and taking off on reduced length runways.

STOP IN TRANSIT The process of stopping enroute to partially load, unload or perform another service.

STOP-OFF OPERATIONS The process of stop-off is a privilege granted to a shipper for the purpose of completing a loading or for partial unloading. A shipper must designate the intended stop-off operation on the bill of lading by designating the points at which the car should be stopped, the name and address of the party who will load or unload at the stop-off point, and the purpose of the stop-off operation. An example would be, "stop this car at Spokane, Washington, to complete loading by the Johnson Produce Company." Freight may be prepaid or otherwise at the stop-off point. If freight is prepaid, a special form is used or a memorandum bill of lading is applied. When goods are stopped for partial unloading, the carrier must obtain a receipt for the unloaded portion of the car. The point at which the car is stopped must be directly intermediate and on the authorized route.

STOP-OVER Many carriers allow a stop-over privilege on carload freight shipments at stations between points of origin and final destination, for the purpose of finishing loading or partly unloading, or taking advantage of transit or other privileges permitted in accordance with tariff rules and regulations.

STOPPAGE IN TRANSIT This term is very different from *stopping in transit*. Stoppage refers to the right of a shipper of goods moving on a straight bill of lading to withhold final delivery and return the shipment to its origin because of the unwillingness or incapacity of the consignee to pay for them.

STORAGE A charge for storage of freight in carrier's warehouse in excess of free time authorized by tariffs.

STORAGE AISLE An aisle used to gain access to a storage bay, pallet slot, pallet rack or bin.

STORAGE BAY That portion of the occupiable storage space that faces either a handling or storage aisle where merchandise can be stored.

STORAGE CHARGE Fee for holding goods at rest.

STORAGE COSTS The sum total of all costs associated with storage. It includes (1) inventory costs, (2) warehouse costs, (3) administrative storage costs, (4) deterioration costs, (5) insurance costs, (6) in-and-out (labor) costs, and (7) taxes. It does not include ordering costs, since these are a part of purchasing costs.

STORAGE EFFICIENCY The degree at which the minimum space can be used for a customer account.

STORAGE-IN-TRANSIT This term is applied to a tariff privilege which permits freight to be stopped enroute for storage without a change in the rate. However, it may involve an added switching charge.

STORAGE REVENUE Money received for the storage of a customer's product.

STORAGE TRACK A track on which cars are placed when not in service, or when held awaiting disposition.

STORE-DOOR DELIVERY The movement of goods to the consignee's place of business, customarily applied to movement by truck.

STOREKEEPER An officer in charge of a bonded warehouse.

STORES Provision and supplies aboard a vessel. List of stores is a document listing stores aboard a vessel at a given time.

STORM TRACK In the northern hemisphere, the cyclone moves in a right curve, while in the southern hemisphere it moves in a left curve. The line of the storm motion is called the storm track. A vessel in the storm track will not experience wind, but the barometer will fall. If in the northern hemisphere, the vessel would put the wind on the starboard quarter and run in a right circle.

STOVE A case or cask broken in from the outside.

STOW To place the vessel gear in its proper place.

STOWAGE The careful arrangement of freight in a ship's hold.

STOWAGE, BROKEN The space in a ship lost between units of cargo.

STOWAGE FACTOR The relation between measurement freight (40 cubic feet of space to the long ton) and the weight of cargo. Stowage factors vary from 9 cubic feet for pig lead to 1000 cubic feet for wicker baskets.

STRAIGHT JOB A truck with the chassis and body permanently attached.

STRAIGHT SHIPMENTS Goods consigned direct to a named consignee.

STRAIGHT TRUCK A vehicle with the cargo body and tractor mounted on the same chassis.

STRAPPING A metal or flexible band used to hold cases together in a unit.

STRADDLE CARRIER A truck lifting device to pickup containers within its own framework.

STRAPPING TOOL A device used to pull strapping tightly on a case or to draw it closely so that seals or other fastenings may be applied.

STRESS The force required to change the shape of an object. It may involve twist, thrust, pull or otherwise.

STRETCH WRAP A process and means of applying a sheet of plastic to a small load of packages in such a way that they are secured together in a convenient unitized manner.

STUB STATION A station in which the tracks are connected at one end only.

STUFFING Loading a container(s).

SUB-BLOCK One of the units contained in a main (express) block and including certain points for rate-making purposes.

SUBLEASED CARS Private line rail cars that are then released to another party, usually for short periods.

SUBPOENA An order to require an individual to present testimony.

SUBROGATE To put in the place of another.

SUBROGATION Putting one thing in place of another; substituting one creditor for another.

SUBSIDY A compensation in which inadequate or no service has been rendered. Under Section 406(b) of the Federal Aviation Act, provision is made for subsidy revenues from the U.S. Government as grants for providing transportation facilities. This grant does not involve revenues for the carriage of mail at service rates, or contractual payments of air service for the U.S. government.

SUCKER BRAKES Vacuum brakes.

SUE Abandoned high and dry.

SUE AND LABOR CLAUSE The action taken to recover the costs of action taken to avert or minimize loss from a casualty is taken under the sue and labor clause by the master against the underwriters.

SUFFERANCE WHARF A wharf licensed and attended by customs authorities.

SUNDRIES Unclassified articles.

SUNSET LAW Law that requires an agency or law to be analyzed and re-justified or else its existence will be automatically terminated.

SUPER CARGO An agent who accompanies cargo to the foreign market to care for and sell it to the best advantage, and to buy a return cargo and accompany it home.

SUPERIOR TRAIN A train given preference by train order.

SUPERVISOR Refers to automated computer processing software. The terms Monitor and Executive are also used by the manufacturer for the processes of multi-tasking and batch processing.

SUPPLEMENT (TARIFF) A publication containing additions to and/or changes in a tariff.

SUPPLEMENTAL AIR CARRIERS A class of air carrier performing passenger and cargo charter services which are supplemental to the scheduled service of the certificated route air carriers. They hold restricted certificates of public convenience and necessity from the Civil Aeronautics Board.

SUPPLEMENTAL ORDER An order made by a court of a regulating body altering or adding to an order which was previously issued by them.

SUPRA A legal term used to signify that a case or ruling has been previously cited in full.

SUPRA PROTEST A form of acceptance by a second party to save the credit of the drawer of a bill of exchange which has been protested.

SURCHARGE A charge above the usual or customary charge.

SURCHARGE, FREIGHT An increase in the freight charge resulting from the rate advances allowed in the Fifteen Percent Case, 1931, Ex Parte 103.

SURTAX An additional or extra tax.

SURVEY An examination requested by the master to the port authorities and his consul, when entering port with such damage as bulwarks or masts down, the vessel leaking, etc. The vessel is checked for proper stowage. The master may extend a protest to the survey.

SURVEYOR In shipping, one who officially examines and reports on applications for marine insurance.

SUSPENSE ACCOUNT An account to record an incomplete transaction awaiting additional information or audit for its adjustment, such as interline freight claims paid prior to settlement with the participating lines.

SUSPENSION The withdrawal of a privilege or opportunity for a short period. Applied to rates, it implies the I.C.C. is holding up a proposed rate from going into effect until a hearing or study is completed.

SUTTLE WEIGHT Weight after tare is deducted.

SWAMPER An assistant who rides with the driver.

SWINDLE SHEET A slang phrase referring to the I.C.C. log.

SWITCH A connection between two lines of track to permit cars or trains to pass from one track to another. Also, to move cars from one place to another within switching limits.

SWITCH CREW The men that move a railcar from one place to another within switching limits.

SWITCH ENGINE An engine used in the service of switching cars.

SWITCHING Movement of cars within terminal areas for loading, unloading, train make-up or breakup. Switching within the plant is intraplant; switching between plants is interplant; switching between points within the terminal area in intraterminal.

SWITCHING AND TERMINAL COMPANY A company performing switching service only, furnishing terminal trackage, bridges or other facilities only, operating ferries exclusively, or performing any combination of these functions, and which may incidentally conduct a regular freight or passenger service.

SWITCHING CHARGE An added switching charge for performing a switching service that is not within the switching limits.

SWITCHING LIMIT Switching limit is the area at a station within which line-haul carload freight is picked up or is switched for loading or unloading without added charge above the line-haul freight rate. It may be the same area as yard or less but rarely greater than the yard limit. Tariffs filed with regulatory bodies define such switching limits at important stations. At intermediate stations it is all tracks within the station layout or yard limit.

SWITCHING LIMITS Boundaries within which switching rules and charges apply.

SWITCHING RECIPROCAL A mutual interchange of carload freight, inbound and outbound, which is switched to or from a siding of another carrier under a regular switching charge. The carrier receiving the line-haul usually absorbs the charge.

SWITCHING SERVICE A railway service performed under yard rules and regulations. It may involve the classification of cars according to commodity and destination; the assembling of cars for train movement; changing the position of cars for purposes of loading, unloading, and weighing; the placing of locomotives and cars for repair and storage; and the moving of equipment in connection with the carrier's work service not constituting a road movement.

SWITCHING TARIFF A schedule containing charges for (switch) movement of cars.

SWITCH ORDER An order to move a car from one place to another within switching limits.

SYNCHRONISM That situation in which the action of the waves and the oscillation of the vessel are in tune. If the ship and waves reach their greatest angle of inclination simultaneously, an excessive roll follows. To correct this, the speed and/or direction of the vessel is changed.

SYNDICATE "A" A U.S. Salvage Association which performs the survey of marine property.

SYNDICATE "B" An association of insurance companies which insures the Shipping Board's equity in a vessel under sale.

SYNDICATE "C" An association of insurance companies that specializes in hulls and machinery for American flags and foreign owned vessels.

SYSTEM (RAILWAY) The entire trackage equipment and facilities of a line of railroad, inclusive of main tracks, side tracks, branch lines, yards and terminals.

SYSTEMS ANALYST The supervisor who approves the instructions, concepts, etc., in the program.

SYSTEMS PROGRAMMER The person preparing the instructions to meet the objectives of a computer program. He also makes up the flow-charts.

—T—

TAB The identification card attached to an article or container shipped.

TABLE, BALL TRANSFER In materials handling, this is a table with freely mounted balls used to facilitate transfer from one conveyor to another.

TACHOGRAPH An instrument used to record miles driven, speed, number of stops, etc. It is placed in the cab of the truck.

TACK Short for tachograph. Also short for tachometer.

TACTICAL DIAMETER The deviation from the course a vessel experiences in traveling through 180 degrees.

TAILBOARD ARTIST Meaning one who regards himself a perfect driver.

TAIL GATE The removable or opening rear wall of the truck body which permits rear end unloading—or permits spill-unloading by raising if it is a dump truck. The tail gate term was originally applied to wagon boxes.

TAILGATING Following too closely in trucking.

TALE QUALE Such as. A term used generally in grain trade to denote that cargo is presumed to correspond with sample and that the buyer takes all risk of subsequent loss or deterioration.

TALLY A tally sheet is made up when goods are received and a record of their condition on arrival is tabulated.

TALLY FORM A record of such items as amount, description, marks, etc., of goods being loaded or unloaded.

TALLY NUMBER Sequential number listing; one given to each tally.

TANDEM A semitrailer or tractor with two rear axles.

TANDEM AXLE A two axle arrangement on the rear of the truck, either, or both of which may be powered.

TANK BODY A tank truck used to carry liquids.

TANK CAR A car consisting of a tank, or more than one tank, mounted on car frame or directly on cradles over truck bolsters, used for the transportation of liquids and gases.

TANK CAR GAUGE BOOK A publication showing capacities, names of owners, series numbers, etc., of tank cars in the country.

TANKER A liquid hauling truck. A tractor with a tank body.

TANK SHIP A vessel used for transporting bulk liquids. It is divided into compartments for facilitating multiple liquids, safety, etc.

TANKTAINER A container with a built-in tank for transporting liquids.

TANK TRAILER A fully enclosed trailer designed for the transportation of liquid commodities in bulk.

TANK TRUCK CARRIER A motor carrier authorized to carry liquid products in bulk. It may also carry dry fluid commodities.

TAPE DRIVE In data processing, the equipment which passes the magnetic tape past the recording heads.

TAPE, GUMMED CLOTH A packaging tape which may take many forms. It may be cloth and paper gummed for packaging, or it may be fiber-filled, clay-filled, etc.

TAPE, GUMMED SEALING A wide tape used for packaging consisting of kraft paper in many weight forms. The most common weight compositions are 35, 60 and 90 pounds.

TAPE, GUMMED SISAL A form of packaging tape composed of sisal fibers of great strength combined with asphaltic or non-asphaltic laminants between sheets of kraft paper.

TAPE, KRAFT A packaging tape made from brown kraft paper gummed with many forms of animal or vegetable glues. They require moistening for use.

TAPE, PRESSURE SENSITIVE A type of packaging tape that does not require moistening when used. Like others, it is covered with adhesive and can be applied with pressure in any temperature or degree of moisture.

TAPE, SEALING A packaging tape made from cloth, paper, etc., and an adhesive which is applied with pressure. It is used for containers and packaging.

TAPE, SHIPPING SACK A heavy duty packaging tape made of creped-kraft, coated with gummed substance. It is applied over the paper ends on multi-walled shipping sacks, usually after the closures are sewn.

TAP LINE A short line railroad, sometimes called a feeder line, usually owned or controlled by the plants served by it.

TARE The amount to deduct from the gross weight of the shipment because of the packaging weight.

TARE WEIGHT The weight of an empty container or an empty car, without any references to the weight of contents, is called the tare weight.

TARIFF Rate books which provide the dollar charge on a given class of transportation movement are called tariffs. Separate tariffs are provided for motor shipments as compared to rail shipments, and for commodity, class, T.O.F.C., in-transit charges, and many other different classes of charges. A tariff is a rate book and should not be confused with the term applicable to international trade which refers to a tax on exports.

TARIFF, AGENCY A tariff published by an agent on behalf of two or more carriers.

TARIFF, ALTERNATIVE A schedule divided into two or more sections, each of which provides for the application of rates in some other section when the use of such rates will produce lower charges.

TARIFF AUTHORITY The tariff or other schedule referred to in support of statement and containing rate or regulation applicable to specific traffic. It is usually sufficient to cite the number under which it is filed with the Interstate Commerce Commission or state regulating body.

TARIFF CIRCULAR (INTERSTATE COMMERCE COMMISSION) A publication of the Interstate Commerce Commission that presents the regulations concerning the publication of tariffs.

TARIFF, CLASS A schedule that contains rates from one point to another for the several groups or classes to which articles are assigned in a classification or an exception sheet.

TARIFF, CLASS AND COMMODITY A schedule that contains both class and commodity rates and provisions for their alternative application.

TARIFF, COMBINATION A tariff containing class and commodity rates.

TARIFF, COMMON A tariff published by an agent for the account of two or more transportation lines as issuing carriers.

TARIFF, CONVENTIONAL A tariff which contains and represents all the concessions provided for by the commercial treaties concluded by the particular country.

TARIFF FILE Copies of tariffs, classifications, supplements, reissues and other schedules, maintained for the purpose of ascertaining, quoting and checking rates and determining the rules and regulations governing traffic.

TARIFF INDEX A list, kept by a carrier, of the tariffs it issues or is a party to, showing I.C.C. and G.F.O. numbers, together with points from, to and between which the rates contained therein apply.

TARP The tarpaulin used to cover the top of the trailer.

TATTLE-TALE The term applied to the tachograph.

TAXI The movement of the aircraft about a landing area on its own thrust. Occurs before take-off and after landing.

TEAM TRACK The team track is not for the sole use of a particular industry, but is provided for the general use of the public for loading and unloading freight cars.

TEAR STRENGTH The measurement of resistance to tear under commonly accepted measurement tests.

TECHNICAL STOP A stop on an airline route for the purpose of crew change and/or fuel; not for passenger enplaning or deplaning.

TELEPROCESSING (TP) In data processing, it involves attaching peripherals online to a CPU by telephone to perform on-line processing services.

TELETYPE (TELETYPEWRITER) An electric typewriter using the telegraph lines to take in messages and provide information continuously or intermittently between two long distance terminals that carry on continuous information transfers. The teletype can handle about 10-15 characters per second.

TELE-TYPEWRITER TWX, high speed typewriter which picks up and sends information through the phone line from one point to another.

TELPHER A traveling carrier, generally operated by electricity, employed at freight stations, piers, and warehouses to transport, load, and unload shipments.

TELPHERAGE The carriage of goods by telpher.

TELPHER SYSTEM An overhead track used for moving a beam-type trolley. It permits hoisting bulk material or containers. It can be operated automatically and remotely if needed.

TEL QUEL The rate charged for a bill of exchange which is of such currency as not to be subject to the *long rate* on three months' bill or upwards, nor subject to the *short rate* which applies to bills up to ten days, but which falls somewhere between those limits.

TEMPERATURE CHIMNEYS A means of determining the temperature of cargo in the hold in water bulk cargo movements by providing pipes into the cargo which permit the lowering of thermometers. The problem is to avoid spontaneous combustion.

TENOR Time and date for payment of a draft, stated in one of the following forms: *At sight (A/S)* — A draft so drawn that it is payable upon presentation to the paying bank. *(No. of days) dayys sight (D/S)* — The draft is payable a fixed number of days after acceptance. *(No. of days) days date (D/D)* — The draft is payable on a certain date; e.g., 30 days from date of invoice or issuance of other shipping documents. *(No. of days) days sight/documents against payment (D/S D/P)* — The term is used in the collections process. The draft must be presented for acceptance to the drawee (usually the buyer). Documents can be released only against payment in full plus charges, if need be. These terms are used mainly in Hong Kong.

TENDER The presentation for transportation by the shipper, or delivery by the carrier, of a shipment. Sometimes it is also used to refer to the obligation of the carrier (or offer of the carrier) to transport goods at the reduced *government shipment rate* under Section 10721, of the Interstate Commerce Act.

TERMINAL Facilities provided by a railway at a terminus or at an intermediate point on its line for the handling of passengers or freight; and for the breaking up, making up, forwarding and servicing trains, and interchanging with other carriers.

TERMINAL CARRIER The carrier making the delivery in a joint carrier movement.

TERMINAL CHARGE The charge for such facilities as docks, wharves, piers, switching tracks, belt-line railroads, hoists, warehouses, and elevators for the loading, unloading, interchange, and storage of freight.

TERMINAL OPERATIONS As applied to a switching and terminal company, the use of the facilities furnished at such locations as a freight or passenger union station, bridge ferry, and other terminal joint facilities, usually measured by the number of cars handled for tenant companies.

TERMINAL SWITCHING The moving of cars originating at destined to points within yard or switching limits.

TERMINAL TRACKAGE Track facilities at terminal stations provided for the joint use of two or more carriers.

TERMINI (POINTS) Synonymous with *terminals* and specifically referring in the case of the *Western Termini* to certain points originally the western terminals of eastern railways and now important in rate construction.

TERRITORIAL A qualifying term and expressive of that which is applicable to a designated section or territory.

TERRITORIAL DIRECTORY A publication embracing description of traffic territories, rate points, crossings, termini, etc., and issued to avoid duplication of matter so extensive that it would not be practicable to incorporate it in each tariff applicable.

TERRITORY In transportation, a designation of a part of section of the country, such as *Trunk Line Territory* or *C.F.A. Territory.*

TEST, DROP A system of testing resistance to damage of containers through controlled drop testing.

TEST, DRUM The process of testing shipping containers by revolving them inside a hexagon drum.

TEST, ELMENDORF TEAR A tear testing system by controlled weight application to various layers of paper or board.

TEST, FLAT CRUSH A crush measurement system by applying incrementally increasing forces to corrugations in a sheet of fiberboard, etc.

TEST, FOLDING ENDURANCE A system of testing the endurance of packaging paper or film to the folding stress. A schopper machine performs a frequent folding operation.

TEST, HYDROSTATIC PRESSURE The I.C.C. requires a hydrostatic pressure test to establish the capacity of metal drums to meet specifications to authorize their use in the movement of dangerous commodities.

TEST, INCLINE IMPACT (COBUR TEST) The purpose of this test is to establish the ability of packaging to resist impact that might occur in freight car movements. The test consists of rolling a dolly down inclined rails so it will impact against a solid wall.

TEST, LEAKAGE A system for testing metal containers for leakage. The specifications for testing and leakage resistance are spelled out by the I.C.C. Underwater seams are tested, and sometimes heavy oil or soapsuds are used for testing.

TEST SHIPMENT A shipment made in a package or form of shipping not specified in the tariff for purposes of evaluating the new package or shipping method.

TEST TENSILE A measurement process of packaging to resist rupture. A measurement of tensile strength.

THEFT Feloniously taking and removing property with intent to deprive the rightful owner; the taking of the entire container or article.

THEORY An exposition of the abstract principles of a science considered apart from practice.

THICKENER A materials handling facility for arranging the solid to liquid concentration by systems of gravity, suction or precipitation.

THIRD LEVEL CARRIER Air carriers that provide passenger and/or freight service between outlying small cities, or from these cities to trunk line cities.

THIRD STRUCTURE TAX The first two levels of tax on motor vehicles consist of registration and fuel taxes. Any other tax on transportation service or the vehicle used in transportation would be a third structure tax.

THREE (OR MORE) TRACKS Three (or more) main tracks, upon any one of which the current of traffic may move in either specified direction.

THROUGH BILL OF LADING A bill of lading drawn up to cover goods from point of origin to final destination when interchange or transfer from one carrier to another is necessary to complete the journey.

THROUGH FARE A single fare for a transportation movement from the point of origin of the passenger to the destination. It is usually lower than the sum of individual fare that might be involved. It could take the form of a joint fare, or the combination of several separate fares.

THROUGH FLIGHT Any flight that does not require the transfer to another plant (or other modal vehicle). It could be very circuitous and involve many stops. It could also involve an equipment interchange movement in which several different carriers are involved, that interchange (jointly use) common equipment.

THROUGH FREIGHT As distinguished from *local,* this class of service is maintained between important junctions and terminals, usually between the great producing and consuming centers of the country. This traffic is largely carload but includes merchandise or package cars.

THROUGH PACKAGE CAR A through package or *merchandise car* is one loaded with less than carload shipments to break bulk at a given point; in some cases containing package freight for one station only and in other cases shipments for many stations beyond.

THROUGH RATES A charge applied to an interline shipment. The sum total of all rates that apply via a through route. A through route is the combination of connecting carriers by which they offer through transportation service from one point on the line of one carrier to the destination on the line of another carrier. In *Southern Pacific Terminal vx. I.C.C.,* 219 U.S. 498 1911, the four essential characteristics of a through rate were established to be: (1) a through bill of lading; (2) uninterrupted movement; (3) continuous possession by the carrier; and (4) unbroken bulk. In a more recent case in 1956 (Denver vs. Union Pacific Railroad Co.), the Supreme Court stated that a through route exists only when the carriers hold themselves out as offering through transportation.

THROUGH TRAIN A train which does not stop at all stations on its route.

THROWING MACHINE, BULK MATERIAL, VANE TYPE A rotating drum that throws bulk material through the use of moving paddles or vanes.

TICKET SCALPER A person who buys and sells the unused parts of railway tickets.

TIE One complete layer of material on a pallet or unit.

TIE (RAILROAD) The wood or concrete cross-member that rests on the surface onto which rails rest.

TIED UP A common expression for a roadway that is blocked.

TIER A layyer of packages placed on a pallet.

TIERS AND BELTS (MERCHANDISE TRAFFIC REPORTS) A numeration of the *Equi-Graphic Rate Blocks,* starting with the northwest corner of the United States. Tiers extend easterly (nos. 11 to 59 inclusive) and belts extend southerly (nos. 11 to 42).

TILT-BED TRAILER An arrangement of a truck trailer on one or more axles, so centered that it may be tilted to facilitate loading or unloading.

TILT CAB A type of cab that will tilt to permit access to the engine.

TIME CHARTER The time charter party in water transportation is a contract for leasing which spells out the terms of the leasing arrangement between the ship owners and the leasee. It would state, for example, the time of the lease in years or voyages.

TIME FREIGHT A term used to signify that payments for the hire of a vessel are being made periodically instead of in one lump sum.

TIME-SHARING A sharing of computer facilities by many different users. It involves a special teleprocessing operation.

TIME-TABLE Authority for the movement of regular trains subject to railway train rules, with a schedule that prescribes train classification, direction, identification, and movement. Time-table schedules usually are in effect for 12 hours after their time at each station, and a train behind schedule for more than the prescribed time limit can proceed only as authorized by train order. Time-table authority may be superseded by rules providing for block signals and interlocking signals.

TIPPER SEAL A device for emptying materials from a hopper by reciprocation without reducing the vacuum.

T.O.F.C. This refers to trailer-on-flatcar. It is also called piggyback. Shipments going T.O.F.C. receive special rates in special tariffs provided for that class of shipment.

TOLERANCE A weight allowance is frequently made to reconcile weight variations of certain commodities due to circumstances that may frequently arise. The deviation allowance in the weight is called the tolerance.

TOLL The charge made for the use of a bridge or roadway.

TOMMING DOWN This is the counterpart (opposite meaning) of shoring up. One would brace under a deck to hold cargo down.

TON A measurement of weight, commonly equivalent to 2000 lbs. avoirdupois (short, or net, ton); 2240 lbs. (long ton); or 2240.6 lbs. (metric ton). The short ton is generally used in domestic transaction, and the long ton in the export trade of the United States. However, since the practices of ocean carriers are not uniform, the long ton is not always used. Countries which have adopted the metric system of weights and measures use a ton on 2204.6 lbs., particularly in weighting exported cargoes.

TONGS, SCISSOR A fork lift attachment that grips the load when the fork is lifted through scissor action.

TON-MILE The movement of one ton of freight a distance of one mile. Ton-miles are computed by multiplying the weight in tons of each shipment transported by the distance hauled.

TON-MILE COST EARNINGS A unit employed in comparing freight earnnings or expenses, i.e., the cost of, or the amount earned from, transporting a ton of freight one mile.

TON-MILE TAX A system for assigning highway costs to motor vehicle operators. It is a criterion for allocating highway costs, and should not be confused with the taxing system for collecting the predetermined user's share. Other systems are the Incremental Method, the Operating Cost Method, and the James Space-Time Method. A new innovation is the Factored-Gross-Ton Mile Method—which applies a factor to gross ton miles that accounts for the added highway costs required by the weight of the heaviest axle (measured in lbs. per square inch of the heaviest axle).

TONNAGE In ocean commerce, the weight a ship carries expressed in tons, or the carrying capacity of a vessel, less specifically, the number of tons of freight handled. Cargo tonnage refers to the quantity of cargo shipped, and vessel tonnage to the tonnage of the ship in which goods are transported.

TONNAGE (CAPACITY), DEAD-WEIGHT The number of tons of cargo which a vessel can carry when loaded to its maximum depth, ascertained by deducting displacement *light* and displacement *loaded* tonnage. Deadweight capacity, expressed in long tons or metric tons, usually serves as the basis for charter rates when vessels are operated on time charters.

TONNAGE, GROSS The total measured cubic capacity of a vessel expressed in tons of 100 cubic feet, found by dividing the cubic measurement of its capacity by 100.

TONNAGE, NET The total cubic contents of those parts of a vessel closed in and devoted to the carrying of cargo and passengers, the weight measure being one gross ton for each 100 cubic feet of capacity. Net tonnage of a vessel is found by deducting from its gross tonnage the cubic contents of certain spaces that are specified in the measurement laws and rules of the various maritime nations or in the measurement rules applicable at the Suez and Panama Canals. Net tonnage may be about 2/3 of gross tonnage, although in the fast transatlantic liners, which have large coal bunkers, machinery, and housing quarters, it is likely to be lower.

TONNAGE TAX A tax assessed on all vessels coming into the United States ports from foreign countries whether owned by Americans or not. Charge is so much per ton at each entry and not to exceed a certain sum per ton in one year.

TON, REGISTER 100 cubic feet, a unit used for measuring the entire internal capacity of ships or for register of tonnage.

TOOLING DOWN THE HIGHWAY Slang for driving a vehicle at the legal or normal speed.

TO PAY AVERAGE A marine insurance term having the same meaning and used alternatively to *with particular average.*

TOP-HAMPER The sum of all gear and spars over the ship's deck.

TOTAL AVERAGE INVENTORY The sum of average order quantity (one-half of order quantity), plus safety stock. Likewise equal to one half of ELQ, plus safety stock. The safety stock is the amount on hand after the arrival of the order. Total average inventory is the average normal use stock, plus the average lead stock, plus safety stock.

TOTAL COST OF DISTRIBUTION The sum of the purchasing, transportation and storage costs in the movement of finished products through the post-production channel. Distribution is only the post-production channel. All direct and indirect (hidden) logistics costs are included in the total distribution costs. This could mean over fifty different logistics costs.

TOTAL LOSS Nothing salvageable; completely destroyed.

TOW The pulling of another vessel by a hawser. The term tow also means the process of a tug pulling barges or other floating material. A tow is also the short ends of manila fiber used in making rope. Usually, tow means the vessel towed.

TOWAGE The fee charged for moving or towing a vessel from one point to another.

TOWLINE Materials handling medium that consists of carts that move via cable line in floor; does not require manual movement on main system.

T&R Truck and rail.

TRACE To follow the movement of a shipment.

TRACER The process of requesting the carrier to give a record of a location of a shipment is a request for a tracer. It would normally ask for the name of the party who signed for the shipment, as well as a record of the arrival and the delivery time. It is not to be confused with expediting.

TRACING The process of following the shipment in order to determine the nature of its movement primarily for the point of determining where it was lost and how it can be recovered is called tracing. While expediting must take place prior to a shipment, tracing takes place after a shipment. While some shippers seem to make a request for tracing for most of their shipments, normally this request should only be made to locate a shipment that has been lost. Among the facilities used in a tracing operation are: (1) passing reports; (2) telegrams; (3) telephone; (4) post cards; (5) records of delivery, from connecting lines. When a tracing act is performed, particularly for motor carriers, the request for a tracing act should include the waybill number, date, tractor number, trailer number, carded data, manifest number, consignee, and destination.

TRACING FREIGHT An endeavor to locate a shipment.

TRACK In motor transportation, this is the precision of the rear axle wheel to follow the preceding axle wheel—particularly when making a turn. Also ties, rails, and fastenings, with all parts in their proper relative positions.

TRACKAGE A charge made by a carrier to another carrier operating over its rails. The carrier using the track acquires *trackage rights.*

TRACKAGE RIGHTS All tracks operated and maintained by others but over which the respondent has the right to operate some or all of its trains. On a road of this class, the respondent has no proprietary rights but only the rights of licensee.

TRACK, BODY Each of the parallel tracks of a railroad yard upon which cars are sorted, switched, or stored.

TRACK CAPACITY The number of cars a length of track will hold.

TRACK, HOLD A track in a storage yard where cars are held pending disposition orders from shippers or receivers.

TRACK, HOUSE A track running alongside or entering a freight house, used by cars that receive or deliver freight at the house.

TRACK, INDUSTRIAL A track that serves one or more industries.

TRACK, LADDER A track connecting the body tracks of a yard in a regular sequence.

TRACK. LEAD A track extended to connect either end of a yard with the main track.

TRACK, PASSING A track auxiliary to the main track for the meeting of passing trains, limited to the distance between two adjacent telegraph stations.

TRACK, SPUR A track of indefinite length extending out from a regular railroad track.

TRACK STORAGE A charge made for exceeding the loading time in rail movements. The car is held on the carrier's line too long for loading or unloading. This charge is not to be confused with demurrage, and is made in addition to demurrage.

TRACK, STUB A track connecting with another at one end only and usually protected by a bumper at the stub end.

TRACK, TEAM A side track for general use of the public in loading and unloading freight directly from cars to highway vehicles and vice versa.

TRACTOR A vehicle designed and used primarily for drawing other vehicles and not so constructed that no part is to carry a load other than a part of the weight of the vehicle and load so drawn.

TRACTOR, AGRICULTURAL In materials handling operations, this four wheeled vehicle is used for pulling loads. Its large rear wheels permit it to operate over very rough ground.

TRADE Buying and selling; commerce.

TRADE ACCEPTANCE A time draft or bill of exchange drawn by the seller of merchandise on the buyer for the purchase price of the goods and having on its fact the signed acceptance of the buyer with the date and place of payment.

TRADE ACCEPTANCE (See "Acceptances.")

TRADE DISCOUNT An allowance made to dealers in the same line.

TRADE MARK Figures, letters, or devices, used on goods and labels which the owner has the sole right to use.

TRADE-OFF The application of off-setting advantages or costs in a planning process. Cost trade-offs involve optimizing total costs by combinations of costs which integrate cost planning. It may involve trading-off transportation costs for storage costs, or trading off faster service for greater transport costs.

TRADER A merchant; a broker.

TRADE ROUTES Lanes of the sea customarily followed by merchant ships.

TRAFFIC Persons and property carried by transportation lines.

TRAFFIC AGREEMENT A working arrangement between carriers relative to the interchange of cars, divisions of revenues and rates, and such items as enter in when traffic is to be handled between the lines.

TRAFFIC EXPERT One who is skilled through practice or experience in traffic matters; one who acts for shippers and receivers in an advisory capacity or takes entire charge of their traffic matters.

TRAFFIC MANAGEMENT In the industrial firm, traffic management involves all functional operations related to the buying and management of transportation services, and/or the management of private transportation services. Consequently, traffic management is responsible for the selection of carriers (if there is no logistics manager), the preparation of shipments for the carrier, loading and unloading on the shipping platforms, tracing, expediting, rate analysis and applications, tariff controls, reconsignment, diversion, preparing and filing bills of ladings, and all other operations related to preparing, documenting, loading, unloading, handling, and approving shipments into and out of the industrial firm. By way of contrast, the traffic department of a motor carrier is responsible for rate determination, whereas the traffic department of a rail carrier firm is primarily involved in sales functions.

TRAFFIC MANAGER (INDUSTRIAL) An official having complete supervision of the shipping and receiving departments and general transportation activities of an industrial concern.

TRAFFIC POOLING An illegal procedure of sharing the revenue between carrier providing a common service on a pre-arranged basis. This eliminates competition by eliminating the possibility of more revenue by seeking out traffic. In fact it encourages directing traffic to the competing line, who would be required to share the revenue after providing the service. It is quite common and accepted as a practice in Europe.

TRAILER A vehicle designed without motive power, to be drawn by another vehicle and so constructed that no part of its weight rests upon the towing vehicle.

TRAILER, ARTICULATED A trailer with a coupling to the tractor by an articulating tractor attachment. The trailer has its own front wheels to permit jockeying around when it is not attached to the tractor.

TRAILER, DROP FRAME (SINGLE) A trailer which facilitates loading or unloading by dropping the platform behind the front wheels.

TRAILER-FLATCAR OPERATION A railroad operation commonly called *piggyback* in which highway semi-trailers of a Motor Carrier (sometimes an affiliate of the rail line) are loaded at shippers' loading docks or place of business and driven by Motor Carrier to railroad loading point where they are loaded on specially equipped flat cars and hauled to unloading point in fast merchandise trains operating on passenger train schedules. At unloading point, semi-trailers are removed from flat cars and driven by Motor Carrier to consignees' place of business.

TRAILER INTERCHANGE In motor transportation, this activity involves the interchange of the shipment between carriers on a joint movement, and it usually involves the transfer of the shipment to the vehicles of the joint carrier.

TRAILER INTERLINE This operation is the transfer of trailers between carriers on a joint movement. This involves large volume interline shipments, since it is a trailer volume interline transfer.

TRAILER POLE This trailer system is used for transporting long loads. It consists of a single steel attachment between two carriages. The trailer is adjustable in length.

TRAILER SHIP A vessel that transports motor trailers, and has ramps for direct drive-on loading and unloading of the trailers.

TRAILER SUPPORT A trailer support device at the front end of the trailer which is retractable.

TRAIN An engine, or more than one engine, coupled with or without cars displaying markers.

TRAIN-MILE The movement of a train one mile.

TRAIN OF SUPERIOR RIGHT A train given preference by train order.

TRAIN ORDER An order issued by or through a proper railway official to govern the movements of a train.

TRAIN SWITCHING Switching service performed by train locomotives at terminals and way stations.

TRAMP LINE A transportation line operating tramp steamers.

TRAMP (VESSEL) A ship not connected with any particular service which carries any cargo to any port and does not operate under a given schedule. Tramp vessels are sometimes chartered by regular carriers and operated as *line ships.*

TRANSFER PRICE Term applied to a charge one part of a firm assesses another for services rendered or products transferred to it; common in private trucking and private warehousing.

TRANSFERS A term used to describe points where shipments are rehandled before reaching final destination. *Transferring* consists of the movement of a shipment or shipments from one car to another or from one depot to another or in the case of a terminal or junction transfer, from one railroad to another.

TRANSFER SLIP A protected landing place for car floats with adjustable apron or bridge connecting the tracks on the land with those on the car float.

TRANSFER UNIT A piece of equipment that facilitates the transfer of a container from a motor chassis to a rail car without heavy lift equipment.

TRANSHIPMENT Shipment of merchandise to the point of destination in another country on more than one vessel or vehicle. The liability may pass from one carrier to the next, or it may be covered by "through bills of lading" issued by the first carrier.

TRANSIT AIR CARGO This is a procedure initiated by the Customs Bureau to expedite international air freight movements. It permits the constant flow of freight traffic between airlines and flights without previously required paperwork.

TRANSIT BALANCE The freight rate applicable under transit rules on shipments moving from transit point to destination. It is the difference between the through rate from origin to destination and the flat rate from origin to transit point.

TRANSIT CHARGES The charges for services given while a shipment is in transit.

TRANSIT DUTIES Taxes imposed on goods passing through a country.

TRANSITING OR TRANSITED Passing or having passed through; applicable particularly to traffic through a canal or waterway.

TRANSIT POINT An intermediate point at which freight is held for finishing processes or other treatment.

TRANSIT PRIVILEGE A privilege specified in a tariff permitting a consignment to be stopped for processing, reloading or other charges, the freight to be reshipped with the application of the through rate from origin to destination. An extra charge may or may not be assessed for the privilege.

TRANSIT RATE A rate restricted in its application to traffic which has been or will be milled, stored or otherwise specially treated in transit.

TRANSIT TIME Travel time to get from shipping point to destination point.

TRANSLOADING On shipments to be stopped in transit to partially unload, a carrier, on request of shipper or at carrier's convenience with consent of shipper, transfers at any point on its line authorized by tariff, the portion of shipment to be partially unloaded or the portion for final destination and forwards each from transfer point in separate cars.

TRANSPORT To move traffic from one place to another.

TRANSPORTATION That activity of commercial life embracing the movement of goods and persons from one point to another.

TRANSPORTATION ACT, 1920 Approved February 28, 1920, 41 Stat. L. 456, provided for the termination of Federal Control, enacted provisions relating to the settlement of disputes between carriers and their employees, and made important amendments to the Interstate Commerce Act.

TRANSPORTATION ACT, 1940 Approved September 18, 1940, 54 Stat. L. 899, provides for declaration of a national transportation policy, regulation of water carriers in interstate and foreign commerce, establishment of a board of investigation and research to investigate the various modes of transportation, government to pay full rates on its traffic and various amendments to the Interstate Commerce Act.

TRANSPORTATION AND EXPORTATION ENTRY In international trade, this is a form which specifies the goods entering the country (U.S., for example) and will be subsequently exported through a domestic port. All warehouses and carriers used must be bonded.

TRANSPORTATION FACILITIES A term which embraces the services rendered by carriers in moving property or persons from one point to another; the cars, vehicles, airplanes or ships used in the act of carriage; and such things as terminals and depots, that form a part of the carrier's plant and are devoted to the act of transport.

TRANSPORTATION OF EXPLOSIVES ACT An act (March 4, 1909) that regulates the transportation of explosives and other dangerous articles in interstate commerce and provides penalties for any violation of the regulations.

TRANSPORTATION OF PERSONS ACT An act, passed in March 1944, which increased the tax on transportation of persons from its former level of 10 percent (imposed by the Revenue Act of 1942) to 15 percent; repealed in 1963.

TRANSPORTATION RATE The rate charged for a line-haul.

TRANSPORTATION WAREHOUSING This represents a warehousing cost saved. It should be termed a transportation warehousing cost saving. Traffic routing under circumstances of reconsignment and diversion offer opportunities for maximizing the time in transit and thereby receiving a free warehousing service. The savings equal the warehousing costs saved by free storage aboard the carrier instead of storing in a private or public warehouse. This is not a savings if the market could have been predetermined and the shipment routed more directly. Under these circumstances, it would represent an added inventory-in-transit cost, rather than a reduced warehousing cost.

TRANSPORT INTERNATIONAL DES ROUTIERS (T.I.R.) An agreement between European countries which authorizes sealed container units to cross boundaries by motor transport without going through inspection, and without paying duties. The inspection and duties are handled at the destination.

TRANSPORT OR CONVEYING LINE Pipes used in materials handling for carrying entrained solids.

TRANSSHIP A term denoting the transfer of freight shipments between boat lines and railroads; the rehandling of goods en route.

TRANSSHIPPING Where there is no steamship line operating between the United States and a foreign port, it is necessary to ship to some point where cargo can be transferred to another carrier for transportation to final destination. The act of transferring is called *transshipping*, and the point where the transfer occurs, the *place of transshipment.*

TRAP CAR This term is used interchangeably with the term ferry cars. It refers to a car loaded by a single shipper at his industrial site containing shipments to various destinations. Another meaning applied to these terms is a car that is loaded by the transportation carrier which contains numerous less-than-carload shipments for various origins.

TRAVELER A commercial agent; a salesman.

TRAVELING This is a term used to describe the motion applied to move the crane.

TREATY A compact or agreement entered into between the governments or sovereigns of two or more states.

TREK To travel by wagon, truck or other conveyance, with accoutrements, (in search of a new settlement).

TRESPASSER As used in connection with accident reports, one who goes on the right of way without right, including pedestrians and occupants of vehicles passing closed gates or similar barriers or attempting to pass over or under trains or cars at highway grade crossings.

TRET Allowance for waste of 4 lbs. in 104 lbs., after tare has been deducted.

TRI-AXLE A three axle trailer or tractor.

TRICK A railroad tour of duty, can range from one day to two or more depending upon the schedules.

TRI-LEVEL CAR A three level freight car used for transporting automobiles.

TRIM The nature of a vessel's float. The trim could be an even keel, or it could be trimmed by the head of stern. The term trim is often omitted by saying a vessel is *by the head.*

TRIMMING CHARGE A charge assessed at so much per ton for distributing coal in a ship so that the load will not shift and in order that the weight will be properly distributed.

TRIP DELAY The loss of driver time after he is available for a trip but is forced to wait for loading, paperwork, trip assignment, repairs, etc.

TRIP LEASE This term refers to equipment leasing. It may be between two carriers, or between a private carrier and a common carrier.

TRIPLICATE To make three copies; the third copy.

TROLLEY BRAKE A means of operating a trailer brake, independent of the tractor brake, by means of a hand valve.

TROLLEY, LOAD (OVERHEAD RUNWAY TYPE) A trolley moving system operating two or more wheels on overhead tracks by a self-powered or manually operated action.

TRUCK, DRIVERLESS An automatically controlled vehicle that can pull trailers or carry loads. The direction comes from control wires in the floor or road surface. It can be applied to any set of directions in this way. These trucks may be operated by remote radio.

TRUCK JOCKEY Slang for a truck driver.

TRUCKLOAD A shipment transported by motor carrier that meets the minimum weight required for the application of a truckload (TL) rate.

TRUCKMAN One who transports goods by means of trucks, drays, carts or wagons.

TRUCK MASTER A truck driver.

TRUCK MAIL This is not the movement of public mail, but the carriers' business mail between terminals or stations in its own vehicles.

TRUCK MILE EARNINGS The earnings per truck mile. Attained by dividing gross revenue by the miles traveled.

TRUCK, SKID An elevating vehicle that may be inserted under the skid that permits raising and then moving the skid.

TRUCK, STACKING A truck with extended legs that may straddle or go under the load. Elevation of the load is performed with hydraulic pump. The forms on the truck may be alternated with a platform.

TRUCK TRACTOR The trailer pulling vehicle. Used to pull trailers and semi-trailers.

TRUE LEASE One in which the lessor has the benefits and risks of ownership; the lesse acquires the use of the asset for a stated period of time without building any equity in the asset.

TRUNK LINE A carrier operating over a large territory. A term now used interchangeably with *Main Line*.

TRUST RECEIPT A document given banks by exporters and importers in exchange for a bill of lading.

TRUTH IN LEASING REGULATION ICC administrative regulations that serve to assist owner-operators who trip lease to carriers; found in 49 CFR 1057, these require specific escrow requirements and divulging of the freight bill.

TUG AND SMALL TRACTOR A small powered unit that tows trailers. The driver may ride or walk. It is battery operated. A bumper permits pushing some loads.

TUGBOAT A small boat used to tow or move other boats, lighters, barges, etc.

TUMBLE OR FALLING HOME The extent the sides of the vessel turn in from the perpendicular.

TUNDISH A container used for collection of liquids from several sources. It is conical in shape.

TURBOFAN The type of airplane engine in which the thrust of the turbojet engine has been increased by applying a low-pressure fan. The turbofan engine may have a separate fan driven by the turbine, or it can have a low-pressure compressor on the front which permits part of the airflow to by-pass the engine.

TURBOJET An engine that has an air compressor to facilitate combustion, with the gas combustion serving to rotate the turbine as well as create the thrusting power.

TURBOPROP A jet engine, not a piston engine, that drives a propeller. The propeller shaft operates the propeller and the compressor for the jet combustion.

TURBULENT FLOW A flow with different direction and magnitude at all points.

TURN A general term used about the vessel. The seaman turns in for the night. The tide turns, etc.

TURN AROUND The combined movement from and to a given terminal. This commonly used term in motor transportation refers to the action of the driver returning to his point of origin after a delivery. Usually it involves the same vehicle, but it may not.

TURNAROUND (VESSEL) The time it takes between the arrival of the vessel and its departure.

TURNING CIRCLE (OF A STEAMER) The circle followed by the vessel when steaming under a hard-over helm.

TURNOUT Another term for a railroad switch.

TURNOVER, ASSETS Total sales of a firm divided by the sum total of assets in the firm; measure of asset profitability.

TURNOVER, INVENTORY The total flow of inventory handled in a given period divided by the average amount held on hand.

TURNTABLES, RUNWAY (MANUALLY OR POWERED) A device which may be rotated to allow the trolley that carries the lifting blocks to be diverted to other tracks which are usually at right angles to the main track. All tracks are on the same level or plane.

TURNTABLE STEERING The front axle of the vehicle pivots around a king pin for a turntable type of rapid direction change.

'TWEEN Means between decks.

TWIN SCREW The power applied to two rear axles in a truck—with the same power source for each axle.

TWO-MAN OPERATION The joint driver operation of two alternating drivers on the same rig on long haul movements. This facilitates a through movement without stopping for rest under single driver operations. Since the vehicle tie-up costs during the stop and rest period exceed the extra driver costs during the total trip time, the operation is sometimes economically feasible.

TWO-WAY OR Y JUNCTION Equipment that permits conveyor load to be diverted to one or two branches.

—U—

UBIQUITOUS MATERIALS Materials that are universally available are ubiquitous. For practical purposes, materials that are somewhat generally available are normally termed ubiquitous. Thus, one might consider water for soft drink production and clay for brick production to be ubiquitous materials. The significance of ubiquitous materials is that it encourages decentralization of production.

U.C.C. Uniform commercial code.

ULLAGE The amount a cask or container lacks of being full.

ULTIMO Last (month).

UMBRELLA RATES When the minimum rate for one carrier mode is held higher than it would prefer in order to permit another carrier, usually with a higher variable cost, to compete, it is called an umbrella rate. It is the process of making rates sufficiently high to protect the high cost agency. This is a pricing policy frequently adopted in cartelized industries. This is most unreasonable when it provides protection for a high cost carrier. In the Ingot Molds Case of 1965, the Supreme Court permitted the Commission to use out-of-pocket cost, fully distributed cost, or some other measurement of cost in setting the minimum level for a rate.

UNBALANCED TRAFFIC A greater movement of traffic in one direction than in the other.

UNCLAIMED FREIGHT Freight that cannot be delivered as a result of improper address, though it has been called for by the receiver or owner.

UNCLAIMED GOODS Goods in government storehouses not called for within three years of time of storing, or on which duties have not been paid.

UNCONCEALED LOSS OR DAMAGE CLAIMS Claims resulting from loss and damage which are apparent on delivery. The consignee specifies in writing on the carrier's delivery receipt the nature of the loss and damage. This should be signed by the consignee representative and delivery time noted. The local freight agent is notified immediately.

UNDERCHARGES Charges for transportation services, which are less than those applicable thereto under the tariffs lawfully on file with the Commission.

UNDERHANG The space on a pallet between the outer edge of the packages and the pallet edges; indicates less than 100% pallet area utilization.

UNDERWAY In water transportation this implies that the anchor has been weighed and the vessel is underway. Even if the vessel has been stopped, it is underway if disconnected with the dock. The terms under weigh and underway are synonymous, but underway is now preferred among seamen. The term weigh generally means the raising of the anchor.

UNDERWRITER An insurance firm. In water transportation, it insures the cargo and vessel. It is common practice in water insurance for several underwriters to cover a portion of the total coverage.

UNDUE OR UNJUST DISCRIMINATION A discrimination which is unwarranted by the facts in a particular case. Under the Interstate Commerce Act it is unlawful for any common carrier subject to the Act to make or give any undue or unreasonable preference or advantage to any particular person, company, firm, corporation or locality, or to subject them to any undue or unreasonable prejudice of disadvantage. Thus, if a carrier establishes different rates on identical services, it would be unjust, and upon complaint the carrier would be ordered to remove the unjust discrimination.

UNIFORM COMMERCIAL CODE (UCC) The body of laws that cover basic contracts, warehouse-goods owner relationships.

UNIFORM CUSTOMS AND PRACTICES FOR DOCUMENTARY CREDITS (U.C.P.) The U.C.P. is a set of rules for letters of credit drawn up by the Commission on Banking Technique and Practices of the International

Chamber of Commerce in consultation with the banking association of many countries. It was revised and became effective in October, 1975 and is published under ICC Publication No. 290. All major trading countries adhere to the U.C.P.

UNIFORM DEMURRAGE RULES Schedules providing rules and charges for demurrage which are in general used throughout the United States, having the approval, but not prescribed by, the Interstate Commerce Commission.

UNIFORM EXPRESS RECEIPT A receipt furnished the shipper for goods entrusted to the Express Company for transportation.

UNIFORM LIVESTOCK CONTRACT The uniform order or straight bills of lading cannot be used to cover the transportation of livestock or wild animals. This class of shipment must be consigned on a straight livestock contract. It is provided for in the rail freight classification. However, the shipment of live poultry or pigeons moves on a uniform domestic straight bill of lading and not a livestock contract. Under a uniform livestock contract, the shipper must declare whether a shipment consists of ordinary livestock or other than ordinary livestock. Ordinary livestock refers to standard farm animals such as cattle, hogs, sheep, goats, horses, etc. No declaration of value is needed when a shipment of ordinary livestock is sent. However, different rates are in effect for shipments of other than ordinary livestock. A declaration of value is entered in the column provided for valuation. The carrier is not held liable for any amount in excess of the specified valuation. Under the uniform livestock contract, the carrier is not responsible for injury resulting from crowding, kicking, escape, etc. However, it would be responsible in the event of negligence. Negligence involves the failure to exercise care in loading or unloading, defects of the car, failure to water and rest.

UNIFORM THROUGH EXPORT BILL OF LADING This unique bill of lading is only used for land and water transportation movements. It is divided into three parts. The first part covers the rail movement to the port. The next part covers the ocean transportation. The third part covers the transportation from the foreign port to the ultimate destination. At the present time the through export bill of lading is used only on rail carload or LCL shipments originating at Denver and points east for export through west coast ports. It is issued in both the straight and order forms. The rail carrier issuing the through bill signs the contracts for all carriers.

UNITED PARCEL SERVICE Referred to as U.P.S.—a commercial firm engaged in shipping packages.

UNITED STATES RAILROAD ADMINISTRATION A body created by Act of Congress and charged with the operation of Federal controlled lines during the period, January 1, 1918, to March 1, 1920.

UNITED STATES SHIPPING BOARD A body created by Act of Congress and charged with the administration and operation of such merchant marine activities as are under the control and jurisdiction of the federal government.

UNITIZATION The consolidation of a number of individual items onto one shipping unit for easier handling. It is also the securing or loading of one or more large items or cargo into a single structure, or carton.

UNITIZE To consolidate by banding, binding, etc., several packages into a single unit for shipment.

UNIT LOAD The process of combining a number of packages, by binding, banding, etc., so the unit package can be moved as a single unit.

UNIT OF TRAFFIC The average number of passengers or tons of freight transported.

UNIT RECORD EQUIPMENT The standard punched card data processing machinery operated by controlled panel, rather than by stored program computers.

UNIT TRAIN Movement of a particular commodity in trainload lots on an arranged schedule.

UNIVERSE In statistical computations, this is the total population from which a sample has been taken.

UNLATCH In motor transportation, this term is applied to the releasing of the lock on the fifth wheel of the trailer to permit dropping the trailer.

UNLAWFUL Opposed to law.

UNLOCATED LOSS OR DAMAGE Injury to goods, person or property occurring at some time or place not exactly known.

UNROUTED A shipment tendered to s carrier without specific shipper routing instructions.

UNSEAWORTHY Unfit for a sea voyage in equipment or condition.

UNSOUND In bad condition.

UNSTUFFING Taking freight out of a container.

UPDATE In data processing, the act of bringing a file of data up-to-date by adding current data and correcting old data is termed *update.*

UPRIGHT Vertical metal frame supporting the bars or shelves of a rack facing.

UPSETTING MOMENT This may be computed by multiplying the tonnage by the upsetting lever (in feet), presented in foot-tons.

USAGE The number of units consumed during a given period of a particular commodity.

USAGE OF TRADE Custom, or the frequent repetition of the same act in business.

USANCE The time allowed by established usage or custom for the payment of a bill of exchange, differing according to the countries.

U.S. CONSULAR INVOICE A statement on merchandise required before a ship may leave any foreign port bound for the United States. It must be sworn to in triplicate or quadruplicate at the American consulate located nearest the point where the goods are assembled for shipment.

U.S. CUSTOMS BONDED WAREHOUSE The federal government retains goods until import duties are paid in a customs bonded warehouse. The importer pays the expense of warehousing, but the U.S. government retains control of the goods. The warehouseman must provide a bond that the goods will not be released until the duties are paid. The customs bond provides no protection to the depositor of the goods.

USEFUL LIFE The length of time in which an asset lasts, as different from depreciable life.

USEFUL LOAD The dead weight tonnage of the vessel.

U.S. FLAG CARRIER In air transportation, the holder of a certificate of public convenience and necessity to transport freight and/or personnel between the U.S. and/or its territories to one or more foreign countries. This operating authority requires both Civil Aeronautics Board and Presidential approval.

U.S. GOVERNMENT BILL OF LADING The United States Government is the world's largest shipper. A special bill of lading is made out for government shipments. It is a draft on the Treasury of the United States. These bills specify the people who are accountable under the government bill of lading contract. It is important that a traffic manager recognize that the government consignee has no latitude in accepting or refusing shipments.

U.S. INTERNAL REVENUE BONDED WAREHOUSE Goods which must be held until internal revenue has been paid are placed in a U.S. Internal Revenue bonded warehouse. This must be on goods produced in the U.S., and it offers no protection to the depositor of the goods.

USURY Interest beyond the lawful rate.

U-WAGON A wheeled vehicle that is U shaped and used to station around a container, lift it, and permit towing to a preferred location.

—V—

VACATION NOTICE OR ORDER (I.C.C.) An order setting aside a ruling of the Interstate Commerce Commission.

VACUUM PACKAGING The process of packaging in a vacuum, or when all air has been removed prior to sealing. It may be performed on flexible or rigid containers.

VALID Binding; good in law.

VALUATION, ACTUAL The value as specified on the bill of lading by the shipper. The transportation rate reflects the value of the commodity.

VALUATION, AGREED The value of an article or shipment agreed upon by shipper and carrier in order to establish a specific liability in case of loss or damage.

VALUATION, DECLARED The valuation placed on an article or shipment when it is delivered to the carrier.

VALUATION, RELEASED A condition which limits the carrier's liability for damage to freight while in transit.

VALUE To estimate; worth.

VALUE ANALYSIS A system that stresses the functions of a product rather than on the systems for creating the ongoing product design. It involves the systematic use of techniques to identify a function, establish its value, and provide the function in the most economic way.

VALUED POLICY A marine insurance policy covering risks to a fixed amount of valuation.

VALUE, EXTRAORDINARY A degree of value which entirely prohibits the movement by freight of goods so classed, or permits it only under certain specified conditions.

VALUE OF SERVICE In transportation pricing charging on the basis of *what the traffic will bear* or, according to Professor Locklin, "not charging what the traffic will not bear" is value of service pricing. There is a common misconception that value of service pricing involves pricing higher than cost of service. This is incorrect because value of service pricing may be at a level below cost of service, it may be equal to cost of service, or it may be above cost of service. In the Hoch-Smith Resolution of 1926, the United States Congress directed the I.C.C. to set rates on agriculture commodities at levels that would move the traffic. At that time this meant setting rates below fully distributed costs.

VALUE RECEIVED A phrase used in bills or notes to express an indefinite consideration.

VALVE A device that serves to control the flow of liquids. In pneumatic or hydraulic operations valves may take the form of sluice, shovel or flat, non-return, ball and disc, plug, gate, and diaphragm.

VALVE, AIR RELIEF A valve that serves to facilitate air escape in the line. It is installed at the highest point in the line.

VALVE, BUTTERFLY A special type valve which has a disc rotating in an axial bearing.

VALVE, COUNTERWEIGHTED FLAP A valve designed to control the outflow of the material in the line, and prevent entry of air or gas.

VALVE, CYCLONE TAIL In materials handling, this valve is installed in the tail leg of a cyclone to allow the solids to leave the cyclone, but prevent the entraining fluid to escape. It also prevents the entry of air.

VALVE, MOTORIZED HOPPER, FOR CONTINUOUS OPERATION A combination of upper and lower valves which provide continuous alternating performance. This gives continuous discharge of the line without permitting reverse flow of the fluid.

VALVE, MULTI-WAY A valve that can serve many lines. It has a rotating chamber with an inlet and outlet, which can be rotated to service many radially spaced conveying lines.

VALVE, PRESSURE RELIEF A valve with an automatic release for fluids when pressure builds up.

VALVE, SLIDE OR SHUTTER A shutter type valve that has a plate that slides across the pipeline or hopper to control the flow.

VALVE, SONIC This is a type of nozzle with an adjustable needle to allow air to flow at high sonic velocity and thus provide constant quantity of air for back pressure.

VALVE, TWO-WAY A device that is able to divert a single stream of material to two alternating flows.

VALVE, VACUUM RELIEF A type of valve which permits fluid to enter the pipeline under vacuum conditions.

VAN A large covered motor vehicle, used principally for moving pianos and household effects.

VAN BODY A motor vehicle body that is fully enclosed, and commonly used in the transportation of general freight.

VAN CONTAINER A container commonly used to transport freight.

VANNING The process of loading a container.

VAPOR Vessel; steamer.

VARIABLE COSTING A method of inventory valuation that applies only variable costs. Variable production costs would include labor, materials, utility costs, etc. The system is helpful for internal management, but is seldom used in external financial costing.

VARIANCE The deviation between planned and actual.

VARNISH FINISH A protective fluid used to coat a surface for both protection and appearance.

VEGETABLE CAR A car equipped with facilities for safe and proper handling of vegetables.

VEHICLE Any carriage or other contrivance capable of being used as a means of transportation on land.

VELOCITY, CRITICAL AIR The critical air velocity which is required to facilitate fluidization.

VELOCITY, CRITICAL SETTLEMENT The level of velocity, which if lowered, will permit the largest particles to settle out.

VELOCITY, OPTIMUM That velocity which requires the lowest power requirement without the process of settlement taking place.

VELOCITY, PARTICLE The velocity of a particle at any specified time.

VENDEE One to whom something is sold, a buyer.

VENDOR The seller. The company supplying the product.

VENDOR LEAD TIME The time expiring from the making out of a purchase requisition until the purchase is received in the warehouse. This is also called the lead time, or the purchasing cycle.

VENDOR PERFORMANCE INDEX A rating of experience factors when dealing with vendors; based upon quality, on-time performance, etc.

VENTILATE To admit air.

VENTILATED CAR A car equipped with openings at top, sides and/or ends to admit air.

VENTILATION The regulation of the circulation of air.

VENUE The place where an action in the law arises.

VERTICLE INTEGRATION The ownership of combinations of complimentary operations in the vertical channel represents vertical integration. Total vertical integration would involve the ownership of the source of raw materials, all storage facilities, all transport facilities, all manufacturing and processing facilities, and all marketing outlets. One form of diversification may involve vertical integration to some degree.

VESSEL, FOREIGN A term sometimes applies to a vessel not registered or licensed, in reference to the privileges derived from the revenue system. In a number of instances the term designates a vessel navigating under the flag and with the papers of a foreign government.

VESSEL, PUBLIC A vessel belonging to a nation or government.

VESSEL'S MANIFEST Statement of a vessel's cargo (revenue, consignee, marks, etc.).

VESSEL TON 100 cubic feet.

VIA By way of.

VISIBLE CAPACITY That which is known or is apparent as to the carrying capacity of a car, its type and the nature of the commodity to be loaded and shipped, considered.

VISUAL REVIEW SYSTEM An inventory control system that involves determining the reorder time by walking around and taking note of the stock levels. This is usually used for low value items and items seldom required.

VOICE GRADE This term applies to a voice telephone line used in data processing that has a capacity of as much as 500 characters per second.

VOLUME RATE A rate applicable in connection with a specified volume (weight) of freight.

VOLUME SHIPMENT A shipment that qualifies for the volume rate, or the minimum rate required for a rate reduction.

VOUCHER A receipt, entry, or other document which establishes the truth of accounts.

VOYAGE In water transportation, the outward and homeward trips are termed a voyage, though the movements between ports are termed voyages in insurance underwriting.

VOYAGE CHARTER A contract for hiring a vessel for a specific voyage. The terms of the contract are specified in the charter.

VOYAGE POLICY An insurance policy based on a voyage, rather than on travel for a specific time period. Normally, a time policy will cover the vessel for a maximum of one year, subject to extension.

—W—

WAIT TIME The time expended while a job awaits processing.

WAIVER The forfeiting of a right.

WAIVER CLAUSE The waiver clause normally used states: "And it is expressly declared and agreed that no acts of the insurer or assured in recovering, saving or preserving the property insured, shall be considered as a waiver or acceptance of abandonment."

WAKE The track which follows the vessel as it moves through the water. The term is also used to refer to the efficiency of the propeller while operating in forward moving water of the wake current. The wake of the hatch is directly behind the hatch opening.

WALL TO WALL INVENTORY A condition when materials, parts or supplies are involved in processing from one end of the plant to the other without involvement in formal stock.

WAREHOUSE A place for the reception and storage of goods.

WAREHOUSE, BONDED A place used for the storage and custody of import merchandise which is subject to duty until the duties are paid or the goods are reshipped without entry. The owners of such warehouses must be approved by the Secretary of the Treasury and must give guarantees or bonds for the strict observance of revenue laws.

WAREHOUSE COST The warehouse cost may be incurred under private or public warehouse storage. The warehouse rate determines the warehouse cost if the public warehouse is used. The average warehouse cost represents the computed cost of rendering a private warehouse service involving the same operations as those provided by the public warehouse under the warehouse rate. The warehouse cost under private facilities for multiple commodity storage circumstances is an average approximation.

WAREHOUSE DELIVERY ORDER A document authorizing the release of merchandise from the warehouse.

WAREHOUSE ENTRY The document or form which identifies goods imported when placed in a bonded warehouse. The duty is not imposed on the products while in the warehouse, but will be collected when they are withdrawn for consumption.

WAREHOUSE LABOR COST This is commonly referred to as the in-and-out costs. It is a flat charge assessed per hundredweight and cannot be influenced by the volume of shipment. Each hundredweight of a shipment must be moved in and out, so the average warehouse labor cost cannot be influenced by the volume of shipment. In most public warehouse tariffs, a separate charge is made for labor costs. Surprising to most people, the labor cost is usually about twice the warehouse rate. However, the average warehouse cost, which is the warehouse rate times the time in storage cost may become larger per hundredweight than the labor cost per hundredweight if the volume of shipment is so large as to require an extended period of time in storage.

WAREHOUSEMAN A person who receives and ships goods and merchandise to be stored in his warehouse for hire.

WAREHOUSE, PUBLIC A place of storage used by the general public. In addition to the service of storage, many public warehouses perform the functions of a distributing agent or forwarder.

WAREHOUSE (RAILROAD) With the changing of the liability of the carrier from that of *common carrier* to that of *warehouseman,* resulting in a decrease in degree of liability, the railroads have provided extensive storage facilities in the shape of warehouses. Two general kinds of storage are available; (1) storage in transit as a necessary part of the service of carriage, manufacturing or milling, and, (2) Enforced Storage, resulting from inability of the carriers to make delivery.

WAREHOUSE RATE The charge for the storage of goods by a public warehouse is the warehouse rate. It is also called the storage rate. The warehouse rate does not change per hundredweight as the volume of shipment changes. It is a fixed cost. Under most circumstances, there is not a reduction in warehouse rate for varying volumes of shipment. The warehouse rate does not include labor costs associated with the in-and-out services on the good. Warehouse cost is the product of the warehouse rate times the volume in storage.

WAREHOUSE RECEIPT A receipt, usually negotiable, given for goods, known as a *lot*, placed in a warehouse for storage.

WAREHOUSING The storing of goods.

WARES Goods, merchandise and commodities, bought, sold and shipped.

WARRANT (WAREHOUSE) A receipt issued by a public or bonded warehouse.

WARRANTY An assurance that merchandise and title are as represented.

WAR RISK INSURANCE Insurance coverage for losses resulting from war activity.

WAR TAX A tax on the total freight charges, including demurrage, etc., assessed on all classes of freight for domestic consumption. (War measure.)

WASHOUT An erosion of the permanent roadbed by storm or flood to such extent as would cause delay of trains, or endanger traffic.

WASH PLATE OR BULKHEAD PLATE This is a baffle plate.

WASH PORT An opening in the bulwark of the ship for the freeing of water. It is usually a barred opening.

WASTAGE Loss in handling; shrinkage or decay.

WATCH (SHOP BOARD) On ship board for equal apportionment of labor and discipline, the crew is mustered in two divisions, the Starboard (right facing bow) and Port, (left). The day commences at noon and is divided into seven watches as follows: Afternoon watch (noon to 4 pm); First Dog watch (4 pm to 6 pm); Second Dog watch (6 pm to 8 pm); First Watch (8 pm to midnight); Middle Watch (Midnight to 4 am); Morning watch (4 am to 8 am); Forenoon watch (8 am to Noon).

WATER BALLAST Water carried in the low flat tanks or double bottom of the vessel for the purpose of trimming the ship. It may be released by pumps or flooded by sea cocks.

WATER BORNE Floating.

WATER CARRIER ACT OF 1940 An act of Congress delegating to the Interstate Commerce Commission regulatory powers applicable to common and contract water carriers operating in domestic trade.

WATER COMPELLED RATE Rate charged by railroads that are depressed in a specific market in response to coastwise or barge competition.

WATERLOGGED A situation in which the vessel is floating only as a result of the buoyancy of its cargo. The vessel has lost its buoyancy.

WATER REACTIVE MATERIAL (SOLID) Means any solid substance (including sludges and pastes) which, by interaction with water, is likely to become spontaneously flammable or to give off flammable or toxic gases in dangerous quantities.

WATERTIGHT COMPARTMENTS Compartments made water free by the application of watertight bulkheads and doors.

WATER TRAFFIC This applies to the movement or handling of goods and persons by vessel.

WAVE PERIOD The time required for two successive waves to crest.

WAY Refers to the ship's action through the water.

WAYBILL The official document which is used to identify the shipper and the consignee, present the routing, describe the goods, present the applicable rate, show the weight of the shipment, and make other useful information notations.

WAYBILL DESTINATION The destination of the shipment.

WEATHER The weather side is the windward side.

WEATHERBOUND Held up by weather.

WEATHER DECK A deck out in the weather—without overhead protection.

WEATHER INTERFERENCE That level of weather activity which retards the loading, unloading or other logistics activity.

WEATHER WORKING DAY Day which permits work operations so far as weather conditions are concerned.

WEIGHING AND INSPECTION BUREAUS A railway organization to secure for its members uniform practices in complying with tariff regulations and requirements of governmental authorities relating to weight, classification, and condition of shipments.

WEIGHT That which it weighs. In shipping, weight is qualified as *gross,* (the weight of the goods and the container); *net,* (the weight of the goods themselves without any container); and *legal,* (similar to *net* and determined in such manner as the law of a particular country may direct).

WEIGHT, AGREED A specific weight agreed upon by shipper and carrier for commodities transported in a particular container or package or in a certain manner.

WEIGHT AGREEMENT A form of agreement between shippers and carriers when shippers desire to use estimated weights not already incorporated in classifications and other traffic schedules.

WEIGHT CAPACITY The carrying capacity of a car designated in weight is referred to as the weight capacity.

WEIGHT CARGO A cargo on which the transportation charge is assessed on the basis of weight.

WEIGHT CERTIFICATE A certificate, sometimes signed by a public weigher, certifying as to the weight of a shipment.

WEIGHTED AVERAGE The statistical process of running an average of many forms of date, with each class of data given a percentage value which jointly equals 100 percent.

WEIGHT, ESTIMATED The weights provided in classification and tariff schedules for goods shipped in certain packages, in a certain manner, or under certain conditions. The general practice of the carriers, however, is to base charges on the gross or combined weights of the articles and containers.

WEIGHT, GROSS In shipping, the total weight of the goods plus the weight of the container and packing materials.

WEIGHT, LANDED The weight of a shipment as the point of landing.

WEIGHT, LEGAL Usually the same as net weight.

WEIGHT LOSING MATERIAL A commodity that tends to loose weight in the production process.

WEIGHT, NET The weight of the goods alone, not including the weight of the container.

WEIGHT NOTE A document issued by dock companies giving details of marks, weights, date of entry, etc., of imported goods.

WEIGHT OR MEASUREMENT, SHIP'S OPTION A term denoting a charge assessed on the basis of weight if the weight of the shipment exceeds its cubic measurement, or on a measurement basis if the cubic measurement exceeds the weight of the shipment.

WEIGHT OUT Term in freight carriage when vehicle reaches weight limit though some empty space still exists in it.

WEIGHT, PAR The steamship par between weight and measurement goods: 56 pounds, found by dividing a long ton (2,240 lbs.) by 40 cubic feet.

WEIGHTS AND WEIGHING Under law, a shipper has a right to have the correct weight of his shipments ascertained so that the charges computed may be correct.

WEIGHT SHEETS The listing with weights of the articles in a shipment. Presented to the weighing bureaus.

WEIGHT, TARE The weight of the container alone.

WELCH FORMULA A formula used to reduce the inventory carried for a number of products. It seeks to reduce ordering costs without increasing inventory, or reduce inventory without increasing set-up costs.

WELL CAR A flat car with a depression or opening in the center to allow the load to extend below the normal floor level in order to come within overhead clearance limits.

WESTBOUND OR WESTWARD The direction of train movements in which the distance by rail from San Francisco is decreasing. A few exceptions have been established on branch lines where this rule would result in confusion because of so-called *westbound* trains actually operating in *eastbound* compass direction.

WESTERN HEMISPHERE TRADE CORPORATION A United States corporate enterprise that performs business anywhere in the Western Hemisphere—North and South America, Central America, or the West Indies—and operates under tax advantages.

WET GOODS Liquids for shipment in bottles or cask.

WET LEASE Airline charter that includes the crew.

WET STRENGTH Wet tensile strength is the measure of resistance of paper when saturated with water. Wet bursting strength applies to containers filled with water.

WHARF A place for berthing vessels in order to facilitate the loading and discharging of passengers and freight; usually a platform of wood, stone, or other material parallel to a stream or other body of water, alongside of which a vessel may wharf for loading or discharging.

WHARFAGE The charge against a vessel for use of a wharf for the purpose of loading, discharging, or docking.

WHARFINGER One who owns and/or operates a wharf.

WHARFINGER'S RECEIPT A document acknowledging receipt of goods for shipment by a wharfinger.

WHEELBARROW A one wheeled device for the handpushing of materials, etc. The elevation of the hand shaft end of the box permits concentrating most weight on the wheel, while the single wheel optimizes manuverability.

WHEEL REPORT A document, made from waybills, which lists the cars in a train as it leaves a yard and on which the conductor posts setoffs and pickups. On trains reaching a yard, the document is known as the inbound (train) consist; on departing trains, as the outbound (train) consist. A copy of the wheel report is sent to the car accountant's office, to be posted to the car record.

WIDE BODY Large jets such as B-747, L-1011 and DC-10.

WIDE-SPREAD Motor truck axles which exceed eight feet apart. (On the trailer.)

WILLIE Railroad slang term for a waybill.

WINCH RIG A straight truck which carries a hoist for pulling or lifting.

WINGS The outer bridge of the vessel. That part of the deck near the sides of the vessel.

WINTER LOAD LINE A load line on a vessel that is lower to provide for rougher weather conditions.

WITHOUT ENGAGEMENT A phrase incorporated in a quotation and used to avoid having to accept an order at the price quoted. A safeguard against prices fluctuating in the interval between the giving of the quotation and the order being placed.

WITHOUT RECOURSE A phrase preceding the signature of a drawer or dorser. It is added to a bill of exchange or a note for endorser protection.

WITHOUT RECOUSE A phrase preceding the signature of a drawer or endorser of a negotiable instrument and signifying that the instrument is passed onto subsequent holders without any liability to the endorser in the event of non-payment or non-delivery. Many negotiable instruments are signed "with recourse," meaning that in the event of non-performance, the holder has a right to make a claim on the last endorser.

WITHOUT RECOURSE CLAUSE, BILL OF LADING (SECTION 7) common carrier bill of lading part; when signed by shipper, carrier can not seek freight bill payment from shipper if consignee fails to pay charges.

WITH PARTICULAR AVERAGE (W.P.A.) Under this insurance arrangement, partial loss or damage to merchandise is covered. It is used in application to loss by seawater. Payment will be forthcoming with little damage. It is often extended to include losses from pilferage, leakage, breakage, theft, non-delivery, etc.

WITNESS A person produced to testify as to the correctness of a statement, fact or action.

WOOD CHIP CARS A converted box car with roof removed used in hauling fuel (sawmill refuse, etc., i.e., wood trimmings, and sawdust used for fuel).

WOODCHUCK A slang term applied to a driver with little seniority.

WORD In data processing, a word is a combination of bytes to facilitate computational requirements. The availability of third generation systems has eliminated the difference between word machines and byte machines.

WORK The action of the vessel or the cargo which results from the movement.

WORK CENTER In production and inventory, the term refers to a section of the plant where a specialized form of work is underway.

WORK ORDER Orders made out for machine processing or maintenance.

WORK SAMPLING The application of random samples to establish frequency of performance.

WORK STATION The place of operation for a worker.

WORST ANALYSIS A means of concentrating effort on the most unstable phase of a system. The use of partial differentials is one way of converging on an unstable system. Applies to data processing.

W&R Water and rail.

WRAP AROUND A wooden cage placed on top of pallet, adding extra support to the product on the pallet enabling higher stacking.

WRECKAGE Merchandise (saved) from a wreck.

WRECKER A special vehicle for towing and pulling disabled vehicles.

WRECK MASTER A person legally appointed to take charge of goods, etc., thrown ashore after a shipwreck.

—Y—

YACHT A quick sailing vessel, used for pleasure.

YARD A system of tracks within defined limits, whether or not part of a terminal, designed for switching services, over which movements not authorized by time-table or by train order may be made, subject to prescribed signals, rules, and regulations.

YARDAGE The charge made in addition to the transportation and other charges for shipping livestock to a stockyard located in various sections of the country. This charge, usually assessed on the basis of so much per head, varies in amount according to the nature of the livestock.

YARD CART A form of trailer used to transport containers in a yard storage area.

YARD, CLASSIFICATION An area in a railroad yard where freight trains are made up according to destinations.

YARD ENGINE An engine assigned to yard service and used for work within yard limits only.

YARD (FREIGHT) A unit of track systems within a certain area used for storing cars, loading and unloading freight, and making up trains, over which movements not authorized by time-table or by train order may be made, subject to prescribed signals and regulations. These units are further qualified according to the service each performs as: *Receiving Yard,* (where trains or cars are received); *Storage Yard,* (where cars are held pending disposition); *Classification Yard,* (where cars are segregated according to their kind, contents and destination); *Hump Yard,* (where trains are broken up, a car being pushed over the *summit* and after uncoupling are run down from the hump by gravity. This is an artificially constructed elevation overtopping a wide expanse of freight yards net worked with tracks and switches); *Make-up Yard,* (where trains are made up); *Gravity Yard,* (where the classification of cars is accomplished by gravity); *Poling Yard,* (where movement of cars is done by use of poles by an engine on an adjacent paralleled track).

YARD HOSTLER a truck tractor of sorts that is used to move trailers around and within a terminal.

YARDING-IN-TRANSIT The process of stopping in-transit to store, load, unload, sort, and otherwise handle forest products.

YARD JOCKEY see YARD HOSTLER

YARD MASTER The one person who is in charge of the yard.

YARD SWITCHING Switching service performed by yard locomotives in yards where regular switching service is maintained, including terminal switching and transfer service in connection with the transportation of revenue freight and incidentally of company freight. See train switching.

YAWL A light, two-masted boat.

YIELD the total revenue derived by a transportation vehicle, plane seat, etc., in a given period.

YIELD POINT That point in stress which identifies the beginning of deformation.

YORK-ANTWERP RULES OF 1890 Rules adopted in Antwerp in 1890 which established the standard basis for adjusting general average. The code states the rules for adjusting claims.

—Z—

ZERO DEFECTS An objective in purchasing and production in which 100% quality is sought.

ZERO SUPPRESS In data processing, this is a utility module used to remove nonsignificant zeros to the left of a number before the printing process takes place.

ZERO-ZERO WEATHER Weather where flying visibility is not effective, in any direction.

ZINCS Plates made of zinc placed between steel and bronze to prevent an electrolytic process.

ZONE OF RATE FREEDOM A zone within which a carrier may raise or lower its rates without them being subject to lawful charges from shippers, consignees or other carriers.

ZONES (EXPRESS) Districts of the United States (blocks and subblocks) used in rate-making in connection with express traffic and rates.

ZONES (PARCEL POST) The eight divisions of the United States and its possessions made for the purpose of establishing parcel-post rates.

ZONE STORAGE Merchandise stored in the warehouse in large areas and given area location.

ZONES (TIME) Districts of the United States used for timemaking purposes, called the Eastern, Central, Mountain and Pacific zones.

TRANSPORTATION RATES —
ALL CARRIER MODES

ACCESSORIAL CHARGES Supplementary services and privileges associated with transportation are accessed an added charge. Examples of such services are loading, unloading, pickup, transit privileges, stopoffs for loading and unloading, inspection, grading, switching, etc. They are not included in the freight charge, and usually take the form of a flat charge not based on a unit of weight.

ACTUAL VALUE RATES The Interstate Commerce Commission authorizes the carriers to base the published rate on the value of the commodity. This requires a grouping of commodities in accordance with value and relating the rate with the value. In the event of loss or damage, the value of the shipment may be recovered, rather than a released or agreed value. This system is the counterpart of released value rates.

AGGREGATE TENDER RATE A reduced rate on separate shipments that are included within a single motor carrier pick up move; the economies of the single consolidated pick up, and often part of the line haul, are passed on to the shipper in this lower rate.

AGREED CHARGES A form of rail contract rate in which a reduced rate is applied in exchange for the shipper routing a certain percent of total movements over a certain carrier.

AIR FREIGHT RATES Air freight carriers have their own special tariffs. Their rates are regulated by the Civil Aeronatics Board, their rate are simpler than surface carriers. Numerous special tariffs prevail, among which are a general commodity tariff (Tariff 2; CAB-8), a pickup and delivery tariff (Tariff 3-C; CAB 19), a specific commodity tariff (Tariff SC3; CAB 158), a container tariff (Tariff CT 4; CAB 131), and a rules tariff (Tariff 1-B; CAB 96). Air freight forwarders have their own tariffs.

ANNUAL VOLUME RATE A rate that is tied to a minimum annual tonnage volume by a shipper; a form of contract rate.

ANY QUANTITY RATES Any quantity (AQ) class ratings apply to those articles for which no minimum or volume is required. They are a substitute for LTL or LCL rates, and a substitute for volume rates. They apply for any volume of shipment. Any quantity rates are also applicable to commodities that usually do not move in carload lots, and may take commodity rate form.

ALTERNATIVE RATES Whenever the tariff rules permit either a class or commodity rate to be substituted for a higher rate in another section of the same tariff, or another tariff, when it is lower, it becomes an alternative rate. The rules sometimes permit circumventing the standard rules for rate priorities.

ARBITRARY RATES An arbitrary rate is added to a base point rate to provide the joint rate to a destination beyond or otherwise within the base point regional zone. Commonly, the arbitrary is given to the short-line carrier. This permits setting rates to a few base points, rather than setting specific rates to each terminal in a region. The movement, of course, need not go through the base point.

ASSEMBLY AND DISTRIBUTION RATES These are rates on multiple shipments which are moving under a consolidated bill of lading. Motor carriers provide A & D rates at about 10 percent lower level than ordinary separate small shipments to account for the lower cost of handling the consolidated movement. They are used on shipments that originate or terminate at points beyond the terminal areas of freight forwarders or consolidators. An industrial shipper that regularly performs a consolidated operation, or uses a consolidator, would reap savings from such rates.

BARGE-RAIL RATES A joint barge-rail movement may have a single joint through rate, or a combination of several rates, computed on various segments of the haul. Congressional legislation requires that barge-rail rates will be lower than all-rail rates between the same points.

BASING RATES (or BASING POINT RATES) Rates which are constructed by assuming the rate to a base point, or adding a differential or arbitrary to a base point are known as basing rates. A basing rate is used in combination with other rates to form a through rate.

BLANKET RATES The establishment of a large *blanket area* from or to which equal rates apply. The blanket area may be the origin, destination, or both origin and destination. The transportation rate would be the same per hundredweight from any point in the blanket area to or from a given point or area. Some regard a blanket rate as being synonymous with a group rate, but is usually considered to cover a greater geographic area than a group rate. A blanket area may cover all points east of the Mississippi River, while a grouped area may cover only the New England states. Blanket and grouped rates encourage dispersion.

BREAKDOWN RATES The provision for incrementally reduced rates for incrementally greater volumes of shipment is a process of breaking down rates. While rail carriers have various types of rates which permit lower rates under varying packaging, container, volume, etc., circumstances, motor carriers are more inclined to have graduated breakdown rates based exclusively on volume of shipment.

CAR-FERRY RATES A transportation movement which combines a rail movement with a water transportation of the rail car on a ferry is assigned a car-ferry rate. They may be the same as an all-rail rate.

CARGO RATES Shipments large enough to employ cargo capacity in water transportation are granted cargo rates. Cargo volume is usually considerably larger than that needed to acquire volume rates for other carrier modes.

CARLOAD RATES In railroad movements, shipments which qualify for a specified minimum volume are entitled to a carload rate. There is no necessary relationship between a minimum carload volume and the amount required to utilize the capacity of a rail car. These rates are appreciably lower than less-than-carload rates.

CLASS RATES Rates applied to groups of commodities between specific points, rather than on specific commodities. The class rate structure assures equal class rates on a given class of commodities for any given distance anywhere in the United States. This does not mean that the same cost per ton-mile would prevail for different lengths of haul, since terminal costs make up varying proportions of the rate for varying lengths of haul.

COLLECTION RATES Rates for inbound movement of many shipments that are consolidated at an intermediate point for long haul; it is the reverse of distribution rates.

COMBINATION RATES Rates determined by adding rates on each segment of a through route make up a combination rate. Often they tend to be greater than a single through rate.

COMMODITY RATES Rates on specific commodities between specific points are commodity rates. They are usually lower than class rates, and put into effect to reflect a lower cost of transportation per hundredweight as a result of the volume of the traffic, reduced handling costs, or otherwise. The commodity rate is a special commodity tariff for the carrier mode.

COMPARATIVE RATES An application for a lower rate in a hearing is justified by documenting that rates for comparable movements by others, or the same carrier exists. Comparative rates are rates used to illustrate a more favorable rate under comparable circumstances.

CORPORATE VOLUME RATE A lower than normal rate charged to shippers that provides increasing discounts with increasing tonnage shipped from each firm over a particular carrier throughout specified time periods.

DIFFERENTIAL RATES Differential pricing is reduced pricing, or at least differences in pricing, based on circumstances which provide an excuse for the reduction. Differential rates in transportation result from a type of movement which seems to offer inferior service at a reduced price. Thus, a more circuitous route, or a joint modal (rail-barge) route, might encourage traffic by giving reduced rates which are not really justified by reduced costs of service.

DEMAND SENSITIVE RATE A rate designed to smooth out the peaks and valleys of seasonal product transportation demands; generally higher in peak season, sometimes lower in low season.

DENSITY RATE A transportation rate that is generally lower per hundredweight for products that are dense (heavy per cubic foot) and vice versa.

DISTANCE RATES Rates which reflect the principle of varying rates with distance, though not in proportion to distance, are termed distance rates. These rates usually reflect a constant amount for a terminal charge, and an added amount to reflect the distance of the haul. The term block rates is often applied to distance rates.

DISTRIBUTION RATES A lower rate provided for the consolidation of many small volume shipments all destined for a single commercial area. The distribution rate covers the distribution process in the terminal area, which is added to the low volume line haul rate. The combination of a consolidated line haul rate, plus the distribution rate for the delivery at the destination on each LTL part of the consolidated shipment make up the total combination rate.

EXCESS-OF-CAPACITY RATES Motor carriers, seeking to compete with railroads, publish rates on minimum weights which exceed the legal capacity of a single vehicle. The I.C.C. has recently approved such rates if they are sufficiently compensatory to cover variable costs. It has been ruled that the entire shipment be moved at one time, and the carrier perform no loading and unloading operations. An example might require a minimum shipment minimum weight of 120,000 pounds transported in three or fewer vehicles.

EXPORT RATES Rates on a domestic portion of an international export shipment are granted lower rates than comparable movements not destined for export. Export and import rates take precedence over other rates—be they class or commodity, import or export rates.

FREIGHT FORWARDER RATES Freight forwarders publish their own tariffs. Today their rates are predominantly governed by motor classifications. Years ago, when rail carriers presented most of the line haul service, the freight forwarder rates were primarily based on the railroad classification. Freight forwarder tariffs are both class and commodity, and provide for both less-than-volume and volume shipments. The freight forwarder pays the line haul carrier TL and CL rates on the line haul service, but the forwarder is forced to provide an assembly and distribution service, which forces the actual cost of the service considerably higher than that of the volume rate. The tariffs must reflect this.

GROUP RATES The granting of identical rates for all points in a grouped area, whether a grouped origin or destination (or both), represents a grouped rate. Grouped rates encourage the dispersion of industry.

GUARANTEED RATE 1) a contract carriage rate; 2) an annual volume rate.

IMPORT RATES (see export rates) The reduction in the domestic portion of an international movement below the rates on domestic traffic between the same points provides a low domestic combination rate which is referred to as an import or export rate. They take precedence over other rates beween the same point—be they either class or commodity import rates.

INCENTIVE RATES Reductions in truckload rates for shipment volumes that exceed the minimum truckload volume by a given amount, or percent. The amount of the reduction in the rate is usually established as a percent of the truckload rate. Thus, a shipment volume that exceeds 28,000 lbs. by at least fifty percent, would be granted a reduction in the truckload rate by 10 percent. Motor carriers commonly employ incentive rates, as they do breakdown rates, but the latter are incremental rate reductions. Incentive rates have the approval of the I.C.C. for both motor and rail shipments.

INTERLINE RATES These rates must involve more than one carrier in the transportation service. They may take the form of a joint rate, or a combination rate (two separate rates).

INTERMEDIATE RATES An intermediate rate is a rate to or from an intermediate point in a movement. According to the *aggregate of the intermediate rule*, if the combination of intermediate rates, whether class or commodity, is lower than the through rate, the lower rate prevails. However, if another tariff contains a specific commodity rate on the through movement, which should take priority over a commodity rate on an intermediate movement, the commodity rate under the intermediate rule will not be applicable.

INTERSTATE RATES Any rate on a movement passing through more than one state. Even if the origin and destination is in one state, if the haul passes through more than one state, it is an interstate haul, with an interstate rate.

INTRASTATE RATES Rates on movements which originate and terminate in the same state, and do not pass through another state, are intrastate rates. According to the Shreveport Principle, any combination of purely intrastate rates which are prejudicial to the interstate rate may be removed by the I.C.C. This is applicable only to rail movements. The I.C.C. is directed to not remove intrastate motor and water rates which are prejudicial to interstate rates.

JOINT RATES Joint rates involve a single through rate—not a combination of separate rates (which are called combination rates). A joint rate is a single rate published for the several carriers involved. Joint rates involve more than one carrier, agreeing on a single through rate.

LAND GRANT RATES Rates on government movements which were lower than the published rates as a condition of the land grants to the railroads were collectively called land grant rates. They were repealed, October 1, 1946. It has been estimated that the total savings to the government under the land grant rates, inclusive of voluntary reductions of rates by competing carriers, amounted to 580 million dollars by the end of June, 1943. Land grant rates should not be confused with Section 10721 (Section 22) rates, which are lower rates given federal, state and local governments by I.C.C. regulated carriers.

LAWFUL RATES A lawful rate is one that conforms with the law, or the approval of the I.C.C. or other regulatory authority. A lawful rate may not be the rate published in the tariff, and thus, may not also be the legal rate.

LEGAL RATE The legal rate is the published rate in the tariff. The carrier is legally bound to collect on the legal rate, whether it conforms to the lawful rate or not.

LESS-THAN-CARLOAD RATES The term carload rates applies to both commodity and class rates. It is commonly said that a truckload minimum weight is based on the weight that can be safely loaded in a trailer of 1,500 cubic feet and conform to the legal limits on the vehicle. The railroad carload classification minimum weight is based on the weight that can safely be loaded on a 40-foot car. This is somewhat academic, however, since minimum carload and truckload weights may be considerably less than this. The less-than-carload rate is the rate applicable to shipments which do not qualify for the minimum weight specified for the carload rate.

LESS-THAN-TRUCKLOAD RATE (See less-than-carload rate above) The less-than-truckload rate is the higher rate that must be paid if the volume of the shipment is not sufficiently large to equal the minimum volume specified for a truckload rate—or the shipper is not willing to pay for the minimum volume specified for a truckload rate. If the actual shipment volume times the less-than-truckload rate exceeds the minimum volume times the truckload rate, the lesser charge of the two systems applies on the shipment.

LOCAL RATES The rate on a transportation movement performed on one carrier line, regardless of the length of the haul, is a local rate. If it is not a local rate, it must be a joint rate or a combination rate. It may involve a combination of two rates as a single combination rate, or it may be two joint rates on the movement—but it must involve only one carrier to be a local rate. One rate, by one carrier, on one movement is a local rate.

MAXIMUM RATES In order to protect the public from exorbitant rates, the regulatory authority frequently will establish a maximum rate that may be charged. This ceiling rate is commonly set to cover the costs of operation, committed capital costs, and provide a fair return on investment. A minimum rate is a floor placed on rates to prevent destructive competition. Between the minimum and maximum rate is the *zone of reasonableness*.

MEASUREMENT RATES A measurement rate is usually quoted on a cubic basis or a gross ton basis. One may find measurement rates on ocean movements and bulk shipments by rail. Other forms of measurement rates might take the form of a rate per cord of wood—based on a specific number of cubic feet per cord. In ocean transportation, the rate may be based on a rate per gross ton of 2240 pounds, or per measurement of 40 cubic feet, whichever produces the highest charge.

MILEAGE RATES Mileage rates are also called distance rates. (See distance rates.) Mileage rates vary directly, but not proportionately, with an increase in the length of haul. They tend to have a fixed terminal cost and an added cost per mile of movement. However, mileage blocks provide an equal rate for all distances within the block. Distance or mileage rates may be class or commodity, flat or proportional, local or joint, and may be import, domestic or export rates. According to Tariff Circular No. 20, the mileage class rate may be used only when no specific through rate or commodity rate prevails. Mileage commodity rates may only be used when there is no specific commodity rate.

MINIMUM RATES A *floor* placed on rates, below which they cannot go, is a minimum rate. It is common to establish that the minimum rate cannot go below the variable costs of performing the transportation service.

MISSIONARY RATE Missionary rates are a form of a promotional rate that is often called a proportional rate. Missionary and proportional are used synonymously, though the term proportional rate is more common. A proportional rate is a lower rate on a segment of a through movement than the rate that terminates at the intermediate point. Thus, an attempt to encourage traffic and give a reduced rate for farm machinery between Chicago and the Pacific Northwest, might give a lower rate to Salt Lake City than the ongoing rate, providing the movement was going on to a point in the Northwest. An added rate, like an arbitrary rate or a combination rate would be applied to the proportional rate to Salt Lake City to determine the total combination rate to Portland or Seattle.

MOTOR CARRIER CLASS (COMMODITY) RATES Motor carriers have their own uniform freight classification, which is a modification of the docket 28300 scale of class rates. The National Motor Freight Classification deviates from the 28300 scale for classifications less than about Class 40 or 45. Motor carriers also issue their own competitive commodity rate tariffs which present commodity rates on specific products between specific points.

MULTIPLE CAR RATE The I.C.C. now permits multiple car rates, which are a lower level of rates for shipment volumes that require more than one car. These rates must at least cover out-of-pocket costs, and must be made available as a result of proven competition. In years gone by, the I.C.C. discouraged these rates because: (1) they were thought to be discriminatory against single car shippers, and (2) it was believed there was little difference in the cost of service between single car and multiple car shipments.

MULTIPLE SHIPMENT RATE A rate for freight whereby a lower rate applies on each shipment when many are tendered at the same time.

MULTIPLE-TRAILER LOAD RATES Rates which are lower for shipments requiring more than one trailer load are multiple trailer load rates. The justification for these lower rates is the same as that presented in multiple car rates discussed above. (See multiple car rates.)

PAPER RATES A rate which is published but has never been used is termed a paper rate.

PER CAR RATE A fixed charge per car on specific commodities, between specific points is a per car rate. Sometimes it is referred to as a sealed carload rate. The flat charge is assessed regardless of the volume of the shipment in the car. This rate is commonly used on fresh fruits and vegetables. It has been an effective weapon against exempt motor carrier movements by the Southeastern railroads.

PREJUDICIAL RATES When a rate exists which is deemed to be in violation of Section 10741 on matters of preference and prejudice, it is generally referred to as a prejudicial rate. The term is used as an adjective.

PROPORTIONAL RATES (see missionary rates above) A lower than normal rate on a segment of a through movement to encourage traffic, or capture competitive traffic, is a proportional rate. Normally, it will allow a rate below the published rate commonly prevailing (though it too is published) that reduces the rate to a geographic intermediate point, for traffic destined to points beyond. This type of rate may be used in international movements, providing a lower rate to the gateway port. The proportional rate may be a percentage of the standard rate, or a flat rate which is lower between given points.

REASONABLE RATES This is a regulatory phrase which deals with the character of a particular rate to be just and reasonable in accordance with the wording and interpretation of the Interstate Commerce Act. While the adequacy of a rate to cover costs is often used to appraise its reasonableness, more often than not, reasonableness is measured by comparing a rate with other rates on comparable commodity characteristics and movements.

RELEASED VALUE RATES Released value rates are based on an agreed value of the commodity shipped. While this provides a lower rate, it also provides a lower liability to the carrier. The ratio of agreed value to actual value is applied to the dollar loss to establish the carrier liability.

SECTION 22 RATES Reduced rates are granted federal, state and local governments under Section 22 of the Interstate Commerce Act, recodified as Section 10721 in RICA. These rates may be made on short notice without being subject to the normal rate suspension rules. They must be filed with the I.C.C. So long as they comply with section 5a of the Interstate Commerce Act, they are exempt from anti-trust action. These rates are not to be confused with the land grant rates which were repealed in 1946.

SHORT NOTICE RATES The statute provides that thirty days notice must be provided before filed rates become effective. The I.C.C. may grant short notice rates to become effective before the thirty day period under circumstances of emergency, etc.

SPACE WEIGHT RATE A rate that applies to weight or cubic measure, usually whichever is greater, to determine total freight charges, common in the ocean industry.

THROUGH RATES A through rate is the total rate applicable on a haul. It may be a single joint through rate, it may be a single local rate, it may involve combination rates or any other charge on a continuous carriage by one or several carriers. When more than one carrier is involved, a through rate has been agreed to by carriers for continuous service.

TRUCKLOAD RATES In motor movements, a shipment volume which qaalifies for a minimum volume required for a truckload rate is granted this lower rate. If the truckload rate times its minimim weight requirement is lower than the actual rate times the LTL rate, the lower rate and payment is the legal and lawful rate. There is no needed relationship between the amount required to fill a truck and the minimum truckload weight. (See less-than-carload rates for further amplification.)

VOLUME RATES Rates based on a minimum volume of shipment (weight) are called volume rates. It is a motor rate, and it includes the loading and unloading by the carrier—in contrast to the railroad carload rate in which the carrier does not load and unload. The term volume rate is also used for lower motor carrier LTL rates based on minimum volumes.

WATER COMPELLED RATE Rate charged by railroads that are depressed in a specific market in response to coastwise or barge competition.

STANDARD ABBREVIATIONS

A Acceptance or accepted in commercial language.

a   At; to. At the rate of.

A.A.A. American Automobile Association.

A.A.F.A. Assistant Auditor Freight Accounts.

A.A.R. Association of American Railroads.

a.a.r. Against all risks.

A1 Top rate. First class condition. The highest rating given by Lloyds of London and other insurance organizations.

A.B. Able bodied seamen.

abn. Airborne.

A.B.S. American Bureau of Shipping.

abst., abstr. Abstract.

A/C, or acct. cur. Account current.

Ac, acc. or acct. Account, accountant.

A.C.C. Air Coordinating Committee.

ACI Air Cargo, Inc.

A/cs. Rec. Accounts receivable.

Act., actg. Acting.

act. wt. Actual weight.

ACW American Chain of Warehouses

A.D. In the year of our Lord. Anno Domini.

a.d. After date.

ad., adv., advt. Advertisement.

add. Addition.

ad inf., or ad fin. (ad infinitum) To the end without limit.

ad int. (ad interim) Meanwhile or in the meantime.

Adm. Admiralty, administration, administrator.

Adm. Ct. or Adm. Co. Admiralty Court.

admr. Administrator.

adv. Advance.

ad val. (ad valorem) According to the value.

adv. chgs(-es). Advance charges.

A.E.C. Atomic Energy Commission.

A.F.A. Auditor of Freight Claims.

A.F.C.A. Assistant Freight Claim Agent.

affd. Affirmed.

AFFT. Affidavit.

A.F.O.C. Auditor Freight Overcharge Claims.

A.F.R. Auditor Freight Receipts.
A.F.T. Auditor Freight Traffic.
A.F.T.B. Atlanta Freight Traffic Bureau.
A.F.T.M. Assistant Freight Traffic Manager.
Ag (argentum) Silver (metal).
A.g.b. Any good brand.
agcy. Agency.
A.G.F.A. Assistant General Freight Agent.
agr., agrl. Agriculture, agricultural.
agt. Agent.
a.h. Aft hatch.
alc. Alcohol.
ALJ Administrative Law Judge (ICC, FMC, etc)
ALPA Airline Pilots Association.
alt. Altitude, alternate.
ALSSA Airline Stewards and Stewardesses Association.
ALTA Association of Local Transport Airlines.
alter. Alternate, alternative.
a.m. Anet meridiem (before noon).
A.M.2 Air Mail Route No. 2.
A.M.A. Automobile Manufacturers Association.
amdt. Amendment.
A.M.F. Air mail field.
amt. Amount.
amt. per veh. Amount per vehicle.
A.N. Arrival notice.
an. (anno) In the year.
anal. Analysis.
Ann. Cas. Annotated cases.
Ann. Rep. Annual Report.
annot. Annotated.
annum Year.
ans. Answer.
ante Before.
A/O Account of.
A.O.C. Auditor of Overcharge Claims.
A/P, A/cs. Pay. Accounts payable.
A.P.A. Administrative Procedure Act.
APICS American Production and Inventory Control Society
App. Div. Appellate Division.
approx. Approximate.
appx. Appendix.
app., appln., appn. Application.
A.Q. Any quantity.

A.R. Auditor of receipts, auditor of revenue, Allegheny Region.

A/R All rail (insurance), All risks (identical with W.P.A.).

ar., arr. Arrives, arrival.

arb., arbry. Arbitrary.

ARInc Aeronautical Radio, Inc.

arrd. Arrived.

Arr. N. Arrival Notice.

art. Article.

A/S After sight.

"as" "Same...as."

A.S.L.R. American Short Line Railroads.

ASTT American Society of Traffic and Transportation

assn., assoc. Association.

asst. Assistant.

asstd. Associated, assorted.

A.T. (marine insurance) American terms.

A.T.A. American Trucking Associations, Inc.; American Transit Association; Air Transport Association (of America).

A.T.A. Auditor of Traffic Accounts.

A.T.A.A. Air Transport Association of America.

A.T.C. Air Transport Command.

A.T.C.A. Air Traffic Conference of America.

Atl. Atlantic.

A.T.M. Assistant Traffic Manager.

A.T.S. Army Transport Service.

att. or atty. Attorney.

at. wt. Atomic weight.

Au (Latin, aurum) Gold.

aud. Auditor.

Aud. Disb. Auditor Disbursements.

Aud. Frt. Accts. Auditor Freight Accounts.

Aud. Frt. Rec. Auditor Freight Receipts.

Aud. Pass. Accts. Auditor Passenger Accounts.

Aud. Rev. Auditor of Revenue.

Aud. Sta. Accts. Auditor Station Accounts.

auth. Authority, authorization.

av. Average, avenue.

A/V Ad valorem.

advps., or avoir. Avoirdupois.

Ave. Avenue.

A/W Actual weight, all water.

A.W.A. American Warehousemen's Association.

A.W.O. American Waterways Operators.

b Bag, bale.

B British, breadth.

B/A Billed at.

Bal. Balance.

B&IB Billing and instruction book.

Barb. Barbados.

B.B. Break bulk, bill book.

bbl., bbls. Barrel, barrels.

BBs. Below bridges.

B.C.C.T. British Columbia Coast Terminals.

B/D Bar-Draft.

bd. Bond, board, bound.

bd. ft. Board foot (feet).

b.d.i. Both dates inclusive.

bdl., bdle., bdls. Bundle, bundles.

bds. Boards.

B.E. Bureau of Explosives.

B/E Bill of Exchange.

bet. Between.

B/F Brought forward.

B.F. or B. Fir. Firkin of butter.

B.F.D.C. Bureau of Foreign & Domestic Commerce.

bg., bgs. Bag, bags.

Bk., Bks., Bank, book; banks, books.

Bkt., bskt. Basket.

B.L., B/L. Bill of Lading.

bl., bls. Bale, bales.

bldg., blg. Building.

blk. Block.

blt. Built.

B.M. Board measurement.

B.M.C. Bureau of Motor Carriers (I.C.C.).

B.O. Buyer's option, bad order, branch office, back order.

B.O.R. Bureau of Operation Rights (I.C.C.).

B of C Bureau of Customs.

B/P, B.P. Bill of Parcels, bills payable.

B.P. Between perpendiculars.

B. Pay. Bills payable.

bque. Barque.

Br. Branch, British.

B/R, B.R., B. Rec. Bill of rights, bills receivable.

br., brs. Branch, branches.

Braz. Brazil.

B.R.E. Bureau of Railway Economics.

Brit. Britain.

B.S. Balance sheet, bill of sale.

B/S Bill of Sale.

Bskt. Basket.

bt. Boat.

b.t. Berth terms.

B.T.E.&S. Bureau of Transport Economics & Statistics (I.C.C.).

bu. Bushel, bureau.

B.W.C. Bureau of Water Carriers.

B.W.I. British West Indies.

bx., bxs. Box, boxes.

C. (Centum) A hundred, currency.

°C Degree Centigrade.

c. Cent(s), centime(s).

c. Coupon, carton.

C.A. Commercial agent, car accountant, claim agent, Central America.

C/A Capital Account, current account.

ca. (metric system) centare.

C.A.A., C.A.Adm. Civil Aeronautics Administration (Authority).

C.A.B. Civil Aeronautics Board.

C.A.D. Cash against document.

C.A.F. (French) Coute (cost), assurance (insurance), fret (freight).

CAF Currency adjustment factor.

Cal., Calif. California.

CAM Commercial air movement.

canclg. Canceling.

C&C Coal and coke.

C&D Collection and delivery.

C&E Clothing and equipage.

C&F Cost and freight.

C&L Canal and lake.

C&SMFA Central & Southern Motor Freight Association.

C&R Canal and rail, canal and river.

Can.F.A. Canadian Freight Association.

cap. Capital, capitol.

Capy. Capacity.

car acct. Car accountant.

car ser. agt. Car service agent.

cash., cashr. Cashier.

CASL Committee of American Steamship Lines

cat. Catalogue.

C.B. Cash book, Customs Bureau.

C.B.D. Cash before delivery.

C.B.E. Cab-beside-engine.

Cbm Cubic meter.

C.C. Chief clerk, connecting carrier.

c.c. Contra credit, current cost, cubic centimeter.

C.C.A. Circuit Court of Appeals.

C.C.B. Canadian Custom Bonded.

CDS Construction differential subsidy.

C.E. Consumption Entry.

cent. (centum) Hundred, century.

cert., certif. Certificate, certified.

c.f. Cubic feet.

cf. (confer) Compare.

C.F., C&F Cost and freight.

C.F.A. Central Freight Association, Canadian Freight Association.

C.F.C. Consolidated Freight Classification.

C.F.I. Cost, Freight & Insurance.

CFR Code of Federal Regulations.

C.F.T.B. Central Freight Tariff Bureau.

C.G. Consul General.

C.H. Custom house, clearing house.

Ch., Chin. China.

ch., chap. Chapter.

Ch. Acct. Off. Chief Accounting Officer.

Cham. Comm. Chamber of Commerce.

Ch. Clk. Chief clerk.

char. Charter.

chg., chgs. Charge, charges.

Chi., Chgo. Chicago.

Chin. Chinese.

chm., chman. Chairman.

C.I. Cost insurance.

C.I.A. Cash in advance.

c/i Certificate of insurance.

Cie. (French, compagnie) Company.

C.I.F., C.I.&F. Cost, insurance and freight.

C.I.F.&C. Cost, insurance, freight and commission.

C.I.F.&E. Cost, insurance, freight and exchange.

C.I.F.C.&I. Cost, insurance, freight, collection and interest.

C.I.F.I.&E. Cost, insurance, freight, interest and exchange.

cir., circl. Circular.

cir. (circa, circum) About.

cit. Citation, citizen.

C.I.T. (Cleaning(-ed) in transit.

ck., cks. Cask(s), check(s).

cl. Claim.

C.L. Carload, connecting line.

class., class'n. Classification.

cld. Cleared.

C.L.F. Connecting line freight.

cl. ht. Ceiling height.

clk. Clerk.

C.L.R. Canal, lake and rail.

C.M. Common meter, certified member.

cm. Centimeter.

CM, AST&T Certified Member, American Society of Traffic and Transportation.

cml. Commercial.

C/N Correction.

Co. Company, county.

c/o (In) care of.

C.O.D. Cash (or collect) on delivery.

C.O.E. Cab-over-engine.

C.O.F.C. Container on flatcar.

C of C. Chamber of Commerce.

C of S. Commissioner of Ships.

col. Column.

coll. Collect.

com., comm. Commission, committee, commerce.

comb. Combination.

com'g. Commencing.

com'l, cml. Commercial.

Com. Merch. Commission Merchant.

commod. Commodity.

commr(s). Commissioner, commissioners.

Comptr. Comptroller.

com. pts. Common points.

con. (contra) Against, in opposition.

conf. Conference.

Cong. Congress.

Cong. Rec. Congressional Record.

const. Consignment.

cont. Controller.

con't., cont'd. Continued.

cor. Corrected.

Cor. L. Corrosive liquid.

corp. Corporation.

C.O.S. Cash on shipment.

coun. Counsel.

C.P. Charter party.

cp. Compare.

C.P.A. Certified (Chartered) Public Account, Combination Publication Authority.

C.P.C.&N. Certificate of Public Convenience and Necessity.

c.p.d. Charters pay dues.

C.P.G. Cotton piece goods.

cr. Creditor, credit, creek.

C.R. Carrier's risk, class (or commodity) rate.

C.R.C. Canadian Railway Commission.

cross., crossg. Crossing.

C.S. Car Service, civil service, cold storage.

cs. Cases.

c/s Cotton seed.

C.S.D. Car Service Department.

C.S.M.F.B. Central States Motor Freight Bureau.

C.S.O. Car Service Order.

C.S.S. Car Service Station.

C.S.T. Central Standard Time.

Ct. Court, count.

ct., cts. (centum) Cents, cent.

ct., cty. County.

C.T.B. Chief of Tariff Bureau, Consulting Traffic Bureau.

C.T.C. Central (or Centralized) Traffic Control.

ctg. Cartage, containing.

ctge. Cartage.

c.t.l.o. Constructive total loss only.

C.T.M. Coal Traffic Manager, Certified (or Consulting) Traffic Manager.

C to S Carting to shipside.

cu. Cubic, (cuprum) copper.

C.U.F. Cushion underframe.

cu. ft. Cubic foot (feet).

cur. Current (this month), currency.

c.v. Chief value.

C.W.O. Cash with order.

C.W.R. Central Western Region.

cwt. Hundredweight (U.S.—100 pounds, U.K.—112 pounds).

cy., cyls. Cylinder, cylinders.

C.Z. Canal Zone.

D. (Roman notation) Five hundred, depth.

d. Day, a penny, or pence.

D1 or 2T1 Double First Class.

D.A. Documents for acceptance.

D/A Days after acceptance.

d/a clause. Vessel must discharge afloat.

D.B. Day book.

D/B/A Doing business as.
D.B.&B. Deals, battens and boards.
dbk. Drawback.
dbl. Double.
D.C. Direct Current.
D.D. Double deck, demand draft.
D/D Days after date, demand draft.
d.d.o. Dispatch discharging only.
D.D. of T. Director, Division of Traffic.
deduct. Deduction(s).
def. Definition, defendant, deferred.
deft. Defendant.
deg. Degree.
D.E.I. Dutch East Indies.
Del. Delaware.
delv'd. Delivered.
dely., delvy. Delivery.
dem. Demurrage.
dep. Depot.
dept. or dpt. Department.
desp. Despatch.
destn. Destination.
D.F.A. Division Freight Agent.
D.F.B. Damage free bracing
dft. Draft.
di., dia., diam. Diameter.
diff. Differential, different.
dig. Digest.
dir. Director, direction.
Dir. of P.S. Director of Public Service.
dis., disc. or disct. Discount.
disp. Dispatch, dispatcher.
dist. District, distance.
distr. Distributor, distribution.
distrb. Distributes.
div. Division, diversion.
dk. Dock.
dkt. Docket.
D.L.O. Dead Letter Office.
d.l.o. Dispatch loading only.
Dm. Dekameter.
dm. Decimeter.
D.M. District (or Division) Manager.
D.N.A. Delta Nu Alpha.

do. (ditto) The same.

Doc. Document, docket.

DOE Department of Energy.

dol., dols. Dollar, dollars.

dom. Domestic.

D.O.T. Department of Transportation.

doz., dz. Dozen.

D.P. Documents for payment.

d.p. Direct port.

dpt. Depth, department, deponent.

Dr. Debtor, debit.

dr. Dram.

D.R. Dock receipt, differential rate.

D.S., Div. Supt. Division Superintendent.

D/S Days after sight.

D.S.T. Daylight Saving Time.

D.T. Director of Traffic (or Transportation).

D.T.A. District Traffic Agent.

dun. Dunnage.

dup. Duplicate.

D/W Dock warrant.

d.w. Dead weight.

dwt Deadweight tons.

dwt. A pennyweight (Latin denarius and English weight).

dz. Dozen.

ea. Each.

E&OE Errors and omissions excepted.

E.A.O.N. Except as otherwise excepted.

E.B. East bound.

E.B.&B.B. Eastbound Basing & Billing Book.

e/c. Emergency charges.

E.C.M.C.A. Eastern Central Motor Carriers Association.

ed. Editor, edition.

E.D. End door(s).

E.D.S.T. Eastern Daylight Saving Time.

edtd. Edited.

E.E. Errors excepted.

E.F.I.B. Eastern Freight Inspection Bureau.

e.g. (Latin, exempli gratia) For example.

E.H. Eggs in hatching (parcel post).

el. Elevated, elevator.

E.L. Eastern Lines.

elec. Electric.

elev. Elevation, elevator.

emb. Embargo.

E.M.F. Electromotive force.

E.N. Exceptions noted.

eng., engr. Engineer.

eq. Equal, equivalent.

equip. Equipment.

E.R. East River (N.Y.C.), Eastern Region

est. Estimated, established.

E.S.T. Eastern Standard Time.

est. wt. Estimated weight.

E.T.A. Estimated time of arrival, emergency temporary authority.

et al. (Latin, et alii) And others.

etc. (Latin, et cetera) And so forth; and other things.

Eth. Ethiopia.

E.T.O. Express Transportation Order.

et seq. (Latin, et sequentia) And the following.

Eur. Europe.

E.W. End width of boxcar, eave to eave.

ex. Example, exception, exchange, extra, express.

ex (Latin) From.

Ex. B.L. Exchange Bill of Lading.

Exc. Exception, except.

excep., except. Exception.

excg. Exchange.

excldg. Excluding.

excpt. Exception.

exd. Examined.

exp. Express, export, expense.

exw. Extreme width.

° F Degree Fahrenheit.

F Fragile (parcel post).

F.A. Freight agent, freight auditor, freight association.

F/A Free astray.

F.A.A. Federal Aviation act (Agency), free of all average.

Fah., Fahr. Fahrenheit.

F.A.K. Freight all kinds.

F.A.M.2 Foreign Air Mail Route No. 2.

F&W Chg. Feeding and watering charge.

F.A.Q. Fair, average quality.

f.a.s. Free alongside (ship).

fath, fth. Fathom.

F.B. Freight bill.

F.C.A. Freight claim agent (or Association).

F.C. Adj. Freight claim adjuster.

F.C. Aud. Freight claim auditor.
F.C.B. Freight Container Bureau (A.A.R.).
F.C.C. Federal Communications Commission.
f.c.&s. Free of capture and seizure.
F.D. Finance docket, freight department.
f.d. Free discharge.
Fe. (Latin, ferrum) Iron.
Fed. Federal Reporter, U.S. District Courts.
Fed. Aud. Federal Auditor.
Fertz. Fertilizer.
F.F. Freight forwarder, folded flat.
F.F.A. Foreign freight agent.
f.f.a. Free from average.
FFI Freight Forwarders Institute.
F.F.L. Fast Freight Line.
F.G.A. Foreign general agent.
F.I. Falkland Islands.
f.i.a. Full interest admitted.
fin. Financial.
f.i.o. Free in and out.
F.I.R. Floating-in-rate.
fir. Firkin.
F.I.T. Fabrication in transit.
f.i.w. Free in wagon.
fl. Florin.
fl. ld. Floor load (in pounds per square foot).
flt. Float.
fltg. Floatage.
fm. From.
F.M. Fine measurement.
F.M.C. Federal Maritime Commission.
fms. Fathoms.
F.O.Adj. Freight overcharge adjuster.
F.O.B. Free on board.
for. Foreign.
F.O.R. Free on rail.
f.o.w. First open water.
F.P.A. Free of particular average.
F.P.A. (A.C.) Free of particular average (American conditions).
F.P.A. (E.C.) Free of particular average (English conditions).
F.R. Federal Register.
fr. Franc, from.
f.r. and c.c. Free of riot and civil commotion.
frt. Freight.

Ft. Assn. Freight association.

F.S. Fourth Section (Interstate Commerce Act).

F.S.A. Fourth Section application.

F.S.O. Fourth Section order.

ft. Foot, feet, fort.

f.t. Full terms, dispatch money payable on all time saved on the chartered time for loading and discharging the cargo.

F.T.B. Freight Tariff (or Traffic) Bureau.

F.T.C. Freight Traffic (or Tariff) Committee, Federal Trade Commission.

F.T.D. Freight traffic department.

F.T.M. Freight traffic manager.

F.T.Z. Federal Trade Zone.

fur. Furlong.

fut. Future.

fwd. Forward.

fwdg. Forwarding.

fwdr. Forwarder.

FX Freight Tariff Concurrence, FX1, FX2, etc.

G. Guineas, gulf.

g. Grain, gage, gauge.

G.A. General agent, general average (marine insurance).

G.A.E. General Air Express.

gal., gals. Gallon(s).

gal. cap. Gallon capacity.

G.A.O. General Accounting Officer (Office).

G. Aud. General auditor.

G.B. Guidebook, Great Britain.

G.B.&I. Great Britain and Ireland.

G.B.L. Government Bill of Lading.

G.B.S. Government Bureau of Standards.

G.C. General circular.

G.C.A. General claim agent.

g.c.m. Greatest common measure.

G.C.T. Greenwich Civil Time.

gds. Goods.

gen., gel'l General.

Gen. Aud. General auditor.

Ger. Germany.

G.F.A. General freight agent.

G.F.D. General freight department.

G.F.F.C. Gulf Foreign Freight Committee.

G.F.O. General freight office.

G.F.T.C.—E.R. General Freight Traffic Committee—Eastern Railroads.

g. gr. Great gross.

gi. Gill (Measure).

G.I.C. Gulf Intercoastal Conference.

G.L. General letter.

G.L.S.A. General Livestock Agent.

gm. Gram.

G.M. General Manager, general merchandise.

G.M. or G. Mdse. General merchandise.

G.O. General order, General office.

G.O.C. General operating committee.

gov., govt. Government.

G.P.D. General passenger department.

G.P.O. General Post Office.

Gr. Greece.

gr. Grain, gross, group.

gr. prod. Grain products.

gr. wt. Gross weight.

G.S. General specials, General superintendent.

G.S.A. General Services Administration.

G.S.F.C. General superintendent of freight claims.

G. Supt., Gen. Supt. General superintendent.

gt. (Latin, gutta) a drop-like marking, great.

G.T. Gross ton.

G.T.&.T.M. General traffic & transportation manager.

g.t.c. Good till canceled.

gtd. Guaranteed.

G.T.D. General traffic department.

G.T.M. General traffic manager.

G.T.I. General transportation importance.

H Hydrogen.

h. Harbor, high, height.

h.a. (Latin, hoc anno) This year.

haz. Hazard.

hbr. Harbor.

H.C. Hauling class (or code).

H.D. High density (Cotton).

heat. Heater charger.

hg. Half.

hg. chts. Half chests.

hg. Hectogram.

hgt. Height.

hhd., hhds. Hogshead, hogsheads.

Hh.G. Household goods.

H.I. Hawaiian Islands.

hl. Hectoliter, metric system.

H.M. His (or Her) Majesty.

H.M.S. His (or Her) Majesty's Ship.

Hon. Honorable.

h.p. Horsepower.

hr., hrs. (Hour(s).

H.R. House of Representatives.

ht. Height.

hund. Hundred.

H.W. High water.

H.W.M. High water mark.

hypoth. Hypothesis or hypothetical.

I&S (articles) Iron and steel (articles).

I&S (docket) Investigation and suspension (Docket) (I.C.C.)

I.A.S. Indicated air speed.

I.A.T.A. International Air Transport Association.

ib., ibid. (Latin, ibidem) In the same place.

I.B. Inbound, in bond.

I.C.A.O. International Civil Aviation Organization.

I.C.C. Interstate Commerce Commission.

I.C.C.-F.F. Used to denote a tariff filed with the Interstate Commerce Commission by freight forwarders.

I.C.C. Rep. Interstate Commerce Commission Report.

I.C.C. Spec'n. Interstate Commerce Commission Specification.

I.C.E.M. Intergovernmental Committee for European Migration.

I.C.H.C.C. International Cargo Handling Coordination Committee.

I.C. Rep. Interstate Commerce Report.

ID Inside diameter.

id. (Latin, idem) The same.

i.e. (Latin, id est) That is.

I.F.A. Illinois Freight Association.

I.F.C. Illinois Freight Committee.

I.H. Ice haulage.

I.L. Interior (inside) length, interline.

ILA International Longshoremen's Association.

ILWU International Longshoremen's and Warehousemen's Union.

imp. Import, imperfect.

impl. Implement.

I.M.R.&T.B. Indiana Motor Rate & Tariff Bureau.

in. Inch, inches.

inc. Incorporated.

incl. Inclusive including.

ind. Index.

indiv. Individual.

inf. (Latin, infra) Beneath, below or hereinafter.

Inf. L. Inflammable liquid.
Inf. S. Inflammable solid.
init. Initial.
in loc. (Latin, in loco) In its place, at the place referred to.
In re (Latin) In regard to.
ins., insp. Inspector.
ins., insur. Insurance.
in situ (Latin) In its original situation.
inst. (Instant) This month.
in sum. (Latin, in summa) In the summary.
int. Interest, intermediate, interior, interchange.
inter. Interstate.
intra. Intrastate.
int'l., intn'l. International.
intra. Intrastate.
in trans. (Latin, in transitu) In passage (movement).
Int. Rev. Internal Revenue.
inv. Invoice.
invest. Investment.
I.P. Identity preserved.
I.P.A. Including particular average.
I.P.D. Individual package delivery.
i.q. (Latin, idem quod) The same as.
I.R.C. Irregular route carrier.
I.R.D. Internal Revenue Department.
I.R.O. Internal Revenue Officer.
I.R.S. Internal Revenue Service.
I.S. Interstate.
I&S Iron and Steel; Investigation and Suspension.
I.&.S. Docket Investigation and Suspension Docket.
I.S.O. International Standards Organization.
isl. Island.
it. Item.
I.T. Immediate transportation, in transit.
itin. Itinerary.
I.W. Interior (inside) width.
J. Judge, justice.
J.A. Joint agent.
j/a Joint account.
jct., jctn., junc. Junction.
jct. pt. Junction point.
J.E.A. Joint export agent.
jt., jnt. Joint.
jt. agt. Joint agent.

jt. r. Joint rate.
K. Kilogram (kilo).
K.D. Knocked down.
K.D.C.L. Knocked down carload.
K.D.F. Knocked down flat.
K.D.L.C.L. Knocked down less than carload.
kg., kgs. (Keg(s).
kg., kilo., kilog. Kilogram (metric system).
kl., kilol. Kiloliter (metric system).
km., kilom. Kilometer (metric system).
kr. Kroner.
kv. Kilovolt.
kw. Kilowatt.
Ky., Ken. Kentucky.
L. Lake, length, loaded, pound sterling.
L.A. Letter of Authority, Local agent.
Lab. Labrador.
L&D Loss and damage.
L&R Lake and rail.
LASH Lighter Aboard Ship.
Lat. Latin.
lat. Latitude. lb., lbs. (Latin, libra) Pound(s).
lbl. gds. Label goods (stored).
lbr. Lumber.
L/C Letter of credit.
LCA Lake Carriers Association.
l.c.l. Less than carload, less than containerload.
lcl. Local.
ld. Load.
L.D. Agt. Agent for long-distance movers (Hh.G.).
ldg. Landing, loading.
ld., lmt. Load limit.
L.F.A. Local Freight Agent.
L.F.T.B. Louisville Freight Tariff Bureau.
lg. tn. Long ton.
L.H.A.R. London, Hull, Antwerp or Rotterdam.
Lr. Lira.
lic. License.
liq. Liquid, liquor.
L.L., ltge., lmts. Lighterage limits.
lon., long. Longitude.
LOOP Louisiana Offshore Oil Port.
L.R. Lloyd's Register.
L.&R. Lake and rail.

L.S. Legal scroll.

L.S.A. Livestock agent.

L.s.d. (Latin, libra, solida, denarii) Pounds, shillings, pence.

L.T., lg. tn. Long ton.

ltd. Limited.

ltge. Lighterage.

L.T.L. Less than truckload.

L to S Lighterage to shipside.

ltr. Lighter.

lt. wt. Light weight.

lv. Leave.

L.W.M. Low water mark.

M. (Latin, mille) A thousand, (meridian) Noon.

m. Month, mile.

M.A.C. Middle Atlantic Conference.

MAC Military Airlift Command.

MA Form A document necessary for exporting into Canada.

MARAD Maritime Administration.

mat. hdlg. Material handling.

max. Maximum.

MBF One thousand board feet.

M.C. Marked capacity, motor carrier.

M.C.B. Master Car Builder.

M.C.B.R. Master Car Builders' Rules.

M.C.C. Motor Carrier Cases (I.C.C.)

M.C.R.B. Motor Carrier Rate Bureau.

M/D Months (after) date.

mdse. Merchandise.

mem., memo. Memorandum.

Memo. B/L Memorandum Bill of Lading.

Messrs. Gentlemen, sirs.

M.F. Motor freight.

M.F.—I.C.C. Designation used on tariffs and schedules filed with the Interstate Commerce Commission by carriers subject to Part II of the Interstate Commerce Act.

M.F.B.M. Thousand feet, board measurement.

mfd., mfrd. Manufactured.

mfg. Manufacturing, manufacture.

M.F.L. Motor Freight Line.

mfr. Manufacturer.

M.F.T. Motor Freight Terminal.

min.Minimum, minute.

min. wt. Minimum weight.

misc., miscl. Miscellaneous.

M.I.T. Milling (or milled) in transit, Military Institute of Technology, Massachusetts Institute of Technology.

mk. Mark.

mkd. Marked.

mkd. wt. Marked weight.

M.L.R.C. Multi-level rail car.

mm. Millimeter.

MM Two thousand.

M.M. Master mechanic.

mo., mos. Month(s).

M.O. Money order.

M.O.4 (Agreement) Managing and operating agreement Number 4.

M.P. Milepost.

MS., MSS. Manuscript, manuscripts.

M/S Months after sight.

M.S.T. Mountain Standard Time.

mt. Mount, mountain.

M.T. Metric ton.

M.T.D. Manager, Traffic (or Transportation) Department.

M.T.M.T.S. Military Traffic Management and Terminal Services.

mties. Empties.

mty. Empty.

M.W.M.F.B. Middlewest Motor Freight Bureau.

mxd. Mixed.

N. North, note.

N.A. North America.

n.a. Not applicable.

n.a.a. Not always afloat.

N.A.C. North Atlantic Coast.

N.A.M.B.O. National Association of Motor Bus Operators.

naut. Nautical.

nav., navig. Navigation.

N.B. Northbound, New Brunswick.

N.C.P.D.M. National Council of Physical Distribution Management.

n.d. No date.

N.D.T.A. National Defense Transportation Association.

N.E. Northeast, New England.

n.e. Nonessential.

N.E.F.A. New England Freight Association.

N.E.M.R.B. New England Motor Rate Bureau.

N.E.S. Not elsewhere specified.

Neth. Netherlands.

N.E.T.R./F.T.C. New England Territory Railroads/Freight Traffic Committee.

net wt. Net weight.
N.F.A. National Freight Association.
N.F.T.B. Niagara Frontier Tariff Bureau.
N.M.F.C. National Motor Freight Classification.
N.Nstd. Not nested.
no., nox. Number(s).
N.O.E. Not elsewhere enumerated.
N.O.F.T.B. New Orleans Freight Tariff Bureau.
N.O.H.P. Not otherwise herein provided.
N.O.I. Not otherwise indexed.
N.O.I.B.N. Not otherwise indexed by name.
N.O.S. Not otherwise specified.
nr. Near.
N.R.A.B. National Railroad Adjustment Board.
N.S. Not Specified.
N.S.P.F. Not specifically provided for.
nstd. Nested.
N.T. Net ton, Northern Territory.
ntfy. Notify.
N.T.P. National Transportation Policy.
NVOCC Non-Vessel Operating Common Carrier.
N.W. Northwest, Northwestern.
n.w. Naked weight.
N.W.R. Northwestern Region.
N.W.T. Northwest Territory.
O&R Ocean and rail.
O.C. Official classification.
O/C Overcharge, Open Charter.
O.C.C. Official Classification Committee.
O.C.P. Overland Common Points.
OD Outside diameter.
ODS Operating differential subsidy.
O.D.T. Office of Defense Transportation.
o.e. Omissions excepted.
o.k. All right, or correct.
O.M. Old measurement.
O.M.I.A. Operating, maintenance, interest and adaptability.
O/N Order notify.
OO Owner-operator.
Oper. Exec. Operating Executive.
Opr. Operator.
O.R. Owner's risk.
O.&R. Ocean and rail.
O.R.B. Owner's risk of breakage.

O.R.C. Owner's risk of chafing.
O.R.D. Owner's risk of damage.
O.R.Det. Owner's risk of deterioration.
O.R.F. Owner's risk of fire (or freezing).
O.R.L. Owner's risk of leakage.
O.R.S. Owner's risk of shifting.
O.R.W. Owner's risk of becoming wet.
O.S. Ordinary seaman.
O.S.&D. Over, short and damage.
o.t. On truck or railway.
OT Open top trailer.
OTR Over the road.
OWB Over without bill.
oxd. m. Oxidizing material.
oz., ozs. Ounce(s).
p. Page.
P Perishable.
P.A. Particular average, purchasing agent, passenger agent, per annum.
Pa., Penna. Pennsylvania.
Pac., Pacif. Pacific.
palts. Pallets.
Pan Am. Pan American.
P&D Pickup and delivery (service).
P&L Profit and loss.
par. Paragraph.
Para. Paraguay.
pass. Passenger.
P.A.Y.E. Pay as you enter.
payt. Payment.
P.B. Privately bonded.
pc., pcs. Piece, pieces.
P.C. Per cent.
P/C Prices current.
P.C.F.B. Pacific Coast Freight Bureau.
pd. Paid.
P.D. (Latin, per diem) By the day, property damage.
pen. Peninsula.
per By the, according to.
per an. (Latin, per annum) By the year.
per ct. (Latin, per centum) By the hundred, percentage.
persh. Perishable.
pf., pfd. Preferred.
P.H.P. Packing house products.
P.I. Publication instructions.

pk., pks. Peck(s).
pkg., pkgs. Package(s).
pkt. Packet.
pl. Place, plural.
P.L. Public Law.
P.L.&P.D. Public liability and property damage.
plff. Plaintiff.
P.M. Postmaster, paymaster.
p.m. (Latin, post meridiem) After noon.
PMA Pacific Maritime Association.
P/N Please note.
pntd. Painted.
P.O. Post Office; purchase order.
P.O.D. Post Office Department, pay on delivery.
Pol. Poland.
P.O.O. Post Office Order.
pop., popl. Population.
pp. Pages.
P.P. Prepay, prepaid, parcel post:
p.p. Picked ports.
PPd, ppd. Prepaid, postpaid.
p.p.i. Policy, proof of interest.
P.P.O. Prepaid order.
pr. Price, pair.
P.R.A. Public Roads Administration.
pre. Prefix.
pres., pres't President.
prev. Previous.
priv. Private.
pro. Progressive.
prod. Product.
prop., propr. Proprietor.
propal., propl. Proportional.
propn. Proportion.
prox. Proximo, next (month).
prov. Province.
ps. Pieces.
P.S. (Latin, post scriptum) Postscript.
P.S.C. Public Service Commission.
P.S.T. Pacific Standard Time.
pt. Port, point, pint, part.
PT Per trailer or container.
PT 20 Per 20 foot trailer or container.
PT 40 Per 40 foot trailer or container.

P.T., P.Tel. Postal telegraph.

P.T.C. Postal telegraph code.

P.T.M. Passenger traffic manager.

P.U. Pickup.

P.U.C. Public Utilities Commission.

P.U.&D. Pickup and delivery.

P.W. Packed weight.

PWC Pacific Westbound Conference.

pymt. Payment.

Q., Qu. Question.

Q.E.D. (Latin, quod erat demonstrandum) Which was to be proved.

Q.F. Quick freeze.

qr. Quire, quarter.

qt. Quart, quantity.

qtr. Quarter.

qts. Quarts.

quar. Quarterly.

R. Rod, road.

R. 25 Rule Twenty-five (Consolidated classification).

R. 26 Rule Twenty-six (Consolidated classification).

R/A Refer to Acceptor.

R&C Rail and canal.

R&L Rail and lake.

R&O Rail and ocean.

R&T Rail and truck.

R&W Rail and water.

R.A.O.A. Railway Accounting Officers Association.

R.C. Relief claim, release clause.

R/C Reconsigned, recovered.

R.C.&L. Rail, canal and lake.

rc'd, rec'd. Received.

RCRA Resource Conservation and Recovery Act.

rd. Road.

R.D. Regional director, rural delivery (P.O.)

R/D Refer to drawer.

rdo. Radio.

re (in re) (Latin) Referring to, in regard to.

R.E. agt. Real estate agent.

rec. Receipt.

recap. Recapitulation.

recon., recong. Reconsign.

red. Reduction.

re-exp. Reexport.

ref. Reference.

refg., refrig. Refrigerating, refrigeration.
refgr. Refrigerator.
refrig'd. Refrigerated.
reg. Regulation.
regd. Registered.
re-imp. Reimport.
rel. Released.
rep. Report, republic, representative.
R.E.R. Railway Equipment Register.
ret., retd. Returned.
Rfgn. Refrigeration (charges).
R.F.T.B. Richmond Freight Tariff Bureau.
RICA Revised Interstate Commerce Act.
R.I.T. Refining in transit.
riv. River.
R.J. Road junction.
R.L.&.R. Rail, lake and rail.
R.M.C. Regulated motor carriers.
RO/RO Roll-on/roll-off.
R.P.M. Revolutions per minute.
R.P.O. Railway Post Office.
rpt., rep. Report.
R.R. Railroad.
R.R.C. Regular route carrier.
Rs. Rupees.
R.S. Right side.
R.S. or L. Rated same or lower.
rtd. Returned.
rte. Route.
R.T.P.A. Railway Travel Promotion Agency.
R.U.I. Railroad Unemployment Insurance.
R-W-R Rail-Water-Rail.
ry., rwy. Railway.
S. State, south.
S.A.C. South Atlantic Coast.
S&C Shipper and Carrier.
S.B. Southbound, shipping board, steamboat, separately binned.
S/B Statement of billing.
S.C. Special circular, Southern Classification, surcharge.
sc., scs. Scale, scales.
S.C.&S. Strapped, corded and sealed.
S.C.C. State Corporation Commission, Southern Classification Committee.
SCD Special Commodities Division.
sch. Schooner.

scl. Scale.

S.C.S. Superintendent of Car Service.

S.D. Single deck, side door.

S/D Sea damaged, statement of differences.

S.D.D. Store door delivery.

sdg. Siding.

S.E. Southeast, Southeastern.

sec. Section, second.

sec., secy. Secretary.

sect. Section.

S.E.F.A. Southeastern Freight Association.

S.E.M.V.F.A. Southeastern Mississippi Valley Freight Association.

S.F.I.B. Southern Freight Inspection Bureau.

shpt. Shipment.

shtg. Shortage.

sh. tn. Short ton (2,000 lbs.).

S.I.T. Stopping in transit, storage in transit.

S.L.&C. Shipper's load and count.

S.L.&T. Shipper's load and tally.

sld. Sailed, sealed.

S.M.C.R.C. Southern Motor Carrier's Rate Conference.

S/N Shipping note.

so., Sou. South, Southern.

S.O. Seller's option, ship's option, shipping order.

SOLE Society of Logistics Engineers.

S.O.S. A distress signal.

Sou. Class'n Southern Classification.

S.P. Supra protest.

s.p.a. Subject to particular average.

sp. gr. Specific gravity.

spgs. Springs.

S.P.L.C. Standard Point Location Code.

spec. Specification.

sp. iron Special iron.

spt. Seaport.

sq. Square.

S.R. Shipping receipt, Southern Region.

S.R.&C.C. Strikes, riots and civil commotions.

S.R.O. Special rate order.

ss. Sworn statement.

S.S. Shipside.

S/S Steamship.

S.S.&C. Same sea and country (or Coast).

ST. Short ton.

St. Saint.

S.T. Stopping (or storage) in transit, Superintendent of transportation, shipping ticket.

st., sts. Street, streets.

sta. Stationer, station.

sta. agt. Station agent.

stat. Statistician.

stats. Statutes.

S.T.C. Single trip container.

S.T.C.C. Standard Transportation Commodity Code.

stds. Standards.

ster., stg. Sterling.

steve., steve. Stevedore.

stg., stge., stor. Storage.

stge. trk. Storage track.

str. Steamer, straight.

str. kpr. Storekeeper.

S.U. Set up.

S.U.C.L. Set up carload.

S.U.L.C.L. Set up in less than carload.

sup., supl., suppl. Supplement.

Sup. Vy. U.S. Supreme Court Reporter System.

Sup. Ct. Rep. Supreme Court Reporter.

supra. Above.

supt. Superindendent.

Supt. Car Ser. Superintendent Car Service.

supvr. Supervisor.

s.v. Sailing vessel.

S.W. Southwest, Southwestern, stenciled weight.

S.W.F.T.B. Southwestern Freight Tariff Bureau.

swg., swtg. Switching.

S.W.M.F.B. Southwestern Motor Freight Bureau.

S.W.R. Southwestern Region.

S.W.T. Southwestern territory.

S.W.T.C. Southwestern Tariff Committee.

sys., syst. System.

T. Terminal, temperature.

T.A., T. Agt. Tax agent, temporary authority.

T.A. or T. Aud. Traffic auditor.

T.A.A. Transportation Association of America.

T&R Truck and rail.

T.B. Traffic (or Tariff) Bureau.

t.b. Trial balance.

TC Tariff (or traffic) circular.

T.C. Traffic counselor (consultant), traffic or transportation commissioner.

tc., tcs. Tierce, tierces.

T-C.F.B. Trans-Continental Freight Bureau.

T. Commr. Traffic commissioner.

T-C.W.&I.B. Trans-Continental Weighing & Inspection Bureau.

T.D. Treasury Department.

T.D. or T. Dir. Traffic director.

T.E.A.E.R. Traffic Executives Association Eastern Railroads.

tel., telg. Telegram, telegraph.

ter., terr. Territory.

term., term'l. Terminal.

tfr., trnfr. Transfer.

T.I.R. International Road Transport.

tk. Truck.

tkt. Ticket.

T.L. Truckload.

T.L.A. Trunk Line Association.

t.l.o. Total loss only.

T.M. Traffic Manager, trainmaster.

T.N. Tariff number.

tnge. Tonnage.

T.O.F.C. Trailer-on-flat-car.

tot. Total.

traf. Traffic.

tran. Transit.

T.R.&W. Truck, rail and water.

trans., transp. Transportation.

transfd., trfd. Transferred.

trans. priv. Transit privileges.

treas. Treasurer.

T.R.F. Transportation Research Forum; Transportation Research Foundation.

trf. Tariff.

trfr. Transfer.

trk. Track.

trk. stge. Track storage.

trm. Terminal.

T.S. area Total storage area.

T.T.B. Texas Tariff Bureau.

TT or TWX Teletype communication system.

U/A Underwriting account.

U/C Undercharge.

UCC Uniform Commercial Code.

U.F.C. Uniform Freight Classification.

U.K./Cont. (B.H.) United Kingdom or Continent (Bordeaux/Hamburg Range).

U.K./Cont. (G.H.) United Kingdom or Continent (Gibraltar/Hamburg Range).

U.K./Cont. (H.H.) United Kingdom or Continent (Havre/Hamburg Range).

U.K.F.O. United Kingdom for Orders—the vessel is to proceed to the U.K. for orders to complete the charter party.

U.L.D. Unit Load Device.

ult., ulto. (Latin, ultimo) Last (month).

unlmtd. Unlimited.

Unrep. Op. Unreported Opinion (I.C.C.).

Urg. Uruguay.

U.S.A. United States of America.

U.S.C. United States Customs.

U.S.C.A. U.S. Code Annotated.

U.S.I.R.B. United States Internal Revenue Bonded.

U.S.M. United States Mail

U.S.M.C. U.S. Maritime Commission.

U.S.N.D. United States Navy Department.

U.S.N.H. United States North of Cape Hatteras.

U.S.S.H. United States South of Cape Hatteras.

U.S.R.A. United States Railroad Administration.

U.S.S. United States Ship.

U.S.S.B. United States Shipping Board.

U.S.S.G. United States Standard Gauge.

U.S.T.D. United States Treasury Department.

U.S.W.A.B. United States Warehouse Act Bonded.

U/W Underwriter.

V Five or fifth.

v., vs. (Latin, versus) Against or in opposition.

val. Value.

V.C. Visible capacity.

v.d. Various dates.

ves. Vessel.

via (Latin) By way of.

viz. (Latin) Namely, to wit.

vol. Volume.

V.P., V. Pres. Vice President.

V.S. Visible Supply.

W. West, western, width, weight.

w.a. With average.

W&F Water and feed.

W&I Weighing and inspection.

W&IB Weighing and Inspection Bureau.
W&R Water and rail.
Wash. Washington.
W.B. Westbound.
W/B Waybill.
w.b. Water ballast.
W.B./E.I. West Britain/East Ireland.
W.C. Western classification.
W.C.C. Western Classification Committee.
W.D.F. Waterfront dock facilities.
wdt. Width.
WERC Warehouse Education and Research Council.
West'n Western.
West'n. Class'n. Western classification.
W.F.T.B. Western Freight Tariff Bureau.
whf. Wharf.
whfg. Wharfage.
whm. Weighmaster.
whse. Warehouse.
W.I. West Indies.
wk. Week, work.
wkds. Weekdays.
W/M, W or M Weight or measurement.
W.O. Wait Order.
W.P.A. With particular average.
W/R Was received.
wrfg. Wharfage.
wt. Weight.
W.T.L. Western Trunk Line.
W.T.L.A. Western Trunk Line Association.
W.T.L.C. Western Trunk Line Committee.
W.U. Western Union.
W.Va. West Virginia.
W/W Warehouse warrant.
w.w. Weather working.
W.W.&I.B. Western Weighing and Inspection Bureau.

X. Extra.
X Car From car.
Xg., Xing. Crossing.

y. Yard.
Y/A York-Antwerp Rules (Marine Insurance).
yd., yds. Yard, yards.

ydg. Yarding.
yr., yrs. Year(s).
Z Zone, zero, zinc.
Zn Zinc.
ZORF Zone of Rate Freedom.

Appendix A

Summary of the Revised
Interstate Commerce Act to December 31, 1980

Citation is 49 U.S.C.A. Section _____

Appendix B

Summary of the Shipping Act of 1916

Introduction/Section 1	Scope of regulation Definitions
Section 2	Controlling interests in corporations
Section 3-8	Repealed
Section 9	Coastwise trade ships may only operate under American documentation Restrictions on transfers of vessels
Sections 10-11	Repealed
Section 12	FMC may investigate and determine cost of building ships, mortgages, insurance, etc.
Section 14	Carriers not to: give rebates, use "fighting ships," retaliate against any shipper, discriminate unjustly and unfairly Dual rate contract agreements allowed
Section 14a	FMC power to investigate and hold hearings on Section 14 matters
Section 14b	Spells out details of dual rate agreements allowed
Section 15	Filing of agreements Discriminatory agreements disapproved
Section 16	Unlawful to false bill Unlawful acts of undue preference and advantage; protests Unfair to obtain lower rates than regular ones Unlawful to influence marine insurance company or agent into giving competing carrier unfavorable rate coverage.
Section 17	Unlawful to charge rates that unjustly discriminatory to exporters of the U.S. or any shippers and ports. Must observe reasonable practices in handling freight
Section 18(a)	Carriers to establish just and reasonable rates, charges, practices, etc. Carriers to file with FMC the maximum rates charged No carrier to charge rates higher than those on file at FMC FMC may prescribe reasonable maximum rate
Section 18(b) (1)	Rates and tariffs to be filed at FMC
(2)	No rates to be changed without new filing
(3)	Carriers to charge and collect only the rates on file at FMC (legal rate)
(4)	FMC to establish the form and format of tariffs
(5)	FMC can disapprove any rate it determines to be unreasonably high or low as to be detrimental to the commerce of the U.S.
Section 19	Restriction on increase of rates reduced to drive out competitor

Appendix C

Title 49 Code of Federal Regulations
Parts 1000-End

These are the administrative regulations put into effect by the ICC. They are found in the Code of Federal Regulations. They are constantly changing; shown here are those in effect on October 1, 1980.

CHAPTER X—INTERSTATE COMMERCE COMMISSION
Subchapter A—General Rules and Regulations
Parts 1000-1019—General Provisions

Appendix D

LIST OF RAILROAD NAMES
AND STANDARD CODES

Railroad	Code
Aberdeen and Rockfish Railroad Company	AR
Adirondack Railway	ADIR
Ahnapee and Western Railway Company (The)	AHW
Akron & Barberton Belt Railroad Company (The)	ABB
Akron Canton & Youngstown Railroad Company (The)	ACY
Alabama Great Southern Railroad (The)	AGS
Alameda Belt Line	ABL
Alaska Railroad (The)	ARR
Alexander Railroad	ARC
Algers Winslow and Western Railway Company	AWW
Algoma Central Railway	AC
Aliquippa and Southern Railroad Company	ALQS
Almanor Railroad Company	AL
Alton & Southern Railway Company	ALS
Amador Central Railroad	AMC
American Rail Heritage, LTD (see Crab Orchard & Egyptian R.R.)	
Angelina & Neches River Railroad	ANR
Ann Arbor Railroad System	AA
Apache Railway Company (The)	APA
Apalachicola Northern Railroad Company	AN
Arcade and Attica Railroad Corporation	ARA
Arcata and Mad River Railroad Company (The)	AMR
Arkansas & Louisiana Missouri Railway Company	ALM
Arkansas & Memphis Railway Bridge & Terminal Company	
Arkansas Western Railway Company (The)	ARW
Aroostook Valley Railroad Company	AVL
Ashley Drew & Northern Railway Company	ADN
Atchison, Topeka and Santa Fe Railway Company (The)	ATSF
Atlanta & Saint Andrews Bay Railway Company (The)	ASAB
Atlanta and West Point Railroad Company	AWP
Atlantic and East Carolina Railway Company	AEC
Atlantic and Western Railway Company	ATW
Augusta Railroad Company	AUG
Auto-Train	
Baltimore and Annapolis Railroad Company (The)	BLA
Baltimore & Ohio Chicago Terminal Railroad Company	BOCT
Baltimore and Ohio Railroad Company (The)	BO

Bangor and Aroostook Railroad Company	BAR
Bath and Hammondsport Railroad Company	BH
Bauxite & Northern Railway Company	BXN
Beaufort & Morehead Railroad Company	BMH
Beech Mountain Railroad Company	BEEM
Belfast & Moosehead Lake Railroad Company	BML
Bellefonte Central Railroad Company	BFC
Belt Railway Company of Chicago (The)	BRC
Belton Railroad Company	BRR
Berlin Mills Railway Inc.	BMS
Bessemer & Lake Erie Railroad Company	BLE
Bevier & Southern Railroad Company	BVS
Birmingham Southern Railroad Company	BS
Black River & Western Railroad	BRW
Boston & Maine Corporation	BM
Brandon Corporation	BRAN
Brillion & Forest Junction Railroad Company	BFJR
British Columbia Hydro and Power Authority	BCE
British Columbia Railway	BCOL
British Columbia Yukon Railway Company	
British Yukon Railway Company (The)	
Brooklyn Eastern District Terminal Railroad	BEDT
Buffalo Creek Railroad	BCK
Burlington Northern Inc.	BN
Burlington Northern (Manitoba). LTD.	BNML
Butte Anaconda & Pacific Railway	BAP
Cadillac & Lake City Railway	CLK
Cadiz Railroad	CAD
California Western Railroad	CWR
Camas Prairie Railroad	CSP
Cambria and Indiana Railroad Company	CI
Camino Placerville & Lake Tahoe Railroad	CPLT
Camp LeJeune Railroad Company	CPLJ
Canada & Gulf Terminal Railway (The)	CGT
Canadian National Railways	CN
Canadian Pacific	CP
Canton Railroad Company	CTN
Cape Breton Development Corporation (The)	DVR
Cape Fear Railways Incorporated	CFR
Carbon County Railway Company	CBC
Carolina Clinchfield & Ohio Railway	CCO
Carrollton Railroad (The)	CARR
Cartier Railway Company	
Cedar Rapids and Iowa City Railway Company	CIC
Central California Traction Company	CCT

Central of Georgia Railroad Company	CGA
Central New York Railroad	CNYK
Central Vermont Railway Inc.	CV
Chattahoochee Industrial Railroad	CIRR
Chattahoochee Valley Railway Company	CHV
Chesapeake and Ohio Railway-Auto Ferries	CO
Chesapeake and Ohio Railway Company (The)	CO
Chesapeake Western Railway	CHW
Chessie System	CO
Chestnut Ridge Railway Company	CHR
Chicago & Illinois Midland Railway Company	CIM
Chicago & Illinois Western Railroad	CIW
Chicago and North Western Transportation Company	CNW
Chicago and Western Indiana Railroad Company	CWI
Chicago Heights Terminal Transfer Railroad	CHTT
Chicago, Madison and Northern Railway Co.	CMNR
Chicago Milwaukee St. Paul & Pacific Railroad	MILW
Chicago, Rock Island and Pacific Railroad Company (Debtor)	RI
Chicago Short Line Railway Company	CSL
Chicago South Shore and South Bend Railroad	CSS
Chicago Union Station Comany	CUST
Chicago West Pullman & Southern Railroad Company	CWP
Chihuahua Pacific Railway Company	CHP
Chippewa River Railroad Co.	
Cincinnati New Orleans & Texas Pacific Railway (The)	CNTP
City of Prineville Railway	COP
Claremont and Concord Railway Company	CLCO
Clarendon and Pittsford Railroad Company (The)	CLP
Cliffside Railroad	CLIF
Clinchfield Railroad Company	CCO
Colorado & Southern Railway Company (The)	CS
Colorado & Wyoming Railway Company	CW
Columbia & Cowlitz Railway Company	CLC
Columbia Newberry & Laurens Railroad	CNL
Columbus and Greenville Railway Company	CAGY
Conemaugh & Black Lick Railroad Company	CBL
Consolidated Rail Corporation	CR
Consolidated Railroads of Cuba	
Cooperstown & Charlotte Valley Railway Corporation	CACV
Corinth and Counce Railroad Company (The)	CCR
Cotton Belt	SSW
CP Express	CP
CP Rail	CP
CP Ships	CP
Crab Orchard & Egyptian Railroad (see American Rail Heritage, Ltd.)	COER

Cuban Railroads
Cuyahoga Valley Railway Company (The)   CUVA

Dansville and Mount Morris Railroad Company   DMM
Dardanelle & Russellville Railroad   DR
Davenport Rock Island North Western Railway   DRI
Delaware and Hudson Railway Company   DH
Delaware Otsego Corporation
Delmarva Route (The)
Delray Connecting Railroad Company   DC
Delta Valley & Southern Railway Company   DVS
Denver and Rio Grande Western Railroad Company   DRGW
De Queen and Eastern Railroad Company   DQE
Des Moines and Central Iowa Railway Company   DCI
Des Moines Union Railway Company   DMU
Detroit and Mackinac Railway Company   DM
Detroit and Toledo Shore Line Railroad Company   DTS
Detroit Terminal Railroad Company   DT
Detroit Toledo and Ironton Railroad Company   DTI
Devco Railway   DVR
Dominion Atlantic Railway   DA
Doniphan Kensett & Searcy Railway   DKS
Duluth & Northeastern Railroad Company   DNE
Duluth Missabe and Iron Range Railway Company   DMIR
Duluth Winnipeg & Pacific Railway   DWP
Durham and Southern Railway Company   DS

East Camden & Highland Railroad Company   EACH
East Cooper and Berkeley Railroad Company   ECBR
East Erie Commercial Railroad   EEC
East Jersey Railroad and Terminal Company   EJR
East St. Louis Junction Railroad Co.   ESLJ
East Tennessee & Western North Carolina Railroad Company   ETWN
Edgmoor & Manetta Railway   EM
El Dorado and Wesson Railway   EDW
Elgin Joliet and Eastern Railway Company   EJE
Escanaba and Lake Superior Railroad   ELS
Esquimalt & Nanaimo Railway   EN
Essex Terminal Railway   ETL

Fairport Painseville & Eastern Railway Company   FPE
Family Lines System
Feather River Route (see Western Pacific R.R.)
Ferdinand Railroad Company   FRDN
Ferroacarril de Chihuahua al Pacifico sa de CV   CHP
Ferrocarril del Pacifico SA de CV   FCP
Ferrocarril Industrial el Potosi y Chihuahua

Ferrocarril Occidental de Mexico SA	FCM
Ferrocarril Sonora Baja California SA de CV	SBC
Ferrocarriles de Costa Rica SA	
Ferrocarriles Nacionales de Cuba	
Ferrocarriles Nacionales de Mexico	NDM
Ferrocarriles Unidos del Sureste sa de cv	SE
Florida East Coast Railway Company	FEC
Fonda Johnstown and Gloversville Railroad Company	FJG
Fore River Railroad Corporation	FOR
Fort Smith and Van Buren Railway Company	FSVB
Fort Worth and Denver Railway Company	FWD
Frankfort and Cincinnati Railroad Company	FCIN
Frisco Transportation Company	SLSF
Gainesville Midland Railroad Company	GM
Galveston Houston & Henderson Railroad	GHH
Galveston Wharves	GWF
Garden City Western Railroad Company (The)	GCW
Genesee and Wyoming Railroad Company	GNWR
Georgetown Railroad Company	GRR
Georgia Railroad	GA
Georgia Southern & Florida Railway	GSF
Gettysburg Railroad Company	GETY
Goodwin Railroad, Inc.	GWIN
Grafton & Upton Railroad Company	GU
Grand River Railroad Company (The)	GRNR
Grand Trunk Western Railroad Company	GTW
Graysonia Nashville & Ashdown Railroad Company	GNA
Great Southwest Railroad Incorporated	GSW
Great Western Railway (The)	GWR
Greater Winnipeg Water District Railway	
Green Bay and Western Railroad Company	GBW
Green Mountain Railroad Corporation	GMRC
Greenville and Northern Railway Company	GRN
Greenwich & Johnsonville Railway	GJ
Guantanamo & Western Railroad	
Hampton & Branchville Railroad Company	HB
Harbor Belt Line Railroad	
Hartford and Slocomb Railroad Company	HS
Hartwell Railway	HRT
Helena Southwestern Railroad Company	HSW
Hershey Cuban Railway	
High Point Thomasville & Denton Railroad	HPTD
Hillsboro and Northeastern Railway Company	HLNE
Hillsdale County Railway Company Inc.	HCRC

Hollis & Eastern Railroad Company	HE
Holton Inter-Urban Railway Company	HI
Houston Belt & Terminal Railway Company	HBT
Hutchinson and Northern Railway Company (The)	HN
Illinois Central Gulf Railroad	ICG
Illinois Terminal Railroad Company	ITC
Indiana & Ohio Railroad	
Indiana Eastern Railroad & Transportation, Inc.	HOSC
Indiana Harbor Belt Railroad	IHB
Indiana Interstate Railway Company Inc.	IIRC
International Bridge & Terminal Company (The)	IBT
Interstate Railroad	INT
Iowa Terminal Railroad Company	IAT
Iowa Transfer Railway Company	
Johnstown and Stony Creek Railroad Company	JSC
Kanawha Central Railway Company	KC
Kankakee, Beaverville and Southern Railroad Company	KSBR
Kansas and Missouri Railway & Terminal Company (The)	KM
Kansas City Connecting Railroad Company	KCC
Kansas City Public Service Freight Operation	
Kansas City Southern Railway Company	KCS
Kansas City Terminal Railway Company	KCT
Kent, Barry, Eaton Connecting Railway Co., Inc.	KBEC
Kentucky & Indiana Terminal Railroad Company	KIT
Kentucky & Tennessee Railway	KT
Kingston Terminal Railroad Corp.	KTER
Klamath Northern Railway Company	KNOR
Lackawaxen and Stourbridge Railroad	LASB
Lake Erie & Eastern Railroad	LEE
Lake Erie and Ft. Wayne Railroad	LEFW
Lake Erie and Northern Railway Company (The)	LEN
Lake Erie Franklin & Clarion Railroad Company	LEF
Lake Superior & Ishpeming Railroad Company	LSI
Lake Superior Terminal & Transfer Railway Company (The)	LSTT
Lake Terminal Railroad Company (The)	LT
Lamoille Valley Railroad Company	LVRC
Lancaster and Chester Railway Company	LC
Laona & Northern Railway	LNO
La Salle and Bureau County Railroad Company (The)	LSBC
Laurinburg and Southern Railroad Company	LRS
Lawndale Transportation Company	LDTC
Lehigh Valley Railroad Company	LV
Lenawee County Railroad Company, Inc.	LCRC

Live Oak Perry and South Georgia Railway Company	LPSG
Livonia Avon & Lakeville Railroad Corporation	LAL
Long Island Railroad (The)	LI
Longview Portland & Northern Railway Company	LPN
Lorain & West Virginia Railway Company (The)	LAWV
Los Angeles Junction Railway	LAJ
Louisiana & Arkansas Railway Company	LA
Louisiana & Northwest Railroad Company (The)	LNW
Louisiana & Pinebluff Railway Company (The)	LPB
Louisiana Midland Railway	LOAM
Louisiana Southern Railway Company	LSO
Louisville and Nashville Railroad Company	LN
Louisville and Wadley Railway Company	LW
Louisville New Albany & Corydon Railroad Company	LNAC
Lowville & Beaver River Railroad	LBR
Ludington and Northern Railway	LUN
Lykens Valley Railroad Company	LKVY
Madison Railroad (Division of City of Madison Port Authority)	CMPA
Magma Arizona Railroad	MAA
Maine Central Railroad Company	MEC
Manufacturers' Junction Railway Company	MJ
Manufacturers' Railway Company (St. Louis)	MRS
Marianna & Blountstown Railroad Company	MBT
Marinette Tomahawk & Western Railroad Company	MTW
Marquette & Huron Mountain Railroad Company Incorporated	MHCO
Maryland and Delaware Railroad Company (see Delmarva Route)	
Maryland and Pennsylvania Railroad Company	MPA
Massachusetts Central Railroad Company	MCER
Massena Terminal Railroad Company (The)	MSTR
Mattagami Railroad Company	
McCloud River Railroad	MCR
McKeesport Connecting Railroad	MKC
Meridian & Bigbee Railroad Company	MBRR
Mercersburg Railway (see Northmont System)	MERW
Mexican Pacific Railroad Company Incorporated	MDP
Michigan Interstate Railway Company	
Michigan Northern Railway Company	MIGN
Middletown and New Jersey Railway Company Incorporated	MNJ
Milwaukee Motor Transportation Company (The)	MILW
Milwaukee Road	MILW
Minneapolis Northfield and Southern Railway, Inc.	MNS
Minnesota Dakota & Western Railway Company	MDW
Minnesota Transfer Railway Company	MTFR
Mississippi & Skuna Valley Railroad Company	MSV
Mississippi Export Railroad Company	MSE

Mississippian Railway	MISS
Missouri-Kansas-Texas Railroad Company	MKT
Missouri Pacific Railroad Company	MP
Mobile & Gulf Railroad Company (The)	MG
Modesto & Empire Traction Company	MET
Monongahela Connecting Railroad Company (The)	MCRR
Monongahela Railway	MGA
Montour Railroad Company	MTR
Montpelier and Barre Railroad Company	MB
Morristown & Erie Railroad	ME
Moscow Camden & San Augustine Railroad	MCSA
Moshassuck Valley Railroad Company	MOV
Muncie and Western Railroad Company	MWR
Napierville Junction Railway Company	NJ
Narragansett Pier Railroad Company Incorporated	NAP
National Railroad Passenger Corporation	
National Railways of Mexico	NDM
Nevada Northern Railway Company	NN
Newburgh and South Shore Railway Company (The)	NSS
New Hope and Ivyland Railroad Company	NHIR
New Jersey Indiana & Illinois Railroad Company	NJII
New York & Lake Erie Railroad	NYLE
New York Dock Railway	NYD
New York Susquehanna and Western Railroad Company	NYSW
Nezperce Railroad Company	NEZP
Norfolk and Portsmouth Belt Line Railroad	NPB
Norfolk and Western Railway Company	NW
Norfolk Franklin and Danville Railway Company	NFD
Norfolk Southern Railway Company	NS
North Country Railroad Corp.	NCRC
North Louisiana & Gulf Railroad Company	NLG
Northern Alberta Railways Company	NAR
Northmont System	
North Stratford Railroad Corporation	NSRC
Northwestern Oklahoma Railroad	NOKL
Northwestern Pacific Railroad Company	NWP
Oakland Terminal Railway (The)	OTR
Octoraro Railway, Inc.	OCTR
Ogden Union Railway & Depot Company (The)	OURD
Oklahoma, Kansas and Texas Railroad Company	OKKT
Omaha Lincoln and Beatrice Railway Company	OLB
Ontario Central Railroad Corp.	ONCT
Ontario Midland Railroad Corp.	OMID
Ontario Northland Railway	ONT

Oregon & Northwestern Railroad Company	ONW
Oregon California & Eastern Railway Company	OCE
Oregon Electric Railway	OE
Oregon Pacific & Eastern Railway	OPE
Oregon Trunk Railway	OT
Otter Valley Railroad Corporation	OV
Pacific and Arctic Railway & Navigation Company	
Pacific Railroad	FCP
Pacific Railway (Costa Rica)	
Pacific Railways of Nicaragua	
Paducah & Illinois Railroad Company	PI
Panama Railroad	
Patapsco & Back Rivers Railroad	PBR
Pearl River Valley Railroad	PRV
Pecos Valley Southern Railway Company	PVS
Pend Oreille Valley Railroad	
Peninsula Terminal Company	PT
Penn Central Transportation Company	PC
Peoria and Pekin Union Railway Company	PPU
Peoria Terminal Company	PTC
Petaluma and Santa Rosa Railroad Company	PSR
Philadelphia Belt Line Railroad Company	PBL
Philadelphia Bethlehem and New England Railroad	PBNE
Pickens Railroad Company	PICK
Pioneer and Fayette Railroad Company (The)	PF
Pittsburgh & Lake Erie Railroad	PLE
Pittsburg & Shawmut Railroad (The)	PS
Pittsburgh Allegheny & McKees Rocks Railroad Company	PAM
Pittsburgh and Ohio Valley Railway Company	POV
Pittsburgh Chartiers & Youghiogheny Railway	PCY
Point Comfort & Northern Railway Company	PCN
Port Authority Trans-Hudson Corporation	
Port Bienville Railroad	PBVR
Port Huron and Detroit Railroad	PHD
Port of San Francisco Belt Railroad	
Port of Tillamook Bay Railroad	POTB
Portland Terminal Company	PTM
Portland Traction Company	PRTD
Prairie Trunk Railway	PARY
Prescott and Northwestern Railroad Company (The)	PNW
Providence and Worcester Company	PW
Quanah Acme & Pacific Railway Company	QAP
Quebec Central Railway Company	QC
Quebec North Shore and Labrador Railway Company	
Quincy Railroad Company	QRR

Rahway Valley Railroad	RV
Richmond Fredericksburg and Potomac Railroad Company	RFP
River Terminal Railway (The)	RT
Roberval and Saguenay Railway Company (The)	RS
Rockdale Sandow & Southern Railroad Company	RSS
Rockton and Rion Railway	ROR
Roscoe Snyder & Pacific Railway Company	RSP
Sabine River & Northern Railroad Company	SRN
Sacramento Northern Railway	SN
St. Joseph Terminal Railroad Company	SJT
St. Lawrence Railroad	SLAW
St. Louis-San Francisco Railway Company	SLSF
St. Louis Southwestern Railway Company	SSW
St. Marys Railroad Company	SM
Saint Paul Union Depot Company	SPUD
Salt Lake Garfield & Western Railway Company	SLGW
San Diego & Arizona Eastern Railway Company	SDAE
San Francisco Belt Railroad	
San Luis Central Railroad Company (The)	SLC
San Manuel Arizona Railroad Company	SMA
Sand Springs Railway Company	SS
Sandersville Railroad Company	SAN
Santa Fe	ATSF
Santa Maria Valley Railroad Company	SMV
Seaboard Coast Line Railroad	SCL
Seacoast Transportation Company	
Seattle & North Coast Railroad Co.	SNCT
Sierra Railroad Company	SERA
Sioux City Terminal Railway Company	SCT
Skaneateles Short Line Railroad	SSL
Sonora-Baja California SA de CV Railway	SBC
Soo Line Railroad Company	SOO
South Branch Valley Railroad	SBVR
South Brooklyn Railway Company	SBK
South Buffalo Railway Company	SB
South Central Tennessee Railroad Company, Inc.	SCTR
Southern Indiana Railway Incorporated	SIND
Southern Pacific Transportation Company	SP
Southern Railway Company	SOU
Southern San Luis Valley Railroad Company	SSLV
Spencerville & Elgin Railroad Company	SPEG
Spokane International Railroad	SI
Springfield Terminal Railway Company (Vermont)	ST
State University Railroad Company	SUR
Staten Island Railroad Corporation (The)	SIRC

Steelton & Highspire Railroad	SH
Stewartstown Railroad	STRT
Stockton Terminal & Eastern Railroad	STE
Strasburg Railroad Company	SRC
Straits Car Ferry Service Corporation	
Strouds Creek & Muddlety Railroad	SCM
Sumter & Choctaw Railway	SC
Sunset Railway	SUN
Tacoma Municipal Beltline Railway	TMBL
Tennessee Alabama & Georgia Railway Company	TAG
Tennessee Railway Company	TENN
Terminal Railroad Association of St. Louis	TRRA
Terminal Railway Alabama State Docks (Port of Mobile)	TASD
Texas & Northern Railway Company	TN
Texas Central Railroad Company	TEXC
Texas City Terminal Railway Company	TCT
Texas Mexican Railway Company (The)	TM
Texas Oklahoma & Eastern Railroad Company	TOE
Texas South-Eastern Railroad Company	TSE
Tidewater Southern Railway Company	TS
Tippecanoe Railroad Company	TIPP
Toledo Peoria & Western Railroad Company	TPW
Toledo Terminal Railroad	TT
Tooele Valley Railway Company	TOV
Toronto Hamilton & Buffalo Railway Company (The)	THB
Towanda-Monroeton Shippers' Lifeline, Inc.	TMSS
Transkentucky Transportation Railroad Co., Inc.	TTIS
Trona Railway Company	TRC
Tucson Cornelia & Gila Bend Railroad	TCG
Tulsa-Sapulpa Union Railway Company	TSU
Tuscola & Saginaw Bay Railway Company Inc.	TSBY
Union Pacific Railroad	UP
Union Railroad Company (Pittsburgh)	URR
Union Railroad of Oregon	UO
Union Pacific Railroad	UP
Union Railroad Company (Pittsburgh)	URR
Union Railroad of Oregon	UO
United South Eastern Railways Company	SE
United States Government Alaska Railroad	ARR
Unity Railways Company	UNI
Upper Merion & Plymouth Railroad Company	UMP
Utah Railway Company	UTAH
Valdosta Southern Railroad	VSO
Valley & Siletz Railroad Company	VS

Valley Railroad Company (The)	VALE
Ventura County Railway Company	VCY
Vermont Railway Incorporated (The)	VTRD
Via Rail Canada, Inc. (see Canadian & CP Rail)	
Virginia and Maryland Railroad (see Delmarva Route)	VAMD
Virginia Blue Ridge Railway	VBR
Virginia Central Railway	VC
Visalia Electric Railroad Company	VE
Wabash Valley Railroad Company	WVRC
Walla Walla Valley Railway Company	WWV
Ware Shoals Railroad	WS
Warren & Saline River Railroad	WSR
Warrenton Railroad	WAR
Warwick Railway Company	WRWK
Washington Idaho & Montana Railway Company	WIM
Washington Terminal Company	WATC
Waterloo Railroad Company	WLO
Weatherford Mineral Wells & Northwestern Railway Company (The)	WMWN
West Virginia Northern Railroad Company	WVN
Western Maryland Railway	WM
Western Pacific Railroad Company (The)	WP
Western Pacific Transport	
Western Railway of Alabama (The)	WA
Western Railway of Mexico	FCM
White Pass & Yukon Route	WPY
Wilkes-Barre Connecting Railroad	WBC
Winchester & Western Railroad Company	WW
Winfield Railroad Company (The)	WNF
Winifrede Railroad Company	WNFR
Winston-Salem Southbound Railway	WSS
Wisconsin Central Railroad Company	WCRC
Wyandotte Southern Railroad Company	WYS
Wyandotte Terminal Railroad Company	WYT
Yakima Valley Transportation Company	YVT
Yancey Railroad Company	YAN
Youngstown & Northern Railroad Company (The)	YN
Youngstown & Southern Railway Company	YS
Yreka Western Railroad Company	YW
Zug Island Road (see Delray Connecting Railroad)	DC

Appendix E

METRIC CONVERSION FACTORS

AREA

When you know	Multiply by	To Find
square inches	6.4516	square centimeters
square feet	0.0929030	square meters
square yards	0.836127	square meters
square miles	2.58888	square kilometers
square centimeters	0.155000	square inches
square meters	10.7639	square feet
square meters	1.19599	square yards
square kilometers	0.386138	square miles

LENGTH

When you know	Multiply by	To Find
inches	2.540000	centimeters
feet	0.304800	meters
yards	0.914400	meters
miles	1.60934	kilometers
centimeters	0.393701	inches
meters	3.380840	feet
meters	1.093610	yards
kilometers	0.621371	miles
statute miles	0.868978	nautical miles
nautical miles	1.150777	statute miles

MASS/WEIGHT

When you know	Multiply by	To Find
pounds	0.453592	kilograms
short tons (2,000 lbs.)	0.907029	metric tons
long tons (2,240 lbs.)	1.016046	metric tons
kilograms	2.20462	pounds
metric tons	1.10250	short tons
metric tons	0.984205	long tons

VOLUME

When you know	Multiply by	To Find
cubic inches	16.3871	cubic centimeters
cubic feet	0.0283168	cubic meters
cubic yards	0.764555	cubic meters
quarts (liquid)	0.946353	liters
gallons	3.78541	liters

cubic centimeters	0.0610237	cubic inches
cubic meters	35.3147	cubic feet
cubic meters	1.30795	cubic yards
liters	1.05669	quarts (liquid)
liters	0.264172	gallons

TEMPERATURE

When you know	Calculate by	To Find
Fahrenheit (F°)	Subtract 32 then multiply by 5/9	Celsius
Celsius (°C)	Multiply by 9/5 then add 32	Fahrenheit

Appendix F

OFFICIAL 2-LETTER POSTAL
SERVICE ABBREVIATIONS

Alabama	AL	Montana	MT
Alaska	AK	Nebraska	NE
Arizona	AZ	Nevada	NV
Arkansas	AR	New Hampshire	NH
California	CA	New Jersey	NJ
Colorado	CO	New Mexico	NM
Connecticut	CT	New York	NY
Delaware	DE	North Carolina	NC
Dist. of Columbia	DC	North Dakota	ND
Florida	FL	Ohio	OH
Georgia	GA	Oklahoma	OK
Hawaii	HI	Oregon	OR
Idaho	ID	Pennsylvania	PA
Illinois	IL	Rhode Island	RI
Indiana	IN	South Carolina	SC
Iowa	IA	South Dakota	SD
Kansas	KS	Tennessee	TN
Kentucky	KY	Texas	TX
Louisiana	LA	Utah	UT
Maine	ME	Vermont	VT
Maryland	MD	Virginia	VA
Massachusetts	MA	Washington	WA
Michigan	MI	West Virginia	WV
Minnesota	MN	Wisconsin	WI
Mississippi	MS	Wyoming	WY
Missouri	MO		

Appendix G

STANDARD TIME DIFFERENCES
United States Cities

Source: Interstate Commerce Commission

At 12 o'clock noon Eastern Standard Time the standard time in U.S. cities is as follows:

Akron, OH	12.00 noon	Memphis, TN	11.00 a.m.
Albuquerque, NM	10.00 a.m.	Miami, FL	12.00 noon
Atlanta, GA	12.00 noon	Milwaukee, WI	11.00 a.m.
Baltimore, MD	12.00 noon	Minneapolis, MN	11.00 a.m.
Birmingham, AL	11.00 a.m.	Newark, N.J.	12.00 noon
Bismarck, ND	11.00 a.m.	New York, NY	12.00 noon
Boise, ID	10.00 a.m.	New Orleans, LA	11.00 a.m.
Boston, MA	12.00 noon	Norfolk, VA	12.00 noon
Buffalo, NY	12.00 noon	Okla. City, OK	11.00 a.m.
Butte, MT	10.00 a.m.	Omaha, NE	11.00 a.m.
Charleston, SC	12.00 noon	Philadelphia, PA	12.00 noon
Charleston, WV	12.00 noon	Phoenix, AZ	10.00 a.m.
Cheyenne, WY	10.00 a.m.	Pierre, SD	11.00 a.m.
Chicago, IL	11.00 a.m.	Pittsburgh, PA	12.00 noon
Cincinnati, OH	12.00 noon	Portland, ME	12.00 noon
Cleveland, OH	12.00 noon	Portland, OR	9.00 a.m.
Columbus, OH	12.00 noon	Providence, RI	12.00 noon
Dallas, TX	11.00 a.m.	Reno, NV	9.00 a.m.
Denver, CO	10.00 a.m.	Richmond, VA	12.00 noon
Des Moines, IA	11.00 a.m.	Rochester, NY	12.00 noon
Detroit, MI	12.00 noon	Santa Fe, NM	10.00 a.m.
Duluth, MN	11.00 a.m.	Sioux Falls, SD	11.00 a.m.
Fort Worth, TX	11.00 a.m.	Spokane, WA	9.00 a.m.
Galveston, TX	11.00 a.m.	St. Paul, MN	11.00 a.m.
Grand Rapids, MI	12.00 noon	St. Louis, MO	11.00 a.m.
Hartford, CT	12.00 noon	Salt Lake City, UT	10.00 a.m.
Helena, MT	10.00 a.m.	San Francisco, CA	9.00 a.m.
Honolulu, HI	7.00 a.m.	Savannah, GA	12.00 noon
Houston, TX	11.00 a.m.	Seattle, WA	9.00 a.m.
Indianapolis, IN	12.00 noon	Tacoma, WA	9.00 a.m.
Jacksonville, FL	12.00 noon	Tampa, FL	12.00 noon
Juneau, AK	7.00 a.m.	Toledo, OH	12.00 noon
Kansas City, MO	11.00 a.m.	Topeka, KS	11.00 a.m.
Knoxville, TN	12.00 noon	Tulsa, OK	11.00 a.m.
Lincoln, NE	11.00 a.m.	Washington, DC	12.00 noon
Little Rock, AR	11.00 a.m.	Wichita, KS	11.00 a.m.
Los Angeles, CA	9.00 a.m.	Wilmington, DE	12.00 noon
Louisville, KY	12.00 noon		

Foreign Cities

Source: U.S. Naval Oceanographic Office

By government decree or proclamation Spain, France, Netherlands and Belgium have advanced their time from the standard meridian by one hour throughout the year. The time indicated in table is fixed by law and is called the legal time, or more generally, Standard Time.

At 12 o'clock noon Eastern Standard Time, the standard time in foreign cities is as follows:

Alexandria	7.00 p.m.	Leningrad	8.00 p.m.
Amsterdam	6.00 p.m.	Lima	12.00 noon
Athens	7.00 p.m.	Lisbon	5.00 p.m.
Auckland	5.00 a.m.*	Liverpool	5.00 p.m.
Baghdad	8.00 p.m.	London	5.00 p.m.
Bangkok	12.00 mid.	Madrid	6.00 p.m.
Belfast	5.00 p.m.	Manila	1.00 a.m.*
Berlin	6.00 p.m.	Melbourne	3.00 a.m.*
Bogota	12.00 noon	Mexico City	11.00 a.m.
Bombay	10.30 p.m.	Montevideo	2.00 p.m.
Bremen	6.00 p.m.	Montreal	12.00 noon
Brussels	6.00 p.m.	Moscow	8.00 p.m.
Bucharest	7.00 p.m.	Oslo	6.00 p.m.
Budapest	6.00 p.m.	Paris	6.00 p.m.
Buenos Aires	1.00 p.m.	Rio deJaneiro	2.00 p.m.
Calcutta	10.30 p.m.	Rome	6.00 p.m.
Cape Town	7.00 p.m.	Santiago (Chile)	1.00 p.m.
Caracas	1.00 p.m.	Shanghai	1.00 a.m.*
Copenhagen	6.00 p.m.	Singapore	12.30 a.m.*
Dawson (Yukon)	8.00 a.m.	Stockholm	6.00 p.m.
Delhi	10.30 p.m.	Sydney (Austrailia)	3.00 a.m.*
Djakarta	12.00 mid.	Teheran	8.30 p.m.
Dublin	5.00 p.m.	Tel Aviv	7.00 p.m.
Gdansk	6.00 p.m.	Tokyo	2.00 a.m.*
Geneva	6.00 p.m.	Valparaiso	1.00 p.m.
Halifax	1.00 p.m.	Vancouver	9.00 a.m.
Havana	12.00 noon	Vienna	6.00 p.m.
Hong Kong	1.00 a.m.*	Warsaw	6.00 p.m.
Istanbul	8.00 p.m.	Wellington (N.Z.)	5.00 a.m.*
Jerusalem	7.00 p.m.	Winnipeg	11.00 a.m.
Johannesburg	7.00 p.m.	Yokohama	2.00 a.m.*
Le Havre	6.00 p.m.	Zurich	6.00 p.m.

*Indicates morning of the following day.